Arguing for Music

Arguing for Culture

ALSO BY SAMUEL LIPMAN

Music After Modernism
(1979)

The House of Music
(1984)

Arguing for Music

Arguing for Culture

Essays by
Samuel Lipman

DAVID R. GODINE, PUBLISHER · BOSTON
in association with
AMERICAN COUNCIL FOR THE ARTS

First published in 1990 by
DAVID R. GODINE, PUBLISHER, INC.
Horticultural Hall
300 Massachusetts Avenue
Boston, Massachusetts 02115
in association with
AMERICAN COUNCIL FOR THE ARTS
1285 Avenue of the Americas
New York, New York 10019

Library of Congress Cataloging-in-Publication Data
Lipman, Samuel
Arguing for music, arguing for culture / Samuel Lipman.
p. cm.
Includes bibliographical references.
ISBN 0-87923-821-6. — ISBN 0-87923-822-4 (soft)
1. Music—United States—20th century—History and criticism.
I. Title
ML60.L465 1990   89-46203
780'.973'0904—dc20

Acknowledgments: The author wishes to acknowledge his debt to the journals in which
the essays that appear in this book first appeared. Each is acknowledged in the headnote
that precedes it and is reprinted with the kind permission of the periodicals concerned.

FIRST EDITION
Printed in the United States of America

Contents

PREFACE
A Concentration on Essentials ix

PROLOGUE
A Certain Independence: An Interview with William Keens 1

I MUSIC IN AMERICA TODAY

1
The Road to Now 19

2
Doing Music, Doing American Music 44

3
American String-Quartet Writing 63

4
The Philharmonic's New Horizons 75

5
Musical New York in Decline 94
The Crisis Continues 103

6
The Harvard Cage 115

7
The Future of Classical Music 123

II THE PROBLEM OF NEW OPERA

8
Opera 1984: Dead or Alive? 131

9
Blitzstein's Cradle   157

10
Einstein's *Long March to Brooklyn*   164

11
Casanova *at the City Opera*   181

12
Lord Byron *Undone*   188

13
A Dissent on Menotti   201

14
Dismal Thoughts on the Present and Future   210

III   PERFORMING AND PERFORMERS

15
Reflections on Bach   219

16
What the Cliburn Contest Thinks of Pianists   226

17
Sad Thoughts on Walter Busterkeys, a.k.a. Liberace   237
Ruminations on the Romantic Piano   241
Vladimir Horowitz 1904–1989   247

18
The Violinist of the Age   254

19
The Met's Failed Walküre   259

20
Dead from Lincoln Center   268

21
Marian Anderson: The Diva from Philadelphia   280
New Life from Old Records   285

22
Leinsdorf at the Philharmonic   294

23
The Berlin Philharmonic Without Karajan 306
Karajan: The Last Time? 313

24
Is the Symphony Orchestra Dead? 318

IV MAKING CULTURE POSSIBLE
25
Funding the Arts: Who Decides? 331
26
Cultural Policy: Whither America, Whither Government? 345
27
Art and Patronage Today 360
28
New York and Its Future 371
29
To Teach the Administrators Art 377
New Thoughts on the Great Audience Hunt 380
The Buck Goes Where? 384
Why Give to the Arts? 387
30
The Case of Nancy Hanks 391
31
The NEA: Looking Back, and Looking Ahead 403

EPILOGUE
Redefining Culture and Democracy 417

INDEX 433

Preface

A CONCENTRATION ON ESSENTIALS

ESSAY COLLECTIONS and the family are in many ways quite similar. In the case of both, familiarity breeds, if not contempt, then something perhaps just as deadening—familiarity. There are other resemblances, too, between essay collections and the family. Like the members of a family, the essays of an individual writer—if he has been at all industrious—are many; like family members, essays come into the light of day over a more or less long period of time; very much like family members, essays share a relationship that is often problematical, distant, and even contradictory; like the founders of families, authors are often sorely tempted to disown writings that once seemed lovable, and now seem just wrong-headed. As is the case in families, there is a great difference in outlook between the old and the young; moreover, there is also that inevitable difference between the old and the new creations that comes not so much from inside but from outside, not so much from what they are in themselves, as from what has happened to them in the surrounding world.

In my first collection of essays, *Music After Modernism* (1979), my unifying theme was the condition of music after the vitality of what used to be called "modern music" had run its course; I believe that I made clear that it seemed to me no viable successor to the modernist movement had as yet emerged. In my second collection, *The House of Music* (1984), I was concerned with examining the pressure of institutions on the making of music; I attempted to show that this pressure had resulted in the substitution of bureaucracy for art. In the present collection, my concerns begin with the fate of American music at the end of the twentieth century, and end with the wider fate of culture.

I cannot deny, nor have I any wish to do so, that the *Leitmotiven* of my musical and intellectual lives have on the whole remained unchanged. My life has been spent in classical music, and it is becoming increasingly plain that it has been spent in what, in the most general sense, now can only be called the classics.

My own definition of such classicism, whether in music or elsewhere, does not suggest a closed canon, but it does suggest a canon rigorously selective, energetically guarded, and slow to change. The great composers I loved in my youth I love today; the cultural bearings I found then—the seriousness of life, the need to combine reason and faith, and in art and civilization greatness above all else—seem equally valid to me today. "Aha! a dyed-in-the-wool conservative," the reader will remark, and with justice.

Perhaps I had better climb for a moment off my perch. Despite my affirmation of the eternal verities, I can hardly deny that times change, and even that I have changed with them. The change of which I am most aware is in the direction of a gathering cultural pessimism. Some of this gloom, which emerges most fully in my concluding section, doubtless is a function of age. But only some. For the young, thank God, everything seems possible; Robert Browning's lines in "Pippa Passes," so redolent of Victorian optimism, speak directly to the young and once spoke directly to me:

The year's at the spring,
And day's at the morn;
Morning's at seven;
The hillside's dew-pearled;
The lark's on the wing;
The snail's on the thorn,
   God's in his heaven—
All's right with the world!

But as we grow older, the concentration on essentials, brought on by increase of experience, dictates an ever more somber assessment of life's future. Still more important, it would be shallow indeed not to recognize that there are consequences to be drawn from our living in a time that uniquely combines material plenitude and spiritual valuelessness. And so we find ourselves fighting for the life of our culture, of our civilization, and, above all, for our future as cultured, civilized beings. I hope that the reader will find that it is this fight, in the largest sense, that this collection of essays is about.

The reader will notice that I often use the word *culture,* and that I end the book with an essay attempting to so define this difficult word that in effect it becomes restricted to what we usually mean by *high culture.* I have hardly been able in my many uses of "culture" to keep to the high-culture definition I now think proper and necessary. For this inconsistency, I beg the reader's pardon, and plead the exigency of a change in my own thinking as I have attempted to confront the situation in which culture—i.e., high culture—found itself during the years in which my essays were appearing.

I am well aware that there is no discussion in this book of the momentous recent developments, still unfolding, regarding the grants by the National Endowment for the Arts for the exhibition of works by photographers Andres Serrano and Robert Mapplethorpe. Though I have taken some part in the public discussion of this issue, it seemed to me that the material of this book represents, despite the importance of the material it discusses for the future, something of a coherent period in our cultural life. There is something artificial in a chronological cutoff; still, the controversy over the proprieties of funding Serrano and Mapplethorpe seems to me to mark the beginning of the 1990s, not, as does the book of essays, the end of the 1980s.

A word is in order about the procedure I have followed in making these essays ready for republication. They stand as written, with only minor changes made in order to correct several errors of fact that have very kindly been pointed out to me; I have not been concerned with rooting out occasional duplications, because their occurrence usually testifies to the importance with which I have regarded the material. I have supplied the essays with very brief introductions, in the hope that I might shed light on my reasons for undertaking them in the first place, and on how what I wrote seems to me to have stood the test of time.

I want to take this opportunity to thank the *New Criterion* and *Commentary,* as well as the other publications in which these essays first appeared, for their cooperation; in particular, I want to thank Erich Eichman, Roger Kimball, Robert Richman, Donna Rifkind, and Christopher Carduff at the *New Criterion* and Norman Podhoretz, Neal Kozodoy, and Brenda Brown at *Commentary* for their invaluable aid in straightening out my language and my thoughts. For reasons which need hardly be mentioned here, this book would not have made it through its final stages of production without Chris Carduff's friendship and labor; I shall never forget his contribution. I am deeply grateful to the American Council for the Arts for its financial support of this book, which inevitably contains much that will seem to some of its members wrong and even pernicious. At the ACA, I am especially grateful to Milton Rhodes and Robert Porter. The continuing interest and kindness of William B. Goodman, my friend and old-fashioned (in the best sense) editor at David R. Godine Publisher in Boston, has made this book come about; I look forward to a long association with him. To Hilton Kramer I can only say that much that may be best in this book has come through his help and his friendship; we have fought many battles together, and I look forward to the many more that we will fight in the future. To my wife and our son I can only express my gratitude and my love.

—*Samuel Lipman*, November 1989

Arguing for Music

Arguing for Culture

Prologue

I decided to begin this book of essays not with an essay, but with an interview going back to 1986. Its origins lie in the exchange I had with the arts-publication consultant William Keens at an arts-advocacy party the preceding year. At this impressively catered event, which took place in a rather impressive Senate Office Building space, he approached me with a microphone extended, and asked if I didn't think that the assembled guests loved art. I answered that I thought they loved parties. The next day I was horrified at the effrontery of what I had said, and when I asked Bill not to make public use of my remark, he agreed. When he came to my office on January 17 to do the interview, which was later published in Vantage Point, *the magazine of the American Council for the Arts, he pressed me to defend myself against the many charges of elitism that had been leveled against me in the advocacy community. In answering, I found myself explaining how my cultural views had been formed, and how I thought developments in the society at large had impinged on art. As I reread the interview now, I am surprised both with my frankness on personal matters and with how little conscious thought I then gave to the way what we call high culture carries and transmits the highest values of society. This book documents, I think, the increasing attention I have paid to this formulation.*

A Certain Independence:
An Interview with William Keens

THERE ARE THOSE who believe that Samuel Lipman is appropriately outspoken. Among my friends, they tend to be artists who maintain, with the late poet and critic Randall Jarrell, that "the good is the enemy of the best." In Lipman they seem to recognize someone who, like themselves, acknowledges the nonnegotiability of talent.

Then there are those who believe that Samuel Lipman has used his power as publisher of the *New Criterion* and as a member of the National Council on the Arts to intimidate others who do not share his more "conservative" cultural philosophy.

· I ·

What might be said of this man? His views have great context: pull at the thread of a thought and the entire skein unfurls. He feels and believes extremely, as one for whom passion has been wedded to principle. His principles admit no ambiguity. He is outraged both by those he believes to be fools and by others who suffer them. His knowledge of music is immense. He simply refuses to be ignored.

We met in his office to talk for an hour about arts education. Three hours later, the landscape of a much larger world, of which arts education is a vital part, had finally emerged.

—*William Keens*

VANTAGE POINT: Three times in the last week, as people learned that you and I would be talking, they told me they had met you recently and how surprised they were: you were nicer than they expected. Doesn't that comment suggest that an image of Samuel Lipman is being formed, perhaps one which is also being cultivated?
LIPMAN: People always expect me to be Samson in the house of the Philistines.
VANTAGE POINT: Is that the role you've taken on?
LIPMAN: I wouldn't have thought so. On the other hand, one has to pay a decent respect to the opinions of mankind.

We've gotten ourselves into a situation in the arts where, if you aren't 100 percent on board, you're 100 percent *off* board. We've become so defensive that in every discussion, the most primitive, short-term conception of loyalty is being applied. If the house is on fire and your spouse needs rescuing, that's not the time to consider whether he's been a good husband or she's been a good wife. But that's where we are in the arts.
VANTAGE POINT: Don't people behave that way when they believe passionately in something and have something at stake?
LIPMAN: They also behave that way when they feel that matters are so insecurely founded that the boat can't take any rocking. Arts advocates have a wonderful role to play, but it's up to artists to get them beyond being committed to parties to being committed to art.
VANTAGE POINT: Why should that be the responsibility of artists?
LIPMAN: Because whether it's about himself or his institution, art or the relationship between art and life, the artist is always educating.

I don't believe that arts advocates at this moment are passionately committed to particular schools of art or even to particular artists. I believe that . . .

VANTAGE POINT: Are conservatives passionately committed to the reorientation of cultural policy in the United States?

LIPMAN: I . . . well . . . I'll answer any aspect of that question you like, but I warn you that you're making a fundamental leap you oughtn't make.

VANTAGE POINT: No, I'm not. I'm trying to underscore what I believe is your own error. I think it would be as incorrect for me to claim that all conservatives feel one way about the arts as for you to say that all arts advocates lack passionate commitment.

LIPMAN: Okay, I'll explain. But first let's deal with this issue of conservatives and cultural policy, which others may not view in the same way.

In the mansion of conservatism there are many rooms. However, it's not even clear if there's a roof over the mansion because conservatism in the twentieth century—especially in the United States—has been defensive, reactive, and essentially concerned with staying alive, not with creating integrated future policies. I'm not talking about extremist movements, by the way, which I don't think fit under conservatism.

In my own way, in my own area, I am involved in trying to change this. My position, the position of the *New Criterion* and its editor, Hilton Kramer, is, we believe, very well grounded. Yet there's not the slightest doubt that it is an idiosyncratic position. We're pretty hostile to other conservative approaches to cultural policy. Where our position is easily assimilable into regular conservatism is on certain domestic, certain foreign policy, and even certain economic issues. But on cultural issues, we are either in the vanguard, or we're out on a limb. We see our job as clarifying the different strands which go into the making of high culture, and the only guarantee we can offer is that we'll try to make our positions clear.

Let's go back to arts advocacy. *If* you are an advocate who has no particular commitment to art or a school of art, then you don't need to take account of people like Sam Lipman. Your own reality is so strong that people like Sam Lipman are farcical. There are no arguments that I can make because what I'm doing is all second-order argument. It's all words. It's not the art.

Obviously I don't feel that way. When I launch into one of my diatribes on American orchestras, there are no defenders of the orchestras. Nobody tells me that Ozawa or Mehta are historically great conductors. So what they do is say, "You're against our having an orchestra. You're trying to pull the whole thing down." Do you see my point? I'm *not* trying to pull the whole thing down. I'm saying that something is not good, and for various reasons no one's willing to consider the consequences. The American orchestral scene is wrongly organized at this moment, which has been the doing of those same people who control arts advocacy. That's what makes for our terrible trouble. The audience is being destroyed by well-meaning attempts to expand it, and those attempts are changing for the worse the basis on which musical art is being done. I think it's going to collapse.

VANTAGE POINT: I wonder if you're concerned, as a writer and critic, that as you carry this banner, your own views may begin to ossify? Some of the same statements crop up again and again in your writing, for example, and I wonder, Whither Samuel Lipman?

LIPMAN: Well, no guarantees, obviously. The pen, as I'm sure you know, to some extent goes by itself.

There are two answers to the problem of ossification. The first is that probably any thinker—if I can be assumed for the sake of this discussion to be a thinker—has probably only one thought. A few of us, a tiny few, have a big thought. Most of us have a little thought. But often the best we can have is *a* thought to which one's life, to a large extent, is devoted.

I don't mean to be mawkish about it, but one's life is obviously a limited passage. The train trip is short. On that trip one really does only one thing, especially if one's a thinker: one has an idea, and life is devoted to fleshing it out. If you live longer, have good health, and are fortunate, then someone publishes you and people may listen.

There's a second answer to the problem of ossification: it's part of reality. I can't kid myself. I've been writing for ten years now, and if I've said a lot of things about one point, finally it goes about the way it did before. So maybe I've affected a few people's minds; as for the rest, the same thing must be said again. The real problem with ossification is a hardening of tone. But then, nobody likes to be ignored.

———

VANTAGE POINT: What do you trace your own "one idea" back to? What was it, and when was it formed?

LIPMAN: I was fifteen in 1949. That was the moment of immense expansion in American cultural and intellectual life, the moment of the G.I. Bill. No matter how important we believe it to have been, the G.I. Bill was even more important than that. It changed the entire idea of who was fit to receive high culture. Guys coming home from the war, the older generation, changed every school they went to because they were serious students. The world of college that I entered in the fifties provided a wonderful societal correlation to my own background, which is Russian Jewish and educationally very upwardly mobile. I discovered that mine was no longer a lonely trek. It was something that the world seemed to be doing.

In the late forties, after being a very successful child prodigy, I suddenly became a music lover. When push came to shove, I found that I loved music more than I loved *making* music myself. Music was deeply connected to everything that I read or saw in our culture. That's the central idea that I had, and that's really what I write about today.

VANTAGE POINT: Are you first generation in this country?

LIPMAN: Yes. My mother was born in Russia but moved first to Canada in about 1905 and didn't come to the United States until she was sixteen or seventeen. She was a music student, a pianist, and a tremendous reader. My father was a reader too—rather a more serious reader than my mother. They were both self-educated people.

My father came to the United States in 1915. He came across Siberia into Manchuria and Japan and worked his way to Seattle on a Japanese freighter. He worked his way down the coast to San Francisco, in truck gardens and as an oiler's helper for the American Can Company. He bought a vegetable stand, caught tuberculosis, was sick for a couple of years and came out flat broke, started a little business—a real American immigrant success story. He sold small electrical appliances before the war, and after the war he owned a drug store. He eventually went into the real estate business and did very well.

The result of all this was that it gave me both an enormous love for America and a certain independence, a certain distance from American life, because to some extent we were still guests.

I think I see more clearly now that we're *all* guests in America. Ours is a strangely consensual society, and a lot of people are here because they *want* to be. The fact that we're all guests, in a way, is responsible for the tremendous vitality of our political life, as well as for its self-correcting aspect, which is enormously gratifying and bodes well for the future—regardless of who wins the next election.

I'm high on America. Our capacity to assimilate our weaknesses, to correct them, to live with them, to make something good out of the bad, to preserve a lot of the good we have—it's extraordinary. The American Constitution doesn't need compliments from me, but the ability of this structure to make adjustments for the most unforeseen changes is remarkable. A divine providence seems to watch over this country as we lurch from stupidity to stupidity. It's marvelous how well it all seems to work out in the long run.

I come out of an immensely conflicted political relationship with the American environment. Much of my family—though not my parents—were very active in the American Communist Party. They were centrally connected, though I don't think any of them are names people would know now.

VANTAGE POINT: How did that conflict express itself in you?

LIPMAN: For me it was a conflict between communism and Zionism, and in that battle I took the Zionist side. After the Korean War, I saw the conflict as being between the Soviet Union and America. Still, I remained reasonably liberal in taking the side of America. I felt a lot of affection for that position running roughly from Roosevelt to Humphrey.

The big change in my political life came with Kennedy's assassination. I had found the aspirations of the Kennedy administration beguiling and seductive, but in the backwash of the assassination, I began to feel a cultural and intellectual hollowness about them. I felt that we were being sold a bill of goods. It was an unhappy passage for culture in those years, and it all fell apart with Johnson and the Vietnam War.

Great tragedies are inevitable, you know. One has to fight like hell to avoid them, and yet one gets swept up in them. It's hard for me not to feel that the tragedy about Vietnam is that something which turned out so terribly for America was probably, in the long run, an enormously constructive event in world history. I think it changed America for the worse but the world for the better. It marked the end of the idea of revolutionary expansion in the rest of the world. The horror was great for the United States, but it was much greater for Asia, and I think that lesson was learned—even though the war was botched terribly.

VANTAGE POINT: Are you saying that it's too bad the Vietnam War was so badly run because it set out from good intentions?

LIPMAN: I happen to believe that. But had it been better run, I don't know that it would have made an enormous difference. The issues were part of the working out of the end of empire and the end of imperialism, and I suppose it worked out in the only way it could.

I'm also saying that I don't think Vietnam was as much cause as symptom. Our American troubles in the sixties were caused by something else—the Pill.

VANTAGE POINT: [Laughter] You know I can't let a statement like that just lie there. Go ahead, I'll take the bait.

LIPMAN: Well, I think that once the normal penalties that men and women had learned were attached to casual sexual activity were removed . . .

VANTAGE POINT: Normal *penalties?*

LIPMAN: Yes. Pregnancy. Right.

VANTAGE POINT: Pregnancy is a penalty?

LIPMAN: Well, sure. To sexual activity. I mean to promiscuous sexual activity. Does that make it clearer? Once you could do those things without thinking of the nine-month consequences, life changed, and I think we're still dealing with that change.

The Pill came out in 1957 or 1958, and it changed everything. I was on the faculty at Berkeley, and I remember that marriages suddenly seemed to be based on consent in a way that they hadn't been the day before.

VANTAGE POINT: Whereas before they had been based on necessity?

LIPMAN: Upon recognition of necessity, yes.

VANTAGE POINT: It seems to me a curious world view that regards the Vietnam War more generously than the birth-control pill.

LIPMAN: Well, one has to look for the root of things, and one may find it in something that others think is trivial. The fact is, people didn't treat it as trivial. It changed their lives.

———

VANTAGE POINT: Let's try to sketch out more completely your views on a few selected topics. What about symphony orchestras?

LIPMAN: Orchestra programs are in enormous flux. Most orchestras now have composers in residence, and most—the Philadelphia Orchestra being something of an exception—are pushing newly composed American music. We're not supporting the status quo in the music itself, but what we are supporting is the same old way of doing business. We're supporting an apparatus for conductors which goes from Columbia Artists Management on Fifty-seventh Street all the way to the managers, executive directors, managing directors— what have you—of the orchestras. It's a very tight network.

Three years ago at the Endowment, I asked that on grant applications the orchestras indicate how much time conductors actually spent with them. I was told we couldn't do that because that would discriminate against those that have superstars, and "without the superstars no one would come to the concerts." When I said that (a) the superstars were not good musicians, and (b) they weren't spending any time with the orchestras anyway, I was asked if I wanted *no one* to come to the concerts. That's the situation we're in. The New York Philharmonic, for example—and I'm only speaking for myself—has an immense problem with Zubin Mehta. They can't replace Zubin Mehta because they can't find anybody with as big a reputation, or bigger—music be damned.

VANTAGE POINT: Okay, art and the state. Your view is that art risks being taken under the wing of the state, which is then propped up by that art. One can be used to legitimize the other.

LIPMAN: Yes. We have to be very careful about what the state does and does not do. We must preserve the state's interest in cultural activities, but we must also preserve the room for an independent private sector. In other words, we need an academy, and we also need an avant-garde. We should not have a kept avant-garde, nor should we have an avant-garde academy. We should have a real academy—one that represents the institutionalization of tradition.

We should also have our universities. But universities are not the place for the avant-garde; they are places where people are taught the past. The avant-garde is the future, and the past and the future don't work well together. One distorts the other. To be an academic, furthermore, is not to be an artistic creator. You can't make a John

Cage a professor at Columbia. Those are different roles and the two can't be contained in one institution.

VANTAGE POINT: Your assumption is that the John Cages are incapable of adopting the frame of mind required of a teacher?

LIPMAN: It's not what academics do. The academy is about conservation, about scholarship, about teaching what has been conserved.

VANTAGE POINT: You have described an art-instead-of-religion or instead-of-state phenomenon by saying that as faith in God or the state declines, "the rhetoric goes up like the hottest of hot-air balloons."

LIPMAN: Because art can heal no one, you see. Art is a mode of thought, not a cure. Art is not a faith. It's especially not a government. I don't think anybody who thought about it for five minutes would want it to be. An artist is an imperial being. An artist says, "Give me everything," and you want people governing you who say, "That's yours, and you can keep it." [Laughter] Artists don't feel that way. Artists include everything unto themselves. That's the great argument for the separation of art from both life and the state.

The phenomenon of casting art in the role of God has its most recent causes in the nineteenth century. God became no more than the hidden hand, and you had your choice: you could have either thought or feeling. Those who opted for thought went the way of science, while those who opted for feeling went the way of art. That's greatly oversimplified, but it helps to put it that way.

Our arts advocates these days find themselves willy-nilly on the side of feeling. As a result, when they talk about arts education, they find themselves saying that it's the training of the feelings. Well, if they thought about it, they wouldn't want to say that. They would really want to say that art is civilization, and instead they talk about art as self-expression: it's a cold, cruel world run by science and impersonality, and art provides personality, self-expression, and feeling. But feeling and self-expression belong to the interior life and can't be easily communicated in words we all understand. The upshot is that a terrible disservice is being done both to art and to education.

VANTAGE POINT: It's also your view that high culture is in danger of being co-opted by the entertaining of America. In "Cultural Policy: Whither America, Whither Government?" [Chapter 26 in this book], you defined high culture as being "concerned with, though not strictly limited to, art, literature, and learning that is either created to endure or that at some point after its creation is widely recognized to have become a permanent part of the civilization that is transmitted by the settled institutions of society." Any further comment?

LIPMAN: Well, I'll tell you. Since I wrote that I had a communication from on high as to what high culture is these days.

VANTAGE POINT: A visitation?

LIPMAN: No, a National Council meeting. A senior executive of the Public Broadcasting Service said, "When we put high culture on television, we make it popular culture." Practically yelling I said, "You can't mean that! You can't mean what you're saying! Do you really mean to say that you take high culture and make it into popular culture? From high you make it low? Is that what you mean to say?" She realized that she had stepped in it because that's exactly what they do.

For instance, last week on "Live from the Met" I saw *L'Italiana in Algeri*, and I asked myself what people see when they watch this. What does it mean to them? They must think it's foolish, because it *is* foolish. Appearing as Rossini appeared on television, with all the high-tech camera work and the false colors and the closeup shots of those not enormously attractive people wearing huge costumes—it's all funny. It's all camp, as a matter of fact. Is that what we want to be doing? What was the relationship of that to Rossini? None. What you had was some kind of peculiar costume show.

VANTAGE POINT: You have written that you feel that the literature, painting, theater, and so forth coming out of America now is pretty poor. There is no "blossoming health," you say, and hasn't been since the fifties. I wonder if what you're describing is really the failure of your own definition of high culture? Can art that is *of* its time ever be certified as enduring or permanent *in* its time? Did painters of the New York School, poets like Randall Jarrell, or playwrights like Arthur Miller really feel any differently about their art than we do about our own today?

LIPMAN: That period was very exciting, and a lot of people knew it. If you look at orchestra programs, poetry readings, lecture series, you can see that they knew in ways that we don't know now.

Nobody in the fifties would have made the argument that you just made, by the way—that the art of the day doesn't fit a definition of high culture. In those days, nobody would have said that nonce art is high culture. Now there are people who say that all the time. They say that there is no more to the art of the day. I don't believe that for a moment.

I think people realize that this is a moment in which great creative initiatives are not being taken. Supposedly the great creative innovation of the last decade is the Robert Wilson–Philip Glass *Einstein on the Beach*. It's perfectly plain, however, that the attitude toward that work is that it's really a style of theatrical production. Whether it is going to be around or not in a few years isn't important, apparently. What's important is that it's going to influence the way we produce theater. That's not a high culture attitude. A high culture attitude is that this is either for the ages or it's not. I know that's a snotty and elitist attitude, but somebody's got to say it.

VANTAGE POINT: I see that you regret having the job thrust upon you.

LIPMAN: Well, if I regretted it, I'd do something else. I'm not a believer in martyrdom.

VANTAGE POINT: Regarding the support of art, you have said that it ought to be based on content and not "the tyranny of numbers."

LIPMAN: It's perfectly clear that the justification for federal support is the number of bodies being served. If you came to Washington and said, "I'd like a grant for opera performance, but I'm not going to have more than fifteen hundred people attending because the great operas of the nineteenth century can only be done properly in fifteen-hundred-seat houses," a lot of people would say you're mad. But if you said that you had a plan for doing operas in the Superdome, why, you could write your own ticket. People would start counting up: "They do football games there, so we must be able to get fifty to sixty thousand people in the Superdome. We could charge them six dollars a ticket—yee, boy, that grosses out at . . ." They'd go nuts. You would go to Congress and say, "Isn't this wonderful? We're going to have as many people watching *Bohème* as watch the Dallas Cowboys." Their minds run to statistics like that.

None of this should have anything to do with what we're after. Everybody doesn't have to do the same thing. It's very important that opera exist and that those who want to can go to it without being barred for financial reasons. It's just like the public library, which I'm in favor of, too. But this idea that we should absolutely destroy what we're doing in order to do it for a lot of people is ridiculous.

VANTAGE POINT: Why are you so convinced that the larger the audience, the more likely it is that the art is being debased?

LIPMAN: You haven't noticed that there is a trade-off in life, a tension between numbers and quality? If somebody promises you a 20 percent return on your money, don't you get a little nervous? You can't have everything. If you have numbers, you're catering to the numbers, because you've got to bring the people in.

VANTAGE POINT: I'm not sure that the conditions of private banking transfer to public performance.

LIPMAN: But these are pretty important rules of life. What is the number one criterion for an arts program on public television? It's got to stop people from changing channels. And if you say to a producer, "We should do such and such a piece," he's likely to say, "Yes, we should—but they'll flip the channel." If you're selling commercial time on television, that's a proper consideration. If they flip the channel, they won't watch the commercials. But I didn't think public television was about that. I thought public television was about making available on the highest possible level that which couldn't be seen elsewhere. Instead I find that it's about keeping the audience watching.

VANTAGE POINT: So, in your view, public television has betrayed its mission?

LIPMAN: Absolutely. Not the slightest doubt.

Take the abysmal broadcasts of the New York Philharmonic with their inane intermission features, where all attempts at education have been given up. Take the Metropolitan Opera performance of *Aida*, which was Leontyne Price's farewell on an opera stage. That was a very sad moment—not so much because it was her farewell, but because she was a great singer no longer singing well, singing a role for which there was no cultural, intellectual interest in her performing. And what did the Met surround her with? Only the most stupid opera quiz in which second-rate show business figures were given the chance to giggle and preen before the camera and talk about their babyhood. I'm aware that that was valuable air time, but why was it valuable? Because it offered a chance to educate, to stimulate, to inspire—and it was lost.

VANTAGE POINT: Under what circumstances would you accept high culture's being directed to a mass audience?

LIPMAN: Well, if it were high culture and the mass audience were properly prepared, I would be all in favor of it.

VANTAGE POINT: What does being "properly prepared" mean?

LIPMAN: They have to be educated. You can't have an offering in mathematics for people who don't know about mathematics.

VANTAGE POINT: So high culture shouldn't be offered to people who haven't been exposed to it?

LIPMAN: The audience should be prepared in some way. Obviously there are limits to what can be done, and probably should be. But the soil has to be readied, which requires a successful attempt at education. Instead we're dragging high culture down out of some well-meaning but misguided idea that if we don't, it will die. It doesn't have to be sold that way.

VANTAGE POINT: What do you believe has gone wrong in the effort to prepare audiences? What has gone wrong in arts education?

LIPMAN: We just stopped doing it. We stopped teaching skills and facts. We just gave up. That's what went wrong. We used to teach kids sight reading and drawing and we don't do it now.

A lot of things went into this. First we decided that we ought to teach self-expression in art. Then we decided that we had to make whatever we taught relevant to the kids, so we taught them popular culture. Then we decided that we didn't have time even to do that, because we had to teach the basics. That's where we are at the moment. Having decided that we can't do anything, we now throw in some entertainment experiences for the kids, and that's what we call the artist-residency programs. On this last point, I think nearly everybody shares my opinion, except those who run the programs. They think they're wonderful.

VANTAGE POINT: I read two pieces of yours recently that I'd like to discuss. One was "Art Education Without the Mess," which appeared in the June 17, 1985, *Washington Times*. The other was "Schooling for All," a review in the January 1983 issue of *Commentary* of Mortimer J. Adler's book *The Paideia Proposal*.

LIPMAN: Oh God, you're the first person who has cited that review.

VANTAGE POINT: It's a good piece—very carefully constructed and very persuasive. You don't say anything outrageous that you don't back up, and as a result one comes around to agreeing with you on many points. In the piece for the *Washington Times*, on the other hand, you take great liberties with your thinking.

LIPMAN: Well, there's a big difference between writing an opinion piece for a newspaper and writing a book review for an intellectual magazine. I mean, really, come on. The occasion is different, the venue is different—I don't think that's a fair shot.

VANTAGE POINT: We all know that book reviews are largely platforms for the expression of opinion that could otherwise be gotten to more directly in a commentary. But let's see if you think this is a fair shot. Quoting from your *Washington Times* piece: "Then the experts came along, preaching self-expression and creativity. Children didn't need skills to do art. What they needed was encouragement and the freedom to make a mess."

LIPMAN: I can assure you that there is an enormous literature in arts education on art as therapy. First you start out by treating the handicapped, and then you find out that every child is handicapped in some way and that normal children can benefit from these same techniques. What you get is therapy on the most enormous scale. If you know the wilder shores of the progressive education movement in the 1960s, you know that it's particularly the messes that show that the child is doing wonderfully, because isn't it marvelous that he feels free to make a mess?

VANTAGE POINT: You have no quarrel with the concept of discipline-based arts education, I presume?

LIPMAN: Oh, certainly not. The problem with the approach that the Getty Trust is taking is that they're not beginning by teaching kids skills-oriented artistic activity. I don't believe that you can teach intellectual skills to ignoramuses; you can't teach philosophy to people who aren't literate. That's the problem. Getty should begin with artistic skills, then branch out to the more intellectualized treatment. Roughly half skills and half intellectual accomplishments would be about right.

I think the Getty Trust is trying to go in the right direction—a direction that used to be called art appreciation. They've moved in a masterful way, but it's not been appreciated in the arts education community. And you know something? As much money as the trust has, that community will kill it. We're even having trouble with discipline-based arts education at the federal level. I think we're going to lose the battle.

VANTAGE POINT: Where would you like to see arts education five years from now?

LIPMAN: I'd like to see general classroom teachers—not specialists—being trained to provide arts education. That's my goal.

VANTAGE POINT: How do we get there from here?

LIPMAN: By developing pilot programs which prove that it can be done. I hope that in-service training for teachers would be followed by changes in certification requirements. If started in the first three grades, then as kids came into the fourth grade their parents would begin saying, "What's my kid going to do with that music he's been learning?" But if we don't start from the beginning, we won't have anything.

VANTAGE POINT: Sam, I come away from this discussion feeling that for you there is always a right way, always a proper sequence.

LIPMAN: Yes. But I have no police powers, remember.

VANTAGE POINT: For which some people are grateful, I suspect.

LIPMAN: I'm grateful, too! I don't want to be a policeman.

VANTAGE POINT: It also seems clear that, in your view, artistic activity and proficiency begin with education . . .

LIPMAN: Basic education.

VANTAGE POINT: . . . move to elaboration, and then to experimentation in a sequential, cumulative fashion.

LIPMAN: Right. Exactly, exactly, exactly.

VANTAGE POINT: And finally, it's your view that we must always guard against allowing art to be overwhelmed by the interests of the state or tainted by day-to-day politics.

LIPMAN: Let me add that the state—which is a greater entity than government—has a proper interest in the survival of high culture and should encourage it. After all, civilization legitimizes whatever it touches. The state then becomes the highest incarnation of our best knowledge about how we are to be governed, how we wish to govern ourselves. That's what the state is—the fleshing out of our wishes.

I

MUSIC IN AMERICA TODAY

I.

I wrote this essay for the Summer 1985 New Criterion, *an issue devoted to "The Arts in America 1945–1985." My essay documents my own conviction that American music has followed a downward trajectory since World War II, and that signs of a change in this depressing state of affairs, despite yards of puffery, are nowhere to be seen. I have found no evidence that the prospects for American classical music are better today than they were when this essay appeared in the mid-eighties; if anything, as the puffery has increased, the musical situation has worsened. I should say too that the relationship between arts advocacy and catered haute cuisine, a mouth-watering example of which comes toward the end of this essay, remains as close as ever.*

The Road to Now

DESPITE ALL the warning signs in musical life—a shortage of significant new music, lowered standards in performance, and the declining commitment and sophistication of audiences and patrons—it is the fashion today to see serious music in America bursting forth at every moment and in every place. In order to sustain the fiction of a splendid present, it is necessary to treat music in this country as if it were an activity without a history. All those statistics so beloved of funders, grants recipients, and the media testify, supposedly, to a growth so splendid and a present so bounteous that any recollection of a usable past seems instantly dwarfed by comparison. Before World War I, it would appear, we had nothing save the barnstorming tours of such foreign celebrities as Kreisler and Paderewski; between the wars was the age of jazz and the big bands; after World War II whatever nascent musical urges we might have had were strangled almost at birth by public incomprehension and its corollary, government's refusal to support art the way any good government should. As the memories of musicians and concertgoers fade, and as the evidence once available on numerous phonograph recordings passes into the dusty hands of institutional archives, some account of the recent musical past we did indeed have seems necessary in the interests of recapturing our lost history and of understanding our extravagantly ballyhooed but nonetheless unanchored present.

In reality, serious music in America was in pretty good shape at the end of World War II. Even new composition, the notorious Achilles' heel of the art in the years since the Great War, was in a tolerable way. The finest European masters living outside the Soviet prison house, among them Paul Hindemith, Igor Stravinsky, and Arnold Schoenberg, were hard at work in our own country writing music which was eagerly awaited, even when not eagerly applauded. Béla Bartók, though already terminally ill, had written the Concerto for Orchestra, perhaps his most accessible masterpiece, as recently as 1943; Darius Milhaud, the genial French *provocateur*, was busy writing his French-sounding music from the coastal wilds of Mills College in California. While the presence of such giants was doubtless pleasing to our national *amour-propre* and important to the vitality of our musical life, it goes without saying that they were not here as a result of the cultural attractiveness of the United States. They were here rather because of the monstrous behavior of Hitler and the Nazis, and because of America's role as the Arsenal of Democracy.

But the health of American musical composition was in fact not simply a matter of composition *in* America. It is important that in 1945 there were flourishing on these shores at least two schools of domestic composition, one nativist and the other rather more internationalist in expression. The most famous figure of the nativist school was Aaron Copland, whose dance scores *Billy the Kid* (1938), *Rodeo* (1942), and *Appalachian Spring* (1944)—not to mention the openly patriotic *Lincoln Portrait* and the *Fanfare for the Common Man* (both 1942)—have come to define what it means for a serious composer to be demonstrably American. In these works Copland integrated the heritage of domestic jazz and folk music with the European symphonic tradition. In 1945 there were great hopes entertained too for the Oklahoma-born Roy Harris, whose Third Symphony (1937) and *Folksong Symphony* (1940) were attempts to write music in an American style. Virgil Thomson was another figure of impeccably European associations who was counted among the musical proclaimers of America. Thomson had found his way back to a kind of artistic nationalism via the improbable route of collaborating (in Paris) with Gertrude Stein on *Four Saints in Three Acts* (1927–28), a mostly hymn-tune-like opera written for Negro singers. His scores for two films by Pare Lorentz, *The Plough that Broke the Plains* (1936) and *The River* (1937), remain milestones of a kind of genre writing familiar in the Central European music of Smetana and Dvořák. In this context, a word must be said also for Douglas Moore, whose opera *The Devil and Daniel Webster* (1938) was perhaps the most successful operatic setting of a regional subject up to that time.

There was a great deal more going on in American music composition in 1945 than the emergence of our first successful nativists. Though now almost forgotten, Walter Piston and Howard Hanson—the first via a neoclassicism acquired from the famous French composition teacher Nadia Boulanger and the second via a Nordic Romanticism derived from his Scandinavian forebears—epitomized the ability of native-born composers to write authentically in an international style. Samuel Barber, that proud product of the great days in the 1930s of the Curtis Institute of Music in Philadelphia, was then best known for his melodically touching *Adagio for Strings* (1936). In Arturo Toscanini's performances and recording of the work, it reached—and touched—millions of listeners who, in the fashion of Molière's Monsieur Jourdain, would have been surprised indeed to be told that they were being moved by American music. Roger Sessions (who passed away just this year at the age of eighty-eight) had by 1945 achieved major standing among musical intellectuals as a cerebral composer remarkable for the individuality of his achievement, despite the influences of both Stravinsky and Schoenberg.

In describing the state of American composition in 1945, it would be a mistake to lose sight of how easy it was for nativist figures, along with their slightly younger colleagues, to jump back and forth across the relatively thin line separating nativist from more cosmopolitan composers. By 1945, Copland had written such notably non-folk-sounding works as the *Piano Variations* (1930) and the Violin Sonata (1943); Harris had written a quantity of nonprogrammatic chamber music. In this regard, the career of William Schuman is instructive. Though in 1945 Schuman was best known for his jazzy *American*

Festival Overture (1939), his Third Symphony (1941) manages to sound recognizably American in its melodic and rhythmic contours without any overt American musical references. Like Copland, Schuman turned his talent to the dance, writing the gripping score for Antony Tudor's *Undertow* (1945).

Schuman, the youngest of the composers referred to above, was thirty-five at the close of World War II. Much younger than Schuman was the prodigy Leonard Bernstein, already famous as a composer in 1945 for parlaying the enormously successful ballet music from *Fancy Free* (1944) into the even more successful Broadway musical *On the Town* at the close of the same year. To be mentioned along with Bernstein is his late (and somewhat older) friend and mentor Marc Blitzstein. It was Blitzstein's curious, though hardly negligible, achievement to have written two much-talked-about, antithetical works: the earlier, Communist Party-inspired musical *The Cradle Will Rock* (1936–37), which in the course of urging a proletarian revolution mocked the American way of life; and the later, war-motivated *Airborne Symphony* (1945), which celebrated the bravery of the United States Army Air Force he had served with in England. Another composer who seemed to bridge the gap between serious and lighter styles was Morton Gould, whose *Lincoln Legend* (1941) predated Copland's treatment of the same subject by one year.

There was another approach in 1945 to the composition of American music, an approach which was apparently of little moment at the time but which in later years began to seem the manifestation of a quintessentially national way of doing things. This approach later became famous—if not infamous—as the American musical avant-garde. Three avant-garde figures, each of them marginal to the composition scene of the day, come immediately to mind. The first, little known then and only later to assume symbolic importance for his dissonantal and anarchic music, was the eccentric and lonely Yankee Charles Ives, then seventy-one; though Ives had ceased composing some years before, he began to acquire a cult reputation among the devotees of new music as early as 1939, with the performance of his *Concord Sonata* (1911–15) in New York's Town Hall by pianist John Kirkpatrick. The second avant-garde figure was the Californian Henry Cowell, the inventor, as early as 1912 (in *The Tides of Manaunaun*), of "tone clusters," groups of contiguous notes on the piano struck with palm, clenched fist, or extended forearm; by 1945 Cowell had become a guru of what he called, in the title of a 1930 book, "New Musical Resources." The third figure in this avant-garde trio was John Cage. This half-whimsical, half-demonic figure was already known by war's end as the inventor of the prepared piano, an instrument so altered by the insertion of foreign objects amongst its strings that the resulting sonority struck listeners as reminiscent of nothing so much as a quaint Balinese gamelan orchestra. By 1939, Cage had given early evidence of his intention to abandon music itself as the raw material for composition in his *Imaginary Landscape No. 1*, a work for muted piano, cymbal, and two variable-speed phonograph turntables.

The bridge between music as composition and music as performance is of course necessary, natural, and ubiquitous. It is not surprising that the relatively happy state of American music composition in 1945—the leaner products of the avant-garde aside—had its corollary in performance. As in composition, American music performance had been enriched for some years by the migration of the great European talents: among conductors, Dimitri Mitropoulos, Pierre Monteux, Fritz Reiner, Arturo Toscanini, and Bruno Walter; among instrumentalists, Adolf Busch, Robert Casadesus, Vladimir Horowitz, Wanda Landowska, Arthur Rubinstein, Artur Schnabel, Rudolf Serkin, Joseph Szigeti, and the members of the Budapest Quartet; among singers, Alexander Kipnis, Lotte Lehmann, Friedrich Schorr, and Elisabeth Schumann. All were exerting major influence in America as performers and in many cases as teachers.

Then, as now, the focus of performing life was on the small group of great American orchestras. Such ensembles as the Boston Symphony Orchestra, the New York Philharmonic, and the Philadelphia Orchestra had become of world class as long ago as the 1920s. In the late 1930s and early 1940s two newer orchestras, the Cleveland Orchestra (founded in 1918) and the NBC Symphony Orchestra (founded in 1937), began to attain the prestige of their older colleagues. The quality of these great orchestras ought not to blind us to the very real distinction at the time of the orchestras of Chicago, Los Angeles, Minneapolis, St. Louis, and San Francisco. Records of important repertory from these groups testify to their high level of playing.

The music directors of these important orchestras were not all foreign nationals taking shelter in the United States from the European storm. In fact, the conductors of the most important old-line orchestras—Serge Koussevitsky in Boston, Artur Rodzinski in New York, and Eugene Ormandy in Philadelphia—had become American residents *before* Hitler's rise in Germany. Leopold Stokowski, who conducted the Philadelphia Orchestra from 1912 to 1936 and who exerted perhaps the most important influence on the mass perception of orchestral music in the United States before the war, had been a domestic resident since well before World War I.

Given the importance that must be attached to the *writing* as well as to the performance of music, the work of two of these conductors deserves to be singled out for its contribution to contemporary composition in general and to American composition in particular. Stokowski enthusiastically introduced new works in Philadelphia to an essentially staid audience, and Koussevitsky gladly performed the same service for American music in equally staid Boston. Their achievements along this line make up a golden chapter in the otherwise troubled relations between twentieth-century composers and performers.

Any account of the condition of American music in 1945 would be incomplete without a sketch of the situation in opera. Then, as now, the Metropolitan, with its secure base of patronage in the world of New York society and its weekly Saturday-afternoon radio broadcasts, was the leader among our opera companies. Times were difficult for the Met during the war, owing to the repertory's dependence on Italian and German singers. The Met dealt with this problem by hiring American singers in large numbers, some of whom went on to become stars, even after the coming of peace made international artistic travel once again possible: the names of Jan Peerce, Eleanor Steber, Risë Stevens, Helen Traubel, Richard Tucker, and Leonard Warren remain high on lists of the Met's great singers. It should also be mentioned that the Met at this time was in the habit of using the services of great conductors, including Sir Thomas Beecham, George Szell, and Bruno Walter.

From the winter of 1944 on, the Met was no longer the only opera in New York. The founding of the New York City Opera did more than provide "dollar opera" for the masses; it also made possible an all-American counterweight to the rather more pretentious and internationalist Met. The fulfillment of the City Opera's promise to produce contemporary repertory, both European and American, was still some years in the future; what was clear from the beginning was that opera—even the European chestnuts—could be "Americanized" with American singers without losing dramatic conviction or musical charm.

Outside New York, grand opera was restricted to San Francisco. A social base similar to that of the Metropolitan Opera had committed itself to the support of a full-scale resident company. The war had treated the San Francisco Opera no less harshly than it had the Met, but with the end of the war the company was poised to exploit the availability of a whole new generation of European artists hitherto isolated in enemy countries. American singers, too, found San Francisco a hospitable environment for their talents. Elsewhere in the United States, operatic excitement was provided by a rise in staged college and university productions, often under the resident leadership of musicians born and trained in Europe.

The move to American performers was hardly restricted to singers. By the end of the war, the careers of such successful instrumentalists as Leon Fleisher, Eugene Istomin, William Kapell, and Isaac Stern were launched. Leonard Bernstein's success as a composer was matched by the huge impression he was making as a conductor in the wake of his spectacular debut with the New York Philharmonic in 1943.

The audience for all these products of American musical life was not restricted to those who attended live performances. Radio broadcasts of symphony concerts were flourishing, with national leadership being taken by the commercially sponsored Sunday broadcasts of the New York Philharmonic and the NBC Symphony Orchestra. Other major orchestras were regularly carried over radio; on the West Coast, for instance, the San Francisco Symphony Orchestra and the Los Angeles Philharmonic alternated weekly one-hour Sunday-evening broadcasts, commercially sponsored by the Standard Oil Company of California. CBS regularly presented American music, played by its staff musicians and conducted by composer Bernard Herrmann. In addition, many local radio stations, among them WOR and WQXR in New York and KPO in San Francisco, employed staff musicians to play regular concerts of serious music, both pre-twentieth-century and contemporary.

With the audience for radio broadcasts went a healthy market for phonograph recordings of American orchestras. At war's end no fewer than *seven* domestic orchestras were under contract to major American companies. The Boston, San Francisco, and NBC orchestras were employed by RCA Victor; the New York, Philadelphia, Pittsburgh, and Cleveland orchestras by CBS/Columbia. In addition, both companies hired pick-up groups of skilled orchestral players to record with such conductors as Stokowski.

Mention should also be made of the relatively halcyon state of music criticism at this time. New York, of course, had many more newspapers than it has now. In addition to the *Times* and the *Herald Tribune*, there were the *World-Telegram* and the *Journal-American* in the afternoon. All of these papers carried extensive coverage of musical events. At the *Times*, Olin Downes actually influenced the state of the musical repertory, the last *Times* critic to have done so; his championing of Sibelius was important in elevating that composer to near-classic status in America. At the *Tribune*, Virgil Thomson was quite simply the best critic in the country, owing to both his perspicacity and prose style; indeed, he was the best critic to have graced an American newspaper within living memory. Across the country, several critics, among them Claudia Cassidy in Chicago, Alfred Frankenstein in San Francisco, Max de Schauensee in Philadelphia, and John Rosenfield in Dallas, established themselves as influential molders of regional and even national musical opinion. There was a flourishing music criticism in magazines as well; musical events were regularly covered not just in such trade organs as the *Musical Courier* and *Musical America* but even in the *Nation*.

Music education too was flourishing. The Curtis Institute was continuing to accept only the most gifted young students, entirely on scholarship. At the Eastman School of Music in Rochester, composer Howard Hanson was making his mark as a tireless conductor of American music. At Juilliard in New York, composer William Schuman had just become the school's president, and was about to embark upon a radical reformulation, the first in American cultural history, of the entire music-theory curriculum. In such an out-of-the-way place as Denton, Texas, Wilfred Bain (with the assistance of piano teacher Silvio Scionti) was making the music school of North Texas State College an exciting adventure in the artistic development of an entire geographical region. In general, everywhere in America the great boom in music education was beginning, with enrollments rising and faculty members in demand. Not only was the situation healthy in professional music training; music education in the nation's elementary schools properly stressed such important ways of learning the first steps to great music as sight reading and sight singing.

Finally, something must be said about the state of patronage for music. Still close enough to the nineteenth century to have some idea of *noblesse oblige* and the Gospel of Wealth, the very rich counted it a privilege to support great musical institutions. There was support from them too for contemporary composers—through, for instance, the League of Composers in New York and its quarterly review *Modern Music*. Just as important, these community leaders were often interested in unobtrusive patronage of highly gifted individuals; in 1945 in San Francisco, for example, both Leon Fleisher and Isaac Stern were the recipients of continuing and generous private philanthropy.

Altogether, the impression one has when looking back at the condition of American music in 1945 is of an art proudly ensconced in the pantheon of classic civilization and in the intellectual world of contemporary cultural art. There was Stravinsky's historic association with Diaghilev and Cocteau, and Schoenberg's relation with Thomas Mann in the brilliant European émigré intellectual community of Southern California during the war; there was Copland's connection to Harold Clurman in theater and Agnes de Mille in dance, Schuman's work for Martha Graham, and Virgil Thomson's collaboration with Gertrude Stein. Whether one chose to look to the past or at the present, at European émigrés or native Americans, music and musicians seemed central to the life of the mind.

It seems clear even from this summary that the mood in American music at the end of 1945 was one of hope. The hope was that our country could produce an independent, autonomous musical life which would take its full place on the stage of world history, both in the sense of adding to the great music already written in Europe and in the sense of providing new, recognizably American music and performers capable of defining the idea of a serious art. Forty years have now passed since 1945. After one has made every necessary allowance for the nostalgia and the fog to which even the best memories—and perhaps especially the memories of the best times—are subject, it seems difficult to avoid the conclusion that we live today in a new musical world, a world vastly different and in many significant ways less rich and certainly less solid.

By the early 1960s, various problems of serious musical development—or rather of its lack—began to appear. In 1961, when Virgil Thomson came to write a new preface for *The State of Music* (1939), his lively exposition of what it was like to be a serious composer in America, he found that while the world really was different from what it had been two decades earlier, the art only looked as if it had changed:

> Mostly what has changed in twenty years is the economic and political background. These changes, however, are so tremendous that almost everybody under thirty-five is dazzled by them, unable to see through them or around them, and tends in consequence to see today's world of art as also full of novelty. . . . [W]hen we see them, as we do today in music, painting, and poetry, mistaking for deep originality and for invention diluted versions of our century's earlier masters (who really *were* radical), then one does feel moved to remind them that we too, when young, had an intellectual life and that an inflated market is merely an inflated market.

What Thomson was referring to in these rather guarded words was the spectacular rise of an avant-garde in serious composition, an avant-garde which prided itself upon breaking the vessels that had previously contained musical art. Thomson himself called these vessels "organization, flexibility, spaciousness, and expressive variety"; he went on to remark that in music since 1914, "there has been no further structural growth, only constriction."

Difficult though it may be to make such distinctions in practice, it is nonetheless necessary to establish the general principle that after 1945 musical composition, not just in the United States but in the whole Western world, separated into two wings: modernism, including its direct descendants, and an avant-garde that attempted not just to create new music but to redefine music as an aesthetic enterprise. In Europe numerous living practitioners of modernism—composers like Kodály in Hungary, Dallapiccola in Italy, Martin in Switzerland,

and Honegger and Poulenc in France—continued to write, as they had before, in styles which, though fully based upon developments in twentieth-century composition, remained predicated upon the existence of a general music-loving audience. In the United States, the major figures of American composition—Copland, Schuman, Bernstein, and others—likewise continued to write a new-sounding music which retained traditional parameters. Of all these composers, only Bernstein found a large audience for his postwar music, and that audience was only attracted to his works for Broadway.

The leading American composers of the mid-1940s were joined by colleagues whose reputations were to be made later in the same decade and in the first years of the 1950s. Merely to list some of these artists is to recollect much beautiful music which still has not found its proper place in our performers' repertories: William Bergsma, David Diamond, Ross Lee Finney, Andrew Imbrie, Leon Kirchner, Peter Mennin, Vincent Persichetti, Ned Rorem, and Hugo Weisgall. Of this generation, only Elliott Carter has managed to stake out an assured position in our concert life; sadly, it is difficult to avoid the conclusion that Carter's numerous performances owe more to the credit performers hope to earn for negotiating their way through the transcendental difficulties of his music than to any real audience comprehension of the works themselves.

In the field of opera, there have been two composers since 1945 who have in fact managed to write works whose surefire audience appeal is responsible for widespread performances. Of this pair, the more successful has been Gian Carlo Menotti, who, although Italian by birth, was educated in America and made his home here. His string of hits has included *The Old Maid and the Thief* (1939), *The Medium* (1946), *The Telephone* (1947), *The Consul* (1950), and *Amahl and the Night Visitors* (1951). The other successful operatic composer is Carlisle Floyd, whose chief success has been the early *Susannah* (1955); among his subsequent operas are *Wuthering Heights* (1958), *Of Mice and Men* (1969), and *Willie Stark* (1981). It is a measure of the limited nature of these composers' achievements, and also of the great gulf which now exists between intellectual musical life and generally accessible new music, that their work is today without any major standing among serious composers and performers.

The real action in composition for many years after 1945 was, of course, with the avant-garde. The two streams of this movement, in the United States as in Europe, took widely differing positions on whether music should be a free or an ordered activity. In Europe, Karlheinz Stockhausen charted a confident course from totally controlled tape compositions to almost totally improvised performance events. Pierre Boulez, by contrast, extended the implications of Schoenberg's (and Anton Webern's) twelve-tone practices to other, non-pitch-related components of music. In the United States, John Cage spoke for freedom, carrying the cause as far as writing his infamous $4'33''$ (1952), a work of pure silence in which only duration and absolute silence are specified. Cage's antithesis was Milton Babbitt, who managed to make twin careers as the composer of carefully planned works of extreme desiccation and as the writer of arcane and forbiddingly self-confident articles on new music. He has the further distinction of having written an essay, a classic avant-garde definition of independence from the audience, entitled "Who Cares If You Listen?" (1958).

The names of some of the followers of this avant-garde should be mentioned. It must be borne in mind that several of these figures managed to leap back and forth across the divide which, one might have thought, separated the practitioners of freedom from the advocates of order. Whether these composers preferred the undisciplined concocting of sounds or the exact formulation of sounds which impressed only their inventors as music, their names describe an era which would now seem past in every way, were it not for the damage it did (and continues to do in the academy): Earle Brown, Charles Dodge, Morton Feldman, Dick Higgins, Lejaren Hiller, Alvin Lucier, Otto Luening, Max Mathews, Pauline Oliveros, Morton Subotnick, and Vladimir Ussachevsky. Nor, I suppose, should the name of Charlotte Moorman be left off this roll of avant-garde honor; her contributions to the art of topless cello playing provided an easy transition to the present generation of performance artists like Laurie Anderson and David Byrne, who compel admiration for their ability to make a success, onstage and in recording, of their musical shortcomings.

By the mid-1960s it was becoming clear that the avant-garde, understood as an assault on the sensibilities even of those who might otherwise appreciate an attack on tradition, was running out of steam.

Even such a figure as Boulez, the very *beau idéal* of the refusal to compromise with the philistines, began at this time to cultivate the international conducting career which would bring him in 1969 to the New York Philharmonic, where he was a propagandist for the music not just of the pathfinders of the Second Viennese School (Schoenberg, Berg, and Webern), but also of such a hitherto despised nineteenth-century romantic as Franz Liszt. Just how far Boulez had gone in giving up his devotion to the present may be gathered from the title of another essay sacred to the postwar avant-garde mythology, his "Schoenberg is Dead" (1952).

In American composition the result of the weakening of the avant-garde was a desire to write music that a new, youthful, politically and socially aware audience might like. The candidates for the Pied Piper of the young varied. George Crumb wrote sensually appealing sound-effects music, depending for appeal on "in" subjects (such as the whale) and texts (such as the poetry of García Lorca). George Rochberg wrote in a neo-romantic style, prompting even such a hardhearted observer of new music as the *Times*'s Harold C. Schonberg to think of Brahms, and to like what he heard. More convincing as descendants of the old avant-garde were Steve Reich and Philip Glass, who wrote a music which embraced the trendy art-world aesthetic of minimalism and the popular rock-music aesthetic of simple-minded harmonic repetitiveness. While the career of Reich has seemed to wane in recent years, that of Glass has waxed in opera houses here and in Germany. Neither composer has succeeded in winning any audience at all from traditional music lovers or from the most respected performers of traditional music.

A new breed of composer has recently come to the fore, writing what we are told is a fresh kind of music. Perhaps the most convenient, if certainly not the most accurate, name for it is "New Romanticism," the phrase the New York Philharmonic used for its 1983 festival of contemporary music. The music assembled for this festival by the composer Jacob Druckman, the Philharmonic's adviser in these matters, seemed neither romantic, lacking any capacity to stir listeners' hearts, nor new, failing to reveal any fresh compositional voices. Even David Del Tredici's composition based on *Alice in Wonderland*, one of the more applauded pieces of the festival, seemed like warmed-over *Salome*. Elsewhere in the Philharmonic concerts, American music was represented by many of the old familiar names from the avant-garde: George Crumb, Lukas Foss, Donald Martino, George Roch-berg, Frederic Rzewski, Morton Subotnick, Charles Wuorinen, and Druckman himself. In a further reminder of the good old days, loudspeakers and electronic consoles, those jolly elements of the most refined avant-garde taste, were much in evidence. There were also at least two composers—John Adams and Nicholas Thorne—whose unbuttoned vulgarity in writing music based upon the hoariest of stock romantic clichés simply defied the imagination. Significantly, by far the best piece on these programs—*Colloquies* (1979)—was by William Schuman, a representative of the 1945 generation. When the Philharmonic repeated the festival in 1984, the superior quality of the earlier American music was underlined again, a major work being Elliott Carter's Brass Quintet, another survivor of the best days of our older modernism. It must also be remarked that the Philharmonic, for whatever reason, did not choose to repeat its festival of new music in 1985.

The same dubious state of affairs obtains in opera. The most traditional producers of grand opera in America today—the Metro-politan in New York, the Lyric Opera of Chicago, and the San Francisco Opera—have pretty much turned their backs on new and old American works, as well as on difficult, post-Berg works in general.

The evidence of this retrograde disposition on the part of great operatic institutions is all around us. The Met, for example, seems happy to let the deadline for delivery on its two new commissions—one from the musically complaisant John Corigliano and the other from Druckman—be extended into the unforeseeable future. In the meantime, it is having the greatest difficulty making up its mind to produce Arnold Schoenberg's classic (if little known) *Moses und Aron* (1932). The Chicago Lyric seems content, under the leadership of Ardis Krainik, to stick to the mainline repertory of the nineteenth century, with an occasional token lunge at the contemporary. In San Francisco, the supercession of longtime director (and conductor) Kurt Herbert Adler by erstwhile record company executive Terence McEwen has meant a return to safe repertory very much in the style of Chicago's. At the New York City Opera, though Beverly Sills's present summer season ventures no further than Puccini's *Turandot*, the fall season does include the New York premiere of an American work, Dominick Argento's *Casanova*. (Tellingly, *Casanova* was commissioned not by the City Opera but by the Minnesota Opera, where it received its first performance.)

There is undoubtedly a great amount of opera production going on around the country, some of it even including new American operas. Much publicity accompanies the performance of these works, and seasoned observers of the operatic scene testify to a new attitude of pleasurable reception by the audiences in attendance. The only rub in this happy story is that this music has such a thin effect to make *qua* music; this verdict applies in much the same way to such otherwise different recent works as Stephen Paulus's *The Postman Always Rings Twice* (1982), Leonard Bernstein's *A Quiet Place* (1983), and Thea Musgrave's *Harriet, the Woman Called Moses* (1985). As for the contribution of experimental music theater, so widely trumpeted just a short while ago, little of any interest, save for *Einstein on the Beach* (1975), the collaboration of Robert Wilson and Philip Glass, seems to have arisen to affect even the wish lists of opera houses and fans.

Despite all the inadequacies of the current music scene, there is indeed a new spirit abroad in music, a spirit of accommodation to the perceived failure of so much recent composition. This spirit is evident not just in the effort of a popularly oriented former avant-gardist like Philip Glass to find a new public. It is evident in the rise of a California school of composition which, as in the music of Robert Erickson played at an Alice Tully Hall concert this past spring, seemingly attempts to provide a music to enjoy hot tubs by. It is also evident in the relationship of much less flamboyant creative figures to the traditional performing institutions which now either commission them for single works or employ them in residencies.

A fascinating look at the way composition is now increasingly being approached was provided this past winter by a live broadcast of a Minnesota Orchestra concert. The chief attraction of the concert was the world premiere of *Symphony: Watermusic*, a large-scale work evidently based on images of Minnesota's many lakes and written by the orchestra's composer-in-residence, Libby Larsen. Despite its ambitious scoring—including (according to the broadcast commentary) an expanded percussion ensemble made up of vibraphone, triangle, tam-tam, bell tree, wind chimes, bass drum, snare drum, tubular bells, cymbals, marimba, crotal, chimes, tom-toms, temple blocks, bongos, sleigh bells, tenor drum, orchestra bells, wind machine, harp, piano, and celesta—the work itself at its best moments did no more than echo Thomson's earlier, and vastly more successful, attempts to write a quasi-original, folk-like music. At its less successful moments, it sounded like note-spinning done to accompany a nonexistent nature film.

The chief interest of this broadcast concert did not lie in Libby Larsen's composition itself, however. It rather emerged in a lengthy intermission interview she gave after the performance. Because what she said seems to capture so exactly the mood in which so much serious music is being made today, it deserves quotation at length:

> INTERVIEWER: There is often the soul-searching that a composer goes through as far as whether his or her music is up-to-date. . . . Is that consideration of any importance to you as a composer?
>
> LIBBY LARSEN: I don't worry about the relative forwardness-or backwardness-looking of my music. What I care very much about, and what many composers I'm working with are taking into account, is that I consider as part of the creative process the audience who is going to hear the piece, and what I'm taking into account [is] the fact that music lives in the moment, it's performed in a single moment and an audience is there that moment to hear the music. And so I don't write music that may be understood a hundred years from now. I write music very much wanting to have it understood now.

It is difficult to disagree with this statement of liberation from the compulsive desire of composers of the past several decades always to be with the latest trends. But Libby Larsen, in being equally clear about how she intends to accomplish this goal of having her music understood now, seems to transform the kind of effort people used to direct toward choosing a style into identifying a market:

> I think a composer these days has a tremendous challenge to decide what his or her style and audience is going to be, so a composer who is being trained academically. . . can make a choice

as to whether he or she is going to elect to have an audience of a very small number, that being one that is interested in the process of composing, whether the piece is serially constructed, whether the piece is based in tonality or not, in other words, caring much more about thinking about the piece rather than hearing it, and that's a very small number of people for a given piece. . . . What I've chosen is to make my living, if possible, and to write my music and create my art in the concert situation.

The difficulty with such egoistic, career-oriented activity is that it must justify itself at some point by reference to an external good. In the case of music composition over the last century and more, that good has been seen to be the education of a growing—and democratically constituted—public in the nature of music and its place in a wider world of culture. For Libby Larsen, such a goal seems inappropriate:

[T]he whole notion . . . is a myth, that the orchestra has a duty to educate the audience concerning contemporary music. It's the duty to educate that's the operative phrase here. That's a phrase that's tossed around a lot among concert-going and concert-giving groups, both chamber groups and orchestra groups: we have a duty to educate. As an audience member myself, I don't particularly come to a concert to be educated. I come to a concert to listen to music and make up my own mind. And, given that, and translating my own feelings as an audience member over to the general audience, I have come to think that it's not important for an orchestra to play what's considered to be an intellectual masterpiece of the twentieth century in order to educate an audience. It's important that the orchestra play that masterpiece because it works on a program, so that the total program has the final outcome similar to what an audience would get if it were to hear an all-Mozart program or an all-baroque classics program. . . . The idea of duty to educate becomes secondary, the idea to put together good listening experiences for the audience becomes primary, and the attitude switches from slightly pejorative—we must educate you—to very optimistic: we want to give you the best work we can.

It is possible to have sympathy for the composer's plight in dealing with an audience well trained in the recent past to be wary of contemporary composers bearing musical offerings. Put another way, it is quite natural for the composer to wish to appear before the public as muse rather than scourge. It is also possible to appreciate the immense amount of intellectual and emotional upheaval which is involved in cutting one's ties to the notion that anything an audience likes must, *ipso facto*, be bad. But even granting all this, it would still seem a mistake, in reacting against the excesses of the musical avant-garde, to give up the idea of education and to replace it entirely with a gospel of amusement. There is more in music education, after all, than delivering an unpleasant and unwanted message to an unwilling audience. Its purpose is the teaching of civilization and beauty; the need exists all the more after the misfires in music composition over the last forty years.

There is another reason why the composer and those who serve him must not lightly give up their duty to educate an audience. The arts—including music—form a relationship with the audience based upon two principles: that of education, and that of entertainment. In the absence of entertainment, a condition certainly familiar to the musical avant-garde, education becomes impossible (and even seems like an unwarranted assertion of arrogance). But in the absence of education, all that is left is entertainment—the mindless pursuit by the audience of empty satisfactions and trivial delights, and by the artist of glamorous success and bloated fame.

Here, I think, is the key to understanding what has happened to our musical life in recent years, and to knowing just where we are today. Where we are is in an era of purposeless performance, an era in which performance entertains and does nothing more than entertain. The continuing shortage of significant new works, most pronounced in opera but equally apparent in orchestral and instrumental music, has thrown the weight of musical activity onto the performance of already validated masterpieces. The full horror of this situation has been masked in America for many years by two extraordinary factors: the existence of an almost inconceivably large corpus of great music and the fortuitous arrival of great European performers on our shores just before World War II. There is hardly any need at this point to preach the virtues of the composers from before the time of Bach to World

War I. But we do sometimes forget the performer's role in bringing this music to us. In a very real sense Landowska brought us the world's greatest performances of Bach and Scarlatti; Walter brought us Mozart; Toscanini, Beethoven; Schnabel, Schubert (and Beethoven too!); Rubinstein, Chopin; Monteux, the French masters and Stravinsky; Adolf Busch and Rudolf Serkin, chamber music; and Lotte Lehmann, *Lieder*. For many years we enjoyed nothing less than an unparalleled golden age of music performance. Sadly, this golden age is over.

By contrast, what we have now in music performance are careers without achievement and glamour without content. The present situation of two of our historically greatest orchestras—the New York Philharmonic and the Boston Symphony Orchestra—is a case in point: both are playing badly, and both are undergoing crises of musical leadership, with administrators and patrons so paralyzed by their knowledge of how dire the situation is that the necessary corrective measure of looking for new music directors seemingly cannot be undertaken. That these orchestras should seriously consider appointing American conductors—or at least full-time American residents—to lead them appears to be unthinkable. In general, the lot of American-born conductors still seems miserable, with most major conducting opportunities closed off to them on the grounds of their supposed lack of distinction and of box-office appeal.

It is true we have had some famous instrumentalists among us. The most famous of these was pianist Van Cliburn, whose victory in the 1958 Tchaikowsky Competition in Moscow (another sign, by the way, of the continuing primacy of foreign influence in our performing life) propelled him into the greatest career an American-born instrumentalist has ever known. There can be little doubt that Cliburn's career had foundered by the mid-1960s, due to the public's insatiable appetite for newer stars and the artist's own inability to say no to the wrong kind of success. Among thriving instrumentalists at the present time, there is the violinist Itzhak Perlman, whose public image as the Luciano Pavarotti of the violin seems securely established. An American resident (though born in Israel), Perlman is unique in the history of violin playing for being the most famous virtuoso of the day without at the same time having had any effect on the playing of other violinists, either in style or repertory. The same can be said of the cellist Yo-Yo Ma, who now seems well on the way to becoming for the cello what Perlman has been for the violin. No American keyboard players have reached the unquestioned eminence of Perlman and Ma, or of violinist Pinchas Zukerman; no domestic pianist since William Kapell has seemed both truly American and equally at home in both traditional romantic and recent repertory.

We are often told of the revolution supposedly brought to performances of older music, and to our perception of that music, by the booming vogue for "authentic" performances on "original" instruments. But even the best of these performances seem to suggest that the old adage about failed pianists taking up the organ applies with at least equal force to the harpsichord, the fortepiano, unaltered string instruments, and original woodwind and brass instruments. Interestingly enough, one of the most talked-about recent performances in a semi-authentic mode—that of Handel's opera *Semele* at Carnegie Hall this past winter—featured a triumphant appearance of a great American singer, contralto Marilyn Horne. Horne's triumph, at least to this listener, stemmed as much from her camp portrayal as from her undoubted vocal excellence. Horne's success as a Handelian notwithstanding, it is difficult to overlook the fact that the authentic-performance movement is headquartered not in the United States but in England and on the Continent; when the Chamber Music Society of Lincoln Center and public radio wished to celebrate the three-hundredth anniversary of Bach's birth with period performances, they did not do so with American forces but instead brought Christopher Hogwood and his Academy of Ancient Music in from London.

Where composition and performance lead, all the rest will follow; where they falter, everything else will falter as well. The complete abdication by major American recording companies to their European betters is a story too well known to require much comment; it is enough to remark that no American orchestra now makes more than isolated recordings for an American company. Rumor now has it that almost all American orchestras, in order to record at all, must themselves pay the musicians. American soloists do in fact continue to record, but not necessarily here. Columbia/CBS has just announced that the new series of orchestral recordings with jazz/classical trumpeter Wynton Marsalis will take place not with an American ensemble but rather with the Philharmonia Orchestra of London, led by Finnish conductor Esa-Pekka Salonen. Similarly, the recent and much-acclaimed Mozart concerto recordings played and conducted by Murray Perahia, the most successful young American pianist of the past two decades, were recorded in England, with the English Chamber Orchestra.

The situation of music criticism—even according to the music critics themselves—is not good. The ability to write interesting, even exciting, criticism for the wide music-loving public seems a thing of the past. Instead we now have two unsatisfactory kinds of music journalism. The first kind, at home in our best newspapers and the *New Yorker*, is infused by academic musicology and ends up striking the reader as overdependent on gleanings from the best reference books; the second, all too prevalent across the country, fills the columns of newspapers with an unattractive combination of musical and literary incompetence.

Music education, too, seems in a bad way. Though the past forty years have seen an enormous expansion of professional music training in this country, there has been no corresponding effort to train a general audience in the basic knowledge and skills of great Western music so necessary to go beyond appreciation to understanding. Instead of a disciplined curriculum there is the cult of the "arts experience," the passive witnessing by schoolchildren and teachers alike of exotic activities of professionals brought in to strut their moment on the stage—and then disappear. The result of not teaching the most basic skills to schoolchildren is by now obvious to every musician: a gradual deterioration of the sophistication of the musical public and a marked decline in the size of the core audience on which day-to-day artistic life depends. Professional training itself shows every sign of being conducted in an atmosphere of basic uncertainty as to whether jobs can ever be found for the thousands of music graduates turned out each year; student populations now seem to be dropping, and increasingly a good teacher is entirely defined as one who can recruit students. Unfortunately, the one area in which music trainees might find employment—that of teaching substantive material in elementary and high schools to every child, not just to those children who will become professionals—is mostly despised as an unrewarding and unfulfilling activity.

Patronage, too, for all the happy statistics of dollars given being ground out, is at a low ebb. The committed private patron, willing to contribute large sums for operating expenses on an annual basis, is in vanishingly short supply. Every musical institution—including the greatest—now knows the very real difficulty of finding board members who will give money and who know enough to know why and to what they are giving. The recent emphasis by arts institutions on corporate contributions has only demonstrated the interest of these funders in creating favorable publicity for the corporation rather than in providing basic support for an ongoing musical life.

As the *quality* of patronage declines, fears naturally arise about the future *quantity* of support. The situation is thus ripe for "development directors," "marketing specialists," and their like. The following material, quoted from a recent press release of the Lyric Opera of Chicago, shows just how far off the artistic track today's fund raisers will go in pursuit of what they see as today's new breed—or perhaps, given the release's shift in interest from art to food, bread—of patron:

William B. Graham, the prominent civic leader and highly respected industrialist, was reelected to the presidency of Lyric Opera of Chicago's board of directors at its unique annual meeting, which took place this year on Wednesday evening, May 1, when some 400 of the world-renowned non-profit Chicago opera-producing organization's voting members (the voting privilege prerequisite is a yearly contribution of $250 or more) came together on the huge stage of the Civic Opera House to be wined and dined in gourmet fashion, while seated at tables set 'gainst the background of the strikingly lighted stage decor for Handel's "Samson," which is to be presented in the coming fall–winter season. Only following the dinner, did the conventional business of an annual corporation meeting begin, and as soon as those deliberations concluded, the assembled "stockholders" became the audience for a mini-concert, presented by soprano Susan Dunn, fast-rising star in the opera firmament. Thus, it can be understood why the press has rightly written that Lyric's annual gathering of its top contributors is "hands down, the world's most glamorous corporate conclave."

At the cocktail hour which preceded the "main event," hors d'oeuvres were served along with drinks in the foyer of the opera house, and those goodies included Country Style Pâté Fingers, garnished with Cornichons on Rye Bread; Tart Shells with Mushroom and Cheese Topping; Artichokes Parmesan; and Prosciutto-Wrapped Brie Cheese. Then the guests streamed down the aisles of the great theatre and onto the brilliantly illuminated stage, traversing the festooned ramps over the orchestra pit. Once everybody was seated at the pearl-gray-covered tables (giving the impression, when glimpsed from out in the house, that the diners might be performers in a grand opera banquet scene) service began with Cold Soup à la Prince from special containers on service plates, garnished with Three Circles of Skin-on Cucumber, Fresh Chives and sprinkled with Bay Shrimp. Then came Sautéed Breast of Chicken with Wing Bone (batted out, with the skin side scored and charred) set on Mushroom Rice Soubise (very moist) and crowned with Bernaise Velouté and Fresh Tarragon. "Veggies" consisted of Fresh Asparagus and Fresh Sugared Carrots with Sage. And, there were baskets of French Bread Melba Sticks, Miniature Twisted Rolls and Individual Butter Rosettes. The dessert delight was a Meringue Circle set on a deep pool of Fudge, topped with a Whole Strawberry, and there was Sabayon Sauce, too. Chairman for the evening's myriad special arrangements was Mrs. Frederick H. Prince and vice-chairman was Mrs. Theodore Tieken, Jr. CITICORP/CITIBANK, which again has underwritten the total costs of the lavish event, was represented by Howard C. Morgan, Senior Vice President and Senior Corporate Officer of Citicorp, and Thomas F. Barnum, Citicorp Division Executive responsible for Citicorp Diners Club.

And then, of course, there is government. In the twenty-year history of the National Endowment for the Arts, founded with such high expectations in 1965, there has been much talk of an increase in the number of institutions, artists, and audiences served, and remarkably little talk of the art produced which would not have existed save for the NEA's money. There is no point in assigning primary blame to the NEA for the present musical situation in the United States; the agency's authorizing legislation states (quite properly) that "no government can call a great artist or scholar into existence." But then the legislation goes on to find it "necessary and appropriate for the Federal Government to help create and sustain not only a climate encouraging freedom of thought, imagination, and inquiry, but also the material conditions facilitating the release of this creative talent." There can be no doubt that government help for the arts, under the conditions of our democracy, has not infringed upon "freedom of thought, imagination, and inquiry." Unfortunately, the NEA's emphasis on "material conditions" has meant that over the past twenty years subsidies have largely gone to already successful institutions and administrators, and to those who serve the interests of these very interested parties.

This natural urge in Washington to serve large audiences, and to do so by encouraging institutions and artists to entertain these audiences, has been well-nigh irresistible; so, alas, has been the tendency (again a result of serving those interests which squawk the loudest) to discharge the NEA's duty to new art by support of an often mindless avant-garde. In the process, a great opportunity for basic education in the various arts has been lost. The result of this policy of neglect clearly has been a loss of comprehension by the audience of both twentieth-century works and even of classic masterpieces. It is significant that because of the increasingly rare ability to read music, today's lengthy concert program notes can rarely include vital notated musical examples. Given the changed national climate for serious education in general, the NEA now has a chance to reclaim its opportunity. It should do so at once.

And so, from the vantage point of a doubtful present, we look to the future of an art we dearly love. Is there no more to be said about the future than that "Music Is a Growth Industry," which was the *New York Times*'s headline on a recent, especially tub-thumping article? Is there no more to be adduced in favor of music than its value for tourism, for urban redevelopment, and for enhanced recruitment possibilities for executives and their families?

There are indeed better arguments to be made for music, if not as a growth industry then at least as an art. First-class music is still being written; recent New York performances have shown the power of the music of two still not yet fully developed composers, the starkly modernist (in the best sense) George Tsontakis and the rather less severe Ellen Taaffe Zwilich. Our great orchestras are still full of wonderful instrumentalists, lacking only serious, dedicated conductors to lead them. Our nation's schools still employ many teachers who only need to be asked to teach the elementary skills of making and understanding music. America's system of private philanthropy still has the resources to do the necessary job of supporting serious culture; the needed sophistication is a matter in the first instance of general education, which is, after all, a national specialty. More and more it seems that what we lack is not the ability to achieve a musical culture but rather the willingness to take music—and our achievements and our failures in it—seriously.

2.

Whereas the preceding was a historical sketch of recent American music, this essay is a personal account, published in the November 1987 New Criterion, of my commitment to a body of twentieth-century music, both European and American, that I have always found of high value. The somewhat plaintive tone that comes through here is a consequence both of the travails of this repertory and of my own difficulties in arousing interest in making it available. Since the essay was written, I have continued my attention to the task at the Waterloo Music Festival, where in the past two seasons we have given extremely well-received performances of two symphonies each by the Americans Walter Piston and David Diamond. Furthermore, Gerard Schwarz, Waterloo's principal conductor and my close comrade-in-arms in these matters, has recently made a best-selling CD of two symphonies of Howard Hanson, an unfairly neglected American composer whose music he first performed at Waterloo.

Doing New Music, Doing American Music

A N Y O N E   W H O fancies himself a thinker, I suppose, should have the experience of mixing his ideas with his labor; particularly is this true in the case of American musical intellectuals, beset as they are by the difficulties of bringing the strengths and weaknesses of the New World to the already existing corpus of European masterpieces. In all the different ways I have worked in music, I have been conscious of the peculiar problems associated with being an American musician. This was true when I was solely a performer. It remained true when, in early middle life, I became a critic. Now, in my fifties, when I am also what is so nicely called an artistic administrator, I find my awareness of this problem taking up a good deal of my thought.

As a musician I have played the piano. As a critic I have judged the compositions and performances of others. As an administrator I have been deciding what music should be played and who should do the playing. My administrative work has come in my role as the artistic director of the Waterloo Festival and School of Music in New Jersey. Here, for six weeks of activity each summer, I have chosen artists and repertory for twelve programs, six of them orchestral (in the beautifully restored Waterloo Village) and six featuring chamber music (this past summer at Princeton University). As a general rule, choice of artists is limited by commercial availability and, it goes without saying, by taste. Choice of repertory is, in one sense, limited only by the musical riches of the past and present; in quite another, it is hemmed in by a tradition—and a present practice—of taking into account the most highly rationalized, though ultimately doomed, considerations of institutional survival and personal self-interest. The consequences of the ways in which repertory is chosen are of particular significance for new music—and for American music, a body of composition much of which is dear to my heart and vital, I believe, to the future of our composers, our performers, and our audience.

My musical knowledge and tastes have been formed by my experiences not just in listening to music, but in playing it, first as a student and then as a professional. My piano-playing life began largely in the way of all such child-prodigy endeavors. From almost my first lessons I studied the old masters of the old country, beginning with Bach, progressing through Haydn and Mozart, quickly going on to the shorter pieces of Chopin—with due allowances being made for the smallness of my hands—and finally arriving in my early and middle teens at Beethoven and Liszt.

But my training was not completely confined, as so many students' is even to this day, to the music of composers alive a century and more before I was born. My first San Francisco piano teacher, realizing the need for new music, did assign me works by such then-contemporary composers as Bartók, Kabalevsky, Prokofiev, Shostakovich, and Villa-Lobos. I found the newer works given to me—all of them, of course, relatively easy—both piquant in sound and great fun to play.

By the time I went on to my second teacher in the late 1940s, I was no longer simply the prisoner of what went on in my piano lessons. Now 78 RPM records of famous pianists began to play a large part in the formation of my pianistic agenda. In the world of modern music, my first phonographic catch was Vladimir Horowitz's 1945 discs of the

Prokofiev Sonata no. 7 in B-flat major, opus 83 (1942). Here was new music—by turns biting, passionately lyrical, and motoric—to stir my young blood. It was pianistically dazzling in Horowitz's performance, for me still one of the great examples of recorded piano playing. I felt I had to learn the sonata, and I had to play it in concert. Though getting it in my fingers cost me much effort, I was successful with it, even with such a severe critic as the conductor Pierre Monteux (with whom I was then working each summer).

This success emboldened me—though I still was very much a product of "classical" Russian piano teaching, and my theoretical studies with the French composer Darius Milhaud were doing curiously little to interest me in the European music then being written—to look for another contemporary virtuoso work. The work I found was, surprisingly enough, American: the 1949 Sonata of Pennsylvania-born Samuel Barber, which I first heard in the extraordinary 1950 Horowitz recording. I fell in love with it and learned it immediately, though it presented even greater technical and musical (especially rhythmic) challenges than the Prokofiev had. Soon after, I played in concert a brilliant and clangorous new sonata by the Stanford University composer Leonard Ratner, and two works of chamber music by Aaron Copland: the *Vitebsk* trio (1929) and the (almost) twelve-tone Piano Quartet (1950). I loved the challenges of all this knotty music; even more I felt comfortable with the characteristic sound of it, which seemed in its jazzy toughness and hard-edged sentiment to be pure America—my America.

Then, at the end of the 1930s, I came east to Juilliard and began studying with another Russian piano teacher, this time the redoubtable Rosina Lhévinne. Here, in this *echt* turn-of-the-century Moscow atmosphere, anything more dissonantal than the Prokofiev and Barber sonatas was frowned on. As I found when I attempted to play even these sonatas—and later, the Bartók Third Concerto (1945) and the Prokofiev Third Concerto (1921)—Mme Lhévinne's only pedagogic interest in such music lay in rounding off its hard rhythmic and harmonic contours. And when I played the Ratner Sonata through for her, she was chilly and dismissive indeed.

All in all, I had little contact with new music at Juilliard, and what little I did have I owed to a class in 1959–60 with the composer Hugo Weisgall. Because of him I heard a private performance by the

Juilliard Quartet of the hermetic but fascinating Second Quartet (1959) of Elliott Carter a few hours before its first public performance; I also heard a performance in Washington—by the New York City Opera—of Weisgall's striking intellectual and compositional *tour de force*, the opera (based on Pirandello's modernist classic) *Six Characters in Search of an Author* (1956). I regret to say that my only personal contact with American music while I was at Juilliard, other than Hugo Weisgall, was meeting composer William Schuman, then Juilliard's president, after my performance of the Liszt A-major Concerto with the school orchestra.

In the early 1960s, I left Juilliard to pursue the chimera of a solo piano career.[1] Wonderful as the best-known masterpieces of the past (and the great performances of them) are and will remain, there can be little doubt that the most significant performing careers are made by finding one's own music to play, rather than by recapitulating the successes of one's elders. Though I had little desire to become a modern-music specialist, I welcomed an opportunity, in the summer of 1964, to tour with a wind orchestra, appearing as soloist in works by Igor Stravinsky, Paul Hindemith, and Olivier Messiaen. Neither the Stravinsky work (the Concerto for Piano and Wind Orchestra [1923–24]) nor the Hindemith (the Concert Music for Piano, Brass, and Two Harps [1930]) represented a truly contemporary style of composition. By contrast, the Messiaen—his *Oiseaux exotiques* (1955–56)—was totally up-to-date in its complete reliance for musical material on birdcalls, expressed in a virtuoso manner but with precious little of the pastoral; while this work possessed a certain shocking brilliance, and was of a kind of horrid interest to those who had previously thought of music as a human (or even divine) creation, Messiaen's tone-full but curiously tuneless birds scarcely provided a viable basis for music's future, or even for the compositions of others.

I was certainly aware of the avant-garde musical ferment in America and in Europe. I was aware, too, of what this meant: the replacement

---

[1] In the context of my trying for a solo career, I hope I may be forgiven for quoting from *The Concise Oxford Dictionary*'s admirable and suggestive definition of the word "chimera":

> "1. (Gk. myth.) Monster with lion's head, goat's body, and serpent's tail.
> 2. Bogy: thing of hybrid character; fanciful conception. . . ."

of melody and harmony by concepts depending for their interest on words rather than music. This trendy following of the two apparently contradictory but ultimately converging tracks of total serialism and amusical experimentation (the tracks represented by, say, Karlheinz Stockhausen in Europe and John Cage in this country) became all the rage then, and for many years thereafter. It seemed to me that the leadership of musical composition had passed from the composers I had known and played to those whom I could only find to be madmen or bores; I have no reason today to revise my judgment of the period.

Save for Shostakovich, there was little new music coming out of Europe that attracted me at this time. Though all the great names of American music were alive and in all cases, I believe, still composing, "traditional" American modern music had begun the long winter of unpopularity it still (except for a very few pieces of Copland) suffers from today. What was painfully evident on concert programs and record companies' lists was made obvious for everyone to see by the spectacular public and critical failures of the two great American music media events of the 1960s, both of them associated with the grand debuts of Lincoln Center halls: the first performances of Copland's difficult *Connotations* by Leonard Bernstein and the New York Philharmonic at the opening of Philharmonic Hall in 1962, and of Barber's lush *Antony and Cleopatra* by the Metropolitan Opera at the opening of its new house in 1966. Furthermore, what we as a nation had already decided for ourselves seemed to be confirmed by Pierre Boulez's total rejection of American music and composers—save, perhaps, for Elliott Carter—upon his assumption of the post of music director of the Philharmonic in 1971.

So there was little choice for me but to look for the new music amongst the old. In 1965 I read somewhere that the Prokofiev Fourth Concerto, written in 1931 for the one-armed pianist Paul Wittgenstein but neither published nor performed during the Stalin–Zhdanov years of terror and murder, was available in the Soviet Union in a two-piano score. By a circuitous route I obtained the music, and even an engagement to play the concerto the next year (its second New York performance, for it had been played in the early 1960s by Rudolf Serkin with the Philadelphia Orchestra) in Carnegie Hall with John Barnett and the National Orchestral Association, a training orchestra then important in New York and American musical life. Though the performance was well received, and though I soon thereafter played the work's first performances in Boston and San Francisco (with Arthur Fiedler) and in Washington (with Richard Bales), its restriction to just the pianist's left hand had the effect of concentrating audience attention on the pianistic tricks (tricks, I should add, of enduring interest only to other pianists) at the expense of the music's considerable, though subtle and even understated, beauty.

In a curious, though rather different, way, the same unwelcome and artistically profitless diversion of attention from music to performer—a diversion highly characteristic of twentieth-century musical life in general—affected the outcome of my next foray into neglected repertory. Sergei Rachmaninoff's Thirteen Preludes, opus 32, were published in 1910 and belong to the period of the composer's Third Piano Concerto (1909). Demonstrating the effect of the various developments associated with Alexander Scriabin and even later with the young Prokofiev, they mark a considerable advance over such earlier and more immediately attractive works as the Second Piano Concerto (1900–1), the Ten Preludes, opus 23 (1901–3), and the Second Symphony (1906–7). I played these pieces a great deal during the early 1970s. But for all their undoubted beauty, the complexity of their harmonic and digital impasto guaranteed that only pianists would find them of major interest.

At this point I should add for the record that the solo recitals I was playing at this time were under auspices—Community Concerts, Inc., a subsidiary of Columbia Artists Management, Inc., my then-managers—particularly hostile to twentieth-century music. In 1973–74, my last season of fairly regular touring for them, it was only with extremely and perhaps unwisely expended effort that I managed to get them to accept my programming of the ten-minute (and charmingly traditional) Sonata no. 2 (1936) by Paul Hindemith.

For many years, I had been looking for an American work to play with orchestra. Through my friend and colleague Jacob Lateiner, I had become aware in 1965 of Elliott Carter's Piano Concerto, a work which Lateiner had commissioned through the Ford Foundation for his own performance. This immensely difficult work (for performers and listeners alike), which Lateiner was to record live at the work's first performances with the Boston Symphony Orchestra under Erich Leinsdorf and subsequently to play extensively here and in Europe, was by the early 1970s no longer included in his repertory.[2] As I heard him talk about it, and as I listened to his heroic recording, the work began to fascinate me, not just in its transcendent pianistic complexity but also in its communicative possibilities. With the help of associates and friends I arranged to play it, in the summer of 1973 in Aspen (where I was a member of the Aspen Music Festival faculty), and then in 1975 in New York.

What happened to me in the course of arranging, preparing, and playing these two concerts, the first concert greatly inspiring and the second troubling in the extreme, does not just sum up my own experiences in playing new music. I also believe that these experiences accurately describe the general experience of other soloists who are sympathetically inclined to new music but who at the same time do not wish to live in the artificially maintained ghetto of modern-music performance.

Since my Aspen performance of the concerto was scheduled to take place the following August, I began the Carter concerto in November of 1972. From the outset I realized that despite the clear notation of the music and of the composer's intentions regarding its performance, my task was close to insuperable. The number of notes the pianist had to play more or less at the same time, the intricate rhythmic patterns often composed of different meters and tempos occurring sim-ultaneously, the numerous tempo changes based only on subtly calculated rather than obviously perceptible relationships, and the whirlwind speeds at which everything had to be played, all of these combined with the almost total absence of exact repetition of even the short passages to render an exact replication of what Carter had written impossible, at least by me.

I persevered for the necessary nine-month gestation period. While on tour giving recitals—often nightly—of music by Beethoven, Chopin, and Liszt, I painstakingly learned the Carter at the average rate of one page of the two-piano score per day. It was easiest for me to get solid work done when I was lucky enough to find an empty practice studio in a hospitable college music department. Piano stores, those jolly refuges of touring pianists, were rather less accommodating

<hr>

[2] Lateiner's recording of the Carter concerto was available some years ago on RCA 3001, and is now deleted; a new recording, by Ursula Oppens with the Cincinnati Symphony Orchestra under Michael Gielen, is available on New World NW 347.

(at least during business hours), for the salesmen felt, not without reason, that the music I was working on did not show their instruments off at their best. Most problematic to work in, of course, were homes, especially when their living rooms and their pianos were the property of lovers of the kind of music I was playing in my recitals. Once I even remember effecting a rather miraculous cure while practicing in such a home. After a few minutes of my working on the Carter, the husband of the house came in and apologetically told me I had to leave, for his wife was confined to bed in the next room by the after-effects of a serious stroke. In something close to despair, I asked him whether I might practice another five minutes; out of pity he agreed. I began to play some Chopin, and well before the five minutes were up his wife appeared at the door, pale but decidedly ambulatory, to tell me that I might stay as long as I wished.

As the Carter was getting learned, I realized that I must practice it with a second piano substituting for the orchestra. My wife, the pianist and teacher Jeaneane Dowis, asked Jacqueline Schmitt, one of her best students, to learn this complex and compacted piano version of the orchestral part. When we tried to put the two parts together, it immediately became clear that the density and the split-second simultaneities meant that a run-through even for two pianos could not be accomplished without a conductor. So I taught my wife how to beat time in the best conductorial fashion, a task which, with her secure rhythm and remarkable muscular coordination, she learned quickly and solidly. Now the piece really began to take shape, and I realized, to my intense excitement, that underneath all the complexity—just how far underneath I did not at this time yet realize—a work of high emotional power lay dormant.

My excitement, along with the kind of nervous trepidation that must accompany such risky life-tasks as being shot off into space, carried over into my preparations in June and July in Aspen. I received a rude jolt when I was informed, just ten days before the performance was to take place, that the conductor assigned to me, the Brazilian modern-music specialist Eleazar Carvalho, had canceled his appearance due to a sudden medical emergency which would keep him in his native country. What happened then has been well described elsewhere;[3]

[3] See "The Rise of a Young Conductor," by Heidi Waleson, in the *New York Times Magazine*, February 23, 1986.

suffice it to say here that I was given as a conductor the then twenty-five-year-old trumpet virtuoso Gerard Schwarz, whose great qualification for the task was a close acquaintance with Carter's music and that of other difficult contemporary composers. From the outset Schwarz took to the Carter concerto like a champion duck to water; the concert was his orchestral conducting debut, and from that tense summer Sunday afternoon in the Aspen Music Festival tent, he has gone on to a brilliant international career.

The concert itself was marvelously successful, and at least on this occasion the concerto emerged as possessing a kind of Coplandesque American rawness and grandeur. It seemed to me highly likely that, armed with the stunning recording of the performance, I would be able to perform the piece widely. Despite my best efforts—which included the pressing of an LP record from the concert tape and the sending of the resulting disc to orchestras large and small—nothing happened. Not only was I too unknown, but the work seemed to impress all the professional listeners I sent it to as incomprehensible, or at best unperformable, at least within the constraints of the abilities of less-than-major orchestras.

As matters turned out, I did secure one more engagement with the Carter. Through the good offices of friends in the cooperative management hierarchy of the American Symphony Orchestra, I was engaged to play the piece in Carnegie Hall with the orchestra in the winter of 1975. Sadly, Schwarz was not allowed by various factions in the orchestra (whose first trumpet he had been just before going on to be co-principal trumpet of the Philharmonic) to conduct. The conductor chosen to do the concert turned out to possess limited English and to be at once rigid and inclined to passivity in rehearsals. Orchestral discipline, too, seemed poor, and when during the concert a mishap in the first movement—unnoticed, I think, by anyone in the audience except my wife, Schwarz, and Carter—threatened to bring the performance to a screeching halt, I finally became aware that, whoever else might be able to carry the Carter concerto to triumph, I was not so able. When the composer called me in Aspen (I think it was in 1976) to fill in, on three weeks' notice, for someone playing the piece in London at a Prom concert, I begged off on the grounds of a schedule conflict. I have never regretted my decision.

I was helped to this far-from-pleasant frame of mind by something that had happened to me two or so weeks before the Carnegie Hall performance. As part of the usual process of selecting a piano which I would feel comfortable playing on the stage, I had tried, and found wanting for my special purposes, several instruments in the Steinway concert basement on Fifty-seventh Street across from Carnegie Hall. My friend David W. Rubin, then the manager of the Steinway concert department, suggested that I try the Carnegie Hall house piano, which he thought I might find suitable. The hall being free at that moment, we went over, and when I went up on the stage to the piano, Rubin asked me whether he could look at a copy of the score as I played. I replied that I only had the copy from which I played, and that I did not know the work by memory. He immediately assured me that after all my work on the piece I did indeed know it by memory. I offered to try, and I gave him the score. I then played the concerto from beginning to end without the notes in front of me, the only time in my study of the piece I even tried to do so. I have to say that the fact I was able to perform this feat even once—without the orchestra, it is true—impressed me as a sign that I knew the piece reasonably well. Imagine my chagrin, then, when almost immediately after this incident in Carnegie Hall I was listening to a tape of it I had just made in my living room and realized that I was unable, as I sat listening to the playback, to find my place immediately in the score.

I must make clear that the point of this story is not that, if I had difficulty finding my place in the score, then no other pianist playing the piece and listening to his own playback would be able to do so either. I am perfectly willing to admit—for I think the odds are overwhelmingly high—that there are others in the world with greater facility and clarity in playing such music, greater familiarity with the idiom, and better hearing with which to disentangle the conflicting elements which make up the work. But then the question becomes, how many such people are there? Surely there are enough to play the piece many times and in many places, but are there enough people with the needed gifts as listeners to make up a willing audience now or at any conceivable time in the future?

I am afraid that there is little real chance ever of the existence of such an audience. I think that here, though perhaps not in the way the author meant the phrase, we find the true significance of the title Pierre Boulez chose from a picture by Paul Klee for his 1955 article on the possibilities and pitfalls of electronic music: "At the ends of fruitful land ... "[4] In his article Boulez suggested that new compositional techniques, applied to both instrumental and electronic media, would bring us to the very edge of musical possibilities. For me, the Piano Concerto of Elliott Carter, in its level of complexity and dissonance, in its rapidity of movement and change, in the demands it makes on both performers and audience, securely occupies the line separating viable from non-viable music. In my own life, I am afraid I have chosen to stay on the near side of this line, even when that has meant giving up the hope of greatness I once entertained for Carter's music. Others, doubtless, perhaps more adventuresome by nature, will put the line of arability on the other side of Carter. I have no doubt at all that whatever the fate of Carter's mature works may be, composition cannot go further in the direction he has adumbrated and remain what can be recognized as music.

My playing of the Carter put "paid" to one period in my life. Soon I began to write, and within a year I had become the regular music critic for *Commentary*. My first article in that magazine was a highly negative review of a musico-political tract by the English avant-garde composer (and Maoist) Cornelius Cardew, a book which castigated Stockhausen (among other musicians) for being elitist lackeys of imperialism. Then, after an article on Richard Wagner, I found the theme which was to resonate increasingly, not just in my writing, but in my musical thoughts. This theme was the golden age of American musical composition, the period when modernism and a musical audience seemed to come together in the music of Aaron Copland and his coevals. My article on Copland, which appeared in *Commentary* and in my 1979 collection of essays, *Music After Modernism*, was called "Copland as American Composer." It perhaps should have been called: "Where Are You Now, Aaron, When We Need You?"

I made my total rejection of the post–Second World War avant-garde of Stockhausen & Co. clear in a 1979 *Commentary* article (also in *Music After Modernism*) titled "Yesterday's New Music." I followed it almost immediately with a sequel (reprinted in my 1984 collection,

---

[4] Originally published in Herbert Eimert and Karlheinz Stockhausen's new music journal *Die Reihe*, no. 1 (1955; English translation, 1958). It was later collected, under the slightly different title "To the farthest reach of the fertile Country," in Boulez's *Notes of an Apprenticeship*, New York, 1968 (original French edition, 1966).

The House of Music) called "From Avant-Garde to Pop." In this article I rejected the static, pop-tending minimalism of Terry Riley, Steve Reich, and Philip Glass. This concentration on the negative aspects of modern music was welcomed, I suppose, by the many sophisticated music lovers whose love can go no further forward in time than the assassination of the Archduke Francis Ferdinand at Sarajevo.

For myself, I had no desire to confine my own musical life to works and styles I knew and treasured. I craved something in music which the great masters of the European tradition, great as they were, could hardly supply. What I craved was the sound of our own time and our own place, a time and place evoked accurately and affectingly not by the self-indulgent chaos and nihilism so successfully conveyed by the various musical avant-gardes, but rather by the composers for whom music and art were affirmations of life and of peoples—and even, in principle, of the divine.

Perhaps a word is in order here about this idea of art, to which I have felt increasingly drawn for many years. It is not easy for someone with a moderate knowledge of political and social movements of the past century to employ, in an aesthetic context, a phrase like "affirmations of life and of peoples." Despite the fact that much, if not indeed most, great art has been created in the process of making just such affirmations, despite the fact that great art is for countless millions a manifestation of the blessings, rather than the afflictions, of human existence, and despite the fact that the beauty of art provides both artists and audience with a glimpse into the real beauty of the world, there can be no doubt that the idea of art as life-enhancing is now sadly compromised. When such an idea does not merely seem fatuous, it seems to smack of Stalinist socialist realism, of the demand, enforced by murder, that art present a happy face to the world and inspire happy thoughts in its captive audience. Art, we are told everywhere, must be autonomous, rootless, and fundamentally irresponsible—even at the cost of being trivial and ugly—if it is to be valued as art at all.

But it seems to me now that art—and most of all music—can little afford the unwillingness of its supporters to make high claims on its behalf. As churchgoers of yesterday well knew, the devil must not be permitted to have all the good tunes. The idea of art as a beneficent force in the life of the individual and of society was not the only constructive idea appropriated—and perverted—by Stalin and his henchmen: these monsters also latched onto peace, economic development, literacy, and scientific knowledge. In Stalinist hands, all these thoroughly praiseworthy goals were used as mere pretexts for enslavement. In a free society, in the hands of free individuals, these goals, in art as well as in politics, economics, and science, when worked toward and achieved, can and do make life better.

I began increasingly to view the history of American music as a battle between those who would carry on music and those who would destroy it. On one side I found what might be called the traditional modernists, whose music had (in varying degrees) strong historical roots in European art music and the American musical past. On the other side I found the avant-gardists—the droll but subtly hostile Cage; the total serialists, who felt that music composition could be planned and analyzed with the precision of scientific experiments; and the electronicists, who managed to combine in their writing every amusical device made possible by developments in technology. This battle seemed to me to be taking place between those who saw music as speaking to the reality of its listeners' lives and those who saw what they chose to call music as mocking the very idea of such a reality.

In 1981, in a paper delivered at a 92nd Street YM–YWHA conference in New York on contemporary music, I tried to sketch my vision of a viable American modernist musical tradition.[5] I took eleven composers born within a decade of 1900—Douglas Moore, Walter Piston, Virgil Thomson, Howard Hanson, Roger Sessions, Henry Cowell, Roy Harris, Carter, Barber, Schuman, and, of course, Copland himself—who together seemed to me to represent a vastly better time than the present in American composition. Including such divergent tendencies as the cerebralism of Sessions, the Nordic romanticism of Hanson, the naïve but touching experimentalism of Cowell, and the equally naïve but touching traditionalism of Thomson, the grouping was hardly unified; indeed, Copland himself did not mention four of these composers—Moore, Cowell, Barber, and Schuman—in the first edition of his pathbreaking book *Our New Music* (1941).

But whatever the aesthetic differences among all these gifted composers, they shared a central position in American musical life,

---

[5] This paper was published in *Commentary* as "American Music: The Years of Hope," March 1981.

and in contemporary music writing as a natural outgrowth of that life. For all of them, new composition was a part of the shared experience of the community, not an activity spawned in the ivory towers of laboratory and academy. It is the dissimilarity of their creative expressions that distinguished these composers' individual musical personalities; their similarity lay in the seriousness of their attempt, often expressed in a sound of rough rhythms and raw melodic shapes, to create an American music at once natural-sounding and new.

In the early 1980s, I continued to play the piano, though less frequently. In 1980, for example, I played the William Schuman Piano Concerto (1938/1942) in Aspen. Just what problems American music still faced were spookily dramatized for me by the behavior of a disturbed music student who blocked my way backstage just before I was to go out to play. He told me that my secret was out: the piece to be played on the concert was not the concerto of William Schuman but rather that of Robert Schumann, and that as a special favor the student would be willing to play what was (in his estimation) the better piece in my place. More important, however, was that as always the rehearsal time for a beautiful American piece had been skimped, and that the European conductor had brought to the preparation and performance of the work every musical virtue save those of familiarity with the score and ease with the jazz rhythms in which the score abounds.

Two years later, in 1983, I played (in Baltimore, New York, Aspen, and at the Waterloo Festival in New Jersey) the Weisgall Piano Sonata, a piece that the composer had just written for me. This large-scaled, highly chromatic, and often touchingly lyrical work, like so much other marvelous American music, is still in search of performers with successful careers, performers who will treat the music with the care and passion it deserves. It must be said that this ignoring by performers of distinguished music affects not only American music. When my wife and I played, again in Aspen, two important albeit difficult works of Darius Milhaud—the Concerto for Two Pianos and Orchestra (1950) and the Concerto no. 2 for Two Pianos and Percussion (1961)—it was all too clear that despite the composer's years in the 1950s and 1960s of devoted service to the Aspen Festival, his music, once he was no longer alive to oversee its performance, was not treated seriously.

In 1982, I was appointed by President Reagan to the National Council on the Arts, the advisory board of the National Endowment for the Arts, for a six-year term. I found there much concern about aiding American music. Unfortunately, that concern expressed itself either in a kind of shotgun approach to funding (as if throwing money at artistic problems could in itself remedy them) or in a pronounced bias toward "experimental," "cutting-edge" programs. The readiness to support every kind of proposal that came the Endowment's way reflected—and still reflects—a strong discomfort with the very idea of making choices in new art between what can only be called good and bad. The tilt toward the avant-garde stems from the natural readiness of government bureaucracies in a democratic society to honor the old maxim, "The squeaky wheel gets the grease." Whereas the practitioners of what is called the "Next Wave" display ideological fervor and rhetorical moxie, mainstream composers are either too busy writing real music or are bewildered at, and enervated by, the grantsmanship of those whom they find it difficult to regard as colleagues.

In 1985, the Waterloo Music Festival and School, of which I had been a faculty member since its founding in 1976, asked me to succeed my friend and co-worker Gerard Schwarz as the head of the organization's artistic administration (with Schwarz becoming principal conductor). I found myself in a position to make concert programs involving vastly more pieces—including works for large orchestra—than I had been able to perform myself in my many years of playing the piano. My thoughts immediately ran to American music—my kind, as it were, of American music. I saw this music as constituting, at Waterloo, the most significant portion of an orchestral and chamber-music repertory emphasizing the best of twentieth-century music and lesser-known masterpieces from earlier periods.

I immediately realized this musical conception placed me in dangerous conflict with the three principles that govern present-day programming. The first two of these principles can be simplified into maxims: Be sure to give the audience the pieces they already know, and be doubly sure to give them plenty of celebrity soloists famous for performing, to instant acclaim, the most predictably crowd-pleasing works ever written. The third principle is one of seemly respect toward the new: Enough contemporary music of an attention-getting character must be played to ensure that everyone will see that a proper attention is being paid to the art of today, but not so much as to interfere in any way with the real business of concert-giving, which remains the presentation of famous works and performers.

But the reasons for pursuing a contrary policy are great, and for me, compelling. Because of the problems of new music, and because of a decline in public sophistication, I am convinced that we are faced with a diminishing core audience: an increasing shortage of those people who attend concerts regularly and who have a fund of knowledge on which to form their reactions. Similarly, because of social and economic pressures, our young orchestral musicians, trained in our best schools as artisans rather than artists, have given up the goal of having a wide knowledge of classical music in favor of a single-minded quest for success in the job market. Patrons—those whose responsibility and pleasure it is to provide the material conditions for serious art—are being told by administrators that their task is one which the pleasure-calculating Jeremy Bentham would have applauded: the greatest entertainment for the greatest number. All these difficulties seem of particular importance in this country, where we are faced with the task of preserving an aging and over-familiar European repertory in a rapidly modernizing and increasingly hedonistic American culture.

I resolved to see whether in its small way the Waterloo Music Festival and School—despite the received wisdom which decrees that summer-festival programming ought to be frothy and entertaining—could be a proving ground for an attempt to reverse these trends. It seems plain to me that since composition is the primary stuff of music, any attempt to change music must begin with what is being played. Therefore my first concern, one which remains paramount for me today, two years later, is the concert repertory, in particular the missing middle of the repertory, the pieces that lie between what is over-familiar to musicians and music lovers and what is deeply (and I think properly) unacceptable.

Two Waterloo seasons—a total of twenty-four orchestral and chamber-music concerts—have now passed. During this short time, and in these few concerts, in our pursuit of the modern and the unfamiliar we played seventeen works, the majority little known, by eleven historically important and representative American composers. These composers have included Barber (Violin Concerto [1939], *Summer Music* [1955], and *Mutations from Bach* [1967]); Ernest Bloch

(*America: an Epic Rhapsody* [1926]); Carter (one of Eight Pieces for Four Timpani [1950–66]); Copland (Piano Sextet [1937], *An Outdoor Overture* [1938], and Symphony no. 3 [1944–46]); Ingolf Dahl (Music for Brass Instruments [1944]); George Gershwin (Lullaby for String Quartet [1919] and Concerto in F [1925]); Hanson (*Lament for Beowulf* [1925] and *Elegy* [1956]); Harris (Piano Quintet [1936]); Piston (Symphony no. 4 [1950]); Wallingford Riegger (Concerto for Piano and Wind Quintet [1953]); and Schuman (*New England Triptych* [1956]).

In the twentieth-century repertory outside American music—in addition to comfortable and familiar compositions by such composers as Falla, Ibert, Rachmaninoff, Respighi, and Sibelius—we did works by the English Malcolm Arnold (Brass Quintet [1961]); the Hungarian Bartók (Violin Sonata no. 2 [1922] and the Sonata for Two Pianos and Percussion [1937]); the German Boris Blacher (Divertimento for Piano, Trumpet, and Trombone [1948]); the Mexican Carlos Chavez (Soli I for Winds and Brass [1933]); the English Edward Elgar (the little-known Cello Concerto [1919]); the German Hans Pfitzner (Three Preludes from *Palestrina* [1917]); the French Francis Poulenc (Brass Trio [1922, rev. 1945] and Piano Sextet [1932–39]); the Russian Prokofiev (Double Bass Quintet [1924] and Symphony no. 5 [1944]); and the Russian Shostakovich (String Quartet no. 1 [1935], Violin Concerto no. 1 [1955], and Symphony no. 15 [1971]).

Taken together, the American with the non-American and the unfamiliar with the familiar, the twentieth-century music we did at Waterloo came close to making up half of our programs. Not only did this change from conventional program making bring about a welcome balance; it supplied a welcome breath of air and a touch of lightness to our concerts. The American music showed itself the equal in importance and beauty of any music written elsewhere at the same time. In this new atmosphere, the many masterpieces of the past we did, and the well-known soloists we occasionally featured, seemed all the more interesting and exciting for not being surrounded by an unchanging diet of the old. And I should add that even when we did perform the old, some of it was out of the ordinary: we opened our season this past summer with the well-known Bach Passacaglia in C minor, not in the usual Stokowski transcription but in the striking and in some ways even shocking reworking by Respighi. Similarly, we began each of six 1987 chamber-music concerts with two fugues from

Bach's great *Art of Fugue*, each pair performed in different instrumental combinations ranging from strings, winds, and brass, to two pianos, chamber orchestra, and pitched percussion.

It is too soon to say how this venture will have fared in the long run. I have heard ominous noises that the size of the audience was held down by my quixotic concentration on interesting repertory at the expense of crowd-pleasing pieces and soloists. One local critic was heard to remark that the reason unfamiliar music is unfamiliar is that it isn't good; one New York critic found some of our American music uneven at best and dreary at worst. In contrast to the detractors, the most important critic in New Jersey came down firmly on our side, and a major New York critic described our programming as among the most interesting at American summer festivals.

But my own feelings about the enterprise are hardly so balanced. I remember the glorious playing of the infinitely touching Barber Violin Concerto by the great American violinist Dylana Jenson; I remember the brilliant performance of the melodic and colorful Piston Symphony no. 4 by Gerard Schwarz and the orchestra; I remember the tumultuous response to the Bloch *America* by an audience that could not have known of Bloch beforehand, let alone of his *America*. I cherish the extraordinary cooperation and sympathy that I received from faculty musicians who play in the most important orchestras in this country and from students who attend the best schools; I cherish their telling me after concerts that the process of discovery upon which we were engaged, in contrast to the routinized playing of routinized programs, was the way the life of music should be lived. Most of all, I was touched by the young cellist who exclaimed: "Oh, Mr. Lipman, this music is so uplifting!" Naïve perhaps, but all the more truthful and inspiring for that.

What about "the cutting edge"? Doesn't everyone have a duty to play what has just been written, to give what has never been heard a chance? Yes, and in fact that duty is now everywhere being fulfilled: more music is being written and almost immediately performed (and just about all of it promptly forgotten) than at any time in the history of Western music. But I think performing musicians have a higher duty to music: to play that which they love in a way that the audience can make its own. It is to find fresh objects for this love that musicians have always worked, and must continue to work today. I have no doubt that the music being written today can include some works that will be capable of satisfying this test, and every thinking musician looks forward to finding them. The stakes are high but simple. They are nothing less than the survival of one of the chief beauties in our lives, and of one of the highest achievements of our civilization.

3.

It is generally accepted that, for the most sophisticated judges, the European classical-music tradition reached its apogee with the string-quartet music of Haydn, Mozart, Beethoven, Schubert, and (perhaps) Brahms. That triumph was essentially completed more than a century ago, though in the quartets of Schoenberg, Bartók, and Shostakovich it is arguable that the creation of this profoundly serious repertory has to some extent continued into our time. It is a measure of the real, albeit submerged, greatness of serious musical composition in our own country that we, too, have produced a major body of quartet writing. This body of writing, as I have tried to show in the following March 1989 New Criterion article, flourished in the 1930s, 1940s, and early 1950s, and then sunk into desuetude. Thus when I heard a new string quartet that seemed instantly to become a part of the great tradition, I was overjoyed; discussing this new work in the New Criterion *seemed even more important because the* New York Times, *that indispensable validator of ontological reality in Manhattan musical life, did not cover what can only be called a rare and happy event.*

American String-Quartet Writing

I HEARD a remarkable new piece of chamber music this past January. The work, the String Quartet no. 4 (1988) by the thirty-seven-year-old composer George Tsontakis, was performed in its world premiere by the American String Quartet at New York's 92nd Street YM–YWHA. By its excellence it not only buoyed my often drooping musical spirits; it also prompted in me some thoughts on the general subject of American quartet music, both old and new.

The composers of American classical music may be pardoned for wondering whether a facetious deity has placed them in an environment rewarding in every way save the most important: that of feeling— somewhere, somehow—that what they have composed has been listened to and not just heard, and that there is at least a chance of their work living on in the collective memory.

Americans have long been a musical people. Occasions spiritual and secular, individual and social, private and public, have always been accompanied by music making and music listening. Classical music, that infinitely noble but always quixotic genre, has ever been a preoccupation of our middle and upper classes, and even of significant sections of our "masses." An *American* classical music, not just simply an American *classical* music, has been a goal of our most gifted musicians since at least the middle of the nineteenth century.

Today, as the twentieth century nears its end, America is full of music. But the sound that so permeates our lives, it goes without saying, is not the sound of traditional classical music, though that too is available in hitherto undreamt-of abundance. Our sonic environment is riddled by rock and pop, those illegitimate offspring of formerly autochthonous folk cultures and the hypertrophied engines of media exploitation. The welter of sound—heard in large and small spaces and via the earphones of the Walkman generation—threatens to destroy our remaining opportunities for sober reflection and private judgment.

Over the past few decades, through the blessings of digital recording and performance technology, the sound of popular music has been changing to an ever increasing loudness and meanness. This change has been paralleled by a new phenomenon, that of minimalist music, which is based on a combination of simple, consonant chords and the obsessive, deadpan repetition of short motivic and harmonic sequences. I should make clear that this music, not as yet commercially successful (except in its application to television commercials and sitcom background scores), hardly lacks champions. The present vogue of Philip Glass, Steve Reich, and most recently John Adams is often seen as a sign of creative energy and audience approbation. The supposed relocation of musical creativity away from the traditional concert-music atmosphere and toward dance spaces, downtown clubs, and the classier rock venues—celebrated by the *New York Times* critic John Rockwell in his 1982 book, *All American Music*—is hailed by many as the first coming of a truly national music. Supposedly this blessed event is all the more bounteously national, and all the more welcome, for its radical discontinuity, expressed musically in a rejection of thematic development and harmonic movement and programmatically in a rejection of a superannuated European tradition.

This radical discontinuity with the past accords well with the wider rejection so visible on college and university campuses today of what is seen as Eurocentrism. Behind the advocacy of changes in music unquestionably lies the hope of a change in society and politics. Our cultural intellectuals, whatever their opinion of Plato as intellectual nourishment for today's youth, seem committed to his analysis of music as it is expressed in *The Republic*. In the following passage, Socrates (the "I" in the conversation) is instructing his two pupils:

So Damon tells me, and I can quite believe him;—he says that when modes of music change, the fundamental laws of the State always change with them.

Yes, said Adeimantus; and you may add my suffrage to Damon's and your own.

Then, I said, our guardians must lay the foundation of their fortress in music?

Yes, he said; the lawlessness of which you speak too easily steals in.

Yes, I replied, in the form of amusement; and at first sight it appears harmless.

Why, yes, he said, and there is no harm; were it not that little by little this spirit of licence, finding a home, imperceptibly penetrates into manners and customs; whence, issuing with greater force, it invades contracts between man and man, and from contracts goes on to laws and constitutions, in utter recklessness, ending at last, Socrates, by an overthrow of all rights, private as well as public.[1]

It will immediately be recognized that this very point has been made recently by Allan Bloom in his best-selling *The Closing of the American Mind*. Bloom properly remarks that the rise of the rock culture is accompanied by a corresponding loss of interest in classical music. This ordered and refined product of civilization, one suspects, does not seem "authentic" to the young. Thus, there is little music written today that at once interests the young and can be seen to be a solid part of the classical-music tradition.

[1] The English translation is by Benjamin Jowett.

Part of our problem is that the classical music we still have is felt by us to belong to others despite its universality. In some important public sense, its true owners remain the lands and the peoples that gave this music birth. It may seem odd to talk about Bach, Mozart, Beethoven, and the other masters of our musical tradition as not fully ours but as *belonging* to other peoples and other times. The fact remains, however, that nothing of the past can belong to the present until it has been, in Goethe's word, earned. Surely this was what T. S. Eliot had in mind when he wrote (in "Tradition and the Individual Talent"):

[W]e shall often find that not only the best, but the most individual parts of [the poet's] work may be those in which the dead poets, his ancestors, assert their immortality most vigorously. . . . Tradition . . . cannot be inherited, and if you want it you must obtain it by great labour. . . . No poet, no artist of any art, has his complete meaning alone. His significance, his appreciation is the appreciation of his relation to the dead poets and artists. . . . [W]hat happens when a new work of art is created is something that happens simultaneously to all the works of art which preceded it. The existing monuments form an ideal order among themselves, which is modified by the introduction of the new (the really new) work of art among them.

How have we fulfilled this obligation to make what we have received our own? Here the evidence suggests a contradiction between our actual achievements in serious music and the opinion some have of us as a creative society. There can be little doubt, it seems to me, that it is precisely this task of what might be called creative possession which our composers are seen as having failed to accomplish. Sometimes this perception of creative failure is formulated with an exaggerated sense of concern for our cultural well-being, as when the literary critic George Steiner found (in his 1980 essay entitled "Archives of Eden") our past record and our future prospects in serious musical creation negligible. Sometimes a virtue is made of necessity, as when the music critic Henry Pleasants (in his 1969 book *Serious Music and All That Jazz*) found that American popular music in its full variety is our true art. Sometimes, too, Americans are patronizingly seen as an art-less people, as when the magazine editor Lewis Lapham, unlike Steiner and

Pleasants an American resident, complacently remarked in 1981:

> The distrust of the arts runs in the American grain. We have tried for two hundred years to improve the country's sensibility, saying to ourselves, "We have money; we have commerce; we have good people—why can't we make art?" Nobody can answer the question, and so, traditionally, the Americans have applied to Europe for poets, painters, dancing masters, violinists, interior decorators, and anybody else who promises to civilize the barbarians.

But matters are hardly so simple. The fact is that over much of this century splendid music has been written in this country. On several occasions, I have written about our achievement and about the general problems of being an American musician.[2] Each time I have done so, I have felt myself in a position of lonely virtue. But this past January, sitting in the 92nd Street Y's Kaufmann Concert Hall, I found myself thinking of the extraordinary American achievement in string-quartet writing.

A book about American string quartets badly needs doing. I have in mind a genre of composition, originally European, for two violins, viola, and cello, stretching back in an unbroken line to the many works of Haydn and Mozart, continuing with the numerous works of Beethoven, Schubert, and Brahms, and finding twentieth-century expression in the four quartets of Arnold Schoenberg, the six of Béla Bartók, and, most recently, the fifteen of Dmitri Shostakovich. All the quartets, along with relatively isolated works by perhaps another dozen composers, form the backbone of the quartet repertory, and as such are played (except perhaps for the Schoenberg works) all over the world by ensembles famous and unknown alike.

One could hardly hope to give a succinct definition of the musical characteristic of a continuously developing genre now two hundred years old. Any plausible list of features, however, would have to include at least the following: an aesthetic of private rather than public

[2] See, for example, "American Music: the Years of Hope" in *Commentary*, March 1981, and Chapters 1, 2, and 12 in this book. For a discussion of the relationship between the American and European musical worlds, see "American Music's Place at Home and in the World" in *The Annals*, Winter 1988.

expression; an emphasis on the thematic and motivic interest of the musical material rather than on the effects of instrumental color and virtuosity; a related concentration on structure, development, and variation rather than on the mere alternation of contrasting large statements; and the treatment of each instrument as an independent linear partner rather than as a cog in a harmonic wheel.

Upon rereading an article I wrote a few years ago largely devoted to the marvelous playing of the old Hollywood Quartet,[3] I now find that, under the influence of my subject, I almost completely ignored American music. Among the many recordings of this group, there appears only one American string quartet—an ingratiating and soulful 1936 work by Paul Creston. The story is the same for the revered Budapest Quartet, American by long residence even though European in origin and personnel, and for two currently well-known American groups, the Guarneri and Cleveland quartets. There have been major exceptions, of course. During the more than four decades of its existence, the Juilliard Quartet has rendered yeoman service to American music, and on a less famous level, the now-disbanded Concord Quartet made many vital recordings of native works. Today, the Emerson Quartet continues to play, and record, a large amount of American music. But in general the performance of American quartets has been left to little-known performing ensembles. The famous rule our composers have learned to their sorrow still applies: with new American compositions, played once, played nevermore.

Perhaps the most conspicuous quartet on the scene today is the fashionable Kronos Quartet. Punk costumes and all, they are marketed as the Talking Heads of chamber music. Hailed by critics as the solution to the problem of bringing in the young to an art marked increasingly by the playing of old pieces for old people, the Kronos eschews the traditional nineteenth-century classics, as well as almost all the major European works of our own time. The group seems particularly careful to avoid the quartet works of the heroic figures of American music, among them Roy Harris, Walter Piston, Roger Sessions, and William Schuman.

Instead the Kronos concentrates, with few exceptions, on what

[3] "The Hollywood and Other Quartets" in *Commentary*, February 1983; reprinted in *The House of Music* (1984).

seem to me rough performances, alternately dreamy and violent, of definitely trivial and often very nasty-sounding music.[4] I do not find any of these performances distinguished either in musical characterization or in technical grace. Their records, like their concerts, mix disparate short works by such avant-garde figures as Glass, the American expatriate Conlon Nancarrow, the Australian Peter Sculthorpe, and the Finn Aulis Sallinen, with even shorter works, usually in arrangements, by jazz, pop, and rock figures, including Ornette Coleman, Astor Piazzolla, John Zorn, and Jimi Hendrix. But whichever composer is played, the studied and provocative eclecticism of the Kronos Quartet does no service to the music, especially to the important works they occasionally do manage to play.

As an American quartet, therefore, the Kronos lacks a center in its repertory. Without doubt, this missing center is twentieth-century American music. In orchestral music, such a center comprises the American symphonism of the composers who are ignored by the Kronos and by their polar opposites on the celebrity chamber-music circuit. The very term "American symphonism," once so full of pride and hope, is now, I fear, reactionary-sounding. This ignoring of our past eliminates from the orchestral repertory all save a handful of the works of Harris, Piston, Sessions, Schuman, and, of course, Aaron Copland. More important for the subject at hand, it eliminates a large body of chamber music written in the first half of this century, including numerous string quartets.

I have already mentioned the lack of a serious book-length study of American quartets. The most recent book on the string quartet in general is by Paul Griffiths, the chief music critic of the London *Times*.[5] Not surprisingly, it gives little coverage to Americans. Like his fellow English writers, Griffiths is concerned only with our avant-garde and its modernist precursors. Thus, detailed consideration is reserved for Milton Babbitt, John Cage, Elliott Carter, Charles Ives, and George

---

[4] I know of only four such exceptions. Three of these—the Webern Six Bagatelles opus 9 (1913), the Bartók Quartet no. 3 (1927), and the slow movement (famous, in its orchestral version, as the *Adagio for Strings*) of the Barber String Quartet (1936)— are available on records. The fourth—Elliott Carter's Quartet no. 4 (1986)—can be heard on a broadcast tape.

[5] *The String Quartet*, by Paul Griffiths; Thames and Hudson, 1983.

Rochberg.[6] Mainstream American composers such as those I have cited above, however, are confined to meager lists, when they are mentioned at all.

Here I ought to take a stab at defining my use of the word *mainstream* as it applies to American classical music. In negative terms, mainstream means not being mired in academicism—the pedantic use of teachable formulas to produce what are in effect textbook illustrations rather than individual statements; it also means not searching for creative authenticity solely in newness.

In positive terms, mainstream means a use of traditional formal structures from Western music since J. S. Bach; an emphasis on a long, often astringent melodic line; a quality of plaintiveness, referred to by some as a "cowboy" quality and by others as the loneliness of the city; a use of dissonance to express a beauty and sweetness similar to that of consonance; a reliance on widely spaced harmonies, what Virgil Thomson has called "struggle counterpoint"; the inclusion of jazz-inspired but regular rhythmic complications to convey musical interest and human vitality; and, above all, a seriousness of utterance, as if each piece being written were the composer's final act. I keep a special place in my heart, too, for the touching music written at the turn of the century by Americans properly trained in Europe but conscious of living in a young and brash country.

Aesthetic definitions, I know, will differ. I can only claim for mine that, as definitions should, it both excludes and includes. It excludes both the mere imitators of European romanticism and the *provocateurs*. It includes a broad range of music: from George Chadwick and Arthur Foote almost a century ago, through the sadly short-lived Charles Griffes and the experimentalist Henry Cowell, to the unabashed Americanist Aaron Copland, the populist Roy Harris, the severely cerebral Roger Sessions, Harvard's Walter Piston, Yale's Quincy Porter, the arch-Romanticist Howard Hanson, the lushly chromatic Samuel Barber, the quintessential New Yorker William Schuman, the Kansas City-born Francophile Virgil Thomson, the post-Bergian

[6] Tellingly, Rochberg is given serious treatment in the Griffiths book not because of any mainstream position but rather because of his widely discussed reaction against Schoenbergian serialism. This has led him, in several of his recent quartets, to write extended passages in the styles of the great composers of the romantic and classical periods.

opera composer Hugo Weisgall, and even, for much of his career, the vastly complex—indeed over-complex—Elliott Carter.

Not all of these composers devoted their energies to the writing of string quartets, though with the exception of Weisgall each of them has made some contribution to the medium. I have made a rather more extensive list of important American string quartets than Mr. Griffiths gives in his book. My list is based on my own record-and-tape collection, and therefore is limited to what has already been recorded or broadcast. Nonetheless, it contains something over fifty pieces by some thirty composers. My list must be supplemented by many works the recordings of which I do not own; more important, it must be supplemented by the other, unrecorded works of already recorded composers. And it is at least arguable that it should be further expanded through the addition of works written on American soil by such European composers as Ernest Bloch, Paul Hindemith, and Darius Milhaud.

In any case it is clear that the American string-quartet literature is rich indeed. Perhaps the largest achievement by an American in this genre is Piston's five quartets, written between 1933 and 1962 and now at last available on records in an excellent performance by the Portland String Quartet.[7] Sessions's two very difficult but always rewarding quartets have been recorded, but only the first is currently in print, and that only on a 1945 disc of a live performance. Of Quincy Porter's nine quartets, only four—no. 3, no. 4, no. 7, and no. 8—have been recorded on LP; I have only been able to obtain the well-played recording of the charming no. 3 by the much-missed Kohon Quartet.[8] None of William Schuman's five quartets is currently available, though no. 3 and no. 4 have been recorded; his most recent quartet—no. 5—was premiered by the Orford Quartet last summer. The performance at the

[7] Arabesque 216, 214, and 208.
[8] CRI-235. This is as good a place as any to pay tribute not just to the Kohon Quartet (shockingly unlisted, I might add, in the *New Grove Dictionary of American Music*) but to two collections of their American string quartet records, issued in the mid-1970s as budget-priced Vox Boxes and now deleted. These two sets of three LP's contain music by Daniel Gregory Mason, Griffes, Foote, Chadwick, Henry Hadley, Charles Loeffler, Copland, Piston, George Gershwin (the immensely touching 1919 Lullaby), Thomson, Schuman, Sessions, Hanson, Peter Mennin, Ives, and Benjamin Franklin (a miserable effort of doubtful attribution!). Many of these works are of great beauty, and the sets are well worth searching out.

92nd Street Y of this long, demanding, and severely beautiful work (which I have heard on tape) was one of the few events of lasting value in the 1988 New York International Festival of the Arts.

Even in this very sketchy *tour d'horizon*, I must also mention the haunting Quartet no. 3 (1953) of William Bergsma, the complicated and deeply moving Quartet no. 1 (1942) of Andrew Imbrie, and Harold Shapero's large-scale Quartet no. 1 (1940).[9] The very impressive David Diamond, still prolific today at the age of seventy-three, has written ten quartets, the latest in 1966; of these, I have heard two—no. 3 (1946) and no. 4 (1951)—in beautiful recordings now unfortunately deleted.

As I mention these works, I am conscious of how many of them were written so many years ago. True, Schuman's fifth quartet was written just last year, but he belongs to an earlier generation (Schuman was born in 1910), as does George Perle (born in 1915), who has published two lovely quartets, one in 1960/67 and another in 1973.[10] Like other American music, the American string quartet showed great promise in the 1930s, 1940s, and early 1950s, and then was destroyed by the combined seductions of the French and German postwar avant-garde and electronic technology. The career of the greatly gifted Lukas Foss is the prime example of this destruction.[11]

So for many years now, the field has been given over to the mocking children of the *méchant* Cage, the squeal-and-beep disciples of Babbitt, and the whoosh-and-rattle followers of Ampex and Moog—

[9] The Bergsma, Imbrie, and Shapero quartets were all available in the Columbia Modern American Music series of the 1950s. The brainchild of Columbia executive (and composer) Goddard Lieberson and very much overseen by Virgil Thomson and several colleagues, this multi-disc series recorded outstanding works of then-contemporary American music. Many of these records were available during the 1970s on special order; they have all been deleted, though a few are now available on the CRI label.
[10] The 1960/67 work is available on Elektra/Nonesuch H-71280, and the 1973 work is on CRI S-387. Mention should be made here of a work of fundamental importance in keeping track of American music on discs: *American Music Recordings: A Discography of 20th-Century U.S. Composers* (1988), edited by Carol J. Oja.
[11] Convincing proof of what happened to Foss, and by extension what happened to so many of his colleagues, is provided by the recordings of two of Foss's string quartets, no. 1 (1947) and no. 3 (1976). No. 1 (formerly available on Columbia ML-5476 and its successors) is full of melody and beauty, whereas no. 3 (currently available on CRI-413) is an intolerably sustained essay in rigidity and ugliness.

or, still more recently, to the minimalist purveyors of music-by-the-yard. Is it any wonder that the Mozart, Beethoven, and Schubert cycles go on and on?

But fortunately the story may not end on this unhappy note. Perhaps it is still possible for a composer who has been trained and come to maturity during the terrible times through which serious music has gone in the last forty years to write a beautiful string quartet. This is just what I think George Tsontakis has done.

I first became aware of the music of George Tsontakis at the Aspen Music Festival, where he has been a faculty member since 1976. A student of Sessions and Weisgall, and briefly of avant-gardists Karlheinz Stockhausen and Franco Donatoni in Europe, Tsontakis has taken from his American teachers their traditional musical seriousness and uncompromising artistic integrity. From his European mentors, he has gained an interest in novel instrumental techniques, and (I think) an awareness of the cul-de-sac of postwar musical thought. Of Greek parentage, he is active as the music director of the (Greek Orthodox) Cathedral of St. John the Theologian in Tenafly, New Jersey.

I am most familiar with his previous two string quartets (a still earlier work, the Quartet no. 1, has never been performed). The Quartet no. 2 (1983), written for the Emerson Quartet, is a work of seemingly pure fury, stating and restating what strikes me as a composer's rage at a time out of joint. Here are hammered expletives from the strings and *pesante* gruntings, and most of all, an entire slow movement built upon the bare opening notes of the finale of Beethoven's last quartet, the opus 135—to which Beethoven appended the words *"Muss es sein?"* ("Must it be?"). Tellingly, in his own finale, Tsontakis cannot respond as Beethoven does—with *"Es muss sein"* ("It must be")—but instead only gets as far as repeated outbursts of two notes conveying better than any words: "It must . . . " But he cannot bring himself to complete the affirmation with the simple "be"; instead the composition ends with repeated expletives that sound like nothing so much as "no, no, no."

The Quartet no. 3 (1986), written for the Blair Quartet, is subtitled *Coraggio* ("Courage"). From the beginning it inhabits a more consonant and tonal world than its freely dissonant predecessor. The consonance, one feels, is merely provisional. Ecstatic wisps of melody struggle throughout with extended passages of obsessive, febrile energy, again reminiscent of late Beethoven, in this case the fast movements of the opus 130, opus 131, and opus 132 quartets. It is as if Tsontakis's musical mind was locked into not just Beethoven but also Adrian Leverkühn, the anti-hero composer of Thomas Mann's great novel *Doktor Faustus* (1947). It is a sign of Tsontakis's integrity that, like Leverkühn, he nowhere in his music takes the two easy ways out that are so common in our time—Dadaism or minimalism.

The Quartet no. 4, written for and splendidly played by the American String Quartet at the 92nd Street Y, proclaims from its opening measures that the way out of our musical predicament lies not in insanity, in petty craziness, or in what might be called (after a collaborative 1920 work by Erik Satie and Darius Milhaud) "furniture music." The work begins with a simple but rich four-part statement of a Russian Orthodox chorale, and the entire work is a set of variations and transformations of this elemental material. The restless timbral experimentation that had marked Tsontakis's two previous quartets is now gone, subsumed in a fluent and idiomatic instrumental style. There are moments of gaiety, of majesty, and of ecstasy; the wonderfully full harmonic texture moves freely and always naturally between consonance and dissonance, with the chords always serving to support and make clear the melodies in which the work abounds. And with a last, lone B-natural played at the top of the violin's range and at the limits of audibility, the work dissolves in pure song.

With his latest quartet, George Tsontakis has, I think, produced a masterpiece. In itself, it exists at the highest—and rarest—level of contemporary composition. Furthermore, it makes us look again at the entire corpus of American string quartet writing to which it now so clearly belongs. In Eliot's terms, it makes a new sense not only of Tsontakis's earlier works but of American music as a whole. His three quartets must immediately be recorded by the ensembles that gave them birth on the stage, for they give hope that what had seemed impossible is truly possible: beautiful new music can be composed (as it used to be said) from the heart to the heart, even today, and we can begin the urgent process of reclaiming our musical heritage.

4.

In the past decade, I have made no secret of my unhappiness with the New York Philharmonic, America's oldest and, I would like to think, its most important orchestra. The Philharmonic is important not just because it has the good or bad luck, as the case may be, to be located in the center of American cultural life; it is also important because as an institution it has for so many years willingly assumed the responsibility of presenting American symphonic music, in concerts and recordings, to a wide music-loving public. When the Philharmonic's excellent musicians do not play very well, as they have not for many years now, their shortcomings affect the entire context in which classical music is done in this country. But one cannot fault the Philharmonic for willingly shouldering more than its share of the new-music burden, as they did during the contemporary music festival that is the subject of this September 1983 essay in the New Criterion. *I might add that their discontinuation of this early-summer series of concerts can hardly be interpreted as a sign of health in American music.*

The Philharmonic's New Horizons

B Y   D E V O T I N G the first two weeks of June to a festival of contemporary music entitled "Horizons '83," the New York Philharmonic demonstrated once again that aesthetic tasks must be their own reward. In seven concerts (more accurately, six concerts and one open rehearsal) the Philharmonic, under the artistic direction of the American composer Jacob Druckman, attempted to give a conspectus of the traditionally oriented music written during the last fifteen years or so in this country and, to a limited extent, abroad. The festival undoubtedly demonstrated the Philharmonic's sense of responsibility toward our time; other, purely artistic, verdicts were much less favorable.

Everything about this festival was on a large scale. The Philharmonic is said to have lost a half-million dollars on the concerts, an amount presumably to be made up by generous subventions from the National Endowment for the Arts, the New York State Council on the Arts, the American Society of Composers, Authors, and Publishers (ASCAP), and several foundations, corporations, and individuals. Twenty-six works (by as many composers) were performed, under the direction of seven conductors—Zubin Mehta, Raymond Leppard, Arthur Weisberg, Larry Newland, Lukas Foss, Gunther Schuller, and Druckman himself. The concerts featured eighteen instrumental and vocal soloists. The Philharmonic was joined by five other performing groups, most of them active in new music: the Group for Contemporary Music, the New Swingle Singers, the New York Choral Artists, the New York New Music Ensemble, and Speculum Musicae. Even the audiences were large, averaging close to two thousand people at the best attended of the concerts. In addition to the concerts, there were symposia and meetings devoted to discussing the music and allied artistic fields.

Following its custom with events of which it is proud, the Philharmonic made sure the public was informed about the efforts it was making in the cause of contemporary music by taking out costly advertisements in the press and sending out elaborate mailings. An advance story in the *New York Times*'s "Arts and Leisure" section and a related piece in the *Times*'s Sunday magazine helped to spread the news. Press coverage after the event was given a boost by the fact that 125 music critics were in New York at the time of "Horizons '83" to attend a professional meeting.

This massive undertaking was clearly not an isolated or idle act by the Philharmonic. Given its scope, it is perhaps best considered in three parts, beginning with the sponsorship of the festival and the reasons behind it, moving on to the music and its performances, and finishing with the reception of the festival by a sophisticated public. As we will see, "Horizons '83" sheds light both on the state of musical composition in our time and on the wide artistic context in which serious music is now being written.

It must be said at the outset that the New York Philharmonic is no Johnny-come-lately to new music. In the years since World War II alone, the orchestra's records in the performance of contemporary works is unmatched by any other American orchestra of comparable stature. Merely to mention the three music directors of the Philharmonic period prior to Zubin Mehta is to recall significant and energetic service (each in a different way) to the compositions of the day. Dimitri Mitropoulos (from 1949 to 1958) zealously programmed pieces by little-known American and European composers, and he brought to New York such then shocking works as Strauss's *Elektra* and Berg's *Wozzeck* in what are increasingly perceived to be, in their energy and discipline, exemplary performances.[1] Leonard Bernstein (from 1958 to 1969) brought to his conducting at the Philharmonic his own stature and interests as one of America's foremost composers; his recordings of the music of Aaron Copland and William Schuman (and of Charles Ives, ignored until then) are but a limited documentary of Bernstein's impassioned and persuasive efforts. Though his heart was clearly not in the creative productions of the avant-garde, he played his share of shocking and provocative works, too.

When the Philharmonic chose the arch-modernist Pierre Boulez as its leader in 1971, it was clear that he had been given—at least at the outset of his tenure—a mandate to program the most difficult and challenging contemporary music. He fulfilled that mandate, and a listing of the modern works he selected (contained in the festival's souvenir booklet) makes for fascinating reading. But Boulez's virtues in performance were restricted to bringing clarity, order, and precision to the music he loved, and the music he loved did not seem to include the beloved standard repertoire of the nineteenth century. Boulez's departure from the Philharmonic in 1978 was thus regretted by neither the orchestra nor the press and public. Unlike Bernstein, Boulez has never returned as a guest conductor to the orchestra he once led.

Under Zubin Mehta, the Philharmonic has continued to play new music, although Mehta's choices have seemed, if not fewer than those of Boulez, somewhat more tame. Vastly more significant than the number of works Mehta has programmed or their style has been the attitude he has brought to their execution. He has seemed both defensive and unwillingly dutiful, as if he were doing an unpleasant task as well as he possibly could. Certain semi-contemporary works

---

[1] Fortunately, broadcast dubbings of these performances are still easily available on LP discs: the *Wozzeck* is on Odyssey Y2-33126; the *Elektra* is circulating on at least one private label.

Mehta has indeed played with enthusiasm—most notably Bartók's *Concerto for Orchestra*—but more often than not he has forced them into a vulgar romantic mold in which distinctions of phrasing and texture are ignored in favor of a merely rhetorical excitement finally resulting in dullness.

This lack on Mehta's part has not gone unnoticed by those in the artistic community committed to new music. Undoubtedly the Philharmonic's management, eager to guard the orchestra's reputation as a champion of contemporary music, has been worried by the discontent. But the problem isn't only Mehta. The Philharmonic's subscribers have so little taste for new music that performing it more often on regular concerts—let alone taking the time to improve the quality of its presentation—has seemed inadvisable, to say the least.

To both problems "Horizons '83" presented a solution. There is a hole in the orchestra's schedule at the end of the regular season that management has been unable to fill successfully since the late André Kostelanetz's Promenade Concerts. The musicians in the orchestra have to be paid for these weeks anyway, concerts or no, so why not (the reasoning must have gone) schedule a festival of new music? Because Mehta was so plainly not the right person to run such a festival, the Philharmonic gave control of it to Jacob Druckman, the orchestra's composer-in-residence. Druckman responded to the challenge by doing more than simply choosing representative recent works. He picked a theme for the festival—"A New Romanticism?"—although it is not at all clear how much the theme affected his musical choices or how accurately this subtitle alludes to the reality of musical composition today. What is clear is that by using the word "Romanticism" Druckman provided a legion of grateful music critics with a hook on which to hang yards of sophisticated discussion.

At this point there seems little to be gained by joining the argument over the exact history or definition of Romanticism. As Jacques Barzun demonstrated at the end of *Romanticism and the Modern Ego* (1943), the word has by now come to mean everything to everyone. In the case of the Philharmonic's festival, what Romanticism is in theory is less important than how the word was used. Druckman explains his own use of it in an essay included in the festival's commemorative booklet, where he contrasts "the Apollonian, the Classical—logical, rational, chaste and explainable" with "the

Dionysian, the Romantic—sensual, mysterious, transcending the explainable." According to Druckman, twentieth-century music prior to the 1960s—including Prokofiev, Shostakovich, Copland, Harris, Schuman, Hindemith, Webern, Boulez, Babbitt, Xenakis, and Carter, as well as the later Schoenberg, Stravinsky, and Bartók—belonged to the domain of rationalism. Then:

> During the mid-1960s the tide began to change. Even though new works and new ideas continue to pour out at break-neck speed, we can sense a gradual change of focus, of spirituality and of goals.
>
> No matter how varied the surface of these musics are [*sic*], one can discern a steady reemergence of those Dionysian qualities: sensuality, mystery, nostalgia, ecstasy, transcendency.

Druckman's essay is a kind of mini-manifesto. The old music, we are told, was rational, thoughtful, intellectual—in a word, dry. Forsaking this lifelessness, the music to be presented at the Philharmonic festival would be of the body and the feelings, affectful and moving in inexplicable ways. If you didn't like the "old" new music because it was boring and ugly, Druckman seems to say, you'll love what we've got to offer. This really involves two claims: that the music to be played at the festival would be significantly different from what had gone before and that it would be differently—that is, more warmly— received than the "old" new music had been. Judging by the evidence of the concerts themselves, both claims are false.

The music of "Horizons '83" began on June 2 with a concert conducted by Raymond Leppard. Four works were presented: *Afterimages* (a world premiere) by the American composer Marc Antonio Consoli; *Ave Maris Stella* (performed by the New York New Music Ensemble, Robert Black conducting) by the English composer Peter Maxwell Davies; *Far calls. Coming Far!* (with violinist Ida Kavafian) by the Japanese composer Toru Takemitsu; and *All in the Golden Afternoon* (with soprano Phyllis Bryn-Julson) by the American composer David Del Tredici.

The Consoli work, related (according to the program notes) to the composer's desire for children and his marital separation, quickly displayed something about the New Romanticism that was to become evident throughout the festival: just how little of the music was new, and how depressingly much was old. The Consoli began like a continuation of Debussy's *Nocturnes* and soon became openly vulgar, with repeated chords and single notes in the brass in the style of Mahler. An ostinato chord motive, whooshing glissandi throughout the orchestra, an amplified celesta—everything seemed to pass without purpose. Despite the lush strings and rich brass, and the fruity percussion of the third movement, the piece amounted to a thick impasto built up out of uninteresting fragments.

Davies's *Ave Maris Stella*, based programmatically on the idea of evoking the dawn and different times of the day, was written in a pallid international style reminiscent of Messiaen but without Messiaen's refulgent musicality. Even the marimba cadenza (brilliantly played by Druckman's son, Daniel) was unable to relieve the general impression of noodling improvisation relying all too much on stock elements—often thirds—stuck on the page without intrinsic connections.

The most up-to-date feature of Takemitsu's *Far calls. Coming Far!* was the work's title, which is taken from *Finnegans Wake*. Otherwise, this rhapsody for violin and orchestra was a reversion to Debussy, bounded by Chausson on one side and by Szymanowski on the other. Its sensitive orchestration and long-lined melodies only added up to superior movie music of a mid-forties vintage. The composition as a whole is at least an effective vehicle for an impassioned violin virtuoso, but Ida Kavafian lacked all the necessary emotional involvement and technical flair to bring off the work's borrowed atmosphere, and Leppard seemed unduly dispassionate and distant.

The real interest of the evening lay in *All in the Golden Afternoon*, a continuation of Del Tredici's settings of Lewis Carroll's words from *Alice in Wonderland*. This piece was clearly the main attraction for the many Del Tredici enthusiasts in the audience, who certainly got their money's worth. It began like the Venusberg music from *Tannhäuser* and progressed via Mahler to *Der Rosenkavalier* and *Salome* of Richard Strauss. It featured an amplified soprano who often got too close to the microphone, producing perhaps unintended whoops and gushes. By the end, the *Salome* mood had become overpowering, and the huge orchestra combined with the larger-than-life soprano to create a monstrous perversion of Carroll's deft and provocative words. Del

Tredici's work is the apotheosis of camp, and the standing and cheering ovation that greeted it was clearly derived more from social than from musical concerns.

The next concert, on June 3, was conducted by Arthur Weisberg, the well-known contemporary music specialist. Again four works were presented, this time all by American composers: *Chords* by Fred Lerdahl; the Concerto for Violin and Orchestra by John Harbison (with violinist Charles Rex); the Triple Concerto for Soprano Clarinet, Bass Clarinet, Contrabass Clarinet, and Chamber Orchestra (performed by Anand Devendra, Dennis Smylie, Les Thimmig, and the Group for Contemporary Music conducted by Harvey Sollberger) by Donald Martino; and *Foci I* by Leonard Rosenman.

In contrast to the limited excitement of the opening night's program, the second concert was routine and lifeless. The Lerdahl was an avant-garde exercise in the manipulation of musical elements. It used consonant chords, which became increasingly dissonant as the piece went along. The work is not fully notated, so many of the notes had been left to chance. As a result, *Chords* had all the rhythmic interest of an anarchic funeral procession. The chords referred to in the title were rarely played together, and the end of the piece tailed off into a boring nothingness.

The Harbison violin concerto is an outstanding example of the music that results from the desire—shared by many composers today—to write an "appealing" music. It began with an attractive brass flourish, followed by the juicy strings so familiar to us from Hollywood. The rhapsodic violin part and the varied orchestral activity were clearly written in an attempt to break out of what many feel to have been the emotional restrictions and intellectual demands of modernism. The solo melodies were often written in octaves, which produced a rich and satisfying sound; the slow movements contained an effective passage pitting the violin's upper register against a powerful bass line in the orchestra. The piece lacked the passionate intensity of, say, comparable music of Berg and Bartók, but it must be said that it was not done full justice at the festival: the soloist (a member of the Philharmonic violin section) was not a compelling player, and Arthur Weisberg's conducting did nothing to animate the proceedings.

The Martino Triple Concerto was very different. It was not "appealing" music and it did not try to be. It was made up of fragmented motives, random entrances and encounters, and angular melodic contours that seemed to come straight out of the constructivist period of the 1960s avant-garde. In its dissection of the musical line, it was not quite pointillistic, but it was pointless. And none of the three forms of the clarinet Martino chose to feature could bear the weight of a solo part.

The return to the 1960s continued with the last work, Rosenman's *Foci I.* This essay in timbral modification, micro-tonality, and rhythmic transitions did achieve a vaguely sinister quality and sometimes even sounded like the kind of modern music that used to scare people who were used to the music of the classical masters. It is hard to say just how adequate the performance actually was, however: as usual, the Philharmonic's string playing was uninvolved and insecure; at one point in the piece the second stand of cellos, having missed a page turn and being evidently lost, started laughing.

The June 4 concert, led by Druckman and Larry Newland, the assistant conductor of the Philharmonic, began with the *Ascent into Air* of Morton Subotnick (conducted by Newland), continued with the *Chromatic Fantasy* of Barbara Kolb (with Tony Randall as narrator), went on to the *Lupercalia* of Sandor Balassa (conducted by Druckman), and ended with the *Grand Pianola Music* of John Adams (with pianists Alan Feinberg and Ursula Oppens, sopranos Jane Bryden and Pamela Wood, and mezzo-soprano Kimball Wheeler).

Morton Subotnick is a cult hero of the old avant-garde. Looking something like a well-dressed Santa Claus, the bearded composer sat at the side of the stage using a computer to modify the sounds of the amplified instruments being played by the musicians. The resulting sound, although relatively consonant, was full of sustained roars and heavings as it came, distorted, out of the large onstage speakers. If the piece had any comprehensibility, it resided not in the music but in the program notes, which shifted easily between philosophical metaphors and allusions to electronic technology. Clearly for Subotnick, as for the many composers today who resemble him, intellectual virtuosity has displaced serious musical creativity.

Barbara Kolb's *Chromatic Fantasy* sets to music a text by someone variously described in the program notes as Robert or Howard Stern. Kolb's piece is scored for narrator, alto flute, oboe, trumpet, soprano saxophone, electric guitar, and vibraphone; the narrator, flute, guitar, and vibraphone are "discreetly" amplified. Musically the work is slight; in its neoclassicism it is clearly indebted to Stravinsky. According to the program notes, Kolb associates her *Chromatic Fantasy* with Stravinsky's *L'Histoire du soldat*, Boulez's *Rituel*, and Bach's own *Chromatic Fantasy*. The psychotic text, describing a fantasy-encounter with one or more young women, distantly suggests still another twentieth-century model, Arnold Schoenberg's *Pierrot lunaire*. In the performance, one element, and that nonmusical, stood out: Tony Randall's narration, both witty and well-projected, reduced the music to subsidiary status.

Balassa's *Lupercalia*, subtitled "Concerto in Memory of Stravinsky," was another faceless piece built on nondescript fragments. Full of blasts from the lower instruments, its sole virtue was that it possessed a certain amount of rhythmic character, although this may have owed more to the strong, if visually crude, conducting of Jacob Druckman than to the music itself.

The conclusion of the third concert was elephantine. Adams's *Grand Pianola Music* is a work out of the school of minimalists Terry Riley, Philip Glass, and Steve Reich. The early moments—one wants to say hours—of the piece were an impasto of pulsing sounds based on agglomerations of notes derived from seventh chords. There were interminable arpeggiated figures speaking across the sonic landscape, singers humming away like the Andrews Sisters gone amok, an E-flat chord sounding for what seemed like eternity, chords up and down both pianos in the fashion of the best Russian concertos, and a modulation indistinguishable from the first progression in Beethoven's "Emperor" Concerto. It all came to a climax on a big tune perilously close to that of the slow movement of the Chopin E-minor Piano Concerto. Adams can rest content with having written the biggest unstaged Busby Berkeley musical in history. The mingled cheers and boos of the audience added up to a mini-sensation.

The next event of the festival, on June 7, was an open rehearsal of new and unperformed works. Zubin Mehta conducted the Philharmonic in *dream of the morning sky* (Cycle V) by Aaron Jay Kernis (with soprano

Gwendolyn Bradley) and *Symphony from Silence* by Nicholas Thorne (with pianist Christopher Oldfather). In between, Arthur Weisberg led a fragment of *A Haunted Landscape*, a work in progress by George Crumb. Matters got under way with a short speech by Druckman, who thanked the Philharmonic for their efforts and then announced that "Mr. Zubin" would introduce each of the composers as they came out.

The first composer to be so honored was Kernis, a slight twenty-three-year-old just out of the Yale music school, where his teachers had been (among others) Druckman and Subotnick. Kernis made a somewhat rambling and incoherent attempt to tell the orchestra members about his piece, describing the work as a progress from amorphous states through various degrees of spiritual enlightenment, leading to the true humanity focused in all of us; his program notes state that the work "is about the process of being born, of becoming human." The composition is in three parts, ending with a setting for soprano of the words of Pulitzer Prize-winning poet N. Scott Momaday. A quotation from this text will help to illuminate the composer's approach to life, if not the sound of his music:

> I am a feather on the bright sky
> I am the blue horse that runs in the plain . . .
> I am an angle of geese in the winter sky
> I am the hunger of a young wolf
> I am the whole dream of these things . . .
> I stand in good relation to the earth
> I stand in good relation to the gods
> I stand in good relation to all that is beautiful
> I am alive, I am alive

Not surprisingly, Kernis's composition sounded at the outset like planetarium music, complete with a representation of the first birds of day. Again, the prime model was Debussy; a huge crescendo suggested that Kernis had also learned his lessons from the film *2001*. Though the amplified singer's words couldn't be understood clearly—her "I" always sounded like "Oi"—the final section ended up sounding like an unsophisticated Richard Rodgers writing "Uniting with the Galaxy."

More interesting than the music was the attitude of "Mr. Zubin" toward the composer and his work. First Mehta played a long section through; his most substantive comment immediately after was that the accents hadn't come out. Then he quickly assumed a patronizing attitude toward Kernis, lecturing him (in front of the audience) on his inadequate technique in orchestration. He responded to Kernis's request for softer playing by telling him that he had written for too many instruments. Though Mehta felt free to make jokes to the audience, he showed no familiarity with the music, finding little to comment on as he riffled through the pages of the score. He made no attempt to clarify balance or correct errors. He remarked that passages weren't together, but he never specified what had gone wrong. Given his evident lack of interest in the task he was publicly performing, one could only wonder why he had chosen to do it in the first place.

Arthur Weisberg began his work on Crumb's *A Haunted Landscape* by saying that he wanted to rehearse orchestral balances before playing the fragment through. In contrast to Mehta, Weisberg knew the music he was conducting. He began by working with the harpists, whom he asked to play louder (they couldn't). He went on to trying to get just the right sound from the pianist, who was hitting the innards of the piano; the best tool for the purpose turned out to be a percussion mallet. Weisberg then discussed how the tam-tam should be bowed, suggesting an up- rather than a downbow. Weisberg even went so far as to ask the strings to play very softly. Unfortunately, their attempts only proved that the Philharmonic cannot play *pianissimo* and together at the same time.

By now, boredom could plainly be seen on the faces of many orchestra members. A functionary came out to tell Weisberg that the time for the break was approaching, so the audience finally got to hear Crumb's eight-minute fragment in its entirety. The score was typical of the composer, combining in a purposeless way percussion effects and reminiscences of other composers, in this case string chords seemingly drawn from Vaughan Williams's *Fantasia on a Theme by Tallis*.

This evening, too, ended with a whale of piece. Thorne's *Symphony from Silence* is another minimalist work, substituting huge volumes of sound played at extraordinary length for any discernible musical activity. After about five minutes of tedious orchestral stasis, the pianist entered with pointless repeated *fortissimo* chords, almost inaudible because of the orchestra's blaring away. When the piano did make itself heard, the tone was mean and dry. There were wayward chord progressions and a huge rattling piano cadenza, informed by a meaningless jumble of demi-Rachmaninoff technical clichés. Mehta stopped about fifteen minutes into the piece to ask the composer for comment. Before Thorne could answer, Mehta said, "Please say it was good," presumably so the orchestra could continue and end the "rehearsal" without going into overtime. *Symphony from Silence* is a piece of such amateurishness that it is difficult to say whether it deserved better than this.

The next night, Mehta conducted a real concert, beginning the program with three *Colloquies* for French horn and orchestra by William Schuman (with Philip Myers, the Philharmonic's principal horn, as soloist). Next came *Canti del Sole* for tenor and orchestra by Bernard Rands (with Paul Sperry). The last work of the evening was *Sinfonia* by the Italian Luciano Berio (with the New Swingle Singers).

From the beginning of the Schuman it was clear that one was listening to the work of a master musician. *Colloquies*, written in 1979, gave an impression of continuity that until now had been lacking in the festival's offerings. The differing timbres of the solo horn combined with the lone, arching, "American" melodic lines to make an integrated, meaningful, and moving music. It must be stressed that *Colloquies* succeeded in this performance despite Mehta's evident lack of care in rehearsal for proper articulation and phrasing, and despite insecure horn playing and ensemble lapses in the strings. To those who would complain that in Schuman's work there is nothing new, that he repeatedly mines the same compositional vein, *Colloquies* made an eloquent rebuttal. Only someone whose taste has been formed by the merely diverting and the trivially provocative could fail to recognize in it the incremental growth of a distinguished creator.

While such splendid marks can hardly be given to Rands's *Canti del Sole*, which followed the Schuman, here at least was highly professional music, using a large and skillfully handled orchestra. In his setting of poems by (among others) Wilfred Owen, Dylan Thomas, Baudelaire, Rimbaud, Montale, and D. H. Lawrence, Rands was concerned, in his own words, to "suggest both the daily (dawn to dusk) and seasonal (winter to autumn) cycles of the sun: 'narratives' which influence our physical and psychological states." The music did suggest Mahler and even the concluding section of Schoenberg's *Gurrelieder*, but it also had a purpose and direction of its own. Unfortunately, Mehta often allowed the orchestra to obscure the singer, so the words were not as clear as they might have been.

The concluding *Sinfonia* of Berio, written in 1968–69, is a classic of the approachable avant-garde. The amplified singers mumble, mutter, hiss, and sometimes sing recognizable words. When the words are clear, they invoke such fashionable icons of the 1960s as Lévi-Strauss, Martin Luther King, and Samuel Beckett. The third section of the work quotes Mahler at length, and also makes reference to the works of Bach, Schoenberg, Debussy, Ravel, Hindemith, Beethoven, Stravinsky, Boulez, Henri Posseur, Vinko Globokar, Stockhausen, and to Berio himself. This pastiche, though relatively conventional, is provocative in the way it discordantly strings together its elements, both musical and verbal. The audience loved it, no doubt in part because so many of the tunes were recognizable.

Lukas Foss's concert of June 10 lost whatever momentum Mehta's program had managed to gain the night before. Here again were four pieces: *Imago Mundi* by George Rochberg, *Baroque Variations* by Foss himself, *Sparrows* by Joseph Schwantner (performed by soprano Lucy Shelton with the Speculum Musicae conducted by Donald Palma), and *The Silence of the Infinite Spaces* by Frederic Rzewski (performed by the New York Choral Artists with the composer as piano soloist).

Imago Mundi was yet another example of George Rochberg's use of borrowed materials, in this case ancient Japanese court music. Unlike his usual borrowings, which at least have the individuality of those whose work has been stolen from, this piece was without even secondhand personal distinction. The string ensemble was once again terrible. The faces of some members of the first violin section betrayed a certain disgust while the music was going on—whether at the composition or at their own playing was not immediately clear.

Foss's own work, *Baroque Variations*, was a recomposition of three pieces: the aria *Larghetto e piano* from Handel's Concerto Grosso, opus 6 no. 12, Scarlatti's Sonata no. 23 in E major, and the Prelude from Bach's Partita in E major for unaccompanied violin. Here was a combination of Gerard Hoffnung and Peter Schickele—but without the fun and high spirits. Instead, Foss brought to these beautiful pieces what can only be called decomposition. Sudden swells on random notes and chords, cruelly wrong harmonies, blatant sounds from an electric organ and electric piano—all comported strangely with leering observances of authentic baroque performance practices. It should be said that reworkings of the classics are not impossible to do in a serious and even profound way: Hans Werner Henze, in *Il Vitalino raddoppiato* (1977), performed the operation on no less a chestnut than the famous Chaconne of Vitali. But Henze produced a real and interesting work very much his own. Foss only mocked what to him are musical pieties, although to others they are works of imperishable beauty.

Schwantner's *Sparrows* was a musical combination of the sonic devices of George Crumb and the structural simplicities of minimalism. Echoes of Mahler—this time *Das Lied von der Erde*—could be heard yet again, along with suggestions of the film music of William Walton. Although the music was a setting of fifteen intriguing Japanese *haikai*, the effect was exceptionally bland, even by the standards of the festival.

"Bland" could hardly be applied to Rzewski's *The Silence of the Infinite Spaces*, heard on this occasion in its New York premiere. The composer is well known for combining avant-garde tastes (he was a founder in 1966 of the Musica Elettronica Viva group in Rome) with what his program biography called a "commitment to social issues." In fact, Rzewski is a dedicated supporter of liberation movements the world over; his most renowned piece so far is a huge set of variations, dating from 1975, on a radical Chilean song of the Allende period, "The People United Will Never Be Defeated." That work was a virtuoso piano piece, immediately attractive, catchy, and essentially simpleminded, despite its use of various modernistic compositional techniques. *The Silence of the Infinite Spaces*, however, was both less ideological and less beguiling. Aleatorically notated, the piece was a virtual barnyard of orchestral effects. In the end it sounded like nothing so much as jungle music, complete with tom-toms and the yelps of victims, this despite the fact that it included as well a tape of sounds recorded in a steel mill. The piece concluded, to many cheers and boos, with a tape of Atlantic Ocean noises, enriched by the sound of a (propeller) airplane passing overhead.

The festival's last concert, on June 15, was conducted by Gunther Schuller. Again, four pieces were programmed: *A Reliquary* for Igor Stravinsky by Charles Wuorinen, *Aureole* by Jacob Druckman, *Adagio* for oboe and string orchestra (played by Philharmonic oboist Joseph Robinson) by Tison Street, and Schuller's own Concerto no. 2 for Orchestra. The only reason for not calling the concert an anticlimax is that the word would flatter too much what had come before.

Wuorinen's *Reliquary* included several small fragments of a piece for orchestra that Stravinsky had projected about 1967. The rest of the piece, while sounding like late Stravinsky, is Wuorinen's own. Although it all seemed rigorously planned—Wuorinen's music always does—and although there were many traditional elements, including a violin cadenza, the result was shapeless and faceless. It is Wuorinen's genius to write so that the very reality of pitch loses musical meaning. In part this is what happens to serial composition in less than gifted hands. But some of the aridity of *Reliquary* is undoubtedly Wuorinen's: he is not a composer whose character and personality emerge in his music.

I have never been convinced by Jacob Druckman's music. He is musically very talented, but he has never been able to put his gift for imaginative orchestral scoring in the service of a long musical or architectural line. His saving grace has been that his music is always sensually appealing and never ugly. And so it was with *Aureole*. It had a vaguely Oriental quality; fragments of big-band jazz peeked out from time to time; at the end there was a long ostinato in the violins against which everybody in the orchestra had a go at displaying various disjointed fragments. *Aureole* was less integrated music than a comment on the elements of music, as if one were to suggest a meal by showing the ingredients one or two at a time.

Tison Street's *Adagio*, mercifully short, certainly sounded like music. The only trouble was that it sounded like other people's music—lock, stock, and barrel. The work relied heavily on slurping solo strings as a foil to the solo oboe. The rich harmonies suggested a late nineteenth-century violin concerto as written by a slick 1940s movie composer. There were many Wagnerisms, and a suggestion of Strauss's *Death and Transfiguration*. If copyrights were nonexpiring, however, the composer with whom Street would have really been in trouble is Mahler, truly one of the patron saints of this festival.

With Schuller's Concerto no. 2 for Orchestra, the concluding work of the entire series, matters were once again back to fragments. The first movement was made up of darting figures, with the winds leading the way and strident full orchestral chords just behind. There was a suggestion of Ravel's *La Valse* gone haywire, and a little later, in the second movement, a bit of his *Pavane*. The third movement featured huge chords, while various percussion instruments were beaten to death. This was followed by a soft, soulful excursion into the mood and music of Act III of Wagner's *Tristan*. At the end, the piece returned to chords, this time, as the program notes stated, "almost in C major." Schuller's conducting, even in his own composition, was tentative and clumsy; time and again, simple orchestral attacks were shaky and not together. Perhaps only Schuller himself really knows whether a better performance would have helped the piece.

Many questions arise from a consideration of this long and dreary story. Perhaps the first one is simply whether all this music was really different from the older, pre-1968 contemporary writing. Viewed one way, the answer is yes. In the Philharmonic festival there were no open provocations, no impassioned attempts to tell the audience that music was dead and that only fools liked such outdated indulgences as melody and consonant harmony. To put it in a word, things were pleasant.

And yet much in these concerts was not a change from what had gone before. For one thing, some of the same people were involved. Morton Subotnick, Luciano Berio, and Frederic Rzewski, for example, are old avant-gardists still in good standing. Old avant-garde devices, too, were clearly in good standing—computers, tape-produced sounds, out-of-the-way instruments, or conventional instruments played in an out-of-the-way manner. Electronic amplification was common for both instruments and voices, and familiar extra-musical shibboleths undergirded the music, shibboleths ranging from political and literary ideas to fashionable ideologies of personal awareness and earth worship. Indeed, the very emphasis of the Philharmonic festival on newness and change was itself a prominent feature of the avant-garde approach to aesthetic phenomena.

There are those, of course, who will point to the *sound* of the music performed in these concerts and say that it is qualitatively different from what had gone on compositionally in the 1960s and just before. Was there not in this music, it will be plaintively asked, melody and harmony, shape and grace, all frankly inspired by an attempt to please? Yes, the answer must be, there were tunes and consonant chords aplenty—though in fact they didn't turn up in every piece. But where these valuable elements were present, they were merely identifiable rather than memorable, interesting more for the manner of their appearance than for their distinctive musical content. And even as style this relatively traditional way of writing was not artistically convincing. The manner so frequently favored in these earnestly attractive compositions was borrowed, after all, from honored predecessors. The ghosts of Debussy, Strauss, and Mahler hung heavy over Avery Fisher Hall.

All this is now being explained away as a happy development. Every style, so it would appear, is now permitted and welcomed, and this is supposedly a good thing, even—as in the cases of George Rochberg and Tison Street—when the composer completely abandons his own voice. But only the naïve should be pleased with what is at best a confession of creative impotence or at worst out-and-out theft. I suppose an argument could be made for this appropriation on the basis of its appeal to the tastes of the public, so long alienated from the new music. But the only available evidence suggests that the audience for serious music, acting as always on the pleasure principle, finds this new music only relatively less painful than what came before. Because this music is tolerated, for a variety of reasons both social and ideological, doesn't mean that it is liked, or still less that it will be demanded.

In this regard, it is instructive to look at the *New York Times*'s critical coverage of the Philharmonic concerts. The *Times*'s chief music critic, Donal Henahan, found only one concert—the last—worthy of covering himself. Even the newspaper's unabashed advocate of new music, John Rockwell, covered only the first three concerts; the remaining concerts were assigned to junior writers. Henahan, although enthusiastically applauding Street's *Adagio* as "a work . . . of obvious musical qualities . . . a score that [may well] be added to the standard repertory," found nothing else on the one program he attended to be either "romantic" or valuable. (Because he heard so little of the festival, he was unable, of course, to write a considered critical analysis at the end of the series.) Rockwell was cool toward many of the pieces in the three concerts he heard, showing real enthusiasm for none of them and offering guarded praise for only a few. Not only was benevolent caution the order of the day for Rockwell, he was careful, in his generally favorable summing-up article, to make clear just how limited he thought the whole Philharmonic effort was:

> Of course, when one speaks of New Romanticism in "music" one means the art music that has commonly been the concern of intellectuals and of composers with a clear sense of connection to the tradition of "serious" composition in the West. The Philharmonic never attempted to address itself to broader questions touching on the newly aspired-to "seriousness" of music arising out of vernacular traditions and third-world Classical tradition, or even the precise connection between the more extreme forms of American experimentalism and conventional "contemporary music."

"Horizons '83" was indeed less than successful musically. Should the Philharmonic have made such an effort on behalf of all these pieces and their composers? Despite the festival's artistic shortcomings, the answer is yes. One of the functions of major musical institutions (and, given the present ossification of the accepted repertory, perhaps the most important one) must be the presentation of that which is actually going on in musical creation at the present time. These institutions must make this effort not just when the effort can confidently be expected to be successful, for then everyone and every group will quite enthusiastically join the act, but even more when the going is rough and the outcome unpredictable, as is now the case in our musical culture.

Viewed in this way, Leonard Bernstein's presentation of avant-garde music in the 1960s deserved doing, just as Pierre Boulez's vigorous and innovative programming in the 1970s deserved doing. *Mutatis mutandis*, "Horizons '83" deserved doing, too. To say this is not to suggest that all the selections, even within the series' own frame of reference, were correctly made, or even that these selections were widely and fairly representative of what is going on in composition today. Nor, most emphatically, is it to say that the works chosen were well served by the performances they received.

Next time around—and it is to be hoped that next time will be next year—the Philharmonic may well find it possible to present, along with music by new discoveries, the recent work of established masters; in this connection, the names of Boulez and Carter immediately come to mind. Perhaps, too, the next series can include the work of other composers, less well known, who have been writing distinguished music over a period of many years. Perhaps the Philharmonic will in the future take the trouble to secure well-rehearsed and powerfully led performances of the difficult contemporary works it programs. And perhaps by the time of a new festival the Philharmonic will once again be playing like the great orchestra its player members surely entitle it to be. Then and only then the musical news from Fisher Hall will be not just news but good news.

5.

*The first of these two short pieces appeared in the October 1983 Commentary
and the second in the January 1989 New Criterion. How much has changed
since these pieces were written? As of this date (November 1989), the New York
City Opera has canceled its fall season because of an intractable labor dispute
with its orchestra musicians, and there has been extended discussion in the local
press about the current exiguousness of the company's artistic mission; the
Metropolitan Opera has a new albeit inexperienced general manager, a
development putting even more responsibility for the future on James Levine, the
Met's enigmatic artistic director; the New York Philharmonic, newly the
subject of* sub rosa *discussion about the quality of its administrative
leadership, has not as yet found a music director to replace the hardly beloved
Zubin Mehta.* Le plus ça change . . .

Musical New York in Decline

N E W Y O R K is the musical capital of the United States. New York
is at the same time one of the most important centers of music in the
world. As the events of the past summer have made abundantly clear,
New York is now musically in a state of crisis.

This crisis has been many years in coming. During the time when
the storm was gathering, crisis wore the face of prosperity, of expansion,
of fame and fortune. The number of events seemed to be increasing,
audiences were growing, press coverage was ever more enthusiastic,
patronage was on the rise, and government and politicians displayed
a touching eagerness to jump on the bandwagon of art.

The evidence for this apparently happy state of affairs has not been
hard to find. Today's leading New York performers—Pavarotti,
Domingo, Horne, Perlman, Zukerman, Levine, Mehta, Yo-Yo Ma,
Larrocha—have all become big stars since the mid-1960s. Noted

careers have recently been made in musical composition too. The two Georges—Rochberg and Crumb—are often programmed, and are enthusiastically received in the *New York Times*. The once lusty avant-garde has had its heroes as well: Philip Glass and Steve Reich have both enjoyed the distinction of being *enfants demi-terribles* for the best part of the past decade. The city's music schools—Juilliard, Manhattan, and Mannes—have continued to attract much of the best talent in the country and even, in the case of Juilliard, in the world; not a few of their students have even become internationally prominent shortly after graduation.

New facilities in which to hear music and see opera have also been built. Gone is the past dependence upon the aging Carnegie Hall, the musty and cramped old Metropolitan Opera House, the poorly located Town Hall, and the barn-like Hunter College Auditorium. In place of these relics, Lincoln Center has arisen from the ashes of an urban slum, housing the New York Philharmonic in Avery Fisher Hall, the Metropolitan Opera in its own palatial building, the New York City Opera (and the New York City Ballet) in the New York State Theater, the Juilliard School in a building designed not only for music but also for dance, theater, and opera, and even the New York City Library of the Performing Arts. The place of Town Hall as a prestigious venue for recitals has been taken by Lincoln Center's Alice Tully Hall, where a successful chamber-music series is now regularly presented. The small Merkin Hall, newly built and adjoining Lincoln Center, provides an inexpensive, good-sounding place to put on smaller events. And the 92nd Street YM–YWHA, reviving its concert activity, has to some extent filled the gap left by Hunter's demise.

Yet despite all this activity and apparent prosperity, something—the most important thing—has been missing. What one calls this central quality is hardly important; it goes variously by the names of vitality, excitement, interest, creativity, or discovery. In the last year or two, not even celebrity musical events have been selling out very often. What new reputations there are increasingly seem pale copies of what has come before. Old recordings more and more sound better than contemporary performances. Old artists like Horowitz, Rubinstein, and Heifetz appear less replaceable as each day passes. And in musical composition, as the recent New York Philharmonic New Romanticism festival showed, new works are praised more for merely being new than as important artistic achievements. In short, every major musical institution in New York is in serious trouble.

Precisely because Lincoln Center is at both the foundation and the pinnacle of local musical life, it seems only fitting that the biggest troubles should be here. And in fact they involve every large musical constituent of the Center.

The most visible of Lincoln Center's recent problems was the strike of orchestra musicians at the New York City Opera. Lasting from the opening of the summer–fall season in July until the end of August, the strike destroyed the Puccini Festival, which general director Beverly Sills had counted on to reverse the plummeting artistic and box-office fortunes of her company. The main issue of this bitter strike was not increased wages and improved working conditions, though these were demanded, or even the loss of the musicians' outside summer employment. What agitated the players was the consolidation of the company's traditionally separate fall and spring seasons into one combined summer–fall season of much shorter duration, leaving them with much less work to do.

Some of the acrimony that characterized this strike was doubtless due to the election of a new slate of militant officers in Local 802 of the Musicians Union, which has jurisdiction over the City Opera contract. Some of the difficulty in getting on with orderly negotiations was doubtless caused also by the unsettled state of the City Opera board, a state of open backbiting and bitchery revealed in a lengthy *Times* article by John Rockwell at the beginning of August.

But while board members complained about each other, union officials attacked the company for financial mismanagement, and orchestra lawyers argued that the expansion of music performances mainly comes about through union pressure, the real cause of the present parlous condition of the City Opera was not, and is not now, ever discussed in public. That cause is nothing less than the total artistic failure of Beverly Sills to put together a company musicians can respect and operagoers wish to support. The sad fact is that the City Opera now employs no one of major musical stature. At best its artists are talents in search of a leadership which could provide vital repertory, effective casting, energetic musical direction, and an overall sense of aesthetic purpose. Instead, Beverly Sills has given the company and the audience only personal publicity, public fund raising, and show-business gimmickry.

It is no surprise, then, that the orchestral musicians have less and less work to do. As the late Sol Hurok is supposed to have said, "If people don't want to come, you can't stop them." When there is a good artistic reason for the public to come and for musicians to take the City Opera seriously, it will be time to talk about length of seasons, contracts, and financial management. As things now stand, the settlement of the strike only papers over a moribund situation.

Matters just a few hundred yards away at the New York Philharmonic are hardly more attractive. There music director Zubin Mehta, about to enter the sixth year of his association with the Philharmonic, is suffering from disaffection on the part of orchestra members, concert audiences, the critical press, and the record-buying public. All this had been much discussed privately by musicians and music-lovers, but it had remained *sub rosa* until the publication of a lengthy article by the *Times* at the end of June. Under a headline reading "Philharmonic Board Hears Musicians' Complaints," Edward Rothstein described the results of a questionnaire distributed to the orchestra. Of the 103 members, nearly half responded; of these, all but six were negative about Mehta.

Rothstein went on to write in some detail about the loss of the Philharmonic's CBS recording contract and the poor sales of Mehta records. Significantly, even the records made by Pierre Boulez with the Philharmonic sell better than those of Mehta—and Boulez's sales figures were a major disappointment to both management and orchestra during the French conductor's tenure.

More interesting, however, than the recounting of this generally known information was Rothstein's presentation of what the Philharmonic board thinks of Mehta and the orchestra. Though the board members quoted by Rothstein were quick to blame the orchestra and not Mehta for the poor morale and the complaints, they also seemed curiously unwilling to praise the conductor either as a musician or as a leader.

In the case of the Philharmonic, as in that of the New York City Opera, there seems no clear insight into the actual state of artistic affairs. Orchestra morale is not a cause but rather a symptom of trouble. An orchestra does not need to like its conductor; it needs to respect him. When that respect is not present, discipline inevitably becomes lax, and minor conflicts of personality begin to grate. Similarly, poor record sales of a well-known orchestra led by a well-known conductor, recorded in up-to-date sound, must be laid to artistic failings, not to mere vagaries of the market. There can be little doubt that the Philharmonic board and management have some hard thinking to do in coming months, not so much about the future of the orchestra as about the future of Zubin Mehta.

The Metropolitan Opera, just entering its centennial year, finds itself faced with the upcoming retirement of Anthony Bliss, general manager since 1981. Although Bliss had originally taken over at the Met in the mid-1970s as part of a troika with James Levine as music director and John Dexter as director of productions, Dexter is now gone from management, and Levine's authority has remained confined to musical matters. Bliss has thus been having the last word at the Met. But now Levine—as revealed in a mid-June *Times* story by Harold C. Schonberg—wishes to be assured that Bliss's replacement will defer to him on all artistic issues.

This insistence by the Met's music director on artistic control, even though art has an impact on the budget, is proper. But it comes at a time when the company is rather more successful at fund raising—its current campaign has now passed $70 million on the road to its goal of $100 million—than at finding a way to present musically and intellectually exciting operatic fare to an increasingly tradition-bound though unsophisticated audience.

The Metropolitan Opera is rarely less than professional; what it does it does on a large and often—as in the case of the Zeffirelli production of *La Bohème* two seasons ago—lavish scale. Both its chorus and its orchestra are composed of highly skilled individuals, and the level of solo singing is as high, it seems, as may be found in the world. Levine is a successful conductor in both concerts and opera here and abroad (though his enthusiasm and vitality are rarely matched by the other conductors who are chosen to fill in at the Met when he does not wish to be on the podium). Production and stage direction seem carefully crafted to appear neither innovative nor old-fashioned, and thus are able to please a wide range of ticket buyers.

All these virtues, considerable as they are, have conspicuously failed to make the Met a significant force in American musical life. The reason is that the Met's repertory is totally devoid of new operas, and of American works regardless of when they were written. It is lacking, too, in major works written since World War I. The Met has never done Schoenberg's *Moses und Aron*, it has done nothing of Hindemith, and even *The Rake's Progress* of Stravinsky, which it performed in the 1950s, has fallen victim to programming caution and even fear. Strangely, this restriction on problematical works has extended to the later works of Richard Strauss; the Met has put on nothing of this master after *Arabella* (1930–32).

When the Met has looked for new repertory, it has tended to find it in such safe modern composers as Britten, Poulenc, and Weill; when it has tried something slightly more venturesome, as in the Stravinsky triple bill of two years ago, it took care to preface the relatively difficult *Oedipus Rex* and *Le Rossignol* with the crowd-pleasing, non-operatic *Le Sacre du printemps*, performed as a ballet. Otherwise, the Met's novelty in repertory is now confined to rediscovering such older works as Francesco Cilea's *Adriana Lecouvreur* (1902) and Mozart's *Idomeneo*, never before done by the Met, even though the opera was first performed (in Munich) in 1781.

Just how Levine feels about the current state of the Met repertory is not a matter of public knowledge; the extent to which the exact makeup of the repertory is an issue in the current administrative battle over the powers of Anthony Bliss's successor is not known either. But if these issues are not now being fought out behind the façade of the famous Met Chagall murals facing Lincoln Center Plaza, it would be just one more sign of the obliviousness to artistic considerations now endemic in New York musical life. If, however, they are on the negotiating table, and even if Levine should win, one cannot be sure, given his propensity to please his supporters, that he would make the tough decisions necessary to bring the Metropolitan Opera into the twentieth century.

One of the requirements of a musical capital is that it have a famous music school, and in the Juilliard School, New York boasts perhaps the most famous such institution in the world. Though its faculty is renowned, the school's distinction perhaps really lies not in its teachers but in its students. Juilliard's students are very often already remarkable performers upon admission, and it seems likely that for the best of these young people Juilliard's contribution can be better described as performance coaching and career placement than as basic musical formation and intellectual development.

For twenty years the distinguished (but remarkably little played) American composer Peter Mennin served as president of Juilliard. In June, just after his sixtieth birthday, Mennin died. With his death, every question, not just about the future of the Juilliard School, but about the proper nature of music education for the most gifted, has become open. Should the Juilliard board merely wish to continue along the course of least resistance Mennin so brilliantly followed, finding his successor will not be easy; his idiosyncratic blend of musical distinction, pedagogic *laissez faire*, and personal charm in the service of fund raising has always been rare. But should the board wish to break genuinely new ground in musical training, neither suitable persons nor inspiring programs come readily to mind.

Certainly one's confidence is hardly raised by several of the prominent names rumored to have been under board consideration for the job. These names include Isaac Stern, Leonard Bernstein, Ezra Laderman, and Vincent Persichetti. Stern, of course, is a famous violinist and is both active and visible in musical politics; Bernstein, both as composer and as conductor, is one of the most gifted figures in the history of American music; Laderman is a well-known composer and for some years was head of the music program of the National Endowment for the Arts; Persichetti is a widely respected and prolific composer who has taught on the Juilliard faculty for many years. It is no denigration of the achievement of the men to remark that their age alone—ranging from fifty-nine in the case of Laderman to sixty-eight in the case of Persichetti—suggests that they are not suited for the immense daily output of energy and strength necessary to change the course of a settled and successful institution. Nor has any of them been known for any new and solid approach to music education. Even Bernstein, famous for explaining music to the millions on television, has functioned more as a music-appreciation lecturer than as a teacher.

One hopes that before it commits itself to a candidate the Juilliard board will take the trouble to think through for itself some of the fundamental questions at stake in music education. They include, but are not limited to, the role of serious music in a society riven by various commercially successful popular cultures; the proper relation (within serious music itself) between unpopular new music and the masterpieces of the past that are still successful with audiences; the currently regnant idea of the best music teaching as a laying-on of hands; and the role of an American music school at a time when many of the best students are not American, or even Occidental.

There are undoubtedly answers to all these questions, but they all involve choosing between the easy course of institutional prosperity and media approval on the one hand, and the hard road of self-limitation and artistic concentration on the other. The future president of Juilliard—willing and able to follow an active policy of rejecting the pressure of commercial culture and fame, of finding and making new music, of conceiving teaching as something other than a repetition of the time-worn formulas of European music schools, and of preserving a distinctively American rather than an internatonal artistic style—will be difficult indeed to find.

Away from Lincoln Center, the problems, while hardly so massive and central, are still troubling enough. Of the two halls in which New York musical life was concentrated before Lincoln Center was built, Carnegie Hall seems much more likely to survive than Town Hall. Carnegie is superior acoustically to Lincoln Center's Fisher Hall. It is centrally located on West Fifty-seventh Street, the business capital of the American music world. It has a busy schedule of rentals, most of them of highly respectable artistic caliber (and so does its small adjunct, Carnegie Recital Hall). It has a rich, well-connected board, with Isaac Stern as president and investment banker James Wolfensohn as chairman.

Furthermore, Carnegie Hall has prided itself upon becoming a businesslike operation, utilizing modern techniques of management and fundraising to replace the personal approach described in a May *Times* story as a "'mom-and-pop store' run by the Sterns [the violinist and his wife] and a coterie of friends." One token of this progress into the computer and business-school age has been the increase in management staff from ten in 1963 to forty-six today. A related indication has been the splitting of upper-level direction into the two positions of managing director and artistic director. Edward Michaelson, the recently chosen managing director, is a former top business executive; Seymour Rosen, the new artistic director, formerly managed the Philadelphia Orchestra. Though they have each been on the job only a short time, the New York musical rumor mongers are now buzzing with apparently well-founded stories of Michaelson's decline in board favor and of his possible supersession by Rosen.

All this might seem merely another example of modern management techniques' not always guaranteeing perfect organization and harmony all around, were it not for the interesting pronouncements Rosen has been making about the proper future of Carnegie Hall. According to the *Times*:

> Mr. Rosen has also been forthright about his intention to steer Carnegie Hall in new directions, democratizing both its programming and its potential audience. . . . "There are areas we have not paid sufficient attention to," he said, citing jazz, ethnic music, experimental and new American music among those whose role he wishes to augment. "We are also going to be doing more outreach," Mr. Rosen added, "moving Carnegie Hall into the community and into the schools."

Perhaps Rosen's statement means no more than an increased emphasis on concerts for the young and "the community." His remarks, however, seem to suggest rather more: a quixotic attempt to go beyond Carnegie Hall's acoustics—the principal reason, after all, for its existence—to implement some grandiose—though no doubt fundable—dream of becoming a citywide presenting institution. Here precisely is the kind of massive overreach, born at the same time of megalomania and an obsession with financing, which is one of the main causes of the crisis in New York musical life.

As for Town Hall, its problem is its unfortunate location in the Times Square area and its run-down condition. Remaining as it does a beautifully clear and sonically faithful ambience for solo recitals and small ensembles, it refuses to die, but at the same time it does not live. In August, another of its periodic attempts to save itself was reported in the *Times* under the headline, "Town Hall Is Scouting for Donors." Though much of the necessary money seems to have been raised, the list of groups to which Town Hall wishes to offer permanent support—among them the New Amsterdam Theater Group and the American Guitar Institute—does not necessarily augur well for its musical future.

To round out this gloomy account, finally, other significant problems in New York musical life could be mentioned as well. The Manhattan School of Music, for example, has been going through a well-organized faculty revolt against its president, and the musician-run American Symphony Orchestra has utterly failed to realize the hopes entertained by its well-wishers that it would become a true second orchestra in New York.

But whatever the particular details may be in each individual case, it is the lack of a significant artistic product which lies in common at the heart of the problems of the New York City Opera, the New York Philharmonic, the Metropolitan Opera, the Juilliard School, Carnegie Hall, and Town Hall. For some of these institutions, such as the City Opera and Town Hall, the crisis is immediate and acute; without some quick discoveries, they simply will not survive. For others, among them the Philharmonic and the Metropolitan, the problem is longer-term. For the time being, their financial health and the loyalty of their subscribers and their boards insure their stability. But unless a serious effort to resolve their artistic problems is made, these institutions too will soon find their survival threatened by the same loss of artistic purpose and creative vitality that has already all but doomed the City Opera under Beverly Sills.

The Crisis Continues

SOME FIVE YEARS ago, I wrote an article for *Commentary* detailing what seemed to me then a crisis in New York musical life. In it, I discussed the general state of apathy among musicians and audiences alike, and I found this mood responsible for a long list of symptoms of institutional ill health. These included the orchestra strike and the contraction in the length of the season at Beverly Sills's City Opera, the stagnation of the repertory and the vacancy in administrative leadership at the Metropolitan Opera, and the rampant player dissatisfaction with conductor Zubin Mehta at the Philharmonic.

In the intervening years much has happened. Hundreds of concerts and opera performances have been given. Artist fees—and administrative salaries—have continued to rise, as have marketing and fund raising costs. There have been two boomlets, one affecting old music and the other new. The truly retrograde development involves the so-called authentic performance of old music—Handel and Bach through Mozart to early Beethoven—on restored original instruments or on copies thereof; the putatively progressive development involves the commissioning and performing of the romantically minimalist music of Philip Glass and John Adams. So far as the old music is concerned, the trend has influenced classically trained performers in the direction of even tighter and paler playing than had been their previous wont; so far as the new music is concerned, the effect of minimalism has been twofold: it has further separated the traditional concertgoing audience from the contemporary-music audience, and it has produced a swarm of untalented compositional disciples who have found in repetition a master key to obtaining fellowships and grants.

All these developments have been heralded—in advance of their actual performance—by hundreds of encomiastic effusions in the *New York Times*, still, alas, the only daily publication in this country to take serious music seriously. The actual music making, however, has regularly been followed in the *Times* by the withdrawal of most of its plaudits and their replacement by a heavy dose of critical sourness. What exceptions there have been to this rule of negativism have been characterized by a palpable fear that knocking local products will result in their disappearance.

Meanwhile, the institutional troubles have continued. At the City Opera, Beverly Sills has announced her departure as general director, and she has been replaced by the conductor Christopher Keene. Miss Sills's future plans remain somewhat vague, though she does talk about hosting a television talk show; in any case, she has promised to remain involved with the City Opera in some capacity. Her successor, Mr. Keene, has not been particularly successful in his many conducting assignments with the company, and it is hard to see in him the necessary spark of imagination that marks every successful ruler of an opera house.

By all accounts, the reign of Miss Sills has been distinguished solely by the kind of massive fund raising necessary these days to keep an opera company going. The day-to-day level of City Opera performances, despite occasional excellent portrayals of individual roles, has failed to excite the current interest of opera lovers or to provide them with the kind of memories that build a tradition of subscriber loyalty. Not only can the City Opera not compete with the neighboring Metropolitan Opera in casting internationally active singers and in the provision of sumptuous and necessarily expensive productions, but the house in which it plays—the New York State Theater—remains vastly too large, and somehow too chilling, for the kind of intimacy that most operas need for the powerful communication of their dramatic passions, and that the company's young singers need to make possible the illusion of vocal size and richness that alone can make opera believable.[1]

Long, long ago, what the City Opera failed to provide in finish it more than made up for in the interest of its repertory. A canny combination of familiar and new (or at least unfamiliar) at cheap ticket prices marked the company from its founding in 1944, which meant it was able both to please new audiences for opera and to showcase the best in twentieth-century works. But in the 1960s, the supply of new operas capable of entering the repertory just about dried up; and audience receptivity to new or unfamiliar works seemed to dry up as well.

To its credit, the City Opera in the past few years has attempted to do new works. Among these have been Philip Glass's *Akhnaten*, Dominick Argento's *Casanova*, Anthony Davis's *X*, Oliver Knussen's *Where the Wild Things Are*, and, most recently, Jay Reise's *Rasputin*. Of these, *Akhnaten*—or at least that part of it that I managed to sit through—was to my ears a great bore in Glass's all too well-known

---

[1] A sad demonstration of the influence of the barnlike atmosphere of the New York State Theater on what was most likely a splendid City Opera effort took place just this past October, when Douglas Moore's charming and deeply affecting 1956 work, *The Ballad of Baby Doe*, seemed dwarfed in the house even when witnessed from an excellent seat in the orchestra.

manner.[2] *Casanova*, a setting of the lover's ups and downs, was well received by what is left of the traditional operagoing public at the City Opera—in spite of, or perhaps because of, its elements of musical pastiche.[3] *X,* a polemical treatment of the life and death of Malcolm X, was musically thin and abrasive in its ideological thrust, although it did manage the not inconsiderable feat of enticing a sizeable black audience into the New York State Theater. *Where the Wild Things Are*, after the 1963 story by Maurice Sendak, treated of a small boy's night dream of glory in a dramatically low-key and compositionally uninspired fashion.

The most recent of the City Opera's efforts to find something new was *Rasputin*. This opera, Jay Reise's first, brought both good news and bad news. The good news was that the story of the mad monk, the rotten-ripe atmosphere at the Tsarist court in the last days of the Romanovs, the catastrophe of World War I, and Lenin's brutal lust for power, taken together, make one hell of a subject for an opera; the bad news was that Mr. Reise proved yet again that writing notes in a medley of styles—in his case, ranging from Mussorgsky to Tchaikowsky, Wagner, Puccini, and the Second Viennese School—is no substitute for a composer's own musical personality.

And so despite the City Opera's efforts under Beverly Sills, the fundamental problem of the company's artistic identity remains what it was at the time she assumed the general directorship in 1979. With Mr. Keene at the helm, there will inevitably be suggestions for novel approaches. One such suggestion came in an October *New York Times* interview with Robert W. Wilson, the chairman of the City Opera board. Mr. Wilson thinks the City Opera has "the bright young American singers, but we are not getting the bright young directors. . . . We are living in a visual age and the challenge is to have something that is visually communicative but does not detract from the music." Unfortunately for Mr. Wilson's idea of beefing up the visuals as a means to save the City Opera, each of the new operas mentioned above as musically uninteresting was distinguished by powerful and imaginative staging which failed to make up for the composer's lacks.

---

[2] For a discussion of *Akhnaten*, and of the Glass phenomenon as a whole, see Chapter 10 in this book.

[3] My consideration of *Casanova* may be found in Chapter 11 of this book.

Though Mr. Wilson professes to be an admirer of Philip Glass and John Adams, whose *Nixon in China* he would like the City Opera to put on, his plan for the company involves doing fewer operas in longer runs:

> If we could do more performances and still sell as many seats, or more, then we could have more rehearsal per opera without increasing the total amount of rehearsal time. . . . Our average now is something below eighty percent of capacity, and that's just about ten percent too low to tolerate. I have almost a moral problem with tolerating it. I think that ticket sales should bear at least half the cost of an evening, and the people who attend operatic performances are not appropriate objects of charity.

Mr. Wilson's implication is clear: the proper function of an opera company is to please its paying customers, and it can do so only by finding out what is popular and doing a lot of it. According to this bottom-line approach, there is no notion that the primary duty of an artistic institution—even an opera company—is the preservation and extension of art, which is the sole reason for the institution's existence and philanthropic status. The implication for the future of the New York City Opera is plain, too: what is important is not opera's future, or even its past, but rather its balance sheet.

A few hundred feet across Lincoln Center Plaza, the vastly richer and more solidly rooted Metropolitan Opera has also just lost a leader. Bruce Crawford, the advertising executive who assumed the post of general manager in 1986, resigned at the beginning of November to take a position as chief executive officer of a New York-based advertising firm. Under his administration, the Met was able to get a grip on spiraling production costs and raise the percentage of its house sold at the box office from 83 to 90 percent—perhaps not coincidentally the number which so enchants Mr. Wilson at the City Opera.

This year, too, the Met is finally managing to get the four operas of Richard Wagner's *Ring*—*Das Rheingold, Die Walküre, Siegfried,* and *Götterdämmerung*—on the stage in one season, in the proper order, and in the same week of performances. This feat, frequently managed by European opera houses, has been beyond the Met's reach since the spring of 1976. The new *Ring*, in a relatively realistic production by Otto Schenk, has won reasonably enthusiastic press notices. But the praise has been inspired, it would seem, rather more by gratitude for one's being able once again to see and hear these marvelous works than by the quality of their performance.[4]

Mr. Crawford is leaving at a time when rumors continue to swirl about the future of conductor James Levine, the Met's artistic director now for some years. It is perhaps not an extravagant compliment to agree with the received opinion that Mr. Levine is the strongest conductor currently active at the Met; his penchant for learning great works by conducting them for the first time in his own opera house seems on the whole well tolerated by today's mostly complaisant music critics, who regularly point with pride to how well, after all, he settles into the scores as he does them night after night. For me, this greatly gifted musician's conducting is increasingly unsatisfactory and even unacceptable. He has replaced his former endearing, if immature, aggressiveness with a boring and stodgy pseudo-profundity.

Singing at the Met seems a gathering problem as well. At the end of November, Donal Henahan, the curmudgeonly music critic of the *New York Times*, stirred from his lair to attack the company, especially its artistic administrator, Jonathan Friend, who is, Henahan wrote, "[p]ossibly beyond his depth . . . [demonstrating] little gift for recognizing good new opera voices or placing established artists in congenial roles. . . . [T]he dismay [over casting] regularly extends to first-night casts and to first performances of new productions."

For me, at least, these problems of musical direction and vocalism are demonstrated in the just-released Metropolitan Opera compact-disc recording of *Die Walküre*.[5] Of the six major roles in this opera— Brünnhilde (Hildegard Behrens), Sieglinde (Jessye Norman), Fricka (Christa Ludwig), Siegmund (Gary Lakes), Wotan (James Morris), and Hunding (Kurt Moll)—none seems adequately portrayed in voice and character. The Brünnhilde, under-equipped for one of the most demanding roles in the operatic literature, is under continuous and plainly audible vocal pressure; the Sieglinde, possessed of an unbounded

---

[4] For my discussion of the Met's 1986 *Die Walküre*, the first of the four operas to be mounted in the new Schenk production, see Chapter 19 in this book.

[5] Deutsche Grammophon 423 398-2 (four compact discs).

voice, substitutes generalized expressiveness for particularized passion; the Fricka is tremulously sung by a once-great singer whose splendid portrayal of the role may be heard on the Solti *Ring* recorded in the late 1950s and the 1960s;[6] the Siegmund, in addition to laboring mightily to get the notes out, lacks vocal color and dramatic personality; the Wotan sounds thin and callow, totally lacking in the necessary fatherly qualities of warmth and worry; the Hunding lacks both the focused dark bass once to be heard from German singers and the quality of horrifying malice so central to the role. And the conducting is par for Mr. Levine's current course: full of stops and starts, gestures without meaning, and shapes without coherent structure.

No observer of the opera scene today needs to be told that there is a shortage of historically great singers. It often goes unremarked, however, that second-rank artists—those below the highest level of fame and audience appeal—lack clear, well-produced voices and stage personalities that are alive with clearly communicated idiomatic conceptions of the requisite style, if not also with personal magnetism. Sadly, the models for the development of this authenticity seem not to exist even in the national homes of the great operas of the repertory. What is going on in opera houses all over the world may charitably be called internalization; less charitably, it may be described as a falling out of touch with the long-dead composers of masterpieces and with the traditions and daily life of the societies out of which our great music has come.

This problem bears with particular force on the Metropolitan Opera, so far from the world which created opera and so close to the corporate balance sheet. Much is made of the Met's present reliance on American singers, including several with large international careers, but the fact remains that European opera performance is for Americans an acquired ability, an ability founded on the lifelong effort to cultivate an authentic style. With no European models to inspire the Met, it is hardly surprising that its performances of works heard many times over many years should seem increasingly pallid and homogenized.

One solution, of course, is an increased attention to the repertory.

[6] A technological marvel for its time, and probably for ours as well, it is now available on fifteen compact discs, as London 414100 2.

It is precisely in this area that the Met's problems have gone unattended for so long. It has been years since the Met has done an American opera, with the single exception of a recent production of Gershwin's *Porgy and Bess*, a work hardly suited either to the plenitude of the Met's resources or to the lushness of its ambience. The contemporary works the Met has chosen to do in recent years—like *Wozzeck* and *Lulu* of Berg and *Peter Grimes* and *Billy Budd* of Britten—are often estimable in their own right, but they have all seemed to belong to the world of European rather than American modernism. Even so, the Met has steadfastly refused to put on Arnold Schoenberg's monumental *Moses und Aron*, a classic of the modern operatic stage and an important work about the tormented twentieth-century relation between prophetic virtue and political leadership.

Now the Met seems intent on breaking with its policy of concentrating entirely on Europe. It has commissioned three new works, the first traditional and the other two belonging to what passes these days for minimalism. The traditional opera, *A Figaro for Antonia*, based on Beaumarchais's *L'Autre Tartufe, ou la Mère coupable* (1792), is to be written by the musically very approachable John Corigliano, with a libretto by William Hoffman. Of the two minimalist operas, one (to be performed in a special season in Brooklyn, not at the Metropolitan Opera House) will be based on the hijacking of the *Achille Lauro*, and is to be written by John Adams and Alice Goodman, the composer/librettist team of *Nixon in China*; the second, called *The Voyage*, will be a celebration of Columbus's discovery of America and is to be written by the ubiquitous Philip Glass with a libretto by David Henry Hwang, the author of the current Broadway musical *M. Butterfly*. No opera can be judged unheard, and one wishes the Met well in these commissions. It is hardly to prejudge their success or failure to remark that the odds on Mr. Crawford's successor's enjoying a quiet introduction to his work as general manager seem very low indeed.

Then there is the plight of the New York Philharmonic, the grandfather of American orchestras and the one with the proudest record of service to symphonic music in general and to American symphonic music in particular. It is no secret that the Philharmonic has been going through a difficult period with Zubin Mehta, who was chosen as music director with high hopes that he would bring to the orchestra the kind of popular artistic and financial success so common during the tenure of Leonard Bernstein (1958–69) and so lacking during that of Pierre Boulez (1970–77). From Mehta's arrival on the New York scene in 1978 to the present time he has not been able to galvanize either orchestra or audience; reviewers, tired of repeating their sour judgments, have tended to ignore his concerts or, at best, to give them short shrift.

Needless to say, Mehta's tenure has had a devastating effect on New York's musical life. The Philharmonic is no longer the nerve center of local concert activity; Philharmonic broadcasts increasingly serve a documentary rather than an inspirational purpose; Philharmonic concerts, at least those conducted by Mehta, don't thrill; Philharmonic programs are now rarely a subject for discussion among music lovers or musicians. Even criticism of the orchestra and its conductor in the press and among friends has begun to seem tired and halfhearted, as if all that needed to be said about the Philharmonic's lack of excitement and musical centrality—about the coarsening of its performance standards under Mehta—has been said already, often and sufficiently.

Of course, the Philharmonic has taken great pains to make clear that Mr. Mehta is leaving of his own volition, and that a new contract has always been his for the asking. However that may be, the Philharmonic now has an opportunity to choose its future path. That choice will not be easy, for just as there is a worldwide shortage of first-rank, charismatic opera singers—and, for that matter, instrumentalists—there are few conductors around who can quicken the pulse of musicians or audiences. Those who can, like Herbert von Karajan, Leonard Bernstein, and Sir Georg Solti, are in their seventies or older. There really aren't many first-rank conductors today. Not very many, that is, compared to a half-century ago, when the list of those who would today be stars included Sir Thomas Beecham, Leo Blech, Artur Bodanzky, Adrian Boult, Wilhelm Furtwängler, Robert Heger, Erich Kleiber, Otto Klemperer, Hans Knappertsbusch, Serge Koussevitsky, Clemens Krauss, Willem Mengelberg, Dimitri Mitropoulos, Pierre Monteux, Charles Munch, Fritz Reiner, Artur Rodzinski, Malcolm Sargent, Tullio Serafin, Leopold Stokowski, George Szell, Arturo Toscanini, and Bruno Walter.

In the difficult search for a successor to Mehta, there are also problems beyond art. The expansion in numbers of orchestras and the lengthening of seasons have combined to stretch the available supply of podium stars even thinner. Despite the vast popular success of Leonard Bernstein (still, in his eighth decade, our musical hope) and the thus far entrenched position of James Levine at the Met, American conductors are still rarely chosen as music directors of our major orchestras, no matter how artistically qualified they may be. As a result of this lingering colonial mentality, the Europeans who are invited here combine their American duties with one or more positions abroad; for our major orchestras, it seems, half a European conductor is better than none.

As difficult as the choice facing the Philharmonic is, there is no escaping it. Perhaps it can best be put in the form of a long question: Does the Philharmonic exist to entertain the largest possible audiences in the largest number of concerts, or does the orchestra exist to give a coherent picture of a great artist's musical vision, and in the process shape the future of what is still to be called classical music?

It will doubtless be argued that if a great orchestra does not entertain its audience, it will die. But is that really so? Mr. Mehta, it can hardly be denied, is an entertainer, and it is as an entertainer that he is now seen to have failed at Lincoln Center. His predecessor, Pierre Boulez, was an artist who attempted to shape New York musical taste, and it was as a shaper of taste that he failed. But can anyone deny that the musical interest in the Philharmonic—and the honorable esteem in which it was held—was greater when Mr. Boulez returned to France than it is now when Mr. Mehta leaves for parts unknown?

Let me answer my own question (one of the few perquisites a critic enjoys). The mission of an orchestra is an *artistic*, not an entertainment, task. The role of a music director is to tell the world what music should be heard, and how it should be heard. A great conductor—like Hans von Bülow, Gustav Mahler, or Artur Nikisch, to take three conductors who were, so to speak, present at the creation—is able through his work on the podium to form an artistic milieu. Such a task can be accomplished by the imprinting of a musical personality on the times—not, I might add, simply on the *New York Times*. A great conductor does not reflect, he *leads*.

It is in relation to this attribute of leading rather than reflecting that I found the contents of a recent Philharmonic concert broadcast so disturbing. The program featured two Bernstein works, the *Chichester Psalms* and the Symphony no. 3 (*Kaddish*), conducted in the current season by Zubin Mehta in honor of the composer's recent birthday. These works—not, it seems to me, Bernstein's best—received routine performances. More troubling than the music was the intermission interview conducted with David Del Tredici, the Philharmonic's recently appointed composer-in-residence.

Curiously, a composer-in-residence is asked to do more than just write some music for the orchestra to play, and to learn from the experience. He is also expected (in the case of Mr. Del Tredici, with the help of an assistant) to evaluate, for the benefit of the music director, the myriad new compositions now being written with subsidies from numerous public and private grant programs. It is obvious that in this process the music director is quite content to abdicate his own role as judge of what he is to play, and, by playing, to urge upon his audience. The interview made clear that, in his selection process, Mr. Del Tredici was required not to choose new music from a committed and personal point of view:

> INTERVIEWER: Are there any particular stylistic fingerprints you're looking for, or is it a general exciting score that attracts your attention?
> MR. DEL TREDICI: Well, I remember Zubin saying to me, after my appointment, he said, "Now, I want you to see every kind of diverse style. I want you to choose in all styles. Can you do that, or will you just choose music like your own?" And as I said to him, I certainly hope that I will choose from a diversity of styles. I mean, I've written in very many styles myself, and I'm interested. And in New York there's such a variety of music being written, it's really dizzying, and the Philharmonic programs will and should reflect all of that diversity.

This, I submit, is not the way for an artist to decide what art will be presented to the public. The process described above is not the making of musical decisions, it is the avoiding of them. The decision about who will next lead the Philharmonic lies, of course, with the board of the Philharmonic. Such tasks always properly fall to those who are ultimately responsible for the fate of every great artistic institution. The candidates (especially the Americans) for the Philharmonic or any other music directorship do not necessarily jump off the pages of the world's newspapers, nor do they jump off the balance sheets of the world's great recording and electronic media conglomerates. The right conductor for the Philharmonic need not be a superstar. The right conductor must be someone who is willing to live or die by the service he provides to music. The Philharmonic has been in the past, and can be now, a uniquely great orchestra. Let the search for its leader begin.

6.

In introducing my description of a lecture by John Cage, that grand master of irrelevancies, I hope I may be pardoned a trifle of my own. When late in the afternoon I left Harvard's Sanders Theatre after gathering my evidence for this December 1988 New Criterion *article, I tried (for a long time unsuccessfully) to find a taxi to take me back to the airport. I finally flagged one down, after much arm-waving in the direction of oncoming traffic, on a busy highway abutting Harvard Yard. As the driver and I were zooming off, he said, "You must be from New York."*

"Yes," I answered, "but how could you tell?"

"Simple," he replied. "People from up here don't start hailing us until after we've passed, but you guys from New York get excited before we can even see you."

The Harvard Cage

IT WASN'T, perhaps, a very fine day to be at Harvard for the first of the six prestigious Charles Eliot Norton Lectures to be given in the current academic year by John Cage, America's foremost avant-garde . . . well, shall we say, influence? Outside, as befits the middle of October in New England, the weather was gray and cold, with a fresh wind blowing. Inside, I found myself standing in gloomy Memorial Hall, waiting for the inner doors to open on Sanders Theatre, where Mr. Cage was to . . . well, shall we say, perform? Perhaps I should not stress the gloom, for the walls of Memorial Hall are also deeply moving, emblazoned as they are with plaques commemorating, by name, birthdate, college major, and battlefield, the Harvard dead in the Civil War, certainly the last of America's wars still considered totally acceptable in today's best schools. With a half-hour still to go, and the doors to Sanders not yet open, people began to gather. Here and there I spotted a well-known contemporary musical figure, costumed in what might be termed intellectual motorcycle garb; elsewhere, as one might have expected, the crowd seemed to be made up of faculty and students, almost all dressed *à la mode*—the men tieless and the women bejeaned—in unobtrusively clean (this was, after all, Harvard) but demonstrably ratty clothes.

As the crowd began to press more closely together, conversations became easier to overhear. My own favorite took place between what I took to be an aging male graduate student and a mature bluestocking lady. "I've heard," the aspiring scholar began after a few pleasantries, "that Nabokov has made a really wonderful translation of *Alice in Wonderland* into Russian. I want to get someone to help me with it, so I can mistranslate it." "Into what language?" approvingly asked the bluestocking. "Into Russian, of course," he shot back.

The note of nonsense so dear to the wily Cage had thus been well struck, and had I not been familiar for many years with photographs of the avant-garde hero's elfin and gleeful face I would have been certain that here, without benefit of ceremony, the lecture had already begun. But as it turned out, after the doors opened and we all noisily filed in, there was to be a kind of ceremony before Mr. Cage was to join his illustrious predecessors in making the personal statement of musical faith for which the series has become famous.

Among those predecessors have been such major twentieth-century composers as Igor Stravinsky (1939–40), Paul Hindemith (1949–50), Aaron Copland (1951–52), Carlos Chavez (1958–59), Roger Sessions (1968–69), and Leonard Bernstein (1972–73). It must be said, too, that outside music the list of Norton lecturers has been equally distinguished, including T. S. Eliot (1932–33), Robert Frost (1936–37), Erwin Panofsky (1947–48), E. E. Cummings (1952–53), Jorge Luis Borges (1967–68), and Lionel Trilling (1969–70).[1]

Indeed, it was in the introduction to Mr. Cage—about which more in a moment—that an innocent onlooker would have found his only

---

[1] In the terms of Charles Chauncey Stillman's 1925 gift establishing the lectures, music constituted one of the disciplines to be discussed. Stillman also stipulated that the Norton lectures be published by the Harvard University Press. Accordingly, Stravinsky's lectures are to be found in *Poetics of Music* (1947), Hindemith's in *A Composer's World* (1952), Copland's in *Music and Imagination* (1952), Chavez's in *Musical Thoughts* (1960), Sessions's in *Questions about Music* (1970), and Bernstein's in *The Unanswered Question* (1976).

intimation of the great academic world which only yesterday had provided the soil not just for the Norton lectures but for the man in whose honor they were named. Charles Eliot Norton (1827–1908), Dante scholar, bibliographer of Michelangelo, biographer of Kipling, and editor of the poems of Donne and the letters of Carlyle, was the first Professor of Fine Arts at Harvard (1873–98). He was also the close personal and intellectual friend of Emerson, Whittier, and Lowell on this side of the Atlantic, and of Carlyle and (especially) Ruskin in England. In *Praeterita* (1885–89), Ruskin called Norton, his junior by eight years, "my first real tutor"; the Ruskin–Norton correspondence, recently republished (1987) in an expanded form by Cambridge University Press, sheds much light on the human ties underlying the high-Victorian transatlantic republic of letters that dominated Anglo–American cultural life until World War I.

Although Norton's life was spent with literature and the visual arts, he was a music lover, and there was much music activity at Harvard in his time, as there has been ever since. Even a cursory glance at the past hundred years makes clear just how much musical composition and thought has taken place in and around Cambridge. The very Sanders Theatre where John Cage was to speak saw in 1871 the first performance of Harvard professor John Knowles Paine's noble incidental music for a production (in the original Greek) of *Oedipus tyrannus*; along with his *Mass* (1865), Paine's Prelude to the Sophocles play is widely recognized today as the earliest American music to have achieved a solid place in the classical repertory.[2] Before and after World War I, the Harvard faculty was the home of the gifted but now forgotten American composer Edward Burlingame Hill.[3] In the 1920s, Harvard students included Walter Piston, Virgil Thomson, and Elliott Carter, and in the 1930s Leonard Bernstein, Harold Shapero, and the sadly short-lived Irving Fine. The greatly gifted and

[2] Fortunately—and given our attitude toward our musical past, surprisingly—this music can be heard on records. The Overture to *Oedipus tyrannus* is available on Angel DS-49263 in an inadequate performance conducted by Kenneth Klein and played by the London Symphony Orchestra. The *Mass* is available on New World 262/3 in an excellent performance by Gunther Schuller and the St. Louis Symphony.

[3] Hill's attractive Sextet for Wind Instruments and Piano, a typically French-influenced work, was available for many years in Columbia's Modern American Music Series on CBS AML 4846.

now vastly underrated Piston taught at Harvard from 1926 to 1960, and served for a time as chairman of the music department.[4]

And so what was now required for Mr. Cage to make his debut as a member of the Harvard faculty was a proper academic introduction. This honor fell to Reinhold Brinkmann, director of graduate studies and professor of music at Harvard. Dressed in an old-fashioned but reassuring jacket and tie and speaking with a scholarly German accent, Professor Brinkmann addressed the audience in a way both jolly and unctuous. He began by describing Mr. Cage's extraordinary contributions to what he so fashionably called "world music"; this phrase, which is to be distinguished from "world musics," an upscale euphemism for what was formerly seen as folk and ethnic art, is used today to identify sounds based on widely disparate rhythmic, harmonic, and procedural elements of, among others, Indian, Tibetan, Japanese, and African music. The result is a "cutting-edge" effort beyond the supposedly narrow prejudices of nations and civilized traditions. After many further jovial compliments and tributes, Mr. Brinkmann ended by telling how he had only discovered that day that the phenomenon of John Cage had been anticipated many years ago. According to Professor Brinkmann, he had just come from playing for his class (on the piano) the ending of Gustav Mahler's *Das Lied von der Erde*, where he found that the closing *pianississimo* chord contained just the notes C, G, E, and A, which, when properly arranged, spelled CAGE!

The rostrum—actually a shabby folding table—was now Mr. Cage's. His first words, delivered in his usual soothing monotone, set the stage for the remaining ninety minutes, as he described the unfolding of his compositional career over these many years. At first, what he had to say had the great advantage, increasingly lost as time

---

[4] Harold Shapero, once hailed as the coming American Beethoven, is just now beginning to reemerge as a composer to be taken seriously. One hopes a by-product of his new reputation will be fresh recordings of some of his major works. A recording of several of Irving Fine's typically lyrical compositions, including the *Notturno* for strings and harp and the String Quartet, has just been issued on Elektra/ Nonesuch 9 79175-1; a beautiful recording of the lovely *Serious Song*, performed by Gerard Schwarz and the Los Angeles Chamber Orchestra, is available on Elektra/ Nonesuch D 79002. Among the currently available Walter Piston records is a complete set of his five marvelous string quartets, well played by the Portland String Quartet on Northeast 216, 214, and 208.

went on, of perfect clarity, save for his tendency to garble an occasional word:

It was here at Harvard, not quite forty years ago, that I went into an anechoic chamber, not expecting in that silent [word indistinct] to hear two sounds, one high, my nervous system in operation, one low, my blood in circulation. The reason I did not expect to hear these two sounds was that they were set into vibration without any intention on my part. That experience gave my life direction, the exploration of economic tension. No one else is true to that. I will do it for us. I did not know immediately what I was doing, nor after all these years have I found much [word indistinct]. I compose music, yes, but how? I gave up making choices; in their place I put the asking of questions. The answers come from the mechanism of the *I Ching*, the most ancient of all books. Tossing three coins six times, yielding numbers from 21 to 64. Something like that occurs for each person as he is conceived.

Now, for what seemed like an eternity but turned out to be less than one-third of his whole presentation, Mr. Cage described in detail how he assembled the text of his Norton lectures, all of them, he was quite frank, made up of the same material. He started, he said, by taking 487 disparate quotations, selected via chance operations from such sources as Ludwig Wittgenstein ("I have long been attracted to his work," Cage said, "reading it with enjoyment, but very little understanding"), Buckminster Fuller, Marshall McLuhan, Thoreau, and Emerson; he couldn't stomach Emerson, he told us, so he ended up with only five usable excerpts from the sage of Concord. To these passages were added excerpts, mostly on international events, from the *New York Times*, the *Wall Street Journal*, and the *Christian Science Monitor*.

All this material, Mr. Cage told us, was subjected to an immense amount of computer-aided manipulation that was partially directed, partially determined by chance. (He was, I might add, gracious in giving credit to his programmers and helpers.) The final selection of the bits that made up his lecture he determined according to what pleased him. The result, he proposed, bore some similarity to astronomer Fred Hoyle's steady-state cosmology, with its suggestion of ever-changing unchangeability. Although scientifically Hoyle seems to be

out of fashion these days, Cage's metaphorical use of his theory—
which, one must assume, started out as a serious scientific
investigation—had the effect of placing Hoyle alongside Fuller and
McLuhan as a prime avatar of the contemporary irrationalist sensibility.

But all good things—by good I mean, in this case, the relative
clarity of Cage's introduction—must come to an end. By now, almost
forty-five minutes in, it was time for the lecture proper to begin.[5] It
was, I must say, a salad composed of sentences that parsed but did not
mean anything, and of recognizable phrases—most recognizable
when they bore some sign of their origins in newspaper stories—
abutted to other equally recognizable but totally unrelated phrases.
Mr. Cage has often told us of his reverence for *Finnegans Wake*. It will
be recalled that Joyce's meaning, embedded in an apparent stream of
consciousness, was multi-layered, perhaps beyond the comprehension
of ordinary mortals. But whatever the merits of that idiosyncratic
excursion beyond rational storytelling and argument, the wit so
omnipresent in Joyce finds no parallel whatsoever in Mr. Cage's
contrived happenstances.

Mr. Cage's delivery was a fitting accompaniment to his content.
Although Mr. Cage has an avid interest in mushrooms—he is a
learned, and evidently brave, mycologist—his presentation was closer
to that of a beekeeper. His voice droned on and on. He tended to start
each sentence or fragment strongly, and then fade away at the end.
Many words he dropped almost completely, whether from design or
a desire to appear "poetic," or perhaps simply from fatigue, I don't
know. But always he plowed doggedly ahead, letting the listener find
his own meanings, if at all, by default.

As time passed, many members of the audience began to doze, and
others started to leave. At first, the exodus was limited to the upstairs
gallery, where the early trickle of emigrants threatened to turn at
times into a steady stream. Then the itch to breathe fresh air affected

---

[5] I was reminded, in the context of Mr. Cage's preliminary lecture to his lecture, of
my friend Lionel Abel's witty story about an evening in a Parisian cultural salon in
the early 1920s, where the offering was to be a performance of a late—and very
difficult—twelve-tone work by Arnold Schoenberg and a lecture by the then chic
theorist and conductor René Leibowitz explaining what had just been played. When
the Schoenberg piece was over, Lionel went up to Leibowitz and asked, "Now that
we've heard the lecture, where's the music?"

the downstairs crowd, who as the first to arrive could be presumed to have been the most eager to come. In my own row—the third, almost in the center—the three people who were next to me got up together and walked out. The young man who'd been sitting between them and me immediately stretched out, his tape recorder still running, lay across the seats they had just vacated, and fell asleep.

I stayed awake—covering John Cage for the *New Criterion* is, after all, a responsible task—and was thus privileged to hear, just as the afternoon came to an end, the glimmerings of some sense in the midst of this randomness. For seasoned Cage watchers, I quote these rare, and rarely gratifying, snippets:

Test fire could become a theater for the deployment of AIDS.

A theater for the deployment of gas.

Israel could become a theater for the deployment of gas.

Washington will pay to buy a 20 percent stake in the Palestinian uprising.

Feelings Washington will pay to buy.

All honor, I suppose, to the *I Ching* for its arrival, through chance operations, at a fashionable *Weltanschauung*, though it is curious that its political position seems to have been formed in the world of American avant-garde social radicalism rather than in the more passive climes of Chinese philosophy. Or perhaps Mr. Cage has been so indefatigable in setting his computers to work churning out material that, like the monkeys at typewriters who eventually end up producing exact copies of all the great works of literature, he has indeed proven that even rank nonsense contains within it the simulacrum of sense.

Whether sense or nonsense, Mr. Cage's coda—if I may be allowed the use of a musical term to describe this nonmusical subject—left a distinctly bitter taste in the mouth. Elfin smiles all too easily seem like nasty leers when they accompany provocations, and finally this first Charles Eliot Norton lecture of John Cage, despite all the brightness and charm of its deliverer, formed yet another chapter in the long line of Cage provocations, stretching back even before his notorious *4'33"*, the totally silent piano composition of 1952, at least to his 1939 *Imaginary Landscape No. 1* for two variable-speed phonograph turntables playing frequency recordings along with muted piano and cymbal.

But it would be a mistake to think that Mr. Cage's primary provocation on this October afternoon was musical, or even political. Indeterminacy and incomprehensibility, after all, are old hat in the avant-garde. What passes today for the cutting edge of music—the various elephantine minimalisms of Glass, Reich, and Adams, for example—is thoroughly, perhaps even over-thoroughly, planned and notated; comprehensibility, and what is even more, likeability, is the widely proclaimed goal of every composer with a claim to being chic. Similarly, Mr. Cage's closing foray into *Village Voice* politics only underscored how little real social thought has gone on in the avant-garde in recent decades.

Mr. Cage's provocation was, I think it is fair to say, directed at his host. The host he had in mind was not so much the Harvard of today, swollen as it is by pride and riches and confused as to its educational mission, its mind more on Wall Street and Hollywood than Athens and Rome; the new Harvard, at least in the person of Cage's introducer Professor Brinkmann and those docile folk in the audience who stayed on to the bitter and boring end, has room for everything under the sun, and for nothing. What was under attack was rather the historical Harvard, the great university of Charles Eliot Norton and so many past Norton lecturers, of the noble pieties of Memorial Hall and Sanders Theatre, of such Harvard presidents as Charles W. Eliot and James Bryant Conant, of the numberless scholars and teachers who have labored to bring an ordered and rational civilization to our always new country.

When Mr. Cage finished, and after the applause had died down, I turned to the people behind me and said, "The whole world's gone mad." No one chose to disagree with me, or to censure my impertinence on a sacred occasion. Instead they just looked at me with open-mouthed stares. Along with everyone else, I went out into the cold night. Where is Charles Eliot Norton, now that we need him?

7.

What follows is the unedited text of my formal contribution to a 1987 discussion with New York Times *music critic John Rockwell at New York's 92nd Street YM–YWHA. The subject of the evening was, just as given below in the title of my piece, "The Future of Classical Music." The edited version of Mr. Rockwell's and my presentations, along with the discussion between us that ensued, may be found in the March and April 1988 issues of* Keynote, *a magazine published by WNCN, the New York classical-music radio station. I would like to say that I'm more optimistic today about the future of classical music, but it will come as no surprise to the reader that I'm not.*

The Future of Classical Music

I WILL BEGIN by describing my own assessment of the musical present, to provide a context in which you might evaluate my thoughts about the future. Each of my diagnostic statements, much as I have tried to speak objectively, is contentious, and each—or all— may well be received as outrageous. I do not speak to you tonight to provoke, but to warn: in human affairs, there is always time to alter the future.

But first I want to take a stab at the thankless task of defining classical music. My working definition is a partial application of the concept of classicism to the field of music; by classical music I mean the works that are widely accepted as belonging to a high and cultivated tradition existing over time. Unlike the now closed traditions of classical antiquity, the tradition of classical music has in recent times been added to in important ways at both its earliest and its latest boundaries. It is at least arguable that it has been added to within living memory; certainly none of us wants to give up the hope that such additions are possible.

So far as these recent and even contemporary accretions are concerned, it is my position that music which becomes a part of the tradition of classical music is written in largely traditional forms and with largely traditional means, though both forms and means are in process of continuous reinterpretation. Furthermore, these new (or at least newer) additions to the canon are written with an awareness—whether that awareness is conscious or unconscious does not, I think, matter—of the existence of the tradition, and with an intention of contributing to that tradition as a whole. It goes without saying that it is possible to produce failed classical music, or rather failed attempts at classical music.

You are all aware of the world my definition encompasses. At the opening of the tradition, medieval music; at flowerings in the Renaissance, polyphonic church music and the emergence of rigorous secular composition; in the age of instrumental counterpoint, Bach; in the nineteenth century and slightly thereafter, the triumphal march of Romanticism; today, the hotly disputed cataloguing and performance of the music of the past.

So here we are, with our major orchestras and opera companies, our great music schools, our plethora of recordings, the diffusion of activity into every hamlet across the country: more persons performing, more persons listening to, and, I suspect, more persons writing music—altogether more persons satisfying their tastes and even earning their livings (often splendid livings) by so doing than ever before in the history of our classical-music tradition. How, then, could there be any problems at all here, let alone problems that might cloud the present and fill the future with anxiety?

The problem, of course, is the situation of new music. There are indeed problems other than composition: performance, education, audiences, and patronage. But these problems, however much they may occupy us, should only be secondary and subsidiary, in that they take their meaning from one simple fact: music is about *what* is played, not about *how* it is played. This fact is particularly relevant to our discussion tonight of the future, for everything in classical music is mortal—except the repertory.

Where are we, then, in musical composition? The usual answer is that we are in an age of pluralism. Ugliness is gone, replaced by the desire to please. Anything goes, including all the highly touted trends of the past half-century: serialism, electronic wizardry, conceptual fantasies, back-to-the-folk simplicities, and the flight to theatricality. At the moment, the palm appears to have been awarded to that curious pastiche of all the above that we call minimalism, and which in its latest large-scale manifestation has, by most reports, managed to cut down to size those two fascinating subjects, Nixon and China. I await the Brooklyn Academy performance of John Adams's work this winter; the limited excerpts I have seen on television and the excised passages I have heard on record hardly promise an exciting evening.

But *Nixon in China* is only a glitzy epiphenomenon of our present public and private system of commissioning new works. Underneath the hype, there is a more sobering reality: there is little concern in the classical-music world with new music at all. Classical-music audiences, and the classical-music performers most admired by their peers and by audiences alike, decisively reject not just the newest music, but all the music written since the 1950s, if not before; it is my impression that the most categorical rejection of all—by a cultivated audience—has taken place in the case of works written using electronic media. I will be told there are exceptions, as powerful as Shostakovich's anguished personal statements and the late works of several American symphonists. However viable with the audience these exceptions may be, there certainly are works that fall under the general ban—including some written by composers who may well be here tonight—that I find beautiful and whose neglect I find heartbreaking. But sadly the statement holds: as anyone who makes programs knows all too well, for our audience and for our musicians, new is bad and old is good.

And so our classical-music core audience—made up of those who support the art by returning time and again—rejects beautiful new music along with the trivial and the ugly, and listens solipsistically to that which it already knows. The much larger casual audience so beloved of arts advocates and legislators attends more on the recommendation of Johnny Carson than of the music being played. Young musicians—as the recent book by Judith Kogan on Juilliard makes plain—study only the old, and are largely taught by the old.[1] In this regard, I must quote from Bernard Holland's review in the *Times* of the Pavarotti master class at our best music school:

[1] *Nothing But the Best: The Struggle for Perfection at the Juilliard School*, by Judith Kogan; Random House, 1987.

MUSIC IN AMERICA TODAY

Famous music teachers, of course, have their uses. There are the professional's tricks of the trade to be passed on, and, more importantly, contacts with managers and concert presenters.

As for patronage today, the best that can be said of our New Age philanthropists is that they give even when they don't like music— and perhaps give most when they don't have to pay any personal attention to music at all.

What, then, of the future? I find myself in a curious position. Perhaps here, as so often in the discussion of modern cultural life, Matthew Arnold described it best: I have in mind his haunting lines in *Stanzas from the Grande Chartreuse*: "Wandering between two worlds, one dead, / the other powerless to be born." I have been trained in the classical music I have earlier tonight tried to define; I have attempted in my own professional life to connect a living musical past with a living present. Though I plan to continue this effort as before, I cannot say that I now find the possibility of success high. All in all, the future I see before us is not a future I happily await.

I see a continuing increase, driven by economic considerations, bureaucratic pressures, and the demands of the media, in the scale on which classical music is done; Ernest Fleischmann's by now well-known speech advocating the creation of giant monopoly orchestras is only one sign that the quickest minds in music administration are now devoting themselves—I almost said in earnest—to the crisis.[2]

I see the only challenge to the primacy of superstar performers coming not from new music and its proponents, but from the advocates of so-called authentic performances of established and rediscovered old music. I doubt whether either musical salvation or commercial success will come, for example, from Roger Norrington's "lite" Beethoven symphonies, from the Salomon Quartet's strident and wheezy Haydn, or from Malcolm Bilson's clumsy fortepiano playing. What must be said, however, is that these new ways of performance, in their laconic and graceless way, are in some small way shaping the future: they have a deconstructive and diminishing effect on our perceptions of what was once taken seriously.

I see music schools increasingly failing to train students to participate

[2] For a detailed discussion of Mr. Fleischmann's proposals, see Chapter 24 in this book.

in the grand tradition, as might have been true in earlier times, or even to train them for stardom, as has been true most recently; I see instead a concentration on careers in the commercial music business, with a special emphasis on the words *commercial* and *business*. In a not unrelated area, I see an imminent collapse, fostered by the glamour of television and the desires of every supposed art form to have a piece of the action, in the present efforts to raise the level of disciplined general music education in our elementary and secondary schools.

I see an audience for music ever larger in numbers but knowing ever less about what it is hearing. I see an increasing attempt to tailor the programs of presenting institutions to the demands of mass marketing. I see brilliant young performing talents beaten down by the pressure to make themselves into imitators of past successes. In this connection, I must remark on the virtual ignoring by the musical press of Vladimir Feltsman's revelatory playing of several parts of Messiaen's *Vingt regards sur l'enfant Jésus* (1944) at his Carnegie Hall concert two weeks ago, in favor of vastly less interesting performance of overly well-known works of Schubert and Schumann; there can be little doubt that artists and their advisors will draw the necessary repertory implications for fame and prosperity from this customary bit of philistinism.

I see composers in the classical music tradition as increasingly unable to write music in a consistent style; consistency of style now promises to be the property of the minimalists—the line stretching from Young through Riley, Glass, and Reich, to Adams—at whose hands this quality has come to mean repetition. I see everywhere a growing inability to write pieces that seem able to get going at the start and close decisively at the end. I see—and this seems to me perhaps the most disturbing—an inability on the part of the most talented young composers to realize their talents as they grow older, to write music on the basis of their own inner voices, rather than according to the artificial considerations of peer-group, critical, and funding pressures.

How does all this come together in the future of classical music? I do not envision the repertory of choice—the music which broad audiences demand and the music in which great performing careers are made—including any music written in the second half of our century; still less do I see it as including music written with electronic means. I think there is reasonably widespread agreement on this dismal prospect insofar as it affects the kind of classical music I have attempted to speak about tonight. I am well aware that there is an enormous world of what might be called nonclassical music out there. This world includes the more ambitious rock- and jazz-influenced genres, as well as the performance art of Laurie Anderson and David Byrne, among others. It also includes a mini-world of "easy listening" music, exemplified (at least in my mind) by George Winston and Andreas Vollenweider. I cannot pretend to speak with authority about any of these figures; for my purposes tonight it is enough to say that I see no sign that any of this work has had, or will have, any influence on the canon of classical music.

From all the evidence I can find, I expect that classical music will proceed on two tracks. The first is that of grandiose entertainment, in which greatly gifted performers will be forced to package themselves for audiences which, if the truth were known, would rather be elsewhere. New music will continue to be performed (and discarded), as it is now, for reasons of self-esteem and the availability of funding. The cumulative effect of this juxtaposition of the adored old and the subsidized new will be to bolt the door of the acknowledged repertory ever tighter. With the canon thus permanently closed, the most to be hoped for is that the greatest Western classical music, because of its intrinsic power, will live as a public, monumental art admired, studied, and even experienced as something wonderful—and dead. In this way, at least the interests of civilization—no small boon—will be served.

There is, however, a second track on which classical music will live in the future, as it lives today. This track is private, rather than public. Here I am speaking about those who are not really interested in large-scale public performance, but are rather devoted to making music by and for themselves. By studying instruments, singing in choruses, playing chamber music, listening to each other, and writing music for reasons more personal than the availability of commissions, these people—they can only be called music lovers—will, I am sure, keep alive the possibility of a small flame of creativity. Through their activities, the living spirit of what we now know as classical music will continue, and with it the possibility of a new music naturally continuing the work of what may not seem a completed past. I have no more cheery tidings to offer.

II

THE PROBLEM OF NEW OPERA

8.

We are told that these are banner years for opera. As I write these words, I have before me a current press release from the Central Opera Service, the research and information department of the Metropolitan Opera, summarizing their 1988–89 statistical survey of opera in the United States. The release speaks of a 17.5 percent increase in performances and a 20.9 percent increase in attendance. One paragraph, excitedly quoting Maria F. Rich, the executive director of the service, summarizes it all:

> *Never before have we witnessed such a burgeoning of the art form within one season. . . . Reporting on the previous year, we spoke of "continuing the constant gains opera made over the last 30 years." But 1988–89 broke out of the "continuing growth pattern" by doubling any earlier one-year increases in performers and audiences. This documents beyond any doubt the success and popularity of opera and music-theater in the United States.*

Only a sourpuss would want to cavil at such a show of prosperity, but then it also seems to require a sourpuss to notice that new operas—even much-vaunted works like Glass's Einstein on the Beach, *Adams's* Nixon in China, *and Argento's* Casanova—*do not make it into the repertory of great opera houses and into the hearts of opera lovers. The conclusion now, as when I wrote this essay for the March 1984* New Criterion, *seems inescapable: the confusion of important with trivial work continues, and the permanent success of new operas remains a matter of an optimism self-induced, and ultimately unsustainable.*

Opera 1984: Dead or Alive?

THE SITUATION of opera at this time is interesting for more than the light it throws on the usual concerns of composers, performers, and audience. Precisely because opera unites music and words, because for its conception and staging it draws upon so many different arts and crafts, because it possesses such a rich repertory of acknowledged masterpieces, and (last but hardly least) because it is so expensive to put on, what is now happening in opera—and what has been happening for the past generation—is a reflection of the place of art in our culture as a whole.

The chief presenting symptom of opera today is easy to see: at a time of larger audiences, more performances, and escalating budgets, there aren't any widely successful new works. This fact is no less apparent to opera administrators than it is to audiences. As a result the repertory has become increasingly constricted, marked everywhere by a reliance on staple crowd-pleasers and—in the most daring opera houses—on an occasional novelty put on a few times and then almost always thrown away.

Just how widespread this backward-facing phenomenon is has been made abundantly clear in *Profile: 1983*, a smartly produced booklet put out by Opera America, a national support and advocacy organization whose roster includes fifty-eight "member companies" and twenty-nine smaller "correspondent companies." There are two important sets of statistics in *Profile: 1983*. The first documents the repertory of the 1981–82 season, the second that of the 1983–84 season.

During 1981–82, Opera America companies presented 146 different fully-staged works performed with orchestra. Of these, seventy-four were written before 1900, and seventy-two were from the present century. But more important than a chronological list of individual works is the nature of the works themselves and the frequency with which they were produced. And here there is no comfort for the friends of a living operatic culture. Of the twelve most frequently produced works in 1981–82—with *Die Fledermaus* at the top of the list and *Tales of Hoffmann* at the bottom—only *Madame Butterfly* (1904) comes from the twentieth century. A quick calculation suggests that the mean year of composition of these twelve operas was 1849.

Matters are no better if we consider the frequency of *performances* rather than *productions*. The most frequently performed work in 1981–82 was *Rigoletto* (1851). Of the forty-seven works receiving at least ten performances, thirteen were indeed written in the twentieth century. Unfortunately, *six* of them are by Puccini: *Madame Butterfly*, *Tosca* (1900), *Turandot* (completed in 1926, after Puccini's death), and the three short operas of *Il Trittico* (1918), *Il Tabarro, Gianni Schicchi,* and *Suor Angelica*. The "contemporaneity" of the list of thirteen is further undermined by the inclusion on it of *The Merry Widow* (1905) and *The Song of Norway* (1944), a badly dated pastiche of Grieg's now almost century-old hits. Of the thirteen, only two—Stravinsky's *The Rake's Progress* (1951) and Blitzstein's *Regina* (1949)—were written after World War II. The mean year of composition of these successful twentieth-century works is 1923.

Six operatic world premieres took place in the 1981–82 season under the sponsorship of Opera America companies. All these works were written by Americans: they include Robert Ward's *Abelard and Heloise* and *Minutes Till Midnight,* Edward Barnes's *Feathertop* and Henry Mollicone's *The Mask of Evil* (both in one act), George Rochberg's *The Confidence Man*, and Stephen Paulus's *The Postman Always Rings Twice*. Of these six, only the Paulus work has so far received more than local exposure, a circumstance owing to its having been performed at the 1983 Edinburgh Festival by the Opera Theatre of St. Louis, the company which commissioned it. The rest seem already to have moved into their composers' musical bibliographies, to emerge only when new reference works are being written.

Among the membership of Opera America, there were no companies producing 1981–82 premieres of new works by non-Americans. Instead, six older works—by Haydn (1782), Rossini (1819), Verdi (1848), Prokofiev (1911–13), Tigranian (1912), and Zandonai (1912)—received first performances here. The mean year of composition of these works is 1864.

Profile: 1983 does not give any information on 1982–83 repertory. It does, however, give listings of the 1983–84 production schedule of each of its members. If the news coming out of the 1981–82 season was bad for the cause of contemporary opera, that coming from the present season can only be called dismal. The lists supplied by United States constituent companies of Opera America (there are several Canadian companies in the organization, as well as a South American company) show that out of 263 presentations, 222 are of works written before (and the vast majority well before) 1930. Only fifteen are works written by non-Americans after 1930; of these, five presentations are of mainstream works by Benjamin Britten. There are twenty-six works by Americans listed in the current season's repertory. Sadly enough, eleven are Broadway musicals and seven are the most popular works of Menotti.

There are no premieres of any significance.

Nowhere is the constriction of repertory more marked than with our very largest opera companies. There are in this country four of these behemoth enterprises: the Metropolitan Opera, the New York City Opera, the Chicago Lyric Opera, and the San Francisco Opera. The Metropolitan, not having performed an American opera since the 1960s, continued to uphold its tradition this year; the entire contribution of this great house to the performance of true twentieth-century repertory consists of Britten's *Peter Grimes* and *Billy Budd*, Poulenc's *Dialogues of the Carmelites*, Weill's *Mahagonny*, and Stravinsky's *Le Rossignol* and *Oedipus Rex*, the last not even an opera but rather a semi-staged oratorio. The New York City Opera, long the hope of a native American opera, is doing (out of nineteen productions) two American works: Bernstein's *Candide* and Floyd's *Of Mice and Men*; of non-American works written after 1930, the City Opera is doing none. The Chicago Lyric Opera is presenting only Shostakovich's *Lady Macbeth*. San Francisco, like Chicago risking no American works, is doing (out of fourteen productions) just one contemporary work: Tippett's *The Midsummer Marriage*.

Clearly, something is wrong in the world of opera. At a time when there is new literature, new poetry, new visual art, new dance, and even (mostly wanly received, it is true) new music, there just isn't much new opera to be seen. Sandwiched in among *Profile: 1983*'s obligatory upbeat descriptions of its own history, organization, staff, programs, and publications is a description of the problem and a suggestion concerning its true cause:

> There is a move toward greater conservatism in programming: so far, only two companies have announced plans for world premieres or American premieres of new works for the 1983–84 season. This compares to 12 premiere productions in both 1981–82 and 1982–83. Companies want to do more American works, but reduced support from government sources has forced them to look more toward earned income to balance their budgets. This means that repertory selection becomes more a matter of choosing works that will guarantee success at the box office—the more familiar, traditional repertoire.

On its face, blaming the problems of the operatic repertory on a shortfall of public funding would seem difficult to sustain. By the evidence contained in *Profile: 1983* itself, recent decreases in public support have been minor and have been largely compensated for by increases in earned and unearned private income. But to say this is hardly to deny the sizeable role public funding does play in artistic life. For enthusiastic testimonials to the magnitude of this influence one need do no more than consult its proponents. One of the most respected of these is Schuyler Chapin, dean of the School of the Arts at Columbia University and chairman of the American Symphony Orchestra League, Opera America's counterpart in the orchestra field. Testifying before the Senate Subcommittee on Education, the Arts, and Humanities on November 17, 1983, Chapin was unstinting in his praise:

> The Endowment has given what I would almost term a new lease on life to the vitality of the arts in this country. There is no question that, on balance, the artistic life of this country has never been stronger, and in my view, the reason for that strength is largely due to the impetus given to the arts by the involvements of the Endowment. . . .
>
> The fact that we have taken a positive position, that the Endowments are in place and working, is probably the single most important thing that has happened to the artistic community in our lifetime.

Concern for opera has been manifest at the National Endowment for the Arts since its inception in 1965. Though funding at first was small—$50,000 in 1966—yearly increases enabled the federal opera budget to reach a million and a half dollars in 1972, to top three million in 1974 (though it dropped to two million the next year), and to go well over six million in 1981. Reagan administration cuts, only partially allowed by Congress, resulted in a reduction of approximately 10 percent for both 1982 and 1983. The 1983 expenditure by the NEA for opera was $5,052,000.

Though I have used the word *opera* to describe the purpose of this federal funding, the program under which opera is now funded is not in fact called "Opera"; it is called "Opera–Musical Theater." Indeed, the process by which the "Opera" of 1966 has become the "Opera–Musical Theater" of 1984 reveals a good deal about official attitudes toward opera and helps explain how opera has reached its present state.

At the beginning the problems seemed relatively simple and the solutions fairly obvious. The first federal initiatives were not unreasonably directed toward the development of regional companies and the expansion of touring. In 1969 the NEA assisted private sources in the establishment of the National Opera Institute, an organization devoted to encouraging apprentice singers, commissioning new works, assisting in the production of new and rarely staged works, and expanding the opera audience.

But it was not enough just to *support* opera. In the words of Janet Brenner's recent official history of the program, "a general concern still remained for the status of opera in the larger American culture, a concern that included raising the awareness of the average American." Toward this end, in 1970, the NEA funded the creation of Opera America to act as "a single, unified voice for the professional opera companies of the United States."

At this point, two considerations—one new, one old—began to alter the way in which the public funding of opera was to be approached. First, operatic activity in the country as a whole increased dramatically and with it the public's attention. The fresh perception of opera's importance seemed to require giving opera an autonomous status in the Endowment's structure, so that it could receive treatment equal to that of music, dance, theater, and the visual arts. Second, there remained the old and lurking problem of the right of musical theater—which had at least historically found its home on Broadway— to government encouragement and financial support. A conflict-ridden discussion of the very nature of opera ensued.

To appreciate the importance of this discussion, it is necessary first to understand how opera has traditionally been understood. In the most simple view, opera is words set to music and staged. Unfortunately, such a definition is broad enough to include as well Broadway musicals and the rock video clips now so common on television. But reality counts in the process of definition too. To the art public, opera is the kind of composition that has traditionally been done in the great opera houses of the world. Indeed, despite our own tendency in America to see opera as composed of both "grand opera" and "light opera," for the cultivated American audience, just as for its counterpart in Europe, opera means the great body of work from Gluck to Puccini and Strauss. It can also include, for a relatively small part of the sophisticated public, works as recent as those of Berg and Schoenberg, Hindemith and Stravinsky, and Shostakovich and Britten. But whatever the exact limits of what is allowed, opera remains an elite art form, European and in some sense romantic in origin, belonging in large measure to the domain of high culture, and recalling the past rather than mirroring contemporary daily life.

There is, of course, a common element of greatness contained in this working definition of opera. The audience is quite aware that the works they love are often marked by absurd plots, pasteboard characters, graceless librettos, and creaky dramatic action. What is common to great opera is great music—distinguished, memorable, and widely seen as belonging to the European classical tradition. Whether the operas in question are by Mozart, Verdi, Wagner, or Strauss, they need not be seen to be experienced; they need only be heard. Neither of the two most important vehicles by which the gospel of opera has been propagated in this country—phonograph records and the weekly Metropolitan Opera radio broadcasts—involves visual elements.

All of this, of course, had been known long before opera's new prominence in official American cultural life. But a large-scale program of support for opera could hardly be content with the premise that opera was based upon a European classical music that didn't seem to be written anymore—even in Europe. So if opera was to receive the injection of public funds worthy of the social distinction and the public-relations talents of its boosters, some way had to be found to domesticate opera, to make it seem not just an adornment to American life but a reflection of the American ethos. At the same time, moreover, a way had to be found to recognize, through support, the Broadway musical theatre, America's only claim to an indigenous opera-like art.

The push for opera's autonomy, resisted by the leadership of the NEA Music Program, came from the representatives of the operatic field. Just how these advocates of opera saw the problem is clear from an official 1976 recommendation of the opera section of the NEA Music Advisory Panel, as quoted in the Brenner history:

Opera, like ballet, is a hybrid form. It is at least as much "theater" as it is "music." As such, it should not be treated as a "pure music" form within other "pure music" forms.

The opera industry is a fast-developing and diverse one, and administering to its special needs would be better accomplished by a separate program structure. The art form has recently begun to attract larger audiences and experience considerable growth via the influx of talented management into the field and via the evolving of a more valid, healthy artistic policy characterized by the use of American artists in highly theatrical productions, the performance of more American works including the best of American musical theater, and the touring of productions to areas having no professional company.

Separate program status, with the accompanying staff attention, could encourage this development at a key point in the industry's—and art form's—development.

It is envisioned that this program would (could) eventually provide support for high-quality projects in the area of American musical theater, which is fast earning its deserved "art form" status.

By 1978, the internal redefinition of opera to deemphasize musical elements seemed complete. In January of that year, Ann Farris Darling, the executive director of Opera America (and now the director of the Opera–Music Theater Program at the NEA) prepared a "Summary–Rationale" to answer doubts about the proposed marriage of opera and musical theater. In answer to the question "What is Opera?" she managed to avoid even a single use of the word *music*:

Opera is:
1) a performing art discipline utilizing literature with voice, orchestra, drama, dance, visual arts, etc.;
2) an expression and artistic exploration of human life, action, values, emotion and thought;
3) an art form that is being complemented by American composers, artists, and producers to embrace the American scene, both in its historical and its contemporary aspects.

Why were spokesmen for opera as traditionally understood so ready to go along with an expansion of their mission that harbored so much potential for artistic dilution and jurisdictional strife? Janet Brenner's account of a 1977 Opera America board meeting offers some clues. Among other things, it shows the curious mixture of opportunism and self-delusion with which artists and administrators go about cutting off the limb on which they sit:

> During the open session of this Opera America meeting, the autonomy issue for Opera/Music Theater was addressed. Although none of the musical theater representatives invited were able to attend, Opera panelists, Music panelists, Endowment Budget Director, and many Opera America members and outside advisors participated.
>
> Several crucial issues and questions were raised during this meeting. An example—whether the inclusion of musical theater in the proposed program might possibly give opera a greater funding leverage. Additionally, it was noted that several opera companies were attempting to help "Americanize" opera by producing musicals, but the exorbitant costs of mounting new, experimental, and/or innovative productions and attracting audiences for these works was an apparent concern.
>
> Alternatives were discussed, but the general consensus from this meeting revealed a strong support from the opera field to form a separate Opera program outside of the Music Program in order to secure appropriate staff, attention and money. It appeared that actual support to musicals was not a priority to these opera representatives. Nevertheless, there was some interest in musical theater as suggestions were raised to broaden the title of the proposed new Program to "Music Theater," but only funding opera until the Program allocation level increased.

As the forces of opera were attempting to get money in other people's names and use it for their own purposes, the proponents of musical theater were staking their claims for funding. A major role in this effort was played by at least two members of the National Council on the Arts, the advisory board of the NEA: Jean Dalrymple, an artists' representative, publicist, and theatrical producer who had at one time been director of the New York City Center Drama and Light Opera companies; and Harold Prince, the noted Broadway director. In a 1977 letter to an NEA Music Program official, Prince wrote, as quoted by Janet Brenner:

> The musical . . . is being priced out on a Broadway level. . . . And for the first time in my experience . . . I see talented composers forced to move to California to write underscoring for movies.

Brenner explains further:

> Moreover, Broadway had met with the imminent decline of the "road" (touring). This, plus the unwillingness of many non-profit institutions to incorporate musicals into their repertory, made even more difficult musical theater's case: to prove that it was, indeed, an integral component of America's culture and therefore was deserving of Endowment assistance.

In April of 1978 a joint meeting of opera and musical-theater professionals was convened at the request of Harold Prince. The assembled experts included only one "classical" composer—Carlisle Floyd, the composer of *Susannah* and *Of Mice and Men*, works which attempted to bridge the gap between the opera and the musical. Not surprisingly, the meeting came out in favor of the proposed marriage between the two musical forms. According to Brenner:

> During the first part of the meeting, the aesthetic and pragmatic compatibilities of opera and musical theater were explored. The consensus of the participants was that the quality of the work is the critical element and there did exist a definite continuum in performers, training, skills and repertoire between opera and musical theater. . . .
>
> Overall, the participants felt that for too long opera and musical theater had been relegated to separate worlds. These disciplines, they felt, could help each other and, therefore, their distinctions should not be perpetuated—instead, a philosophical and administrative consolidation should ensue.
>
> Suggestions as to the name of the new Program included "Lyric Theater," "Opera/Music Theater" and "Music Theater." The majority of the participants endorsed "Music Theater" for the appropriate title as they felt it most clearly described the makeup of the proposed Program. However, the opera

representatives did not want to eliminate the name "opera" from the title. They explained that for years, the American opera companies worked hard to try and diminish the stigma associated with opera [and] thus "legitimize" it as a true American art form. Excluding "opera" on a national level would undermine what they had finally begun to achieve. The participants acquiesced in the title "Opera/Musical Theater" and concluded that the name was not the crucial issue as long as the public was aware of the Program and who it funds. The goal—a unified Program, of opera and musical theater, which would hopefully encourage some new perspectives and directions for the art form.

By May of 1978 the combined program was born.[1] The first guidelines represented a triumph for all except the silent adherents of a traditional idea of opera:

> The National Endowment for the Arts, through its Opera–Musical Theater Program, is committed to broadening the concept of musical theater in the nation and, in the process, to making all manifestations of this unique art form, created and produced at the highest artistic level, available and accessible to a wide and ever-expanding audience.
>
> Whether comic or serious, earthy or elevated, music theater, from the time it moved from the courts to the public arena almost two and a half centuries ago, has been part of a continuing tradition of people's art at its best, and has flourished most when it has been an integral part of the fabric of public life. The Opera–Musical Theater Program hopes to help eliminate, or at least reduce, the artificial barriers which have grown up in our society to separate the various forms of music theater, and to help create an atmosphere of mutual respect and appreciation which extends to artist and public alike.

It hardly seems possible to quarrel with the somewhat vapid goal of

[1] Even the discussion over the new program's name represented the new and altered definition of opera. As reported by Brenner, "this new Program recommended that what had been a 'slash' in the program's name (Opera/Musical Theater), now be changed to a 'dash' (Opera–Musical Theater), as they agreed this more closely reflected the content and concern of the New Program without a loss to opera's name and identity."

respect and appreciation for the artist and public, but one can only wonder about an artistic and intellectual sensibility that calls the choice between *Fidelio* and *Oklahoma!* a result of "artificial barriers." Here, in the work of our artistic leaders in Washington, was a perfect example of the 1970s mélange of cultural blend and level.

The specific policies that the NEA has promulgated since then have gone far to put music in its place. Although it is true that the large and famous companies continue to receive large subsidies for their traditional activities, the truly innovative effort of the NEA has been put into the creation, development, and production of new works. *Creation*, in this context, does not mean giving composers money to write operas. Rather, it means assisting "institutions to commission creative artists such as composers, librettists and lyricists." *Development* means funding "laboratory or workshop productions of the new work." And *production* means helping "institutions with pre-opening costs such as for copying and for orchestrations." In the world of musicals, because that world has not yet been institutionalized, money has gone to "attract," in Brenner's words, "the individual producers who, in actuality, were the leading forces behind developing new musicals."

When, as a member, I first attended a meeting of the National Council on the Arts in February of last year, the first item of discussion in the opening public session was the guidelines for Opera–Musical Theater during the 1984 fiscal year. Much of the language for the guidelines had been borrowed from the previous version. But several new sentences had been added at the opening:

> In the United States, at the end of the twentieth century, we are witnessing a proliferation of many forms of music theater, both traditional and avant garde. The older forms of opera and operetta have been enriched by the work of composers, performers, and directors who are constantly expanding the boundaries of the art form with their own fresh vision and the new technology. Moreover, music theater in this country is shaped by a heritage which is unique and specifically American: the Broadway musical.

This upbeat language was consistent with various passages in the 1983 Opera–Musical Theater program review. The NEA "overview panel" posited thirty-five ideal outcomes for the discipline by 1990. They included such happy ideas as letting "opera take its place as the cutting edge of all art forms," encouraging a "new environment within music theater for the creative process and its audiences," allowing a "broader definition of opera and music theater," and seeking the "involvement of other creative artists not currently challenged by music theater to work within the art form."

It came as something of a shock, then, to read that the first point in the overview panel's subsequent list of current conditions in the field was contradictory, not only to the optimism being merchandised elsewhere but even within itself. The condition was stated as a "lack of high-quality New American Works submitted to the Opera–Musical Theater Program, and the need for exposure and acceptance of contemporary works being written." Indeed, the pessimism of the opening half of this statement was amply confirmed by the two examples of current work shown, via video clips, to the Council. The first was a short section of a musical dealing with the moonings of a lovesick teenaged girl. This musical was being "workshopped" in a nonprofit environment in Cambridge, Massachusetts. The musical and dramatic puerility of this seemingly amateur confection was painful to behold. Nor were matters much better with the clip of the Houston Opera's premiere production of Carlisle Floyd's *Willie Stark*. This work, centering on a powerful incident in American history— the assassination of Huey Long—fails for basically one reason: its musically uncompelling and emptily conventional score. From the discussion that followed it was clear that the other examples of the new creation in music theater weren't much better. It all reminded me of the disaster suffered by the New York City Opera in 1980 when it made its last attempt (so far) to put on new American opera. This triple bill of derivative one-acters, weak on music but heavy on conceits, pleased neither operagoers nor musicians. Indeed, it seemed at times as if the works had been chosen for the purpose of giving the cause of native opera a black eye.

When the problems are seemingly insoluble, the committees of inquiry are many. In April of last year, little more than two months after the National Council on the Arts meeting in Washington, the National Opera Institute (in conjunction with the Theatre

Communications Group, another government-sponsored service organization) devoted its sixth national colloquium to the subject of "New Alliances for Music Theater." The keynote speech was given by Harold Prince, the institute's chairman. He began with the glad tidings that at its last board meeting the National Opera Institute had voted to change its name to the National Institute for Music Theater (with the name followed by the phrase "Supporting Opera and All Forms of America Musical Theater"). Prince made his concern clear at the outset:

> Many people think of opera houses as museums, but I believe that while we are all keepers of historic flame (whether we're doing opera or musicals), we also have to promulgate new work.

To the question of how this should be done, Prince advanced an answer consistent with his whole approach to the subject of opera's future:

> The same problem hit the non-Music Theater world decades ago, and the solution has been found in the two hundred resident professional theaters spread all over our country. From these theaters now come the new works which Broadway wants but has a hard time creating. The big boys with the big money come and see them and try to determine which one will work on Broadway. They guess right some of the time, and, happily enough, authors get to be richer because of it, and good things happen in the commercial arena for them. So the business becomes more attractive and viable for new talent, more able to compete with Hollywood and TV for the new talent. In just the same way we need thirty or forty organizations to solve the problem Music Theater now faces.

What Prince envisioned as coming out of this music theater was hardly the art form that is now a component of high culture. He had already made clear where his tastes lay:

> To everyone's astonishment, opera companies are introducing the likes of *Sweeney Todd* and *Candide* into their repertoires. Audiences which five years ago would have denied any interest in this fare are quickly becoming excited by it and even inviting

it. Now that's a terrific turnabout, but we will have to encourage it.

Given these marching orders, the group's proposals were preordained. Institutions were to be encouraged to "offer a broader repertoire including all forms of music theater" in large part by

> [setting] up regional workshops to share successful experiences, production techniques, and positive attitudes . . . ; [developing] peer pressure with emphasis on those opera and theater companies which have done well with a variety of Music Theater styles, e.g., Houston Grand Opera, which has produced large "standard repertoire" pieces as well as new, often experimental works and Broadway musicals . . . ; [mounting] a national public relations effort to increase awareness of successful involvement in a wide variety of Music Theater production . . . ; [and involving] critics in open discussion to increase their awareness of the destructive efforts of premature reviews and reviews by individuals whose scope is limited (e.g., a non-musical theater critic or a non-theatrical music critic).

Yet another meeting to plan for artistic production in the music theater field, sponsored by Opera America with support from the Rockefeller Foundation and the NEA, took place at the end of August in Detroit. Once again the suggested plan of action was to expand the notion of music theater and bring new players to the creative table. The goal was clearly a broadened, collaborative effort, with music reduced to its proper role:

> [T]he best approach to new works development [is] to start with new sources of up-front funding to encourage new forms of collaboration among creative people, as well as alternative processes for bringing new works into being. . . . [Recommended were] several alternative models describing how the various actors in the creative process could come together in the pre-commissioning and commissioning stages. In general . . . new arrangements that involved a wide variety of creative artists in the very early stages of a new work's development, such as laboratories within opera companies, and other innovative workshop settings [were favored]. . . .

[A] central problem with new American works is their lack of strong dramatic element. To deal with this . . . several ways of encouraging greater interaction between theater and opera companies [were proposed, including specifically] a program of apprenticeships of composers with theater companies, and a parallel program to enable stage directors to work with opera companies.

One more meeting of inquiry—inquest might be a better term—was held, this time under the direct auspices of the NEA itself. The Opera–Musical Theater Seminar was held in Chicago on November 14 and 15 in a large room provided by the Lyric Opera of Chicago. Those in attendance included Anthony Bliss, the general manager of the Metropolitan Opera, Ardis Krainik, the general director of the Lyric Opera of Chicago, and John Crosby, the founder and present general director of the Santa Fe Opera. Also attending was Kurt Herbert Adler, the distinguished conductor and general director emeritus of the San Francisco Opera. Three newer and smaller companies were represented as well: Richard Gaddes came from the Opera Theatre of St. Louis, David Gockley from the Houston Grand Opera, and Joan Harris from the Chicago Opera Theater. From the world of education there was Robert Fitzpatrick, the president of the California Institute of the Arts, an institution founded with Walt Disney money but now closely associated with multimedia productions and the avant-garde. Three composers were in attendance: Conrad Susa, a theater-music specialist, and the successful Broadway writers Gary William Friedman and Micki Grant. The stage directors present were Tom O'Horgan, Rhoda Levine, and George Coates. From the theater, too, came playwright Megan Terry and designer John Conklin. Two vastly successful producers were there also: Joseph Papp, the head of the New York Shakespeare Festival, and Stuart Ostrow, the producer of such Broadway smash hits as *Pippin* and *1776*. Alan Eisenberg of Actors Equity and Gene Boucher of the American Guild of Musical Artists represented the performing union. Timothy Nolen, who created the title role in Floyd's *Willie Stark*, spoke for singers; Paul Walter, a businessman and patron who is the chairman of the board of The Kitchen, spoke for patrons; and Nash Cox, the executive director of the Kentucky Arts Council, spoke for state arts agencies. Suzanne

Weill, a senior vice president for programming, articulated the views of the Public Broadcasting Service, and Jessie Woods, of the Chicago-based Urban Gateways, brought the message of arts education for the young. I attended in my capacity as a music critic. The meeting was chaired by Francis S. M. Hodsoll, the chairman of the NEA, and was open to the press; excellent briefing material, including the Brenner history from which I have been quoting, was provided for the seminarians.

All the familiar issues and problems—the drought of new operatic works, the escalation of costs, the lack of enduring audience success for experimental pieces, the hope that joint efforts and audience tryouts might provide a substitute for artistic inspiration, the downgrading of music in favor of theater and drama—were articulated at the Chicago meeting, even to the point of boredom. What was surprising— at least to me—was the dissension among those assembled. It went far beyond the occasional misunderstandings and talking at cross-purposes common in any gathering of people intent on their individual tasks.

The order of the day in Chicago, in fact, was factional splits, kept controllable only by a general agreement that the irreducible condition for increased federal funding of any was the increased federal funding of all. The disagreement had to do with the very definition of the terms necessary to carry on the discussion. Whether these terms were opera or music theater, music or drama, tradition or innovation, establishment or avant-garde, art or craft, artist or audience, creator or producer, each speaker seemed to speak as a kind of frustrated monad, internally omnipotent and externally blocked.

There were, of course, some rough similarities among what might be thought of as the different camps represented. Those speaking for the traditionally oriented opera companies—Bliss of the Metropolitan, Krainik of Chicago, Crosby of Santa Fe—seemed above the discussion. Bliss seemed only to want to talk about boards of directors and how the Metropolitan gets its own directors to give large sums without interfering. Krainik made clear that the Lyric Opera had recovered under her stewardship from near-bankruptcy only by following the safe policy of presenting internationally celebrated casts in accessible operas. Crosby talked little. Taken together, these purveyors of undoubted quality (and in the case of Santa Fe, a rare amount of innovation within the serious repertory) conveyed the message that they wanted nothing so much as to be left alone.

The composers present proclaimed themselves martyrs to an uncomprehending and even cynical artistic establishment whose work was at best irrelevant and at worst offensive. From the theater people at the meeting one heard a largely inchoate case for dramatic and production values. From Houston's David Gockley came the message that sopranos and conductors should not be allowed to run the show. Singer Timothy Nolen, speaking out of his experience with the Lake George Opera, said that the producer now can't trust the creator of a work to come out with a full-blown masterpiece. Alan Eisenberg spoke in the most cautious way about the limited help the performing unions might give to new works in their early stages of exposure. Stuart Ostrow seemed to speak for another era and another creative world when he lamented the absence today on Broadway—and everywhere else for that matter—of musical scores that "sing." Ostrow's remedy, one advanced by many others at the gathering for their own creative problems, was "workshopping," a process that gives collaborators, committees, and onlookers the possibility of adding to the creative outcome over a long period of artistic development. An observer with a more traditional idea of creative genius might wonder just how many zeroes it takes to add up to one. At the end of the meeting demands were heard for the NEA to require the presentation of new American works as a condition of its funding, as if the cause of an American art were best served by an enforced entitlement program.

Those who wished to make a case for the avant-garde—whatever they thought it to be—did so by a general attack on the old rather than by any description of the new. Indeed, the whole idea of tradition was under pressure from everyone except the three opera companies represented by Bliss, Krainik, and Crosby. When I remarked that the primary function of opera organizations was to preserve the treasures of civilization, I was answered by Joseph Papp (throughout the meeting the strongest advocate of the nonmusic and noncomposer approach to music theater) with the rejoinder that the very notion of "treasures of civilization" could be nauseating. When I suggested that opera was now suffering from an unwillingness by opera companies to present the major, if little-known, works of this already very far advanced century, no one seemed willing to discuss them. Perhaps no one was able to.

The last gathering on the state of opera was the annual conference of Opera America in New York the second week of December. I attended three events of the meeting: a speech by Senator Daniel Patrick Moynihan, a press conference to announce a grant from the Rockefeller Foundation, and a showcase of new works. Moynihan's speech demanded an eightfold increase by the year 2000 in federal arts support. For some reason, the month-late Opera America press release describing the senator's speech neglected to mention either that he offered to introduce the necessary legislation himself or that he thought those interested in the arts ought to give serious thought to making campaign contributions to candidates. The Rockefeller-grant press conference, dealing as it did with funds for implementing the proposals coming out of the National Institute for Music Theater Conference in Detroit last August, was chiefly interesting for the amount of opposition it provoked from such Opera America members as Terence McEwen, general director of the San Francisco Opera, and the way in which the opposition was put down from the chair. It might also be added that Opera America's press release on this matter failed to mention anything about the less than enthusiastic reception the Rockefeller initiative received from those who, like McEwen, worried that Opera America might be intruding in their own work.

The Opera America showcase, given unstaged on December 12 at the acoustically excellent Merkin Concert Hall, seemed at least to me to be (in the hoary phrase of the 1960s) part of the problem rather than part of the solution. Excerpts from five works were presented. The first piece was *Private Lives*, an inane "video opera" by the avant-gardist Robert Ashley. The music veered between soft rock and jazzy piano, the television sets (the only performers on stage) showed bright jumbles of images, and the words seemed to be concerned with "Gwyn," a girl who worked in a bank "helping people count their money." The long synopsis of the "action" contained in the program ran to some 750 words. I must admit to being charmed, though, by the thought of an opening night at the Met with the usual gala audience assembled to watch the TV sets do their stuff in front of the footlights. Just think of the anxiety for the management. If Sony has a short, will Zenith step in?

The next work was *X*, a piece about the life of the famous Malcolm composed by Anthony Davis, with libretto by Thulani Davis-Jarman and book by Christopher Davis, as well as additional lyrics by Deborah Atherton. Two scenes from the work were given. The first, "Chickens Come Home to Roost," was an account of Malcolm's reaction to the Kennedy assassination, the murder of Medgar Evers, and the Birmingham bombing. The second, "Mecca," concerned a confrontation between Malcolm and Elijah Muhammed over the latter's sins. The music was repetitive, with a stressing of single unaccompanied lines. The singing was generally excellent, though untrained. The general effect, given the repetition, the syncopated music, the earnest performance, and the general clumsiness, was of an updated version of American ballad opera of the 1940s and 1950s. Indeed, all that was new—if that is the right word—about Davis's work was the story line. As with the Floyd opera on Huey Long, the very power of the story swamped whatever music might have been available to clothe it.

Meredith Monk's *Dolmen Music*, the next offering, was described in the program as "an original work utilizing the solo voice as an instrument, working with the unique quality of each voice and playing with the ensemble possibilities of unison, texture, counterpoint, weaving, etc." It was written for six voices, with cello and percussion. Again, according to the program, there were "Special Music Requirements": "Singers who have been taught Meredith Monk's vocal technique." And here, of course, is the key to the special character of the work. Though Monk has an avant-garde reputation as a dancer and composer going back two decades, her work here consists of little but the use of nontraditional vocal sounds, based on nonsense syllables, carrying melodic lines often harmonized in parallel fifths. The entire effect, while properly minimalist and owing much to the work of La Monte Young, is not always lulling. The general impression is of a very busy old-fashioned marketplace. I might add that there was no story line here at all.

Now followed an excerpt from Jon Gibson's *Voyage of the Beagle*, a group of episodes combining bits of Victoriana with scenes from Darwin's intellectual life. The excerpt given at the showcase consisted of a singer vocalizing the opening of the first book of Genesis against the background of a prerecorded tape. The music was minimalist in style (and in invention too) but maximalist in decibel level. Again, there were endless chains of parallel fifths, sometimes emerging, with the addition of the third, as triads. The repetition was on a cosmic scale. Still, the singer's frequent deviation from exact pitch on the note he kept sounding over and over, though very likely a function of the impossibility of a human being's doing anything in exactly the same way over a long time span, did add a dollop of harmonic interest. Perhaps it's a frivolous response, but as the singer kept intoning "In the Beginning" I did sometimes wish that in the music's beginning had also been its end.

The last musical event of the evening was by far the most interesting. It consisted of excerpts from *Oedipus at Colonus*, the most successful presentation in the Brooklyn Academy's "Next Wave" festival this past fall. This retelling, via black gospel singing, of Sophocles's great play did have one great thing going for it: the remarkable improvisatorial singing of Clarence Fountain and the Five Blind Boys of Alabama. In the excerpt presented here, one was conscious less of Sophocles or of Oedipus than of the immense cry of pain, stemming from slavery, that is still locked up inside the black self-image. Here, for all to hear, was the stuff, not of operatic art or of avant-garde performance, but of an entire people's suffering. I don't know what its relevance is to opera or to the avant-garde; I don't even know what its relevance was on this night to an audience of arts administrators, New York downtown music types, and stray critics. One thing I do know. So powerful was the impact of Fountain and the Blind Boys' singing that the ensuing excerpt from *Oedipus* seemed, in its Bob Telson score and the vocalism of the J. D. Steele Singers, like a return to commercial pop and ethnic exploitation.

And so the question remains, now in 1984 as before, Whither opera? Where so many doctors have failed in the cure, it would be quixotic to deny that the patient is sick. An ossified repertory, a lack of new creation, a resulting attempt to find the exciting by going further and further back for interesting material, an increased questioning of the mounting costs involved—all these are real problems. Despite our permanent need to perform the classics of opera because they are among the exemplars of high culture, some attempt at an *aggiornamento* of the repertory is nevertheless required.

In this difficult attempt, the guiding principle to follow must be that of not forcing the art form to compromise its own history and integrity under the pressure of outside forces. A stop must be put to the attempts of those who do not come out of, and do not sympathize with, the ethos of great opera to *mandate* the replacement of what is alien to them with something that conforms to their own ideas of how the future of the art ought to look.[2] It is no more necessary to make opera houses and companies put on musicals than it is to make Broadway theaters do Mozart, Verdi, and Wagner. It is both improper and pointless to make opera audiences sit still for video operas and theatrical provocations; it is just as wrong to require The Kitchen to put on Handel and Rossini. It is not, of course, that we should bar the door to the development of new forms, either in music theater or in art in general; it is rather that we must let opera be opera, as we must let every other art be itself. Because we cannot plan the creative future,[3] because we can never know what will be an art work until it has been made, it behooves us to look to the present and to the immediate past for whatever little we can hope to know about the future.

If we will just look at what has been going on in opera in the last fifty years abroad as well as in America, we will immediately find a tremendous lack in our own knowledge and experience, a lack that extends not just to audiences and performers, but even to the very composers upon whom we must depend for the future. The sorry fact is that by and large our greatest opera institutions have a bad record of making available to the opera public the acknowledged major works of our time. Though there are some happy exceptions—the San Francisco Opera under Adler made a valiant attempt to do at least one "difficult" work every fall season, and the New York City Opera until recently took justifiable pride in its record of service to a contemporary repertory—the exceptions, alas, remain just that.

Lacking has been any leadership from the top. The Metropolitan Opera has steadfastly refused, whether under Bing or Chapin or now under Bliss and his music director James Levine, to take responsibility

---

[2] A good place to begin the necessary tasks in opera might be at the National Endowment for the Arts itself, with a divorce of the shotgun administrative marriage of opera and musical theater, and the return of opera to the Music Program, whence it came and where it belongs.

[3] In this regard, Kurt Herbert Adler's point at a recent National Council on the Arts meeting is significant: European governments, despite their generous support of new opera writing, have not been any more able than we are to bring about a supply of viable new works.

for the twentieth century in opera. No American works at all since the 1960s, only the tamest of post-World War II works, no *Moses und Aron* of Schoenberg, no exploration of the Henze of recent times or even of the Hindemith of a half-century ago, no Richard Strauss after *Arabella*, no Bartók or Shostakovich or Prokofiev: surely, of all the world's famous opera houses, only the Bolshoi in Moscow can beat the Met for ignoring what is under its own nose—and one can hardly doubt that the Bolshoi's record in Russian opera is miles better than the Met's in American.[4] Even the Met's recent commissioning of operas from Jacob Druckman and John Corigliano, delivery date uncertain, seems hardly taken seriously by the Met management itself.

At the New York City Opera, Beverly Sills has in fact scheduled Philip Glass's *Akhnaten* for next season, following its European premiere this spring. This American performance comes after several years of the City Opera's almost completely ignoring contemporary operas, and it represents little more than a determined effort to jump on Glass's lavishly funded bandwagon. There is no sign of any attempt on the part of the City Opera management to reach into the rich recent repertory of the company for the excitement of unfamiliar material. It is difficult indeed to believe that just sixteen years ago the City Opera presented a spring season entirely devoted to *ten* American operas, including several that were performed by the company for the first time. Among these works were such operas as Menotti's *Maria Golovin*, Moore's *Ballad of Baby Doe* and *The Devil and Daniel Webster*, Dello Joio's *The Triumph of Saint Joan*, Blitzstein's *Regina*, and Weisgall's *Six Characters in Search of an Author*; the last was a world premiere. Such a course would seem revolutionary indeed today.

What is now needed, it seems to me, is a general attempt on the part of American companies large and small to present, to the extent that it is within their power, a yearly conspectus of the life of opera from its beginnings to the present day. An effort ought to be made to avoid both all old-masterpiece seasons and the present practice of sandwiching in whatever difficult new works are done between thick pieces of attractively sentimental works. Although this doubtless well-

---

[4] It must be emphasized that the Met's recent widely trumpeted negotiations for a limited presentation of a new Robert Wilson stage extravaganza involve only a rental of the house, not a Metropolitan production.

intentioned practice may not have the effect of pacifying a hostile audience, it does prove to that audience by propinquity—Puccini on one side of the new work and Verdi or Mozart on the other—that the old works were indeed in a different league. If a continuum of works were to be presented, the audience and the performers would be trained by steps to deal with the unknown. A climate of intelligent understanding just might thus be created, in which the new works would not have to rival *Pagliacci*.

It must be said too that a shifting of part of each season's repertory to the twentieth century would have the welcome function of lessening the pressure to make old operas new by either giving them *outré* productions and stage direction or presenting them in fabulously expensive "authentic" guises. All this ingenuity is not wrong; it is just misdirected.

A close observer of the finances of opera companies would doubtless be justified in asking who, indeed, might pay for this idealistic redirection of repertory away from the surefire to the speculative. The answer is simple, but would require a revolution in how opera funding is accomplished. For many years now, a prime requirement for philanthropic funding—whether private or governmental—has been a high percentage of earned income on the opera company's annual report. That earned income, it goes without saying, must come from ticket sales; there should be little surprise in the fact that more tickets are sold to familiar operas than to unknown ones. The attitude of patrons has increasingly come to resemble that enshrined in the old saw about banks: banks are places that lend money to people who already have money. This attitude will no longer do, in the arts in general or in opera in particular. The first order of business of arts advocates ought not to be, as it is today, supporting arts institutions because they already go a long way toward paying for themselves; it ought to be convincing patrons that it is their responsibility to fund what is artistically necessary and would not exist without their support. Arts institutions, after all, are not businesses. They are, and should be when they are doing what is required of them, charities.

Perhaps the best way to end would be with a listing of operas, all completed in this century, that might provide a pool from which the works necessary to bring about a leavening of the present repertory might be chosen. I have divided this pool into European and American lists. I have included on both lists works grand and intimate, long and short, little-known and half-familiar, more and less difficult for audiences and performers. The lists are not complete, and they include works that have been performed and dropped, or that have never received the kind of performance they deserve, or that ought to have been done but have never been done in this country at all.

Here are the European works, with their composers listed in alphabetical order and their dates in parentheses:

Bartók	*Bluebeard's Castle* (1918)
Busoni	*Turandot* (1917)
	Doktor Faust (1916–24; completed by Jarnach)
Dukas	*Ariane et Barbe-bleue* (1906)
Falla	*La Vida Breve* (1905)
Henze	*Boulevard Solitude* (1951)
	Elegy for Young Lovers (1961)
	Der junge Lord (1964)
Hindemith	*Cardillac* (1926)
	Mathis der Maler (1935)
Kodály	*Háry János* (1926)
Kokkonen	*The Last Temptations* (1975)
Korngold	*Violanta* (1916)
Milhaud	*Christophe Colomb* (1928)
Pfitzner	*Die Rose vom Liebesgarten* (1900)
	Palestrina (1915)
Prokofiev	*The Fiery Angel* (1923)
	War and Peace (1943)
Reimann	*Lear* (1978)
Sallinen	*The Horseman* (1974)
	The Red Line (1978)
Schoenberg	*Moses und Aron* (1932)
Strauss	*Feuersnot* (1901)
	Intermezzo (1923)
	Die ägyptische Helena (1927)
	Die schweigsame Frau (1934)
	Friedenstag (1936)
	Daphne (1937)
	Die Liebe der Danae (1940)
	Capriccio (1941)

Stravinsky	*The Rake's Progress* (1951)
Tippett	*The Midsummer Marriage* (1952)
	The Knot Garden (1969)

And the American works:

Argento	*The Voyage of Edgar Allan Poe* (1976)
	Miss Havisham's Fire (1979)
Barber	*Vanessa* (1957)
	Antony and Cleopatra (1966)
Copland	*The Tender Land* (1954)
Gruenberg	*The Emperor Jones* (1931)
Sessions	*The Trial of Lucullus* (1947)
	Montezuma (1963)
Taylor	*Peter Ibbetson* (1931)
Thomson	*Four Saints in Three Acts* (1927–28)
	The Mother of Us All (1947)
Weisgall	*Six Characters in Search of an Author* (1956)
	Athaliah (1963)

One point deserves stress. Little good for either the present or the future of opera will be accomplished by merely presenting one individual opera chosen from these lists or from the much wider lists that doubtless could be fashioned. The need of the art is for the presentation of a broad twentieth-century repertory. There are, of course, no guarantees in my—or in anyone else's—selections. There can only be interest. Isn't that enough?

9.

Marc Blitzstein, lately the subject of an admiring biography by Eric A. Gordon, continues his shadowy presence in American musical theater, or at least in that branch of it that attempts work of "social significance." There is both in art and in politics an understandable tendency to prefer old radicalism to new: after all, we know we have survived the old, and we can't be sure about the new. Still, there is a crass brutality in The Cradle Will Rock, *the subject of this June 1983* New Criterion *article, that seems the archetype of the intellectual search for simple solutions in art or in politics to complicated problems. And simple solutions, after all, have hardly ever lacked admirers.*

Blitzstein's Cradle

MARC BLITZSTEIN'S *The Cradle Will Rock*, a quintessential piece of 1930s Communist agitprop, was presented through May by John Houseman and The Acting Company at the American Place Theater in New York. It was neat and tightly paced, musically well performed, and clearly communicative. Despite its virtues, however, the event was an artistic failure, and even as an ideological enterprise it occasioned none of the political fervor Blitzstein must have hoped to inspire, only the smirks and snickers of an obviously knowing audience. The production's importance lay elsewhere—in the realm of cultural politics, where Blitzstein himself has won such a considerable reputation.

Something in the nature of a myth now attaches to Marc Blitzstein as both creator and man. An assiduous propagator of that myth has been Blitzstein's close friend and associate, Leonard Bernstein. A tribute from Bernstein is published in his new book, *Findings*, and is reprinted in the program for *The Cradle Will Rock*:

> I was amazed at the slightness of this man I had imagined, through his music, to be a giant. . . . [W]e walked, all afternoon,

by the Charles River. Now that image leaps up in my mind: Marc lying on the banks of the Charles, talking, bequeathing to me his knowledge, insight, warmth—endlessly, with endless strength drawn, like that of Antaeus, from his contact with the earth. And gradually he became a giant again; and so he continued to be whenever he touched earth, sea, woods, snow. That was the secret of the giant who had written those notes which seduced my soul.

Blitzstein was born in 1905, the son of wealthy Philadelphia parents; he died in 1964 in a brawl (whether politically or socially caused remains unclear) with three sailors in a Martinique bar. He had proper musical training with pianist Alexander Siloti (Rachmaninoff's cousin) and then at the Curtis Institute in composition with Rosario Scalero. Like so many Americans in the 1920s, he studied with Nadia Boulanger in Paris; like very few, he also studied with Arnold Schoenberg in Berlin.

All this produced a modernist Blitzstein we know nothing of today. Our Blitzstein, if such he may be called, is rather the product of a timely marriage between the dramatic influence of Bertolt Brecht and the musical influence of Hanns Eisler and Kurt Weill. But to describe matters so clinically is to ignore the true formation of Blitzstein's artistic persona. Brecht and Eisler were Communists. Weill's work with Brecht in *Die Dreigroschenoper* (Berlin, 1928) had shown how a revolutionary social and political statement could be clothed in a music of power—and appeal.

For Blitzstein the result of these influences was the story and music of *The Cradle Will Rock*, written in 1936–37 under the auspices of the Federal Theatre Project (an arm of the WPA). *Cradle* is set in "Steeltown, USA, on the night of a union drive." The characters are pasteboard figures of a Marxist morality play: a capitalist and his worthless family, supported by a cast of lackeys willing not only to be bought but also to sell out their loved ones. Policemen, a minister, an editor, a musician, a painter, a doctor, a druggist, a college president and his hired professors—these sinister characters are balanced by a soulful prostitute, a touching young Polish couple marked for a violent death (which is to be blamed on the union organizers), the druggist's dutiful young son, who is killed in an attempt to save the Poles, a woman (representing true proletarian family feeling) who demands justice for her union-supporter brother, and the steelworker head of the union drive, the true hero of the piece, who exudes simultaneously the toughness needed for struggle with the class enemy and the gentleness born of hope for a better world.

Just how far Blitzstein intended to render these characters as political symbols is eloquently conveyed by their names. The capitalist is dubbed Mr. Mister, his wife Mrs. Mister; his two children are Junior Mister and Sister Mister. The prostitute's name is Moll, and her john is called Gent. The policemen are Dick and Cop, the minister is Reverend Salvation. The editor is named Daily, the violinist Yasha, the painter Dauber, the college president President Prexy. The touching Poles are Gus and Sadie Polock, and the hero of labor is Larry Foreman.

This "labor opera," written with Brecht's encouragement, is in ten scenes (divided into two acts) variously located around Steeltown. The work opens with the prostitute, who is having trouble getting a living wage from her customer because of the Depression; when they argue, a detective demands a bribe from the man in order to let him go, and then himself makes a pass at the girl. Now the real business of Blitzstein's evening begins: in a grotesque but fitting mis-understanding, the police, acting on Mr. Mister's orders to arrest anyone showing up to hear union speakers, bring in the entire Liberty Committee, an organization of town worthies all under the capitalist thumb.

In Night Court, the tables are turned. As envisioned in the Communist Manifesto, the expropriators are expropriated; the bourgeoisie itself is on trial. The minister, in a series of flashbacks, is shown supporting World War I (and Mr. Mister's armaments profits) in return for Mrs. Mister's daintily dangled checks. The Mister children are shown frolicking in a depressed way on their father's lawns. The druggist is shown willing to send the Polish couple to their doom in order to save his store and seeing his son killed as a result. The artist and the musician are shown squabbling for Mrs. Mister's favors. After Mr. Mister (delayed by the union organizing drive) finally turns up to get his Liberty Committee stooges released, we see him first select a professor (named Scoot) to deliver a pep talk to students on the subject of military preparedness (read anti-union repression) and then behave like a coward as he undergoes a physical examination from Dr.

Specialist. It all ends happily when, back in Night Court, Larry Foreman refuses Mr. Mister's bribe and vows to continue the fight for unions and solidarity. The final chorus consists of the menacing slogan "The Cradle Will Rock!" The audience is left with no doubt that this cradle is the social structure that upholds a moribund yet vicious bourgeoisie.

It is hardly surprising, given the political nature of its characters and action, that nothing about *The Cradle Will Rock* has caused more notoriety than the circumstances of its entry into the world of show business. Indeed, before the audience is vouchsafed one word or note of Blitzstein's in the current production, it is presented with a ten-minute speech read by John Houseman detailing the attempts to block the first performance. Not only did the Federal Theatre Project and WPA administrators try to block it, but the unions representing the actors and the musicians cooperated in the embargo by demanding full wages for their work. The irony of prefacing Blitzstein's union exhortation with the implied claim that the unions' demanding scale was somehow unprogressive appeared lost both on Mr. Houseman and on the audience. Saying that he and Orson Welles (who collaborated with him on the original *Cradle*) were not terribly political, Mr. Houseman went on to describe the search for a theater to replace the one closed to them by the government, and the frenzied preparations to do the show without orchestra and without onstage actors. In the end, of course, Blitzstein himself played all the music on an old upright piano, and the actors performed from the audience. Everything ended happily: the audience was large and enthusiastic, the press copious and ecstatic. The show ran in various theaters for more than a hundred performances.

The current production re-creates certain aspects of the premiere. The music is provided by a pianist seated at an upright, his back to the audience[1]; the first son, that of the prostitute, comes from the audience. Almost all the action thereafter takes place on the nearly empty stage. The cast delivered the lines forcefully and with conviction. The dance sequences involving the Mister children were properly

---

[1] The pianist in this production, Michael Barrett, also serves as music director. He plays the piano marvelously, with accuracy, brilliance, and rhythmic verve. One must assume that he shares some responsibility for the excellent singing of the cast.

frenetic, and even funny. The actors seemed well prepared to exploit the stereotypical possibilities inherent in the characters they were playing. Mr. Mister was fat and bullying; Mrs. Mister was a nice combination of Joan Mondale as arts advocate and Hermione Gingold as la-de-da opportunist; Reverend Salvation was appropriately unctuous and creepy; Gus and Sadie Polock were almost unbearably clean-cut, vulnerable, and loving; Patti LuPone, playing the two opposing roles of Moll and Sister Mister, managed to be fully authentic in both. And Larry Foreman, acted by Randle Mell, was the very model of the craggy and handsome worker-hero, not quite clean-shaven and possessing a voice perfectly suited to putting all the girls to bed.

But it didn't work. *The Cradle Will Rock* is not a moving moment in the theater. Part of the problem undoubtedly lies with the music. So much attention has been focused on Blitzstein's sociodramatic debt to Brecht that one might overlook Blitzstein's abject musical robbery from the less political Weill. The score of *Cradle* is inconceivable without the prior existence of *Die Dreigroschenoper*. The sound of Macheath and Brown's *Kanonen-Song* is all over *Cradle*; Peachum's *Morgenchoral* is all too clearly the model for Reverend Salvation's pious crooning of the virtues of peace. Blitzstein's score, however, is Weill's *Dreigroschenoper* without the music. Limited as Weill was as a composer, he did manage on this occasion a tuneful, jazzy, and altogether memorable piece; Blitzstein's *Cradle* score, by comparison, passes by the ears hardly noticed.

Much of the problem of *Cradle* lies with Blitzstein's conscious decision to replace the individuality of his characters with their class identification and function. The idea of calling the capitalist owner Mr. Mister is witty, but it is also brittle; when applied to a whole world of people, and when made the ruling gimmick of an entire dramatic work, the conclusion cannot be avoided that "man" has replaced men, and that politics has replaced life. Blitzstein, in company with a whole line of Stalinist writers ranging from Brecht to the Soviets themselves, must have been aware than in so doing he was depriving his work of what remains most moving on the stage: the lonely encounter of a distinct individual with the world. To make up for this curious self-denial, Communist art must wallow in bathos and sentimentality. Blitzstein's *Cradle* is full of just such false sentiment, of stock emotions being summoned up to animate stock ideas. The result is soap-opera feeling at Broadway prices.

What is really interesting about *The Cradle Will Rock* is thus hardly its achievement as art, or even its present influence on our culture. The biggest prizes of the Great White Way, after all, went to Rodgers and Hammerstein, Frank Loesser, Lerner and Loewe, and not Eisler and Brecht, or even Weill. And as for its politics, that too seems hardly in the forefront now. The *New York Times* quotes John Houseman saying:

> The only aspect of the work that's dated is Marc's excessive love of unions. . . . There are other themes—the fact that artists sometimes sponge off the rich and that doctors and newspaper editors don't always have the most impeccable morals—which still make sense to us today. Actually, the play's only message is that a town run by a boss is not a good town. It's really that simple.

Unfortunately, it is really *not* that simple. Heinrich Heine, no mean observer of human affairs, once wrote about the recurrent vagaries of love:

> *Es ist eine alte Geschichte,*
> *Doch bleibt sie immer neu;*
> *Und wem sie just passieret,*
> *Dem bricht das Herz entzwei.*

> (It's an old story,
> And yet it's always new;
> He to whom it happens,
> His heart breaks in two.)

For aesthetic devotees of Stalinism like Blitzstein, the problem is not the heart, but the art. The wages of the Party line are not just heartbreak, but creative bankruptcy. A decade of artistic disappointment after the Bolshevik revolution, followed by more than a half-century of the Soviet intellectual desert, might have been thought enough to get the lesson across. But political education, after all, is continuing education, which is one reason why *The Cradle Will Rock* once again requires consideration.

The real significance of *The Cradle Will Rock* lies in its appeal to that intellectual stratum that sees itself as peculiarly qualified to package the truth for a mass public. This stratum does not attend the theater for an aesthetic experience. Thus, the audience for *Cradle* the night I attended seemed largely drawn, not from the public at large, but from the world of the theater and from allied activities. Its response was not that of feeling, but rather of *knowing*. It knew, in other words, just which buttons were being pushed, and it showed its admiration for the techniques displayed by what can only be described as a kind of politically smutty laughter.

Here, indeed, is a Stalinism, not of politics, but of culture. Writers, Stalin is credited with having said, are the engineers of human souls. His literary category is certainly flexible enough to include actors and musicians as well. Too many of these people, by virtue of their supposed facility in the manipulation of symbols, go through life conscious on the one hand of their desire to influence the masses and acutely aware on the other of just how unemployed those powers are in capitalist-bourgeois society. Indeed, it is the evil genius of Communism to hold before these intellectuals the prospect of a work they dearly love.

Marc Blitzstein and *The Cradle Will Rock*, by plugging into this vicious seduction, are ensured a revival any time intellectuals are conscious of being out of their true work. Surely there must be a better way of finding a job.

IO.

Philip Glass remains a name to conjure with in new American opera, at least in the loose way that term is presently defined. He has been described as the most successful opera composer since Puccini, though whether this is a compliment to him or a comment on the fate of his colleagues remains a matter for discussion. It is my own opinion that the vogue for his static, adramatic musical tableaux has passed, and that Glass's recent works—indeed, all his operas since Einstein—*have been a disappointment to his young admirers. Many Glass commissions, of course, are still in the funding pipeline, and as a result we may expect to see what I am tempted to call new Glass spectacles arriving for some years to come.* Einstein on the Beach, *his collaboration with the very gifted though eccentric Robert Wilson, and about which I wrote this February 1985* New Criterion *article, thus remains both the first and the last of his conquests.*

Einstein*'s Long March to Brooklyn*

BROOKLYN, though having lost a famous baseball team (and, before that, an infamous football team), need weep no longer: it now has the up-to-date Brooklyn Academy of Music, the national leader in the presentation of guaranteed media-succulent avant-garde theater-*cum*-dance-*cum*-"music" extravaganzas. Indeed, so successful has the institution been under the guidance of Harvey Lichtenstein, its president and chief executive officer, that *Blam!*—the title chosen for an exhibition of pop, minimalist, and performance art at the Whitney Museum this fall—might have been thought to refer not to the famous 1960s (Roy) Lichtenstein cartoon painting but to the 1980s Brooklyn (Harvey) Lichtenstein Academy of Music.

Jokes aside, the Brooklyn Academy's record in presenting what it has chosen to call the "Next Wave" has been notable. A successful series sailing under this name took place in 1983; it featured eleven attractions, among them such icons of the new as dancers Trisha

Brown, Lucinda Childs, Carolyn Carlson, and Molissa Fenley, and theatrical *animateurs* Lee Breuer (of Mabou Mines fame) and George Coates. This year—with one exception—the presentation roster seemed a bit slimmer in hype value; on the whole the names of the artists—dancers Remy Charlip, Bill T. Jones, Arnie Zane, Mark Morris, and Elisa Monte, videographer Tim Morris, far-out saxophonist Richard Landry, and even composer Steve Reich—appeared to come out of the debate within the experimental art world rather than to stand perched, as their predecessors of the year before had been, on what might be called the brink of true media stardom.

The one exception, of course, was the presentation of the now-mythic—at least in some circles—*Einstein on the Beach*, the mid-1970s collaboration between composer Philip Glass and director-designer-visual artist Robert Wilson. The 1983 Brooklyn festival had begun with Glass's *The Photographer*, a kind of tribute to the nineteenth-century figure Eadweard Muybridge, who first proved by the evidence of the camera that a horse, when trotting, has all four hooves off the ground at the same time. This work, in its static artificiality, seemed to impress even the composer's fans as something more of a whimper than a bang. *Einstein*, however, was different. Through its use of the terrifying images associated with the scientist's work, it had managed, in two 1976 performances at the (rented) Metropolitan Opera House, to enter into the consciousness of artistically knowing New Yorkers. A measure of the fame the work has gained with the passing of time is that so many people now claim to have been present that these performances must have been given, not at the Met, but at Madison Square Garden. The choice of *Einstein* to close the 1984 festival with some twelve performances thus seemed a deliberate attempt to end with strength, to make up once and for all for whatever was less than exciting in the earlier part of the season. Artistic merit aside, the effort succeeded at the box office. *Einstein* seems to have sold out every performance, in the process enabling the entire festival to gross over a million dollars.

Apart from their collaboration on *Einstein*, Glass and Wilson have separately made enviable public careers. Glass is the most visible of the musical minimalists, those composers who have found a way out of the complexities, disintegrations, and unpopularity of post-World War II modernism. Following in the footsteps of La Monte Young and

Terry Riley, and evolving on a parallel course with Steve Reich, Glass used the simplest harmonic materials, iterated at stupefying length, and orchestrated for instruments sometimes electronic and always electrically amplified. Prior to the mid-1970s, his music was instrumental, written for and performed by an ensemble led by him and bearing his name. The result of all this was a growing reputation on the New York downtown music scene and several LPs available only in the more sophisticated record stores. In Europe, too, where Glass had worked with Nadia Boulanger and first become inspired to follow his present course through association with Ravi Shankar, a cult began to form around him and his ideas. This cult abroad was perhaps most interesting as yet another example of the European readiness to be charmed by American simplicities at once eccentric and divine.

Whereas Glass's artistic education at the Juilliard School in New York and with Boulanger in Paris was nothing if not establishment, Robert Wilson was from the beginning of his theater career in the 1960s something of an autodidact. Born in Texas in 1941, he had almost graduated from the University of Texas with a degree in business administration when he decided to come to New York to study architecture; though he did take a degree in it at Pratt Institute and even served as an apprentice with an architect, his interests lay more with the visual arts, and more specifically with body movements. For him, such movements were not "dance" but rather a means toward freeing blocked impulses and capacities. He had worked with handicapped, deprived, and disturbed children to support himself, and in the process developed an aesthetic of slow-motion gesture and action, wherein each detail carried a portentous but usually nonexplicit, quasi-symbolic meaning.

When Wilson's therapy-induced movements were grafted onto his background in architecture and his time spent in painting in New York during the yeasty mid-1960s, the result was a theatrical conception of painterly stage designs, massive constructed sets, and wordless dance, all unfolding without very much action but at heavenly length. Wilson's titles for his stage works all seemed to suggest more content than the works themselves made any attempt to provide: *The Life and Times of Sigmund Freud* (1969), *Deafman Glance* (1970), and *The Life and Times of Joseph Stalin* (1973). All were huge stage pageants using for the most part untrained actors and dancers who did Wilson's bidding more through the force of his personality, deployed during unlimited rehearsal time, than through any professional experience of their own. The critics—especially those of the avant-garde stripe—were interested, and audiences here and abroad attended in enough numbers to convince private and governmental backers that Wilson was indeed onto something.

Wilson likes to call his earlier works "operas," though the music that accompanied them was, by common consent, little more than trivial, even for those critics whose standards were anti-profundity. In this regard the collaboration with Glass on *Einstein* awakened expectations—which many critics later found wholly fulfilled—of a Wagnerian *Gesamtkunstwerk*, that is, a unity of music, theater, and dance in which the aesthetic whole was vastly greater than the sum of its parts. Whatever the justice done in this instance to the wooly formation ascribed to Wagner—his great *oeuvre*, after all, demonstrated nothing if not the primacy of music—the general feeling after the first performances of *Einstein* was that the multimedia avant-garde had at last come of age.

Even for those who were enthusiastic in saluting *Einstein* on its first appearance, the creative results from Wilson and Glass working separately thereafter—they had entered upon a period of strained relations that precluded their further collaboration for the time being—fell short of complete satisfaction. Wilson, for his part, retired to Europe, where funding, mostly from state sources, was easier to find than in America. He conceived and staged several less ambitious works on the Continent, and even turned his busy imagination to making video clips capable of being shown in any order and at any length. Then Wilson devoted the major part of his attention to a project grandiose even for him, an extravaganza that was to be the centerpiece of the cultural offerings at the 1984 Olympic Games in Los Angeles. It was designed to do nothing less than sum up the entire world-historical experience.

In any case, *the CIVIL warS: a tree is best measured when it is down* was first conceived by Wilson as an agglomeration, lasting twelve hours, of six related theater pieces with music; the six parts were to be produced (and financed) in six different countries, then shipped to Los Angeles, where their assembling was to be funded by the Olympic

Arts Committee and presented at the Shrine Auditorium. Though individual segments had been produced in Rotterdam, Cologne, Rome, and Minneapolis, their putting together at the Olympics defied even the financial abilities of the doughty Robert Fitzpatrick, president of the California Institute of the Arts (a school founded some years ago with Walt Disney money) and director of the Olympic Arts Festival. The work was scaled down to eight hours, and further cuts were envisioned, but to no avail. Despite more than three million dollars from the producing countries, two hundred thousand dollars from Los Angeles, and almost a million and a half dollars from donations and projected ticket sales, the entire project was scrubbed amidst massive publicity. The French Communist Party daily, *l'Humanité* (as quoted by *American Theatre*, the magazine of the nonprofit Theatre Communications Group) wrote that the cancellation was "a crime against the spirit."

Whatever the expert status of *l'Humanité* in matters of the spirit, the segment of *the CIVIL warS* produced last spring in Minneapolis suggested a different conclusion. There, in the small auditorium of the Walker Arts Center, one could hear and see a collection of entr'actes from *the CIVIL warS*. Wilson called these "knee plays" because they serve as the "joints" between the work's five acts.

It is doubtless less than fair to judge an art work lasting twelve hours (some estimates go as high as sixteen) by intervening excerpts alone. But a passage in the program notes, presumably written by Wilson, explicitly argues for these entr'actes' existing on their own: "*the Knee Plays* is like a substory that is woven through the tapestry of *the CIVIL warS* . . . . [T]hey serve in some cases as an introduction to the larger scenes, but on their own they tell a story together that can be seen separately." The knee plays include music composed and led by David Byrne (of Talking Heads fame) and played by seven musicians, six brass, and one percussion. The narration was written and spoken by Byrne as well. The scenario and the direction were solely by Wilson; the design and lighting were by Wilson and a group of (presumably subordinate) collaborators. The choreography for the evening was by Suzushi Hanayagi, variously described in the program as "one of Japan's foremost classically trained Kabuki dancers" and as "one of Japan's foremost classical dancers." Rehearsal time for the Walker performances had apparently been generous: rehearsals had begun (after much planning here and abroad) fully one month before the opening.

There is no point in attempting to describe the story line of the knee plays, for it is part and parcel of Wilson's aesthetic that there is none. Instead, the watcher is confronted by a motley assortment of symbols drawn from the stock inventory of emotionally charged detritus floating about in every half-educated intellectual's mind. On this occasion, the material consisted of a tree becoming a boat becoming a book and then ending up once again a tree. More consequential for the viewer was the heavy Oriental influence on the proceedings, an influence mostly enthroned in the choreography and in the *mise en scène*. To my Western and doubtless parochial eyes, it all seemed stiff, arbitrary, and unconvincing. The movements of the dancers, full of jerks and bodily poutings, seemed like some clumsy imitation of Japanese samurai movies on late-night television. The sets included bird-puppetry carried around the audience and a clumsily constructed boat that insisted (on the night I attended) on repeatedly falling apart. It was all creaky, and its minimalism extended well beyond its conception of its craftsmanship.

A special word, I suppose, is necessary to describe the music and the narration. Byrne's composition—it must be remembered that he wrote only the music for the knee plays: the music for the five major acts of the whole work came from other composers, including Glass— was a combination of charmless hymn tunes and the minimalist overworking of already thin material. And the narration, at least on the level of literary interest, added nothing to the evening's vitality. Seemingly heavily drawn from the deadpan monologues of performance artist Laurie Anderson—another icon of the new avant-garde artistic sensibility—Byrne's words would have been laconic had there not been quite so many of them. A quotation from the opening of the first knee play defines the curiously androgynous camp effect:

Today is an important occasion.
She thinks that she must wear the right clothes.
The right combination of clothes
. . . will make her lucky.

A quotation from the beginning of the fourth knee play adumbrates an element of schizoid alienation never very far from Wilson's work:

> I thought that if I ate the food of the area I was visiting
> That I might assimilate the point of view of the people there
> As if the point of view was somehow in the food
> So I would make no choices myself regarding what I ate.
> I would simply follow the examples of those around me.

The reception by the audience of Wilson partisans in Minneapolis fell short of delirium on the night I attended. Even the *New York Times*'s usually ebullient (at least on this subject) John Rockwell seemed to have some difficulty getting his praise started:

> Mr. Wilson is a creator of massive spectacles, and sometimes his more intimate work has looked schematic and simplistic. There was a bit of that during the first few "knee plays" on Thursday. But then Mr. Wilson exerted his spell, or one began to comprehend what he was about.

For my part, I found the whole effect both boring and amateurish, with remarkably little to show onstage for the month-long efforts of something like fifty people. Indeed, so aimless did everything seem that I could not help wondering later whether the key to both the aridity onstage in Minneapolis and the spectacular financial demands that caused the cancellation of the Olympic Arts Festival presentation was not simply Wilson's oft-trumpeted insistence on developing the final form of his works in rehearsal. This implied an emphasis on casualness and at the same time an inevitability of outcome too profound to be communicated to the participants in words. In artistic matters, after all, the line separating egoistic self-indulgence and merely not knowing what one wants is often a fine one indeed.

In the meantime, while Wilson had been preparing *the CIVIL warS*, Glass was devoting himself to opera. The first major fruit of his attempt to write for conventional opera houses was *Satyagraha*, a set of tableaux drawn from Gandhi's experiences in South Africa from 1893 to 1914. The work was commissioned by the city of Rotterdam and first performed by the Netherlands Opera in 1980; the American premiere took place in 1981 at Artpark in upstate New York; the New York premiere was given at the Brooklyn Academy in the fall of the same year. *Satyagraha*'s "libretto" was written by Glass and his associate and friend Constance DeJong, with sets and costumes by Robert Israel, and staging by Hans Nieuwenhuis.

Satyagraha's vocal text is completely drawn from the Indian *Bhagavad-Gita* and sung in Sanskrit, a language known neither by Glass nor by the participants in the performance. By Glass's own testimony he does not wish the audience to be distracted by understanding. The work's three acts are each overseen onstage by a different benevolent, totemic figure: Tolstoy, the Indian philosopher Rabindranath Tagore, and Martin Luther King, Jr. The mimed (in slow motion) Gandhi material is, of course, heavily fraught with anticipation of the American civil-rights struggles of the 1960s. The music is in Glass's repetitious and mostly motoric style, this time with the motor set on *Molto adagio*. Only the score's ingenious (though Broadway-commercial sounding) orchestration—and a moving theme at the end seemingly drawn from the apotheosis of Tchaikowsky's *Swan Lake*—saved the evening from the total tedium Glass's admirers call ecstasy. In fairness, it must be added that ten thousand tickets were purchased for the work's sold-out Brooklyn performance.

Satyagraha was the second of what Glass calls his "portrait" operas, *Einstein* being the first. The third, and latest, of these is *Akhnaten*, a work based on *Oedipus and Akhnaton*, a 1960 book of psychoanalytic speculations by Immanuel Velikovsky, a best-selling author famous for *Worlds in Collision*, an attempt to prove that the Red Sea actually did part. The work was first produced in Germany early last year. Its American performance was the result of a co-production by the Houston Grand Opera and the New York City Opera. *Akhnaten* thus arrived at the New York State Theater in November and, like all of Glass's recent operatic works, promptly sold out.

As far as my own experience of *Akhnaten* is concerned, I must confess that I only managed to last through the first act. Musically the work began with an endless arpeggiated A-minor chord. The number of notes in the arpeggios varied and sometimes quick repeated chords—also in A minor—were sounded. The stage was full of piles of sand, to which scantily clad Egyptians added water to make what one presumes were monotheistic mudpies; the eponymous hero throughout behaved in the manner of what Andrew Porter called in the *New Yorker* a hermaphrodite, a description which seems both kind and understated. The first act ended with several minutes—Andrew Porter, again displaying British caution, thought it seemed like only five—of what can only be dubbed a romp around the pyramid. At the end of the act the audience was either too stupefied or too moved or too exalted to do more than give a few rattlings of applause, which sounded like nothing so much—or so little—as the fluttering of aged pigeons' wings.

Donal Henahan in the *Times* and Peter Davis in *New York* hated it all. Henahan, no slouch with a cutting phrase, summed up the musical side of the evening this way:

> *Akhnaten* . . . is not a work whose music asks to be listened to seriously. Despite the publicity that Mr. Glass's works have received, his operas to date add up to little more than pageants with backgrounds of continually repeated, barely varied sound patterns. They stand to music as the sentence "See Spot run" stands to literature. . . .
>
> Considered strictly as an almost primitively tonal protest against the self-defeating complexity of most contemporary music, *Akhnaten* may act as a tonic, if you will forgive the pun. But it is one more example of going-nowhere music. . . .

Davis made his verdict into a prediction of the composer's future: "Glass may have reached the end of his limited resources and can think of nowhere else to go." Speaking for advanced opinion, Andrew Porter wrote respectfully and at some length on the opera, describing the work's sources and blaming the unsatisfactory nature of the outcome on the problems of the production. Porter even described the music, but the closest he could some to saying he liked it wasn't really very close at all:

> The only section of the score I've seen, the Akhnaten–Nefertiti love duet, is two hundred and seventy-five bars stuck in an arpeggiated E minor, colored by passing notes and added notes. There are pedals and some slow, occasionally dissonant counterpoints in the form of climbing chromatic scales. The lovers' voices shine out above this in a slow chorale-like melody, crossing, overlapping . . . and ending each phrase on a unison, octave, or fifth. The metres and the phrase lengths vary. It's a carefully composed, carefully proportioned stretch of music.

My own reaction to the third of *Akhnaten* I was able to endure will come as no surprise. It was rising boredom, passing through the various degrees of irritation to fidgets and anger. Is it that I was merely reacting to the presence of a strong creative personality? I hardly think so. Rather it was just the normal response of a Diogenes trying to find, not an honest man—that would by comparison be easy—but a performance of Glass or Wilson that would justify the hype. Neither man by himself had been able to bring it off. Would a collaboration succeed where each had failed?

So in the long run it all came down to *Einstein on the Beach* in Brooklyn. For months the buildup had been intense, and a veritable Niagara of printed material on the pair, all produced clearly with the cooperation of its busy subjects, had prepared the scene. The sets and the costumes from the 1976 performances had been stored, and so were available to re-create the original production. The lighting design, by Beverly Emmons, and the sound design, by Kurt Munkacsi, were repeats of 1976; many of the musicians, too, were back for the revival. The 1976 choreography (except for one dance at the beginning of Act I) had been the work of Andrew deGroat, a dancer much favored for his ability to twirl endlessly in one place; in the present performances, Lucinda Childs (who had been a lead dancer in the 1976 production and had choreographed the beginning of Act I) was the choreographer for the entire work. Several actors repeated their earlier roles; and most of the words they spoke were carried over from 1976.

The performance I attended was billed as the opening, though several performances, called previews, had been given earlier. While the news could hardly have been a total surprise, it still came as something of a shock to be informed by a sign in the lobby that the performance would last four and a half hours without intermission. Fortunately, this disciplined call to duty was leavened by a generous concession printed in the program:

As *Einstein on the Beach* is performed without intermission, the audience is invited to leave and re-enter the auditorium quietly, as necessary. The food service will remain open during performances.

With comfort and nourishment thus assured, it was possible to settle down to the performance. Though the opera was scheduled to begin at two o'clock, the music seemed already to have started when I arrived ten minutes early. This music consisted of low organ-like tones, only slowly changing, coming out of an electronic console in the orchestra pit. Anyone not familiar with the recording of Glass's score made after the Met performances in 1976 might have been pardoned for assuming that this quasi-doodling was just pre-performance tuning.

Several minutes later—but still before the official starting time—the audience's filing into the hall was matched onstage by the appearance in front of the curtain, but to one side, of Childs and Sheryl Sutton, the two dancer-actresses who were to be onstage for almost the entire length of the marathon. They sat down in front of a table in the two chairs which had been prepared for them; their costumes, clearly chosen to awaken memories of Einstein's dowdy dress, consisted of men's pants, open-necked white shirts, and suspenders. Both wore telephone-operator headsets, complete with microphones. As they sat they began to make slow, laborious motions with their hands and arms, giving the impression of being in considerable pain. At the same time they began to count numbers very slowly; sometimes other words were audible, including the fascinating phrase "Take a Toyota." As this action went on before the closed curtain, a chorus, also dressed in Einstein costume, began to file stiffly into the orchestra pit. The chorus began to sing numbers as well.

Suddenly—it was now about 2:10, and the sold-out house was still only about two-thirds full—the curtain went up, and the music, which up till now had been quite delicate, became alive with an enormous amplified rush. Childs, repeating her dance from the 1976 production, kept up a constant movement diagonally from the back of the stage to the front, and then back again; her dancing was frenetic, as was the music. From the side a crudely schematic steam locomotive, looking like an enormous child's toy, advanced ever so slowly to the center of the stage. On the back curtain a narrow band of light, like some fugitive element from a Morris Louis or Kenneth Noland painting, descended from the top to the floor.

Now a violinist dressed—surprise!—like Einstein appeared on an elevated platform in the pit, and began to play an endless solo consisting of slow single notes, mostly in scales. From the many loudspeakers could be heard nonsense containing the name "Mr. Bojangles." The male judge began, in a sententious tone, to tell a story about a modest woman—so modest that she wore a blindfold when bathing—who gave a speech in Kalamazoo on the rights of women. After describing how the woman wanted to lead her listeners in singing the national women's song, the judge went on to quote her as recommending that women should tell men, if they don't behave right, to take "their kisses right back where they came from."[1]

Now there was a huge dance sequence, illuminated by a vaporous persimmon light, which proved for me by far the highlight of the entire event. Danced by the members of the Lucinda Childs Dance Company, the choreography seemed a brilliant evocation of the post-World War II New York dance scene in all its athleticism, buoyancy, and optimism. Though it all went on too long, and though Glass's music kept up a constant drumbeat of triviality, one could not help feeling that dance, as brought to Brooklyn by Lucinda Childs, had staked its claim to full artistic stature.

From this point on things went downhill. There was a jail scene featuring what looked like two male dancers, one of whom was stated in the program to be a woman. In this scene Childs went on muttering lines typical in their combination of nonsense and alienation:

> I was in this prematurely air-conditioned supermarket and there were all these aisles and there were these bathing caps you could

[1] Interestingly, this somewhat ambivalent pitch for women was not in the 1976 recording, and presumably not in the 1976 production either. In its place was an equally sententious speech devoted to what I suppose must be called equality of sexual choice:

> In Paris there is a number of young men who are very beautiful, very charming, and very lovable. Paris is called "the city of lights." But these young men who are very beautiful, very charming, and very lovable, prefer the darkness for their social activities. . . .
>
> One of the beautiful things of Paris is a lady. She is not too broad, bordered with smiles, and very, very, very pleasant to look at. When a gentleman contemplates a lady of Paris, the gentleman is apt to exclaim "Oo la la," for the ladies of Paris are very charming. And the ladies of Paris are dedicated to the classic declaration, expressed in the words "L'amour, toujours l'amour!"

Whether or not the avant-garde is attempting to tell us that feminism has replaced free sexuality as a cause I leave to the reader to determine.

THE PROBLEM OF NEW OPERA

buy that had these kind of Fourth of July plumes on them that were red and yellow and blue and I wasn't tempted to buy one but I was reminded of the fact that I had been avoiding the beach.

As if to show that the Third World guerrilla movement is still with us, she picked up an automatic weapon and pointed it first at her colleagues onstage, then at the orchestra pit, and then finally at the paying customers.

Perhaps I tired, or perhaps the profusion of visual material and incessant music unmatched by any real story line made connected notetaking impossible. Much of the rest seemed hardly worth writing down. There was a long scene with a couple standing on the platform of a railway observation car, and another scene in which a long horizontal bar, lighted in front and meant to represent a bed, was raised ever so slowly by a cable at one side so that it became vertical; it was then raised into the flies. Toward the end of the afternoon, a little missile, perhaps two feet long, flew across the front of the stage on a guy wire against a sky-blue backdrop. This was succeeded by a nuclear explosion, and then by a new drop curtain which in the center depicted a mushroom cloud, on the top right an American bomber, and on the top left a detailed explanation in words of technical aspects of an atomic blast.

So here at last was the point of the whole work. Einstein, the shabby, music-loving, humble philosopher-scientist, had come home to roost with a vengeance. The putative disaster of the century—the threat of annihilation which produces the alienation of the person—can now be seen to rest at the feet of the greatest scientific mind of the century. If this is what comes of logical thinking, I suppose the argument would run, who could condemn Robert Wilson for putting on a melodrama without a story line, and Philip Glass for writing hours of music using only a few harmonies and even fewer harmonic and rhythmic devices?

The end of the opera, on the stage as in the recording, found Childs and Sutton sitting on a bench, not touching, as a bus driver intoned drippy words expressive of young love. It was all frightfully maudlin, and the final words seemed risible indeed.

Once more her voice was heard. "Kiss me, John," she implored. And leaning over, he pressed his lips warmly to hers in fervent osculation. . . .

At the final curtain almost all the seats in the house were still occupied, and the applause was deafening. John Rockwell wrote in the *New York Times* the next morning:

> I find it constantly involving and almost religiously moving. For those who feel the same, the performances in Brooklyn will be experiences to cherish for a lifetime.

For those who do *not* feel the same, the problem will be to understand just what took place in *Einstein* and why this work appears to have such a powerful effect on certain people. The verdict on *Einstein* as an art work must be that, as a collaboration, it represents a vastly more interesting work than either has been able to achieve on his own. As music heard apart from the stage spectacle (and at low volume on one's home phonograph), Glass's score seems not only harmless but even appealing, as if it were quite content to function as a sentimental pop anodyne; heard in the visual context of Wilson's shameless exploitation of contemporary anomie, the music takes on a character no more musically impressive, but vastly more evocative of a certain kind of cultural despair. As stage spectacle, Wilson's aimless cramming together of overworked metaphors is tied together and even integrated by the frenzied electronic sameness of the music. The result doubtless is the putting into art of a unique moment in modern culture: the moment in the 1970s when it had become clear to all the participants that the best, if not the only, causes were those undertaken strictly for oneself.

The social characteristics of the audience for *Einstein* are, I think, quite clear. Affluent, relatively educated, moderately successful in the professions, old enough to know about the 1960s, too young to know that the events of the 1960s had a historical context beyond personal concerns. The other side of this concentration on self is a loss of faith in a transcendent order, a loss which hardly renders less necessary the satisfaction of human needs for comfort and reassurance. It is about this situation that Stephen Holden wrote in the *Times* on the Sunday of the *Einstein* opening (in an admiring article titled "The Avant-Garde Is Big Box Office"):

> Whether mystical or nonsensical, the idea of evoking a totality of experience is the essential thrust behind works like "Einstein

on the Beach." . . . But that reality isn't a rarefied perception of truth and God toward which high art has traditionally directed audiences, but a multiplicity of images and sounds, from cartoons to Mozart. Its appeal may come from its attempt to embrace not only the familiar but—everything we don't know and can only imagine.

Doubtless *Einstein*, like other products of the counterculture and its fossil remnants, has a political cast attractive to its viewers. But those who are determined to find in this ideology manifestations of an orthodox left-wing, state-oriented disposition will be wrong: the politics of *Einstein* and its kindred is that beguiling, irresponsible variety of anarchism so endemic in an educated middle class which, no matter how existentially alienated, still wants someone else to pay for its amenities, whether these amenities be urban redevelopment or cultural offerings.

In this regard, it is significant that the requisite financial support for the entire range of Brooklyn Academy "Next Wave" offerings does not come from the audience, which pays only a part of the cost of mounting the various events. Even the huge gross for *Einstein* failed to cover the costs of reviving a previously paid-for production. It is significant, too, that it was not the audience that was to cover the expenses of *the CIVIL warS* at the Los Angeles Olympics. Indeed, in neither case was the lion's share of the money to come from private patrons of vast means. Rather the money was to come from corporations, foundations, and, most especially, governments. In the case of *the CIVIL warS*, most of the necessary money had already come from foreign governments via their own lavish support of culture. In the case of *Einstein* a glance at the acknowledgments page in the 1984 "Next Wave" souvenir booklet discloses that the first seven donor names saluted are the National Endowment for the Arts, the National Endowment for the Humanities, the Rockefeller Foundation, the Howard Gilman Foundation, the Ford Foundation, the Pew Memorial Trusts, and AT&T.

If this analysis of the audience is correct, one can understand why the *New York Times*, Gotham's mission to (and trading post for) the Yuppies, is in the forefront of the publicity wave for the "Next Wave" festival, and also why the *Wall Street Journal*, that former bastion of bourgeois respectability, has published material extolling Glass on tour as well as the doings in Brooklyn. Whether the *Journal*'s writer is experimental music critic (and *Village Voice* regular) Gregory Sandow or opera and dance buff Dale Harris, the tone is one of wonder and gratitude for the new—and popular—riches being proffered. Clearly these newspapers have identified an audience, not just for a certain kind of culture, but for themselves.

Given the current success of *Einstein*, two questions about the movement it exemplifies remain to be discussed: its future as box office and its future as art. Despite all the claims made for the burgeoning commercial success of this branch of the avant-garde, the fact remains that its productions, from solo appearances to fully staged events, require hefty subsidies from nonprofit sources. The one example usually cited as showing the financial potential of this material is the hit English single "O Superman" by Laurie Anderson. Though it briefly was near the top of the English rock-singles charts and inspired Warner Bros. to sign her to a contract here, it has proved incapable of replication either by Anderson or by any of her colleagues and imitators. The costs necessary to put these events on, whether in lighting, staging, dancing, or audio, are onerous, and audiences for intellectually trendy attractions are notoriously fickle. Furthermore, there is no sign that this material is capable of appealing to an uneducated mass audience on the one hand or to traditionally oriented music lovers on the other. It must be added, too, that any artistic product so tied up with the particular historical and personal experiences of its devotees tends to find it hard to attract new audiences who must come fresh to the offering.

None of the above considerations, of course, has any necessary relationship to artistic validity and potential. Whatever the stature of *Einstein on the Beach* as an art work in itself may be, it seems clear enough that it has not had progeny as successful as it was immediately upon its birth. It is equally clear, it bears repeating, that neither Wilson nor Glass, working separately, has been able to achieve the success on his own that they have earned together. Once again, we may take the word of John Rockwell that at least so far *Einstein* is *sui generis*: for him, "This Wilson–Glass collaboration is the major achievement in the performing arts of the minimalist esthetic." Wilson and Glass may, it is conceivable, decide to work together again on something new; it should be borne in mind, however, that sequels which have as their only purpose the repetition of an earlier success usually fizzle.

And so, the 1984 "Next Wave" festival in Brooklyn is history. But the grants go on, and the yards of favorable publicity already generated guarantee no shortage of future events in Brooklyn and elsewhere. Whether one calls *Einstein on the Beach* performance art or multimedia, there can be little doubt that it symbolizes the nearest we have yet come in this country to an art form crafted to the tastes of what has been called the new class, that group which, we are told, alone possesses the skills to run our society. The new class certainly will have progeny; will its art?

II.

The New York City Opera, as I have said earlier, remains a problem child in New York and American musical life. Of its two chief functions, doing familiar operas for a large public and new or unfamiliar operas for sophisticates, the latter is by far the more difficult. Worthwhile new works, alas, cannot be created to order, but must be created by fallible artists working in difficult times. In the case of Dominick Argento's Casanova, *the subject of this January 1986* New Criterion *article, the time seemed ripe to welcome a work of enduring substance to the operatic canon. But in spite of critical enthusiasm on all sides, the very cynicism somehow central to* Casanova *as a work of art militated against its permanence, and once again the opera world was left with a flash—a glittering one, to be sure—in the pan.*

Casanova *at the City Opera*

THERE IS A CURIOUS, though little-noticed, aspect to the reports that come out of performances of new American operas. As with political candidates who are always winning (to hear them tell it) until the very instant they absolutely must concede, the mood emanating from first performances and new productions of contemporary American works is always determinedly upbeat. In the case of each new opera, we are told that the audience loved it; that the cast and orchestra applauded the composer with *real* enthusiasm; that the critics thrilled to the sound of their own praise; that this time at least the cause of new native opera *really* has a winner. Unfortunately, time and time again over the last twenty-five years, the love of the audience, the applause of the performers, the thrill of the critics, and the operas themselves are forgotten. And after every disappointment the cycle starts up again with the same threadbare optimism, only to end with the same weary resignation.

Dominick Argento's *Casanova*, performed three times in the first two weeks of November by the New York City Opera in the State Theater at Lincoln Center, seems to be another possible exception to this rule of failed optimism followed by oblivion. Originally entitled *Casanova's Homecoming*, the work was written as a commission from the Minnesota Opera, by whom it was performed last spring in a co-production with the St. Paul Chamber Orchestra. Its November performances by the City Opera marked its New York premiere, and its first appearances after the world premiere. Critical reception in New York ranged from enthusiastic to overwhelming, and there now seems little doubt that the City Opera will repeat *Casanova* next season, and that the example of Beverly Sills's company will inspire other productions across the United States in the coming years.

The work that now enjoys such happy prospects is an operatic setting—to a libretto written by composer Argento himself—of Casanova's return home to Venice in 1774 as a relatively old man of forty-nine. Partly true and partly invented, the plot involves three major episodes, one per act. The subject of Act I is Casanova's seduction of an opera singer who Casanova's enemies think is a castrato, but who turns out to be just what the always-wise Casanova thought, a very feminine and passionate woman. In Act II Casanova, an adept at necromancy and the occult, conceives and carries out an elaborate scheme for tricking a rich old woman, who wants to be reborn into the body of a male infant, into giving up her jewels to provide a dowry for one of Casanova's godchildren. In Act III, it seems at first that Casanova's time has come, for he is accused of practicing magic, of defrauding the old woman, and of murdering her by exposing her to a storm on the Grand Canal during the process of robbing her. But then Casanova talks his way out of the charges by showing—falsely—that he had only received a small amount of money from the woman, and that the "magic" he had practiced on her had only been making love to her. The opera thus ends happily, with everyone beaming. Casanova is shown to be a rogue so good-hearted as not to be a rogue at all, but instead a philosopher who teaches us how to get the best out of life.

In order to present on the stage a story so rife with possibilities for broad humor and comedy, the production of *Casanova* employed richly costumed crowds, numerous sight gags, acting marked by broad gestures and mugging, and technical effects that included storm-tossed waves and, at the final celebration of the Casanova philosophy, fireworks. The guiding principle of the stage direction seemed everywhere to be a maximum of busy movement, a veritable froth of activity designed to provide a full dollar's worth of entertainment in the theater.

To deal with the bedeviling problem of what to do with the words, which now seem to be so necessary in opera, this production resorted to the currently red-hot practice of surtitles, called subtitles in the evening's program. These snippets of the sung text are displayed in two lines of relatively dim letters projected on a broad band at the top of the proscenium, extending across its entire width. The obvious reason for the insertion of this mechanical device between singers and audience—even when the opera being done is in English, as *Casanova* was—is the difficulty performers have in pronouncing the text clearly as they sing, a difficulty frequently compounded by the large houses in which opera is done in this country and by the impossibility (in any space) of being heard against the large accompanying orchestras. But opera has survived across the decades without the singers' words being very much more clearly heard than they are today. Why then the present rage for understanding, and for the surtitles which, it is hoped, will allow such understanding?

The answer, quite plainly, is that the audience must clearly understand the words because the *music* can no longer be counted on to make the necessary dramatic effect. Remarkably, this is true for today's expanded opera public even in the cases of the great *musical* masterpieces of the repertory. No longer can Mozart's, or Verdi's, or Wagner's, or Puccini's, or Strauss's music be counted on to satisfy an increasingly ill-educated and unsophisticated audience. Untutored and vacant minds wander, and the best way of keeping them attached to the performance seems to be to make them hang on every word.

What is true for accepted—and supposedly familiar—masterpieces is doubly true for new and recent works, written in contemporary and often difficult musical styles. It is no secret that new music—to adapt Paul Klee's phrase about the visual arts—*trägt kein Volk*: new composition is not supported by the audience, as we have all learned to our sorrow. Thus for twentieth-century operas an understanding of the words as they are being sung seems to provide the only possibility of exciting public interest.

In the case of the City Opera production of *Casanova*, the surtitles undoubtedly did their job. Time and again, one had the feeling that the audience was laughing at the words not as they came out of the singers' mouths but rather as they appeared on the screen some forty feet above the performers' heads. Since it seems unlikely that a viewer of opera can look simultaneously at the screen and at the singers onstage—a difficulty immeasurably greater the closer one sits—this performance of *Casanova* presented the anomaly of an audience reacting not to what it heard (and saw) being sung, but rather to what it was reading at more or less the same time.

What was slighted here was not just the text as sung. The chief casualty of these frenzied attempts to involve the audience in the opera was the requirement of taking Argento's music seriously. Perhaps this really was a blessing in disguise, for as music what Argento wrote seemed largely pastiche. The impression resulted from what must have been a conscious attempt on the composer's part to quote from musical and operatic styles of Casanova's day, and also from the influence of those twentieth-century composers—Richard Strauss and Igor Stravinsky come immediately to mind—whose own compositions were often based on borrowings. The danger for Argento's music was that it would be heard—at least by sophisticated listeners—not simply in its own terms but in the terms of its models. A further danger was that it would be judged not merely against its eighteenth-century models but against the way Strauss and Stravinsky used the work of others to find their individual styles.

Faced with this competition, it cannot be said that Argento's music comes out very well. In Act I, for example, the writing "in the style of" Niccolò Jommelli (1714–1774), "one of Casanova's favorite composers" (according to an article in the City Opera magazine *Spotlight*), not only seems scrappy and lacking in any long line; it signally fails to achieve the piquancy and affecting charm of Strauss's extraordinary appropriation of Jean-Baptiste Lully (1632–1687)—and others—in the music for Molière's *Le Bourgeois Gentilhomme* (1912–18). In the climactic moments of Act III, it is again Strauss who provides the successful material by which Argento must be judged. At the very end of the opera, when one can feel Argento attempting to invoke every talent he possesses to write lyrically affecting music, the crucial phrase seems to have been lifted from the tumultuous moment in

Strauss's *Elektra* (1909) just after Aegistheus and Klytemnaestra have been killed by Orestes.

Because Argento's music is built up out of so many short and disparate bursts, the listener is reminded of Stravinsky as well as of Strauss. It was Stravinsky, after all, who wrote *The Rake's Progress* (1951), an opera on a similar subject. That *Rake*, in which so much depends upon the device of the bearded lady, was not so far from Argento's mind is shown by Casanova's words as he watches a *commedia dell'arte* troupe present their own mocking version of his seduction of a purported castrato: "Not bad! That's *almost* the way it was, but you forget one thing—she also had a *long* beard!" Argento's use of eighteenth-century music in Act I, too, cannot but summon up recollections of how Stravinsky used the models of Gluck and Mozart in *Rake* to an altogether more interesting—and more musically satisfying—purpose. Perhaps not less important, Argento's music suffers by comparison with Stravinsky's heroic achievement in *Pulcinella* (his ballet after Pergolesi, 1920) of reforming our entire modern idea of the way old music, played in its original form, should sound.

Taken on its own merits, without regard to the question of the superiority of its models, Argento's music lacks the long line (composed of both melody and architectonic structure) which is the chief bringer of musical power. The ability to write this long line, whether original or derivative, is a specifically musical gift. Necessary as long line is to pure music, it—and not an excellent libretto or a sure feeling for stagecraft—is the *sine qua non* of operatic composition. Its absence is most conspicuously marked at the great emotional and musical denouements of opera. And so it is in *Casanova*: the moment Argento's *musical* talent should take over, in order to justify the entire work, is in Casanova's concluding statement of his philosophy:

The important thing is: to live; to love;
And most of all—to love living.

"My system, if it can be called a system,
Has been to glide away unconcernedly on the stream of life—
  Sequere Deum—
Trusting to the wind wherever it led.

For happy or miserable,
Life is the only blessing man possesses

And those who do not love it are unworthy of it."

Prize it above all things. And

Praise it as much for the darkness as the light.

Whatever the merits of these paltry sentiments as a guide for life, they deserve—if *Casanova* is to prevail as a work of art—a powerful musical treatment. But this does not happen: instead the music is thin, plain, and even angular, thus giving the impression that the composer himself can't believe what his hero is saying at the climax of the opera.

Here, then, is the problem of pastiche in music: the problem not just of Argento's use of pastiche, but of everyone's. The Strauss of the complete score for *Le Bourgeois Gentilhomme* and the Stravinsky of *The Rake's Progress*, though they are recognized as great composers who have written, in these cases, fascinating and beautiful works, have both found it uphill sledding to convince the music-loving public that these works come directly from the heart.[1] The problem with the works of Strauss and Stravinsky is writ large in *Casanova*: it is that of projecting an integrated and consistent view toward the characters and their situation, a view which can only be expressed by the composer through an integrated and consistent musical style. The extraneous elements brought into the score by a conscious dependence on the art music of others—no matter how apt this borrowed music might be for the dramatic situation at any given moment, and no matter how much better it might be as music than any original music written by the composer whose name goes on the title page—must inevitably destroy the unity which is the proudest hallmark of a great work of art.

So in the end the problem of Dominick Argento's *Casanova* is not that it is musically conservative, or even that the vocal writing often seems to be swamped by the instrumental parts which lie beneath. It is rather that the composer Argento never makes clear to us that he believes the words that the librettist Argento has so cleverly written. And so everything in *Casanova* is a joke, and by the end of the opera

---

[1] Significantly, the complete music Strauss wrote for *Le Bourgeois Gentilhomme*, despite the many felicities it contains (occurring in passages not present in the frequently played suite of "Incidental Music" from the play) and despite the interest which should attach to this collaboration of Strauss, Hugo van Hofmannsthal, and Max Reinhardt, is almost never performed, and remains unrecorded to this day.

it hardly matters whether the jokes are meant to be jokes or are just the mock-serious mouthings of silly and foppish people onstage.

When snappily performed, as it was in November at the New York City Opera, *Casanova* is in fact a superior evening of entertainment in the musical theater. Given the paucity of even entertainment in the new works being presented at opera houses these days, this might seem like rather a lot to say. And indeed it is, if the purpose of opera— under the new dispensation of public culture for ever larger audiences— is to be the diversion of audiences. If the purpose is, as it should be, enlightenment about the highest human and aesthetic values and achievements, then *Casanova*, in its very success, marks yet another nail driven in the coffin of a serious American opera. But then the funeral business has always been a profitable one, much in demand.

12.

Virgil Thomson died in 1989 at the age of ninety-two, rich in friends and honors—but not in performances. In retrospect, it seems clear that his two operatic settings of Gertrude Stein texts, Four Saints in Three Acts *and* The Mother of Us All, *have survived on the fringes of the repertory because of their unique combination of artistic merit and social timeliness:* Four Saints, *with an all-black cast at its premiere in 1934, and* The Mother, *with its evocation of suffragism in the past and its hints of latter-day feminism yet to come. No such added social value can be claimed for* Lord Byron, *about whose second New York production—a semi-production at that—I wrote in the Spring 1986* Grand Street. *And so this touching work languishes, despite its passages of real beauty and its tender nostalgia. My closing remarks about the cowardly unwillingness of operatic administrators to face a world without the guarantee of public-relations success remain at least as applicable to the breed today.*

Lord Byron *Undone*

L ORD B YRON , Virgil Thomson's third, and one must assume final, opera, was given by the New York Opera Repertory Theatre, in a semistaged concert production at Alice Tully Hall in New York last December 7, to celebrate the composer's eighty-ninth birthday. This performance was long awaited, for the opera had not been done since its premiere, in a full production, by the Juilliard American Opera Center in 1972. Despite remarkably little advance publicity in the *New York Times* (and elsewhere), the house was full, and the audio portion of the performance was broadcast live across the United States on the American Public Radio network, a new and energetic competitor to the older National Public Radio.

Thomson's two earlier works, *Four Saints in Three Acts* (1927–28, orchestrated 1933) and *The Mother of Us All* (1947), both to librettos by Gertrude Stein, now seem exceptions to the languishing condition of most recent American operas. Though it cannot be said that either opera has been widely produced, each possesses many sophisticated and even passionate admirers; at present, *Four Saints* is something of a modernist classic and *The Mother of Us All* is well on the road to folk-opera status.

By contrast, it has proven difficult to get *Lord Byron* so much as a hearing. Written between 1961 and 1968 to a libretto by Jack Larson, the work was first envisioned as a Metropolitan Opera commission. According to the composer, the enthusiasm for *Lord Byron* of the Met's then general manager, Rudolf Bing, cooled when a prospective backer for the production turned out to be more interested in a work by someone else. According to another version, the European-oriented Mr. Bing hadn't liked the piece very much from the first. Whatever the reason, the Met got out of the picture, and *Lord Byron* had to wait several years for its 1972 Juilliard premiere.

Sadly, the first performance of *Lord Byron* was a repetition on a smaller scale of the debacle in 1966 at the Metropolitan Opera premiere of Samuel Barber's *Antony and Cleopatra*. The opening of the Met's new house in Lincoln Center was the moment for the largest, most consequential failure in the history of American opera. Mitigating circumstances—fancy new stage machinery didn't work properly, the audience for that gala of all galas was hardly in the mood for anything new and challenging, and for months before the event itself had been oversold—could not disguise the magnitude of the disaster: the fate of *Antony and Cleopatra* had proven to everyone's satisfaction that the most ambitious American opera, even as done by the Met, could not work.

The lesson taken from Barber's very grand work was underscored six years later with Thomson's smaller-scale effort. As was often the case, the *New York Times*'s chief critic Harold C. Schonberg was representative of what passes for enlightened opinion in America's cultural capital. Schonberg found himself little interested in *Byron*'s libretto and was content to do no more than introduce his own summary with the minatory words "Byron was a protean figure, and a librettist dealing with him has his work cut out." About Thomson's music, however, Schonberg was willing to make some normative judgments *sub specie aeternitatis*:

Mr. Thomson has provided a very bland score. He has used some heavier dissonance than is to be found in his two previous operas, but there is also a good amount of the "white key" music that is basic to his style. What is missing is the charm and sophistication of "Four Saints in Three Acts" and "The Mother of Us All". . . .

The vocal settings are done with the skill of a composer who understands words. But the music is often distressingly banal (those waltzes!) and frequently gaggingly cutesy. . . .

Melodically . . . the content is very thin, and the tunes, hard as they try to fly, bump the ground. It is hard to imagine Mr. Thomson writing a conventional opera, but with "Lord Byron" he has nobly succeeded.

So dismissive was the initial reaction to *Lord Byron* that it was something of a surprise when Andrew Porter, writing in the *New Yorker* in 1977, found a tape of the Juilliard performance (as broadcast in celebration of the composer's eightieth birthday) "a welcome rehearing of an opera that I felt was generally underrated at the time of its premiere." Though Porter continued with a tribute to the work's real distinction, he encapsulated within that tribute what can only be deemed an apology:

Lord Byron must inevitably disappoint anyone expecting a redly romantic, heart-on-sleeve, conventionally "Byronic" opera; it has nothing in common with Berlioz's *Le Corsaire* or *Harold en Italie*, Verdi's *Il corsaro* or *I due Foscari*, Schumann's or Tchaikovsky's *Manfred*, or any of the other numerous nineteenth-century compositions that Byron's poetry inspired. Thomson and his librettist, Jack Larson, have not dramatized the poet as the poet dramatized himself. Their opera, an elegant and cultivated piece, affords pleasures kin to those of witty, lively, precise, shapely conversation on an interesting subject.

Toward the end of his long and considered review, Porter once again offered praise, this time musical, but praise clearly mixed with major reservations:

Thomson has the gift to be simple; his notes come down where they ought to be, in the place just right. But his simplicity is that of a master, not a naïf. The music is not artless but careful, refined and purified by a process that has not destroyed its zest. *Lord Byron*, while decorous and controlled, is also lively; Thomson's evident joy in setting down a witty musical idea as neatly as possible proves infectious. The opera may lack the fresh, free lyric inspiration of *The Mother of Us All*, his masterpiece, and it is certainly a less moving work.[1]

It was only to be expected, given the interest that always attaches in a premiere to the work itself, that the performance afforded *Lord Byron* at Juilliard would have come in for relatively little attention. Thus Schonberg, though best known as a critic for his concern with performance, confined himself to a single paragraph at the end of his review, beginning with the summary judgment, "Of the singers and orchestra, nothing but praise. Gerhard Samuel [the conductor] led a controlled performance, and the singers were uniformly excellent." Porter, usually less concerned with performance than the more virtuoso-inclined Schonberg, had not even this much to say, merely noting (and then only between parentheses) that "the Juilliard cast managed the notes with accomplishment, the style less securely." It must also be added that listening to the tape of the Juilliard performance thirteen years after it was made suggests that for all the good intentions of those involved, and for all the sizeable talents of many of the singers, one's impression is of a difficult work uncomfortably, and ultimately inadequately, rendered.

In any case, so negative was the reaction to the Juilliard premiere that the composer himself embarked upon major revisions to *Lord Byron*. These revisions, with one exception, involved frequent small-scale cutting, as if Thomson thought that the problems of the opera's reception had been caused by the short attention span of the audience. He also made one long excision, removing the ballet at the end of the closing act; this cut (as Porter pointed out) at least made sense because it involved the removal of music written many years before that did not cohere stylistically with the rest of the work. All these cuts are retained in the published version of the score which formed the basis for the December Alice Tully Hall performance. This performance

---

[1] Schonberg's review was not reprinted in his collected criticism, *Facing the Music* (1981), and so may be found only in the *New York Times* of April 22, 1972; Porter's review is reprinted in his 1978 collection, *Music of Three Seasons 1974–1977*.

was not only severely cut; Thomson, still attempting to find a winning shape for *Lord Byron*, recast the work's original three acts into two, telescoping the action still more.

Whether in the form performed at Juilliard or at Alice Tully Hall, *Lord Byron* is a musical setting of events, real and imagined, taking place in 1824 immediately after the arrival of the poet's body in London from Greece. The opera opens[2] in Westminster Abbey, as the ghosts of England's great poets mourn their dead colleague. Byron's half-sister Augusta Leigh and his estranged wife Annabella, his friends John Cam Hobhouse and the poet Thomas Moore, and his publisher (and thus not quite friend) John Murray wish him to be buried in the Abbey surrounded by the greats of Poets' Corner. The mourners are joined by Byron's mistress Teresa Guiccioli and her brother, who have brought Byron's body back from Greece, along with a statue of him. To the discomfiture of all, they learn that Byron has left behind a memoir containing the true story of his life and loves. A flashback now presents a party scene at Lord Melbourne's in 1812, where the famous Byron is surrounded by young women asking him to dance the then new waltz, but because of his clubfoot he refuses. In the next flashback, occurring two years later, Lady Melbourne advises Byron to escape the scandal about his incestuous relationship with his half-sister by marrying Annabella Milbanke, Lady Melbourne's niece; Byron and Annabella meet, and Act I ends as they fall in love.

Act II of *Lord Byron* begins with two more flashbacks. The first takes place on the night before Byron's and Annabella's wedding, as Byron and his friends amuse themselves at an alcoholic bachelor dinner by railing against women, and, at another party taking place simultaneously, Augusta Leigh and Lady Melbourne join Annabella in admiring her trousseau. The next flashback describes a scene after the wedding, in which the pregnant Lady Byron surprises Byron and Augusta Leigh in a compromising situation; Byron asks Augusta to elope with him to the Continent, but she refuses. He has no choice but to go into exile. The opera ends back in Westminster Abbey in 1824, as Byron's friends and associates decide—not without protest from

---

[2] My description of the action follows the two-act Alice Tully Hall version, rather than the three-act version presented at Juilliard.

Moore and Teresa Guiccioli—to burn the incriminating memoirs. As Hobhouse begins the act of destruction, the Dean of the Abbey notices what he is doing, uses the burning as an admission of Byron's sinful life, and refuses burial in the hallowed church. Teresa Guiccioli leaves, taking the statue with her, and the opera ends as the poets' lament for Byron's fate is put to an end by the ghost of Shelley who, along with the poets of England's past, welcomes Byron into the company of the immortals.

Jack Larson's libretto for *Lord Byron* uses many bits of the poet's own verse and surrounds these bits with words written in a style always comfortable in the Byronic context. But the problems of writing a libretto on the subject of Byron are hardly confined to stylistic integrity and even to poetic aspiration. The difficulty is with the character of Byron; there can be no doubt that Schonberg was right when he remarked that anyone wanting to write a libretto about Byron "has his work cut out." This difficulty is very likely one particular to our own time. The nineteenth century could deal with the scandal of an artist's life by prettifying it and minimizing that which it could not make edifying. The facts of Byron's extravagantly wild personal conduct were sufficiently well known to the early Victorians, and even before. His way with women, like his fight for Greek national independence, was a central element in the myth of his poetry. His relationship with his half-sister, no less than his homosexual passions while in school and at the squalid end of his life in Missolonghi, were either on the printed record or readily deducible from what was. But the nineteenth century was interested in the life of the poet not for itself but for what it added to the poetry. It was the poetry that carried the man, not the man the poetry. The nineteenth-century appetite for poetry was insatiable; we today who lament the present economic plight of poetry and the poet can hardly ignore the startling fact that the British public bought ten thousand copies of Byron's *The Corsair* on the first day of publication in 1814; by the end of the first month the poem had gone into seven editions and sold twenty-five thousand copies.

Today much of Byron's life cannot be seen simply as that of a great poet who happened, *inter alia*, to be a rake. Now, of course, we find it easier to be concerned more with the rake than the poet; indeed, as shown by the recent flurry of interest (including the lead review in the

New York Review of Books) in Louis Crompton's tendentious if readable *Byron and Greek Love*, our excitement over Byron is more likely to be awakened by the possibility of his being a homosexual libertine. Interestingly enough—perhaps showing just how much they were behind the times—Thomson and his librettist Jack Larson decided to treat Byron the lover in a traditional manner. Thomson made this decision explicit in an interview with the writer and critic John Gruen in the *Times* just before the Juilliard premiere:

> Actually, his homosexual amours were limited to his schooldays in England and maybe a little bit in college, which is normal enough for an Englishman of his class. The opera makes a passing reference to one such liaison. But his big amours, and later amours, were always with women.

What is daring about Thomson's *Lord Byron* is therefore not the piquancy of its libretto; it is rather the music. The musical mood of much of the score is that of what used to be called at the turn of the century "Heart Songs": English, Scottish, and Irish folk melodies, love ballads, Stephen Foster, all tender sentiments clothed in Protestant hymn-tune progressions. Some may cavil at Thomson's use of the lovely Irish melody of "Believe Me If All Those Endearing Young Charms"—verse by Thomas Moore—to set words written by the opera's librettist. But the effect of this use of material which in anyone else's hands would be called—and rightly so—pastiche is touchingly authentic because Virgil Thomson's musical world, in all its simplicity and familiar plainness, is deeply rooted in those nineteenth-century Americanisms formed by the interaction between our social experience and our cultural inheritance.

Nowadays musical nationalism—at least for Americans—is despised. There was a time when it seemed that America would bring forth an art music based on our own common experience. But that dream, despite early successes, was dashed after the Second World War by our failing to find a middle way between the twin avant-gardes of European system building and cranky American experimentalism. Thomson, because of his perception of the linkage, and perhaps even the identity, between an important part of nineteenth-century American musical life and the rest of our shared cultural tradition, is practically the last survivor of our sometime dream. Using a style recognizably his own, in *Lord Byron* Thomson has found the musical means to write an opera that makes clear the poet's central position not just in nineteenth-century English language poetry but also in our shared American cultural tradition.

It must be stressed that what Thomson has achieved in *Lord Byron* is so to enhance an existing subject through the medium of music that a new, and greater, subject is created. This is perhaps the highest goal of opera, and twice before Thomson has accomplished it, both times using the quasi-nonsense words of Gertrude Stein. His achievement in *Four Saints* was to create a distinctive American amalgam of the sophistication of Stein's linguistic modernism and the childlike innocence of the pure, relatively untrained, sound of black voices; his achievement in *The Mother of Us All* was to combine Stein's words with the pageantlike presentation of figures from the American political past. Now, in *Lord Byron*, he has made the poet live anew for our time by reminding us of a vernacular Byron, a free-flowing, bountiful genius who in belonging to us all happily in no way resembles the ideal type of the alienated poet so beloved of fashionable literary critics.

It would be a pleasure to report that Thomson's achievement in *Lord Byron* was done justice in the New York Opera Repertory Theatre performance. But such was not the case. What one saw on the stage seemed rudimentary at best, stiff in conception and halting in dramatic realization. Even the best-disposed viewer could hardly indulge that suspension of disbelief necessary in so seemingly artificial an art as opera. A short stairway going nowhere, some columns and chairs, the spectral English poetic greats dressed rather like cricketers, Byron's chief associates in tuxedos, and three English ladies in shiny peach dresses—it all seemed uncomfortably like a refined variety of dinner theater. And, as is true in dinner theater, few of the singers seemed able to provide any characterization of the roles they played; indeed (with one exception, that of the portrayer of Byron himself) it might have been an evening of oratorio rather than opera.

The music of *Lord Byron* was hardly better served by the Alice Tully Hall performance. Though the singing was uneven, the chief musical culprit of the night was the conductor (and co-director of the New York Opera Repertory Theatre), Leigh Gibbs Gore. Throughout the work the orchestra, which included many excellent New York free-lance musicians, played too loudly and too heavily. Part of this loudness and heaviness was doubtless caused by the presence of the orchestra on the stage just behind the singers, rather than in the acoustically less forward environment of the pit. But much of the trouble was a consequence of the musical direction; there could be little doubt that the excellent players were egged on to greater and more labored exertions by the large and vehement motions of the conductor. And the conductor too was responsible for the prevailingly quick tempos, tempos which seemed time and again to put the singers (and the chorus) under uncomfortable pressure.

Some of the singing was excellent. I was particularly taken with baritone Herbert Perry (Hobhouse), tenor Charles Walker (Murray), and mezzo-soprano Candice Burrows (Lady Jane). I could only sympathize with tenor Paul Spenser Adkins in the immensely difficult leading role. The role is both vocally onerous, because so much of it lies so high, and theatrically difficult, because of the need for Byron to look commanding at the same time as he must win sympathy for his pronounced limp. It cannot be said that Adkins triumphantly surmounted the vocal challenges. His high C's were not held long enough, and they sounded strangled into the bargain. Even when he was more successful with the notes as written, the quality of his voice was hardly euphonious and often seemed to have a grating quality.

It cannot be denied that Adkins, alone of all the singers onstage, did manage to convey a dramatic image of the character he portrayed. But his Byron seemed soft, troubled, even anxiety-ridden, a creature of pity rather than of majesty. In his attempt to project the poet's limp, Adkins seemed always to move in a kind of tense and pressured, though clumsy, glide, as if he were responding to some inner imperative never to move naturally and never to show a moment's pleasure. His Byron was the poet as petulant child, rather than as the artist in whose honor our ancestors coined the adjective *Byronic*.

Throughout most of the evening the singers' diction was nothing short of atrocious. Considering the felicity with which Thomson sets English, this failure came as a surprise. Much of the problem doubtless was caused by the loud playing of the orchestra and its prominent position onstage; much too was caused by the little attention given to clear enunciation of the words in today's education of singers. It is a tribute to the quality of Thomson's music that the work makes sense—and projects a strong dramatic impact in such scenes as those involving Byron and Annabella Milbanke and Byron and Augusta Leigh—even when nothing in the libretto can be understood. Whether a composer who takes language as seriously as Thomson does should have to struggle against this kind of handicap is another matter.

However laudable the intentions of the New York Opera Repertory Theatre in putting on *Lord Byron*, and however laudable the intention of the Juilliard American Opera Center in attempting the same task more than a decade ago, it is clear that vastly more in the way of ensemble experience and professional resources are necessary to put this opera on in the way it requires and deserves than is available either to an ad hoc group of free-lancers or to even our best music school. Opera production is hardly an occasional matter, and here as elsewhere what is needed is a fully staged production at the highest level of musical and theatrical expertise.

And so the critic, just as the opera lover, is faced with the old question: why does a notable American work find it almost impossible to receive a performance consonant with its distinction—when it manages to receive a performance at all? I have alluded earlier to the difficulties of Barber's *Antony and Cleopatra*; fortunately, a recording made at the 1983 Spoleto Festival in Italy, now available on New World Records, manages to keep the work a presence in our ears, if not for our eyes. Two other postwar American operas of the greatest importance, Roger Sessions's *Montezuma* (1963) and Hugo Weisgall's *Six Characters in Search of an Author* (1956), lack even recorded representation in our repertory. Significantly, Thomson's earlier two operas, relatively "popular" as they undoubtedly are, have not only never been done by the Metropolitan Opera (that goes without saying) but have also never been done by the New York City Opera, whose very *raison d'être* should be the doing of just such works. It is small consolation that *Lord Byron* is not alone on this infamous roster of artistic neglect. It is small consolation, too, that other—and inferior— works are done, in highly advertised productions, by the City Opera and other leading American companies. Just a few years ago, for example, much approving attention was garnered by the Opera Theatre of St. Louis production of Stephen Paulus's *The Postman Always Rings Twice*; the Houston Grand Opera production of Carlisle

Floyd's *Willie Stark* even managed to be shown on PBS network television. Last season the attention of the press was focused on the Virginia Opera world premiere of Thea Musgrave's *Harriet, the Woman Called Moses*; and just this past fall, everyone seemed to be applauding the City Opera's presentation of Dominick Argento's *Casanova*.

Why then have these works been put on to what seems like general approval even if not commercial success, when others have not? The answer—at least based upon my own serious listening to the tapes of all of them—cannot be musical distinction, for of this rare quality they have passing little. Of the theatrical qualities of two of these works I cannot speak, not having seen *The Postman Always Rings Twice* or *Harriet, the Woman Called Moses*. But I have seen *Willie Stark* on television and *Casanova* live in the opera house; *Willie Stark* is indeed a work of great dramatic force, a virtue which it owes entirely to its Huey Long-based story rather than to its music, and *Casanova* is full of fetching stage business and delicious lines, if not of any memorable music. But clearly the problem is not simply one of theatrical effectiveness, for *Six Characters* and *Montezuma*—both of which I have seen—are of gripping dramatic force when staged, in addition to their high musical quality.

So if the distinguishing feature of the operas that do get put on is not musical superiority or theatrical superiority, what is it? The answer is, I think, inescapable: the operas that are put on reflect the personal taste, and the artistic judgment, of those in charge. That taste and judgment are basically vulgar and deeply anti-intellectual. It is remarkable that of the operas which I have mentioned as belonging to the class of those which despite their merit are ignored, all—I repeat, all—are in an important sense intellectual in their subject matter and its treatment. *Antony and Cleopatra* is an ambitious setting of Shakespeare; *Six Characters* is based on Pirandello's classic modernist play; *Montezuma* deals with the epochal encounter between the Spanish and the Aztec in the New World; *Lord Byron*, as we have seen, is concerned with the life and literary immortality of a great poet. All these operas, employing widely different musical styles, treat subjects demanding serious thought, based on broad and deep culture, not just from librettist and composer, but from performers, audiences, and, most of all, from administrative and philanthropic decision makers.

Alas, whereas the words "serious thought, based on broad and deep culture" are easy to write, the qualities of intellectual thought and cultural courage they suggest are currently in short supply. Composers, caught between the richness of the past and the emptiness of the present, are told to look to the false gods of the uncultured mass public and the miracle of electronic technology for their salvation. Performing musicians (a category, contrary to the old saw, very much including singers) are educated in this country to replicate a model of celebrity career success irrelevant to our times and in any case achievable by few. Their duty is to play and sing, and not to reason why. In a Faustian bargain they have been paid off in money and (in some cases) fame; in return they are more than ever at the beck and call of those who, whether in the private sector or in government, have taken responsibility for bringing a debased musical culture to the broadest, and the least comprehending, audience.

In opera, a loss of faith in the possibility of serious musical creation has forced a concentration on improvised and often cheap theatrical effect at the expense of the intellectual content of the music and the literary ideas that stimulate the music. Increasingly, the sovereignty of composers and performers, and the importance of the librettist's contribution, has been replaced by the dominance of noncreators, of dramaturges, directors, and producers, of administrators whose forte is marketing rather than art, and of boards whose idea of community service has room neither for artistic knowledge nor for taste. Mere gimmicks—"one-aria operas," workshopping as the substitute for audience reaction for the lonely work of individual creation, tame avant-garde treatment of topical subjects, and reshaping of older works to fit supposedly up-to-date taste—are trumpeted as solutions to the problem of contemporary opera. Above all, safe works of the past—this season, it seems to be *Faust* and *Carmen*—are endlessly recycled to provide the illusion, if not the reality, of discovery.

Deprived of the chance to see the many classics of twentieth-century modernism, the audience becomes ever less educated and therefore ever less sophisticated and increasingly thinks of opera as a diversion accompanied by pretty music. For this general public, opera becomes a staple diet of tuneful hits, a diet only infrequently broken by supposedly theatrically effective new works meant at most to cause a momentary *frisson* and then pass into the limbo of rejected works.

There is indeed a crisis of new work in opera today, not just in America but in the world at large. This crisis is one of musical composition as a whole, not just of operatic composition in particular. The solution to this crisis is a matter for composers to solve, not for administrators and bureaucrats. But there is another crisis in opera, one caused precisely by these administrators and bureaucrats. It is a crisis of the repertory, and it is responsible for the difficulty the *Lord Byron* of Virgil Thomson, among other important works, has had in receiving the decency of an adequate production. We hear much these days about the "cutting edge" of art and the need for "risk taking" in artistic enterprise. Unfortunately, all the available evidence points to the fact that these fine phrases mean nothing more than the right to waste artistic and institutional capital in trying for meretricious and trivial success in public relations. In fact, the courage to produce a work such as *Lord Byron* is not to be found anywhere in the land.

13.

I am amazed that this article on the premiere in Washington of Menotti's
Goya, *which I wrote for the January 1987* New Criterion, *remains nearly
the only favorable assessment of the opera to be found. I find it a bit unsettling
to be in the role of a Menottian, for his post-Puccinian aesthetic is not one
particularly close to my heart. But fair is fair: I can pay no higher a compliment
to Menotti in his* Goya *than to say that to this day, some three years later, I
remember, and often recollect with great pleasure, both the melodies and the
harmonies from many lyrical passages in the opera. I need not add that such
pleasurable memory is a fundamental test of the value of music, and it is a test
dwarfing in value any considerations of mere interest and controversy. At the
end of my article I speculated that what on the one hand disqualified Menotti's
use of a romantic and sentimental musical style, and on the other allowed it
to be appropriated by such admired "neo-romantic" composers as Argento, was
Menotti's true belief in his models, and his colleagues' cynicism about theirs.
I'm afraid that I was right.*

A Dissent on Menotti

BY MOST STANDARDS, a banner event in the history of American
opera was scheduled to take place this past November. Everything
seemed in place: a major work on the subject of one of the great
painters of the Western tradition, written (libretto as well as music)
by a composer rich in years and in innumerable popularly successful
performances of his previous operas, presenting in the title role one of
the most celebrated tenors of the last half-century, conducted by a
major European conductor and produced (under the composer's
direction) by the distinguished opera company resident in our nation's
capital, with the whole package to be broadcast (on a delayed basis) by
PBS on network television.

Curiously, the result was called a disaster. Gian Carlo Menotti's

Goya was given its first performance, in the year of the composer's seventy-fifth birthday, on November 15 (and broadcast on PBS on November 28) at the Kennedy Center Opera House in Washington, D. C., by the Washington Opera. The work—starring the great Placido Domingo in a brilliant and well-nigh unsurpassable performance of the title role, and featuring the distinguished conductor Rafael Frühbeck de Burgos in the pit—was largely condemned, when not ignored altogether, by major critical opinion and relegated to the garbage heap of operatic history. It is painful to quote from the journalistic barrage, but for the record two quotations will give the flavor of the onslaught:

> "Goya," as soon became clear, had everything in its favor except a composer and a librettist capable of dealing in depth with its operatically promising subject. Mr. Menotti, functioning as usual in both capacities, has produced a rather stupefying exercise in banality, similar in its superficiality to his other recent works, though on a larger canvas. . . . This time, Mr. Menotti has composed a parody of a Menotti opera.
>
> —Donal Henahan, in the *New York Times*

> It's hard to imagine how such an experienced, if chronically uninspired, opera fabricator, libretto as well as music—the best of which are minor but viable achievements—could have signed his name to the sad exhibit that was unveiled November 15 at the Kennedy Center Opera House. How are the mediocre fallen!
>
> —Leighton Kerner, in the *Village Voice*

As negative as these verdicts are, they are in fact an accurate reflection of other reviews, and of private, not-for-publication, expert opinion as well.

And so a compositional career which began with the youthful 1937 *Amelia Goes to the Ball*, a work so successful on its initial performances in Philadelphia and New York that it was immediately picked up for production in the 1937–38 season by the Metropolitan Opera, now seems to have described that most tragic of artistic trajectories, the descent from initial triumph to final failure. Of little account now, or so educated opinion would have it, is an achievement that along the way produced the long-running Broadway successes of *The Medium*

(1946), *The Telephone* (1947), and *The Consul* (1950); into the discard pile (at least for intellectual opinion) is thrown the NBC-commissioned television opera *Amahl and the Night Visitors* (1951), perhaps the most performed operatic work written in the twentieth century. Even Menotti's current performance statistics seem of curiously little weight: the fact that (according to the most recent *Opera News* survey) in the 1985–86 season *The Medium*, *The Telephone*, and *Amahl* together racked up *798* performances in the United States alone is a datum good only for proving how much opera activity there is in the United States. It apparently does not serve to prove the staying power of Menotti.

I cannot say that in the past my own opinion of Menotti has been different from the prevailing critical rejection of him which seemed to set in during the 1960s, and which seems to have gained strength ever since. When *Menotti*, John Gruen's interesting biography of the composer, came out in 1978, I bought such records of Menotti's works as were then available—and in truth, except for his most popular operas, there is little to be purchased—only to find myself unwilling to accept as authentic a music which seemed so purposeful in its pursuit of an easily flowing vein of melody and in its rejection of all the developments in music of the last half-century and more.

Nor was my opinion of the composer's works better when I experienced them in live performance. I found the extravagant and often hysterical *Juana la Loca* (1979), written as a vehicle for Beverly Sills's operatic farewell and produced first in San Diego and then at the New York City Opera, fragmented and unimpressive; the 1980 performances of the sardonic and distanced *The Hero* (1971) by the Juilliard American Opera Center struck me as trivial and jejune; the easy sentiment of *Amahl and the Night Visitors* has always been difficult for me to accept.

When I received a request at the beginning of November from the Voice of America to give an interview about Menotti, to be broadcast on a special program in connection with the *Goya* premiere in Washington, my initial reaction was to say that Menotti was a composer who had wasted whatever talent he had in an attempt to be popular, and that in the process he had been unable to go beyond rewriting Puccini for television. Fused with this moral judgment was an intellectual conviction that to turn one's back on the present, as Menotti surely had done, was to guarantee one's irrelevance. But even one's own cherished critical opinions ought not to be taken as holy writ. And so, before actually giving the interview, I returned once more to the recordings—augmented by some new acquisitions and by a tape of the City Opera broadcast of *La Loca*—of the music I had previously found so unconvincing.

This time around, I found ample evidence for a more positive view of Menotti, not just as a master of theater-*cum*-music, but as a musician and composer. Even a not very well played 1955 Leopold Stokowski recording of the Suite from the ballet *Sebastian* (1944)[1] now managed to convey the composer's great melodic power. The gripping original cast recording (made about the time of the work's 1947 Broadway run) of *The Medium*[2] made a persuasive case for the composer's ability to weld drama (in this case melodrama) with music so that the quintessentially nagging observation about twentieth-century opera did not arise: namely, that if the libretto is theatrically first-rate, the music is hardly needed, but if the libretto isn't independently distinguished, then the music somehow doesn't seem strong enough to stand on its own. Sad to say, I found that the original cast recording of *The Telephone*[3] didn't change my original opinion of the arch and campy nature of the work. What was a surprise to me, however, was the tremendous lyrical power of Magda Sorel's great aria from *The Consul*, Menotti's protest against the bureaucratized police state. Heard in Patricia Neway's glorious performance from the original cast recording,[4] this excerpt—written to Menotti's lines, "To this we've come/that men withhold the world from men"—is in itself proof that newly written opera cast in traditional molds continues to have the power to move our emotions.

[1] This recording was originally released on RCA LM-1858, and rereleased—but now deleted—on RCA ARL 1-2715.

[2] This recording, with the inimitable Marie Powers in the title role, is fortunately still available on CBS Odyssey Y2-35239.

[3] This recording, conducted by Emanuel Balaban (as was the original cast recording of *The Medium*), is currently available on CBS Odyssey Y2-35239, packaged with *The Medium*.

[4] This excerpt, along with fascinating passages sung by other artists from works by Victor Herbert, Deems Taylor, Louis Gruenberg, Aaron Copland, and Howard Hanson, is available on New World Records NW241, under the title *Toward an American Opera 1911–1954*.

When I returned to the impressive 1955 recording of *The Saint of Bleecker Street* (1954),[5] I heard evidence of a growing musical solidity which was present throughout the work and not limited, as it had been, to climactic dramatic moments. The prevailing texture of musical writing seemed increasingly characterized by melodic as well as rhetorical power. The music, singing voices, and orchestra seemed to carry more weight, and the conversational patter (something for which Menotti was much admired in his first triumphs on Broadway) less. Only one important attribute of musical value (in my opinion) was still missing: the ability of musical phrases in themselves, not just in connection with the dramatic scenes they accompany, to stick in the listener's mind.

With this newly favorable opinion in mind, I listened to the tape of *La Loca*, made as if was at a time of Beverly Sills's decline as a singing artist. I immediately realized that much of my negative opinion of the work had been based upon an adverse judgment of Miss Sills's singing, a singing which for vocal spread and pitchless shrieks can have few parallels in recent New York operatic history. But a determined attempt on my part to isolate this admittedly basic element of the performance enabled me to recognize that Menotti's work was now marked by a new and powerful lyricism, complete with memorable melodic passages. One can only regret that a well-sung production of *La Loca* has not yet been mounted in New York to correct the performance-bound impression created by the 1979 City Opera version; that a new verdict on this much-maligned opera might be possible for the independent in spirit was suggested by a tantalizingly short excerpt from *La Loca*, hardly more than a few seconds long, which was shown, along with several other valuable film clips of Menotti's operas, on a recent ninety-minute PBS special devoted to the composer's career.

The television showing of *Goya* at the end of November impressed me not as the nadir of Menotti's compositional career, as the reviews would have it, but rather as its triumph. Here, in approximately one

---

[5] Excellently conducted by the late Thomas Schippers, Menotti's onetime protégé, this recording was first available on RCA LM-6032 and later on RCA CBM-2-2714. It is now no longer listed in the Schwann catalogue.

hundred minutes of music, was a complete world of rich emotion and gorgeous melody. Indeed, not since Puccini's *Turandot* has there been Italian operatic song of this density and uninterrupted flow. In *Goya*, Menotti has managed to strip from his creation every irrelevant, merely diverting element, and to concentrate upon the pure vein of music which he possesses.

Fortunately, Menotti decided to make an opera, not a historical treatise. The story is simple, and makes no pretense to historical accuracy. The five scenes of the opera, divided into three acts, show the painter in a tavern, meeting the beautiful Duchess of Alba, who was disguised as a chambermaid, falling in love with her over again when he meets her in the splendor of her palace, spurning the advice of the King of Spain to throw her over, losing her to the Queen's poison plot, and then as an old man, blind and deaf, judging his past and finding that his life had been well spent for art. Along the way there are opportunities for Spanish dances in the tavern, pageantry in the royal palace, a mad scene as Goya realizes that he is going deaf, a ballet in which, now aged, he recollects the demons of his life, and the confrontation between the young Goya and what Menotti calls the painter's "deaf and blind carcass."

There will be no pedantic scholarship, of the kind now so fashionable in operatic criticism, expended on the libretto of *Goya*. The plot makes sense, not as history, but as a portrayal (in a musical setting) of the heights—and the depths—of an artist's life. At the very beginning of the Prelude to *Goya* we hear the great melody which throughout the opera most often represents the hero's love for the Duchess; again and again it returns, often in alternation with another theme, which seems to represent the Duchess herself and which is sounded to moving effect upon her death. Though these two themes are the cornerstones of the opera, the writing throughout is melodically distinguished and memorable, with great tenor and soprano arias as well as immensely attractive passages of dance music both popular (as in the tavern scene) and stately (as in the Act II entrance music for the Queen and for the Duchess of Alba).

The point of the opera, of course, is Goya's love, not just for the Duchess and for women, but for art. And so, fittingly, the greatest moments of the opera occur at the end as the specter of the Duchess appears to Goya as he is about to die. She sings, to the melody which has accompanied her progress through the opera, a hymn of forgiveness and blessing:

> I am the guilty one, I understood too late.
> Too late I prized your love,
> I filled your heart with pain.
> The silent cry of your raging brush,
> More than the soldier or the priest,
> Will forever fight the fiend.
> Join the immortal company!
> Come, receive your crown, your glorious rest.

To these words Goya answers, in soaring melodic phrases:

> O Art! O Beauty!
> My only truth, my only love.
> Pity the artist's humanity,
> And lead him to God's perfection.

And then he dies.

Some words must be given to the transcendent performance of Placido Domingo in the title role. Ringing high notes, faultless legato production, what seemed to be immense stamina, believable acting (though some critics found it wooden), consistently beautiful vocal quality—all these, on this night, were his. It must be stressed that the role, written as it was at his suggestion, is grateful (for the right artist) beyond measure. If there is one factor alone which makes the opera difficult to produce, it is the need for a great tenor to sing Goya—a need all the greater because of Domingo's tour de force in the premiere.

Elsewhere the televised performance was of remarkably high quality. Victoria Vergara, as the Duchess of Alba, sang beautifully and touchingly; the other vocal roles, too, were well filled. The conducting of Frühbeck de Burgos was splendid, as was the playing of the orchestra. A particular commendation must be given to everyone involved for the excellence of the performance because of the usual lateness with which the composer finished his work. It seems that the week preceding the premiere found all the best New York music copyists in Washington, laboring around the clock to have the orchestra parts ready in time for opening night. I must say, too, that

I found the television image of the sets and costumes consistently satisfying, and Menotti's direction edifying.

It remains, I suppose, to explain just why so moving a work was so unsuccessful with educated opinion. Much of the reason lies with Menotti's ostentatiously rich melodic and harmonic vocabulary. It is not, of course, that one is not allowed to write in a pastiche of bygone compositional styles; Dominick Argento, to name just one example, has recently done so to the greatest success in his *Casanova*, given for the first time last season at the City Opera.[6] But it cannot be too strongly emphasized that Menotti is *not* a writer of pastiche, for pastiche connotes a distanced, and usually mocking, treatment of that which is copied.

Menotti, by contrast, possesses a deeply authentic style, a style continuous with Puccini and other masters of late Italian opera. For our writers on music, alas, everything can be forgiven in a composer save sincerity. Because Menotti so clearly loves the immediate past out of which he writes, he stands condemned in the court of critical opinion.

I suppose something of the violence of the rejection of *Goya* can be traced to the conventional nature of the sentiments the opera's admittedly conventional music enshrines. In a time of flaunted anti-conventionalism, Menotti's opera has a lot to answer for: an artist gaining his renown through attendance upon the aristocracy, a lover shamelessly indulging his pursuit of beautiful women, and a life justified—and highly valued—in terms of its production of great art. And yet, the fact remains that it is Menotti's sentiments which carry on the great tradition of operatic rhetoric: his musical exploitation of the dramatic conventions of love and art tie him firmly to a past in which opera was at once popular and refined, at once for the masses and for the cognoscenti.

To pay such a high tribute to Gian Carlo Menotti is hardly to say that his music, any more than his drama, is up-to-date. It is even less to say that Puccini is a viable model for others who wish to write serious music in general or opera in particular. It is still less to demand that the music of the present or of the future contain lush melodies and

[6] For my discussion of *Casanova* and its production at the City Opera, see Chapter II in this book.

warmly appealing harmonies. To admire *Goya* highly does not mean that one cannot ardently wish to see works produced, whether by Schoenberg or Hindemith, Busoni or Milhaud, Sessions or Weisgall, that engage modern culture and society on its own terms.

To be capable of liking *Goya*, I trust, is not to be reactionary. It is simply to be able to listen with open ears to a beautiful piece of lyric theater. To reject *Goya*, as I suspect it is now being rejected, merely *because* it is beautiful at a time when musical art does not have the right to be beautiful is itself to be more than reactionary; it is to be obscurantist. Such obscurantism raises a fundamental question about new music and its reception in our time: can any new music, or any possible new music, satisfy the demands our seasoned observers place upon it? The reception of *Goya* goes far to suggest a dismal answer to this most dismal question.

14.

The following piece is an edited transcript of an interview with Dodie Kazanjian, which appeared in the Winter 1987 Arts Review, *a now-discontinued publication of the National Endowment for the Arts. As I read it now, I am impressed by the overwhelmingly contentious nature of my comments and of the way in which I made them. I think the reasons for a level of abrasiveness I don't often reach are to be found in my awareness of the way the movement toward what might be called the "music theaterizing" of opera was gathering steam in and outside the NEA. It is this transformation, one that I see as merely substituting grand kitsch for grand opera, that explains the present prosperity of the opera field that I mentioned in my introduction to the opening piece in this section. I should say too that whereas "Opera 1984: Dead or Alive?" represented the way operatic matters appeared to me close to the beginning of my term on the National Council on the Arts, "Dismal Thoughts" caught how these matters looked to me close to the end of my term.*

Dismal Thoughts on the Present and Future

SOME PEOPLE say opera appears to be dying, but that's a very south-of-Fourteenth-Street perspective. However, in my opinion, most new opera seems to be dead. The fact that most new opera is dead only means that there's a problem in writing new opera. I don't think that one can back-date this problem and say that because new opera is dead, old opera is dead.

I'm very much impressed by the fact that, of new operatic work over the last twenty-five years or more, nothing has gone into repertory. That is, nothing has gone into the ordinary, year-after-year production of major opera houses. It's my impression that the last piece to have done so was *Billy Budd* or even *Peter Grimes* of Britten.

The fact that something's being done is not the same thing as its being in repertory. "Something done" means done once. It may even be done twice. There are the Philip Glass works. I personally am not convinced they're to be called "operas." They have no action in them. But perhaps we will now redefine opera. That's all right with me. My impression is that such new works are done only when some kind of particular statement is felt to be necessary by the presenter, the statement being, "We're with it. Look, we do new things. There is a wonderful new audience." Then all the stops are pulled out. All the money is spent to do this.

In fact, it's a life-support system that makes the production of these works possible. I'm quite aware that there is a lot of press coverage and that people who go to these performances tend to feel they have done something meritorious.

But these works don't seem to stick after their isolated performances. I don't see performers and conductors making great careers out of doing these pieces. I don't see that (for example) these Philip Glass pieces cast the kind of glory upon the performers that in the past really successful works have always done.

What we know as opera today is larger-than-life characters singing beautiful tunes with stage action. I don't see any other way to define it. Insofar as Broadway musicals have managed this, they do begin to approach opera. I just want to point out that if one thinks about Broadway musicals, it's very hard to think of the individual characters. When one thinks of traditional operas, at least from Mozart to Britten, one finds that the leading characters have been projected by the composer and to some extent by the librettist into mythic status: the *Lulu* of Berg, the composer, has cast its origins in Wedekind, the playwright, into the shade. If we think of Wotan in the *Ring*, the Wotan of the sagas from which Wagner took the material has been replaced in the same way that Shakespeare's Henry V has replaced the Henry V of Holinshed.

I'm not down on the future of opera. People want to sing, and melody is not dead. Even if we might not be writing melody at the moment, we're listening to melody and we're still moved by melody. In the same way, I don't think harmony is dead, because clearly we're moved by harmony. In a peculiar way, the rise of minimalist music proves the power of harmony. The trouble with minimalist music is that the harmonies are abstracted. They're taken out of the matrix of melody and development in which harmony has its fullest flowering.

One has to realize that this is a discussion in which there are a lot of interested parties. The traditional-opera people and new-opera composers are clearly interested parties. My guess is it's hard to find singers to talk about the problem of opera because singers are happy that there's material for them to sing so they can be successful. That's provided by traditional opera. They don't wish to rock the boat.

We really have to compare the appeal of rock music as art or as failed art with the appeal of opera. The problem is that rock, whatever its virtues so far as the audience is concerned, is deeply tied to one particular period in people's lives—the adolescent and immediate postadolescent period. After that, it becomes nostalgia at best—if it's not forgotten. Rock is not a music for the whole lifespan of the individual. Rock is something which has its moment in the sun as far as the listener is concerned, and then afterward disappears. That is not the fate of high civilization. High civilization is clearly subject matter for one's whole life, from first exposure to death. That's something that the proponents of rock as art haven't considered enough.

Listening to rock is like playing basketball. I used to do a bit of it. Shooting baskets is a great idea. But at some point, you can't do it any more.

Life changes. One has other things. High culture is different. High culture has in it nourishment and attractive power throughout the participant's life.

Opera today is in a difficult way because of the lack of new operas that really catch on. Opera today is repeating the classics. Opera today is repeating a smaller and smaller cut of the classics. If you're on mailing lists as I am, you get the schedules of opera companies in the United States. You will see an increased concentration on the *Bohème*s and the *Carmen*s and the *Tosca*s and the *Rigoletto*s.

Music in the whole world is in a dreadful state. I was going to say it's only my opinion. I believe firmly that everybody agrees with me—the people who know about these things—but they don't want to say it. They don't want to talk about it because they feel that will get in the way of what might happen. There isn't any wonderful music being written anywhere. That's why there's no new opera, when you really get right down to it.

Now we have the practice of workshops for new operas. At first the idea was that in workshops the participants learned from each other.

Then it became fashionable to workshop the audience. You get the reaction of the audience and you see what tickles the audience, what works. Now there is a new phenomenon that I call "workshopping the critics." What they're really doing is stirring up media interest. They're giving the critics something to write about so that the critics will write more. It really is an attempt to play up to the people in the media with the hope of lots of coverage.

The workshop idea is certainly not about bringing opera to the people. It's illusory to think that there are any "people" out there who are going to come to see *Nixon in China*. That's a foolish idea. What all this is about is creating the appearance of an audience. It's about creating so much media splash that publicity can substitute for the audience. The media is controllable in the United States in a way that the audience is not. You can get to the media. You can't get to the audience. Getting to the media is simply a matter of knowing how to do it and putting the resources into it. Getting to the audience has nothing to do with either knowing how or resources. The audience comes or it doesn't come.

How important is the critic? Not very. The critic is a kind of historian. The critic tells you what's happened. Even when he tells you what's happening he's telling you what's happened because by the time he tells you, it's already happened. The critic has a lot of influence on people outside the field—those whom I would call the carriers of culture and civilization. The critic has a lot of influence on them. Critics have lots of influence on how society sees itself. They have almost no influence directly on how creators create because creators creating is a private, not a public, matter. We cannot influence it and when we try, we stultify the process.

The idea of workshopping the critic is really a terrible idea. The critic is in effect being manipulated, although the critic is, I guess, happy about it. The other point that has to be made about the *Nixon in China* episode in the history of our dealing with opera is that this isn't opera by the composer. This isn't opera even by the librettist. This is opera by the director. This is opera by Peter Sellars. Peter Sellars is the master of ceremonies. Peter Sellars is the *animateur*, the person who gives life to the entire enterprise. On a television program about *Nixon in China*, he said at one point, "We've had a lot of trouble with this particular scene. John Adams, the composer, has rewritten it four times." I don't think that's the right way to go about it. Rewriting is what is done in commercial music. It's known as writing to fit.

There are a few people today writing opera of major significance. New works come out of a modernist world which suppressed the writing of tunes. If what we're looking for is new Puccinis, that hasn't happened yet. Opera doesn't have to be all new Puccinis. Britten was not a Puccini either, writing great tunes that are performed not just by singers but on every instrument because the tunes themselves are so memorable. An opera like Hugo Weisgall's *Six Characters*, from the Pirandello play, has the extraordinary quality of creating myth. Pirandello did it in writing the play, and the Weisgall opera goes past the play in making a deeper myth out of the situation and the characters. This is an opera that doubtless will always be somewhat special.

It doesn't fill the role that a *Tosca* fills. I think it's hard for us at this moment either to have a *Tosca* or to have an intellectually satisfying opera. We have a little more chance for the intellectually satisfying works now than we have of the *Tosca*s. I don't see the person who is going to write these great tunes. There were some wonderful tunes on Broadway. Kurt Weill wrote wonderful tunes. That's kept Kurt Weill going. The wonderful tunes in *The Threepenny Opera* keep the piece going even though it's hardly a pleasant libretto. There's no doubt that people who listen to "Mac the Knife" don't think of the words in it. They think of the tune.

Menotti's *Goya* presents the litmus test for the critic because *Goya* is a piece with wonderful tunes. It's a piece with sumptuous staging and action. It's a piece that provides wonderful roles. It's now been one year since I saw *Goya* and wrote about it. I still remember the big tunes. *Goya* is about the kind of subject opera ought to be about, the larger-than-life subject. At the end, Goya, a great figure of civilization, sings the climax of the opera, "O Art! O Beauty!" That's what opera ought to be about.

Goya was trashed by the critics, but very successful with the audience. It is now probably unperformable for some years—I was about the only one to write favorably about it—because of the critics.

The critics ought not to be listened to because they're getting in the way of creation. This will certainly affect Martin Feinstein at the

Washington Opera when he thinks of people to commission. In the case of *Goya*, I don't know any of my intellectual friends who watched the telecast. I don't know any musicians who listened to it. I have forced them to listen to the tape, and they say, "Gee, that's gorgeous! Gee, that's wonderful!" But they didn't listen on their own. I have had discussions with important people in the theatre who didn't bother to see the telecast. That means that Menotti and what he does is out of fashion. I only want to point out that recently, in just one year, there were something like eight hundred performances of the operas of Menotti in the United States. That's what I call being in repertory.

The traditional audience doesn't go to see things like *Einstein on the Beach*. If there is enough hype, some will doubtless go. People leaving Glass's *Akhnaten* at the City Opera at the end of the first act were legion. There were people running on all sides. Those people didn't leave because they were happy.

Smaller houses are extremely important for the communication of opera. There's no doubt in my mind that some of the lack of immediate relation between the performers and the audience in America has to do with the size of the houses. They're just too large.

But I can't see a move to smaller houses. The whole economic situation—real estate, construction, union costs, artist fees, administrative costs—all works against that. I see it going the other direction. That's very, very bad. It is so hopeless that I don't even know that it's worth discussion.

It's a tremendous problem. New opera houses are huge and very unpleasant. The works cannot be heard.

Amplification is not the answer. You might as well stay home. It's more comfortable. Already, people *want* to stay home. Already, it's much better in certain senses to listen to recordings. Is that what we want to encourage? The same thing with surtitles. Now we're seeing surtitles when the operas are in English. So all we need are surtitles, amplification, and a television monitor nearby to watch the close-ups. Then going to the opera will be just like staying home. Then if we just add beer and peanuts, we'll truly have all the comforts of home.

III

Performing and Performers

15.

There can be little doubt that the authentic performance movement now carries the day in our concert halls and on new recordings. Indeed, the move to playing old music on original instruments (or more likely on copies thereof) in a musicologically approved way has reached the point where an artist performing Beethoven sonatas on the modern piano in New York runs the risk of being chastised in the press for lack of historical respect. In this article from the September 1989 New Criterion *I described the consequences of this attitude for the kind of repertory performers play, and for the kind of performances audiences get to hear.*

Reflections on Bach

HAS SO APPARENTLY unexceptional an act as playing Bach in a more or less traditional way now taken on an exceptional, indeed an oppositional, character? Of course, Bach is now played everywhere; along with Mozart and Beethoven, his music attracts both audiences and critics. And yet there is hardly any music today that is approached by the most talented performers with greater trepidation and anxiety. I have become more aware than ever of this curious phenomenon in the course of my work as artistic director of the Waterloo Music Festival in New Jersey, where for the past three summers we have begun each of our chamber music concerts with glorious but little performed music by Bach. In my concert program notes this past summer, I attempted to discuss the situation in contemporary Bach performances. What follows is drawn from these notes.

I

In 1989, Johann Sebastian Bach once again began each of Waterloo's six chamber music concerts. In 1987 and 1988, we had traversed the entire *Art of Fugue*, performing this profound and fascinating collection of contrapuntal ingenuities in a variety of instrumental combinations, ranging from strings, winds, and brass to two pianos and even percussion. This past summer we shifted our attention to the no less significant *Musical Offering*, a group of thirteen individually perfect works based on a theme given to Bach in 1747 for improvisation by that accomplished musical amateur, Frederick the Great of Prussia.

Several of the mostly short components of the *Musical Offering* were written to be performed on the keyboard, and others were written to be performed by instrumental ensembles. The keyboard Bach had in mind for the opening *Ricercar à 3* was either a harpsichord or an early version of the fortepiano, which some years in the future was to replace the harpsichord and which in its turn was to be replaced by the modern iron-framed piano. In this summer's opening concert we heard this work twice, first on a double-manual harpsichord and then, in a bow to the instrument whose triumph in the nineteenth century made possible the growth of a discerning mass audience for classical music, on a nine-foot Steinway concert grand. In the ensuing four concerts, we heard the various canons of the *Musical Offering*, as well as the four-movement Trio Sonata, in instrumentation suggested either by Bach or by recent performing editions. Finally, in our last concert, we heard the closing *Ricercar à 6* in a transcription for small orchestra by Gerard Schwarz, Waterloo's principal conductor.

Save for the harpsichord version of the *Ricercar à 3*, all our performances were on modern instruments. Some may feel that this attitude toward performance forces displays a lack of respect toward the composer's intentions, as divined by modern scholarship. One critic even called it "bizarre." I think, however, that Bach's music, because it is so beautiful, and because it has so much to teach, and because it is, in a word, so universal, must be performed by as wide a range of players as possible.

II

In the almost 250 years since his death in 1750, Bach has provided sustenance for the players of every instrument and every combination of instruments. As new instruments were called into being in the last century by the explosive growth in the concert music repertory, it seemed ever more natural to perform Bach in whatever medium came to hand. The nineteenth century, after all, was the age of the instrumental transcription; no instrument profited more from the availability of Bach than the piano, that omnipresent successor to the clavichord, the harpsichord, and the organ, and replacement for the orchestra and the voice. But as the twentieth century followed, we entered a proud age of academic specialization. Now, as the demand for intellectual purity is taken for granted, Bach performance has become the property of a self-appointed and self-perpetuating guild.

Like every guild before it, the doughty band devoted to the so-called authentic performance of old music on original instruments, or copies of them, combines the codification of rigorous internal standards with the proclamation of an elaborate rationale designed to exclude interlopers and dilettantes. The interlopers and dilettantes, it is hardly necessary to add, are those who choose *not* to play Bach in the approved authentic style on the approved original instruments.

For musicians and audiences alike, the result of the new performance-oriented musicology is the restriction of Bach playing to relatively few musicians, and those few are usually neither technically nor artistically of the first rank. As one conductor recently remarked: "Musicology provides players with an excuse for playing out of tune." And, I might add, an excuse to play in a monotonous, jerky, and unnatural rhythm as well. Unfortunate as this situation is for an audience thus deprived of communicative performances of Bach's masterpieces, it is even worse for executant musicians who address themselves to a mainstream, mostly nineteenth-century, repertory. Bullied by scholars and derided by critics, they no longer learn and perform Bach, a literature that contains within itself, as a drop of water contains the ocean, all our music.

III

It is difficult not to feel these days that Bach is as much a great scholarly industry as he is a great composer. Thoroughly vetted and "definitive" textual recensions, abstruse accounts of the master's compositional procedures, manuals detailing exactly how his music is to be realized in an authentically free manner—all of this, taken together, supposedly amounts to a great deal about what we hope is the real Bach.

Along with this explosion, there is another—in Bach performance. The Bach guild prospers: recording companies market "complete

Bach editions," and artists make careers programming—and recording—an amount of Bach's music so great that one wonders how they can comprehend even a small number of the notes they perform. And so the Bach sound flows on, a seamless tapestry—or is it an engulfing ocean?—of music.

Yet performers know in their hearts that there is hardly any music in the repertory so difficult as that of Bach. Hardly any music is so difficult to penetrate in spirit and meaning. For the simple fact is that Bach is always infinitely varied in local pattern and large-scale design. No two pieces, no two passages, no two instants in Bach are ever in any important way alike; no two counterpoints, no two melodies, no two transitions are ever quite the same. Though it can hardly be literally true, it seems as if no chord ever leads harmonically to its successors in quite the same way.

To this endless compositional variability in Bach is added a refinement and subtlety of expression so great as to reveal new depth each time a performer opens the pages of a given piece. In every performer's heart is graven the awareness (and perhaps the fear) that a lifetime of study is not enough to plumb the depths of even a short piece by Bach. Perhaps this sad but strangely uplifting fact should be remembered every time we are told that a Bach recording is "complete" or "definitive."

IV

Bach was once the recipient of an ambivalent tribute from John Cage, the American avant-garde composer, mycologist, and prankster. Sometime in the 1960s, I heard him remark in a broadcast lecture, apropos of what I no longer remember, "Bach did the right thing with counterpoint: he taught it." Whimsical though Cage's aperçu may have been, he struck at a profound, albeit obvious, truth: Bach is the great teacher of our musical tradition.

But to demean Bach's educational value by making of him no more than a musty theory teacher is to trivialize a great master. What Bach teaches us is the primacy of the musical material, the value of each note and each combination of notes, of each melodic line and each combination of melodic lines. The beauty of Bach inheres as much in the parts as in the whole. Every separate line possesses its own interest, vitality, and autonomy; every moment is capable of standing alone before music's and Bach's God. Thus what we learn from Bach is that every note, every player, every musical thought counts.

V

Aside from the overall incommensurability of Bach's art, there are many specific problems in performing his music. Chief among these problems is that of sentiment—the role of what used to be called "feeling" in communicating the true essence of the music. Our age, though it rewards maudlin sentimentality in its entertainment culture, increasingly seems to find in scholarship the only allowable point of entry into the great art of the past. Unabashed sentiment, a manifest indulgence in beauty, is seen as the disfiguring of pure texts.

Matters were otherwise in the nineteenth century. Hallowed masterpieces in painting, literature, and music were perceived as glorious vessels fit to contain the most typical and extravagant contemporary emotions. Thus Liszt could write his *Sposalizio*, a sensuous and extroverted piano piece inspired by Raphael's painting of the marriage of the Virgin; the great Oxford teacher Benjamin Jowett could find in Plato an exemplar of high Victorian values; Bach's choral works could be performed not by the small choruses natural to the composer's small-scale world but by the growing hordes characteristic of post-1789 bourgeois society.

What we see now in Bach is his infinity of notes, not his infinity of thoughts. Accordingly, our modern taste in Bach performance is for the mechanical and antiseptic, not the eloquent and grand. Does this mean that, just as the romantic era accommodated Bach to its own age of florid expression, we are accommodating Bach to our own age of the typewriter and the computer?

VI

It is perhaps curious that a position such as mine, so friendly in general to performances of Bach on modern instruments, nonetheless finds it difficult to countenance—perhaps stomach is a better word—renditions of Bach on keyboard synthesizers, in the fashion of Wendy Carlos and Tomita. After all, if what Bach wrote is wonderful on the Steinway piano, that marvel of nineteenth-century metallurgy and acoustical research, why should not it be wonderful on the Moog or the Yamaha synthesizers, those marvels of late twentieth-century electronics?

Once the purity of the original sound has been violated, as the very passage of time makes inevitable, what is to be said against the latest fashion in performance replacing the one before?

It will doubtless be said that much of the resistance to electronic Bach is pure snobbery, like fish forks at fancy dinners. Electronics, so the argument against this supposedly snobbish disdain would go, is both for the masses and of the masses; it is cheap, widely available, endlessly duplicable, and exactly obedient to the will of the artist. And so what began (in the case of Bach) with the harpsichord in the palaces of the aristocracy and expanded with the piano into the living rooms of the middle class ends today with CD and cassette players on jogging paths and car speakers. Is there anything inherently wrong with this progression?

Although there is much to be said about the benefits of elite culture remaining the preserve of a self-selecting and self-sacrificing elite, the crucial issue regarding the electronic performance of Bach is not one of Veblenite sociology but one of music and art, and therefore of civilization. The contribution of electricity to music making, it should be emphasized, is simply not continuous with the nineteenth-century improvement of instruments. Regardless of how much louder a piano is than a harpsichord, or how much easier and more reliable a valved horn is than a natural horn, the nexus linking physical effort and artistic result remained the same: what the player put in, the listener got out. Similarly, in the case of music composition, notes had to be written down, with all the frightful physical and mental labor such inscription involves.

With the coming of electricity this nexus was decisively broken. The first break came in the 1920s with the microphone, wireless broadcasting, and the electrical-recording process: for the first time in the history of music what had been originally played soft could be heard loud. With the coming of recording on magnetic tape in the 1940s, errors could be snipped out, leaving a seamlessly correct result. And yet, despite the decisiveness of the change brought by early electronics, something of the old order remained: at least what sounded on recordings or the radio like playing and singing had to be somewhere, somehow, played or sung.

After the arrival of electronic keyboards and sine-wave generators in the 1950s, the working musician, as traditionally understood, became irrelevant to the making of what was now to pass in academic laboratories for music. Failed scientists with a smattering of music, and failed musicians with a smattering of science, decided that composition was a matter of ideas, not talent. And yet, despite all the equipment and all the critical acclaim, the new music made by electronic means has vanished without a trace.

But the illusion that electronics provided—of a music making no longer bound by physical limitations on endurance, accuracy, and strength—has remained, and has inevitably invaded the realm of Bach performance. Because music gains its greatness from the musician's battle to tame and transcend his body, Bach when plugged in is nothing more than a feelingless robot, a mechanical trick calculated to deceive the innocent. Because Bach wrote so many notes, and because his many notes are so difficult to penetrate, he has been a prime candidate for this rootless brand of performance. It is in synthesized Bach that we hear the death rattle of sublime genius reduced to the level of wallpaper. Emptied of meaning and purged by quack science of humanity and divinity alike, electric Bach is fast, loud, cold, and square. It lacks even the devil's power to shock.

16.

I wrote this article about the Van Cliburn International Piano Competition for the September 1985 New Criterion. *In it I questioned whether those responsible for the contest really thought very much of the musical virtues of their contestants. My evidence for guessing that they really didn't was the astonishingly offhand treatment given these struggling and presumably talented souls in the PBS television coverage of the contest, which appeared shortly after the contest was over. In my article, I particularly objected to the program's habit of artificially assembling a whole performance of a composition by seamlessly splicing one pianist into another, as if the individuality of each artist hardly made any difference anyway. Now, in the PBS coverage of the 1989 Cliburn contest, this practice was extended; this time it was compositions—acknowledged pieces of art, after all—that were seamlessly spliced one into the other. Perhaps the grand sachems of the Cliburn contest ought to go into organ transplant surgery.*

What the Cliburn Contest Thinks of Pianists

I T M I G H T S E E M an unlikely proposition, but it could be argued that those responsible for the 1985 Van Cliburn International Piano Competition—held late this past spring in Fort Worth, Texas—have somehow been influenced in their marketing strategy by the deathless advice the great English humorist Stephen Potter gave to failed tennis players: "If you can't volley, wear velvet socks." In the case of the Cliburn contest, volleying might well stand for the proper business of a piano competition: choosing, with some regularity, first-prize winners of musical authority and personal magnetism. Potter's notion of velvet socks surely can be applied to the lavish but meretricious coverage the competition received (and doubtless strove for) on nationwide public television at the end of the festive proceedings in early June.

To understand the present manifestation of this now most famous of American music contests, one must begin, not with the relatively brief history of the Cliburn award itself, but with the history of music performance competitions over the past fifty years or so. In the late 1930s, by all odds the most important competition in the world was the Queen Elisabeth contest in Brussels. Founded in 1937 as the Concours Eugène Ysaÿe (in honor of the great Belgian violinist), it gained luster from the association of the Queen with such famous performers of the day as Pablo Casals and Arthur Rubinstein. From the first years its prizes were an object of the ambitions of the Soviet Union, then embarked on a policy of cultural exportation in furtherance of the Popular Front against Hitler and Mussolini. Indeed, the USSR hit pay dirt in the first two events in Brussels: the first prize went to violinist David Oistrakh in 1937, to pianist Emil Gilels in 1938.

Not every winner in Brussels went on to achieve the fame of Oistrakh and Gilels. For example, in 1952 and 1955 the contest was won by Americans: the pianist Leon Fleisher and the violinist Berl Senofsky, neither of whom made great solo careers. (Fleisher's fate was sealed by a persistent hand problem, which has proven incurable to this day, despite much-ballyhooed attempts at medical intervention.) In 1956 the gold medal was won by the then very young—and still very Soviet—pianist Vladimir Ashkenazy; though Ashkenazy was later to become a kind of superstar in London, his first appearances after his 1956 victory were ambiguous successes at best.

Whether because of its undeniable musical seriousness or because its most recent winners had hardly set the musical world on fire, the Queen Elisabeth contest was devastatingly upstaged in the spring of 1958 by the first Tchaikowsky contest in Moscow. This was of course Van Cliburn's moment in history. The young American from Texas seemed to personify not only pianistic accomplishment and Southern charm but also the desires of mankind (skillfully shepherded by Nikita Khrushchev) for a thaw in the Cold War and an end to the arms race. When Cliburn returned to the United States for a hero's welcome, he brought with him a certified performance of the famous Tchaikowsky Piano Concerto, a piece which some say he played more excitingly before he left for the USSR. Though he eventually played and recorded many other virtuoso concertos, the Tchaikowsky and its close relative, the Third Concerto of Rachmaninoff, were to be the center of a decade-long career of fantastic show-business proportions. With the triumph of Van Cliburn, indeed, contests and prizes for the first time bid fair to supplant concerts as the road to musical success and riches.

Because of the importance of the USSR in what is after all still a bipolar world and the formidable powers of the Russian publicity apparatus, the Tchaikowsky competition remains *primus inter pares* in the contest world. The success of the Tchaikowsky, combined with certain well-known organic weaknesses of creativity in composition and individuality in performance, has inspired the creation of innumerable similar events, large and small, serious and frivolous, of greater and lesser distinction, all across the world. When added to such already existing competitions as the Chopin contest in Warsaw, the Marguerite Long-Jacques Thibaud contest in Paris, and the Busoni competition in Bolzano, these contests have helped to make the category of contest winner—even that of contest entrant—a recognized artistic profession.

What about American events in this cornucopia of musical prizes? For some years our chief domestic musical contests were the Leventritt and Naumburg prizes, both established by patrician New York families of German–Jewish origin. Although some of their winners have done well in domestic musical life, the most famous winner of the Leventritt prize is none other than Van Cliburn, whose victory in 1954 failed to establish him as a major concert artist. Sadly for America's cultural independence, it took Khrushchev's kisses of peace to make Cliburn a stage personality in his homeland.

Given the role of a contest in Cliburn's career, it is hardly surprising that at the beginning of the 1960s a kind of supercontest was founded in Texas in the name of that state's most famous musical son. It is ironic indeed that today, after the collapse of Cliburn's pianistic career—he has not played publicly for many years—it is the contest established in his name, and furthered with his enthusiastic participation, that keeps his name in front of his once adoring public.

As Cliburn's own career has gone from shaky to nonexistent his contest has become ever more splashy. The first prize of the 1962 Van Cliburn International Piano Competition was no less than $10,000; now, twenty-three years later, the first prize is described by the contest's sponsors as "in excess of $200,000," including (according to the organization's press release), a

> cash award of $12,000, Van Cliburn Gold Medal, Lank-ford–Allison Memorial Cup, debut recital appearance in Carnegie Hall, concert tours in North America and Europe for a period of 30 months, air travel by American Airlines' domestic routes, recording on the Vox Cum Laude label and studio recording of a recital in Hilversum, The Netherlands.

As the first prize has grown in value, so too has grown the interest of the contest's sponsors and administrators in securing publicity. Already in 1981 the contest was covered across the United States on public television; in addition, the *New York Times* published an extensive series of articles on the contest by Harold C. Schonberg, who had recently retired as the paper's senior music critic. Not surprisingly, it is now standard practice for the Cliburn competition to supplement its own public relations with the services of a high-powered New York publicity firm.

To date, there have been seven Cliburn contests, including the most recent one. It goes without saying that it is much too early to tell what the long-term result of the 1985 competition will turn out to be. But it is clear that the winners of the first six contests, taken as a group, leave much to be desired. Of these six gold medal winners, only one— the Romanian pianist Radu Lupu in 1966—has gone on to make a major international career. Just listing the names of the other winners— the American Ralph Votapek in 1962, the Brazilian Cristina Ortiz in 1969, the Russian Vladimir Viardo in 1973, the South African Steven De Groote in 1977, and the American André-Michel Schub in 1981— serves to chronicle the disappointment of high hopes. It can safely be said that the success rate of the Cliburn contest in picking career winners, while perhaps not markedly worse than that of other contests, is certainly no better.

This unhappy verdict would hardly come as a surprise to those responsible for the Cliburn contest. Thus, when the decision was made to publicize the 1985 contest on public television, the big question must have been how a nationally televised program could be made to seem wholly absorbing and fascinating in the absence of any sterling musical record. The answer, whether intended or not, was to treat the contest, and the process of running it and competing in it, as the whole story. To do this it was necessary to subordinate music and musicians to what came across the television screen as a kind of beauty contest/talent show, a show in which everything was anonymous save the contest itself.

Even a brief description of the program—aired on PBS in June—is sufficient to convey its atmosphere of musical facelessness. It began with voice-overs taken from telephone conversations in which several foreign contestants were informed of their acceptance into the preliminary round by the Van Cliburn Foundation's English director, Andrew Raeburn. Then we were shown pictures of the arrival of several contestants at the Dallas–Fort Worth Airport. Here the emphasis was on demonstrating the contestants' wary gratitude for all the kindnesses about to be heaped on them by their hosts. The prevailing tone of it all was demonstrated by the confident and at the same time embarrassed words of one of the greeters: "I'm Joan, I'm Joan, and I'll be your momma for three weeks."

The scene now shifted to the room in which each contestant picked a piano from those provided by various manufacturers including Steinway, Baldwin, Bechstein, Bösendorfer, and Yamaha. Here the contestants were unnamed for the television viewer, as they would remain, with few exceptions, until the very end of the program. There seemed little rhyme or reason to the choice of any particular instrument; as picked up by the television microphones, the tone of these very different pianos was much the same. Indeed, it was clear from the way this process was presented that the prevailing emphasis of the program was to be on the similarity of the contestants and their experiences, on the miraculous interchangeability of all these brilliantly gifted young people.

The next scene—which showed the drawing of lots for the order in which the contestants were to play—concentrated on the immense discomfort, sometimes marked by open anxiety and sometimes by pointless bravado, that musical contests engender in even the most insouciant participants. Here attention was focused for a moment on the poor unfortunate—her name, alas, *was* given—who had the ill luck to be assigned the opening slot. It was clear from her crestfallen reaction that she knew her fate was to play her best and then have the performance forgotten as pianist after pianist followed in her wake.

Next came Mr. Raeburn's introduction, in all too suitably orotund accents, of several jury members. As if to emphasize the "international" character of everything, two of the jurors were described as each representing two countries. One was said to represent Hungary and the United States, the other West Germany and the United States. Neither, it might be added, was in any real sense American. With these nobly universal sentiments, the contest was at last declared open and the music began.

A young lady—the drawer of the unlucky opening performance slot—started playing the C-major Etude, opus 10, no. 1, of Chopin. This work, of immensely difficult arpeggios in the right hand set against a slowly striding octave bass, provides a challenge (especially when played as an opening selection) which few pianists of this or any other time can satisfy. Her performance hardly began remarkably; but before she had gotten very far in this short étude the master stroke of this year's Cliburn contest television coverage—the "velvet socks," as it were, of Stephen Potter—was revealed: by the miracle of up-to-date electronic technology, the television screen now showed *another* pianist taking up, without any audible jump, where the first pianist had left off. Before the étude had lumbered to its end, a total of what I think were *five* different pianists—all save the first unknown to us— had each played part of the piece more or less well. The piece too, I might add, was unidentified.

Next followed snippets from mostly well-known piano works, all unidentified, played by several contestants, also unidentified. There was Liszt's étude "La Campanella" in a sloppy rendition, a well-played bit of the first movement of the *Pathétique* Sonata of Beethoven, some of the opening of the *Chromatic Fantasy and Fugue* of Bach played by four pianists, each imperceptibly shading into the other. There was a passage from the Chopin Scherzo in C-sharp minor, some of the opening movement of the famous Haydn E-flat major Sonata (the best piano playing on the program to this point), and the end of the *Mephisto Waltz* of Liszt. In this performance of the Liszt the lyrical moment before the coda was languid to the point of discontinuity and the coda itself something of a mess. The final bit of music given in this segment of the program was a small part of the so-called Dante Sonata of Liszt; this rendition, first stodgy and then inaccurate, did little justice to what in the right hands can be an enthralling composition.

At this time the names of the twelve semifinalists were announced, again by the commanding Mr. Raeburn. On the screen could be seen shots of the tearful non-survivors; their sadness was, of course, counterbalanced by the glee of the new, temporary victors.

The scene now shifted to a demonstration of one of the distinguishing features of the Cliburn competition, the contestants' performance of chamber music with a respected string quartet. The ensemble on this occasion was the Tokyo String Quartet; significantly, this well-known group's name was mentioned only once on the program, and then only by a contestant in passing.

The first piece of chamber music was the *Scherzo* of the Schumann Quintet; once again, the music, like the performers, went nameless. The movement's opening was roughly played by a female contestant, who was allowed to get as far as the beginning of the first trio section before another pianist, this time a man and a more idiomatic player, was spliced in. He got through the return of the opening, whereupon his place was taken for the second trio by another male contestant. This pianist seemed unable to keep both the syncopated phrasing and the necessary accented downbeats in mind at the same time. Nevertheless, he was allowed to get up to the last seven bars of the movement, when his place was taken by pianist number two, who played the next two bars of the seven, followed by pianist number three for two bars, and finally pianist number one for the last three bars, consisting simply of four tonic chords.

This dog's breakfast of music making (for which, of course, the pianists could not be blamed) was followed by a similar presentation of the *Scherzo* of the Brahms F-minor Quintet. Here, it must be said, the program did vouchsafe the identity of the piece being played, since one contestant implied in passing that he was playing the work. This time the music was played by no less than *seven* pianists, with the same return of various hands to play tiny parts of the ending bars. Under these conditions, there could be no possibility of listening to the music as music, of actually hearing a work of art on its own terms. And even as a way of comparing the performances of different pianists, this rapid and putatively seamless succession of different abilities, technical approaches, and expressive styles could only end by confusing even sophisticated viewers.

At this point four judges appeared on the program: Soulima Stravinsky (a pianist and the son of Igor Stravinsky), John Giordano (conductor of the Fort Worth Symphony), Malcolm Frager (a pianist and winner of the 1959 Leventritt contest), and Wolfgang Stresemann (formerly the manager of the Berlin Philharmonic and the son of Gustav Stresemann, German chancellor in 1923 and then foreign minister from 1923 to 1929). They talked, each for a few seconds, about such weighty matters as the extraordinary gifts needed to win such a contest. Finally Stresemann allowed as how, because genius will out anyway, it was not necessary to feel such terrible responsibility as a judge.

Then the six finalists were announced, though so little camera time was spent on each contestant that it was still difficult to match faces to names. Suddenly there was a shot of one of the finalists playing her concerto in a rehearsal room for the man who would conduct her performance in the final round; though his identity was not to be revealed until the printed credits at the end of the program, the conductor was in fact Stanislaw Skrowaczewski, formerly the music director of the Minnesota Orchestra.

Now came the performances of the concertos. In itself, this emphasis on concerto playing as the highest public criterion for winning contests speaks volumes concerning what contest managements feel their work is all about. Important as the ability to play excitingly with orchestra is in the making of careers, it remains true that only a relatively small number of virtuoso concertos—whether for the piano or for the other major solo instrument, the violin—contain the very greatest music; concertos in the repertories of popular soloists are played today largely for the purpose of whipping up an audience. Most of the great music for the piano is truly solo music, written to be performed by the pianist with no one coming between him (or her) and the audience. This music includes Bach (if, that is, contemporary taste deigns to allow his work to be performed on the piano at all), the sonatas and shorter works of Schubert, Chopin, and Brahms, and even a surprisingly large number of compositions written in the twentieth century. To place the public weight on concertos, as this television program did, is at worst to distort the work of the pianist, and at best to make clear that the pianist as artist stands foursquare in the world of show business.

The concertos performed at the end of the program were, with one exception, drawn from this virtuoso stockpile. Two finalists, like Siamese twins, shared part of the last movement of the Third Concerto of Prokofiev; one finalist played the closing pages of the Third Concerto of Rachmaninoff; two finalists alternated in the finale of the Brahms D-minor Concerto; and last of all the pianist who turned out to be the gold medal winner played the last quarter of the first movement of—surprise—the Tchaikowsky B-flat minor Concerto of Van Cliburn's glory days.

There is little point here in second-guessing the judges' decisions; clearly they heard much more from all the contestants—and heard it live rather than from a television set—than what was presented on this program. On the basis of what I heard, the best playing came from the sixth-prize winner, Hans-Christian Wille, twenty-seven, of West Germany, and the third-prize winner, Barry Douglas, twenty-five, from the United Kingdom. Wille played the end of the Prokofiev (after the segment had been soggily begun by fourth-prize winner Emma Takhmizian, twenty-seven, from Bulgaria) with great force and clarity. Douglas began his portion of the Brahms last movement with real musical authority and technical command; when he was succeeded in the piece by second-prize winner Philippe Bianconi, twenty-five, of France, there was a significant drop-off in dramatic tension and pianistic finish. The fifth-prize winner, Károly Mocsári, twenty-two, of Hungary, seemed technically overmatched in the last part of the Rachmaninoff Third Concerto, a work of course also associated with Cliburn's own triumphs; one had the feeling that the piece was playing Mocsári, and that both thereby lost.

And so it all came down to the Tchaikowsky Concerto. The passage allotted to the grand winner, José Feghali, twenty-four, of Brazil, ran from the reprise of the beautiful lyrical theme through the brilliant and taxing cadenza to the coda. What distinguished Feghali's performance most were the emotions and signs of commitment to the music that showed on his face as he played. He looked, rather than played, an exciting performance.[1] Pianistically he seemed cautious

---

[1] Without in any way suggesting that there is only one way of playing the Tchaikowsky Concerto, it might nevertheless be useful to stress that the work, in a proper performance, can affect listeners even today with the force of an electric shock. Such a performance was regularly given by Vladimir Horowitz in his earlier

and often retrograde in his handling of the gathering excitement that the composer has written into the music; the cadenza, which can provide a stunning vehicle for an athletic keyboard player, lacked both hard-edged brilliance and ease and flow.

After a few *pro forma* words from Van Cliburn (his only real role in the program), the awards themselves were announced—not in a very accomplished manner—by F. Murray Abraham, the actor who won an Academy Award this year for his performance as Salieri in *Amadeus*. The program ended with a short segment from Mr. Feghali's performance of the end of the second movement of the Tchaikowsky, followed by a long, slow list of credits in which were named, in addition to the Fort Worth Symphony and Skrowaczewski, the numerous technical personnel who made the film. Special thanks were expressed to Mr. Raeburn for his services as "creative consultant." Mention was made too of grants from Mobil and the Tandy Corporation which made the program possible.

What lessons are to be learned from this television offering? How can one explain the obstinate refusal of those responsible for the program to present important music at sufficient length to make its *musical* effect? Why did those in charge fail to provide enough identification of those who played to enable a viewer who liked their performances to remember them and look for them in the future? Perhaps all these questions come down to one big one: *cui bono?*

The intended winner in this interlocking set of artistic failures was, clearly, the Cliburn contest itself. Like all important (or self-important) musical institutions, the Cliburn contest sees its survival as an institution as the highest good; to effect that single purpose, everything—it matters little whether it is the art or the artist—must be integrated, suppressed, and, if necessary, destroyed.

So the meaning of this television coverage is indeed simple. It is that

---

days; lovers of piano playing—and of the Tchaikowsky Concerto—are fortunate there are three recorded documentations of his traversal of the work: the 1941 Carnegie Hall recording with Toscanini and the NBC Symphony (RCA CRM4-0914); the 1943 War Bond Rally live performance, again in Carnegie Hall with Toscanini and the NBC (RCA LM-2319); and a "private" recording of a 1953 broadcast performance with George Szell and the New York Philharmonic, once more in Carnegie Hall (CLS RPCL 2027).

music and pianists alike must take a back seat to the survival and perpetuation of the contest which was given birth to serve them. Unfortunately for those who would thus fit artistic life into an institutional Procrustean bed, contests are not art, administrators are not artists, and television editors are not musical arbiters. Here, perhaps, is something for the folks at the Cliburn to ponder as they begin to prepare for the next time: less thought must be given to the contest itself, and more—much more—to the contestants and the music they play. Then and only then, whether or not the contest is on the tip of every tongue, whether or not its winners all hit career jackpots, will the Van Cliburn International Piano Competition truly accomplish the purposes of art it should.

17.

This chapter contains three New Criterion *articles that discuss the recent state of the piano, as reflected through the prism of three pianists. No one older than fifty, however refined his taste, could have read the news of Liberace's death without a twinge. He so perfectly encapsulated the peculiar combination of show-biz glitter and uplift that marked the 1950s; his choice of the piano as his medium for achieving stardom now seems the last, though hardly the finest, moment of the piano as universal civilizer. As my short April 1987 article makes clear, I had respect, albeit grudging, for his piano playing, and I would only wish that his gifts had been turned to a higher goal. In the equally short February 1988 article that follows, I was concerned to talk about the loss attendant upon the way today's most talented pianists have forsaken interesting modern repertory. I particularly saluted the estimable Vladimir Feltsman for his marvelous performance of parts of Olivier Messiaen's* Vingt regards sur l'enfant Jesus. *Such courage deserves congratulation. Finally, in a somewhat longer January 1990 piece, I attempted an assessment, written shortly after his death, of Vladimir Horowitz's fabled career.*

Sad Thoughts on Walter Busterkeys, a.k.a. Liberace

MUSICAL SUCCESS, it has often been noted, is hardly a respecter of the high-minded. For composers and performers alike, the brass rings of fame and money are often not at the disposal of the noble in aspiration or even the uncommonly attractive, but rather of the attractively common.

And so it was, I am afraid, with the pianist Wladziu Valentino Liberace, who was born in West Allis, Wisconsin, in 1919, and who died in Palm Springs, California, this past February. As I write these words, the newspapers are full of stories that the pianist was indeed a victim of the dreaded disease AIDS, despite what his personal physician wrote on the death certificate.

This embarrassment to Liberace's memory seems only a pendant to a career that thrived on another, and quite different, kind of shame. For the embarrassment of Liberace's life was that of a success without respect, a success achieved through flouting the very idea of earning the respect of one's colleagues or of a sophisticated audience. What Liberace courted, and won, was the love of the world out of which he grew, and whose faithful son he remained to the end of his life.

But first some facts about Liberace, culled from a long *New York Times* obituary. His father was a musician in the Sousa concert band; his mother played the piano. He began piano lessons when he was four. As a teenager, he worked as a pianist in silent-movie theaters, and when he was fourteen he played, under the scarcely believable pseudonym of Walter Busterkeys, in a Wausau, Wisconsin, cocktail lounge. According to *The New Grove Dictionary of American Music*, he also played in an ice-cream parlor. Hard as it may be to imagine, he appeared with the Chicago Symphony Orchestra as a soloist (according to the *Times*) under the *echtmusikalisch* Frederick Stock in 1936, playing the Liszt First Concerto; according to the *Grove Dictionary* article, the concert (conductor unnamed) took place in 1940, and the piece was the Liszt Second Concerto. In the *Grove Dictionary* account, he adopted the name Walter Busterkeys after moving to New York in 1940 to perform in nightclubs.

Most performing musicians, like the specialists they are trained to be, continue assiduously to cultivate their failures even when the evidence for those failures is overwhelming. Not so Liberace. According to the *Times*, three years after his Chicago Symphony debut, he "stumbled onto the musical formula that made him famous":

> It happened at a recital in La Crosse, Wis. The audience yelled for Liberace to play the popular novelty song "Three Little Fishies" as an encore, and he did. This break with concert tradition "really shook 'em up," Liberace said later, and he realized he was on the road to riches, rhinestones, and Rolls-Royces.

Whatever his initial progress on the road to fame, Liberace hit the jackpot in the mid-1950s with weekly programs on national television, combining his playing of arrangements of classical pieces with a line of patter so sugary-sweet as to seem hostile to those outside the social context of his charm. He often spoke in hyperbolic terms of his mother and of his close relationship to her. And what one can only call Liberace's *mise en scène* always included gaudy costumes, which in the end became gowns, and a quasi-votive candelabrum on the piano.

As a young pianist in the 1950s, I could hardly avoid being aware of Liberace. What thrust him to my attention was not simply his success, for television (like pop music and the movies before) was always unearthing assorted phenomena for the worship of the masses and the spiteful delectation of the elite. Liberace, alas, quickly became a personal matter for me everywhere I went outside the limited musical circles in which I moved, for his very success—often he played compositions I had played myself, among them demanding works of Chopin—was a shining model of what a pianist might aspire to, and a mocking example of what no classical pianist might attain.

Had Liberace played badly, my discomfiture might have been easily handled: serious artists can always reassure themselves by pointing to the triumph of the incompetent. Unfortunately for my feelings, Liberace played rather well. He displayed at all times a large, accurate, and brilliant technique, even indulging himself from time to time in impressive displays of octaves, scales, and complicated passagework. His tone, it is true, was prevailingly hard-edged, but that could easily be explained by the hard-edged tone of the piano he had chosen to play. All in all, his playing purled and glittered just the way an accomplished pianist's should. As for his meretricious choice of repertory and the lack of any spiritual quality in his playing, his rapturous audience reception had a curious way of putting such metaphysical deficiencies into limbo.

What now in retrospect seems clear to me is that Liberace's great commercial success from 1956 on—using as it did television and hyped personal appearances to sell a debased version of classical music—made possible the great commercial success two years later of a vastly more traditional crowd-pleasing pianist. It will be remembered that Van Cliburn—born in Louisiana and raised in Texas—won the International Tchaikowsky Competition in Moscow in April of 1958, and was suddenly catapulted into national prominence not only as a great pianist but as a *popular* pianist. Cliburn's initial repertory was the famous Tchaikowsky B-flat minor Concerto and the Rachmaninoff Third Concerto, both high-romantic works hugely appealing to an enormous public. Cliburn's manner on and off the platform, at once soft-spoken and easy, seemed not just authentically American but, like Liberace's, authentically non-New York American. Cliburn's mother, like Liberace's, had been a pianist, and indeed was his only teacher until he was seventeen. She remained a constant presence in his life as he toured the country. Though Cliburn did (somewhat stiffly) essay Beethoven and Brahms, it was as a performer of Tchaikowsky, Rachmaninoff, and, of course, Chopin that his career was made. While many serious musicians respected his unpretentious musicality and his unforced piano tone, his greatest personal success was made with those who had hitherto been strangers to concert halls. It is difficult to avoid the conclusion that Cliburn's fans, like Liberace's, have remained strangers to concert halls ever since, at least when those concert halls are occupied by serious musical programs.

If the legacy of Liberace has been the power of television to make great careers on the fringes of classical music (a power which has recently been displayed in the case of Luciano Pavarotti), the most important legacy of Cliburn, undoubtedly stemming from the size of his post-Moscow career, has been the contest mania among young performers all over the world. This mania, which places more emphasis on contest competition than on mature artistry, has resulted in an explosion of contests and winners, and a dearth of interesting performers growing up at their own pace.

And so it is easy now to see the different but also curiously similar careers of Liberace and Cliburn—the one ended by death and the other by what one can only assume is a combination of physical and emotional problems (Cliburn has not played in public since 1978)—as having provided spectacularly inapplicable models for the careers of serious musicians. Such is the tragedy of it all. There is also a strange irony in these two great but ultimately ephemeral reputations.

The irony is simply that both Liberace and Cliburn were able to capitalize—and were perhaps the last pianists to do so—on the splendid epoch of the piano as *the* musical instrument par excellence. The epoch lasted from the beginning of the nineteenth century to World War II. During those 140 years the piano was indispensable to creators and performers for the making of both music and careers; it was indispensable, too, across middle-class society as the carrier of a music serious in origin and popular in reception. The piano in the living room, like the candelabrum (so beloved by Liberace and his fans) in the dining room, became an emblem of cultural advancement and participation. It was this touching aspiration which made possible two huge successes, one now ended and the other, we can only hope, in abeyance. Whatever the future holds in store for music in general, the piano will probably never again enjoy such popularity and prestige.

Ruminations on the Romantic Piano

R ECENTLY I FOUND myself on a pre-concert panel, discussing the glorious past and problematic present of what the panel's organizers called "the romantic piano." The panel took place in an atmosphere resembling more an inquest than a celebration, for lately there has been much talk—and more evidence—of a major shift in attitudes toward this quintessential instrument of nineteenth-century music.

Some of this shift involves the hard facts of commerce. After many years of declining activity by American piano makers, and their gathering replacement by highly rationed suppliers in the Far East, it is now accepted that annual piano sales will never again achieve the levels of the past. What the older among us think of as a true piano— a mechanical agglomeration of wood, metal, and felt—has now been rechristened the "acoustic" piano. This antique (and expensive) Victorian behemoth is being supplanted by inexpensive electronic keyboards vastly easier to house and to play. If one is to trust the sales literature, playing these gadgets of the transistor age is more a matter of choosing software than practicing finger exercises or learning harmony. Thus an advertisement in last month's *Stereo Review* spoke glowingly of just how gratifying music making can be with these new keyboards (at a cost of under two hundred dollars):

It's chopsticks time in musicland. Now you can play any of 12 totally different instruments, and have 12 different rhythm sections backing you up automatically.

And what if you don't play? Well, if you sing, this incredible new chordmaker will combine auto-rhythm with your choice of chords to accompany you.

It's amazing. It's like having a skilled band backing you up. If you want to sing in the key of G, just touch G, and let the concert begin.

As the instruments being played have changed, so have the people doing the playing. On the level of serious music study, the increased presence here of pianos from the Far East has been paralleled by the arrival of great numbers of Japanese and Korean piano students in our music schools. And there is increasing doubt that the brightest American students are choosing to play the piano, or to devote their lives to serious music at all. Among the population at large—uninterested in an arduous *Gradus ad Parnassum*, the title composer Muzio Clementi (1752–1832) chose for his standard piano exercises—the availability of cheap and easy-to-play instruments has spawned a new, and properly democratic, class of users quick to bend these new toys to the service of a loud, repetitive, and stripped-down musical product. This product is more the result, or so it seems to many, of emotional and intellectual primitivism than of the technological sophistication that makes all the noise possible.

Curiously, amidst all these changes in keyboard instruments and their players, two closely associated areas of musical life have been little changed, save perhaps in the direction of slow contraction. Here I refer equally to the concert audience and to the concert repertory. In the case of the audience for the piano, I have the impression that piano recitals today are fewer in number than they once were, their place having been taken by ensemble and nonmusical group attractions, most of them dance and theater. Those who do go to hear the piano come, so the studies show, from the same relatively well-educated, musically sophisticated, and economically affluent groups that have supported the piano since the beginning of its conquest of the public two centuries ago; this group now seems less sure of itself, less willing to use its tastes in the service of cultural leadership, than was once the case.

As far as the repertory is concerned, the situation is simple: the famous pieces sell, and the selling pieces are famous. Teachers specialize in the great pieces of the repertory, and piano students pay them a kind of dedicated attention they show to no other music. Audiences react in an unbuttoned way to what they know, and critics display their finest bits of knowledge in evaluating the performances of accepted masterpieces. Just what these accepted masterpieces are is known by everyone: among solo pieces a few sonatas of Beethoven, many of the works of Chopin, several large suites of Schumann, the most brilliant (and tacky) pieces of Liszt, *Le Tombeau de Couperin* and *Gaspard de la nuit* of Ravel. Among concertos the list is equally restricted, to works by Beethoven, Schumann, Brahms, Liszt, and, of course, Mozart.

This is the core of "the romantic piano." Written over a period of hardly more than 125 years, this is the music specialized in, with different kinds of concentration, by the greatest "romantic" twentieth-century pianists of the various national schools—Russian (Hofmann, Rachmaninoff, and Horowitz), German (Schnabel and Fischer), and French (Cortot, Casadesus, and the German-born Gieseking); a brilliant musical polymath like Arthur Rubinstein (who, though deeply Polish, did not really arise out of any national school) played the whole of this core repertory, adding to it music of the early twentieth century, including that of the Spaniard Falla, the Brazilian Villa-Lobos, and the most fetching work of the French charmer Poulenc. Elsewhere, great pianists added to this canon the solo music of Bach, Mozart, and Schubert. What changes there have been in the repertory to the present day have mostly taken place in the concerto literature, with the addition of the concertos of Rachmaninoff, along with the B-flat minor Concerto of Tchaikowsky, the Second and the Third concertos of Prokofiev, and perhaps—just perhaps—the Second Concerto of Bartók.

Of all the pieces included above, the most recently composed—the Bartók Second Concerto (1931) and the Rachmaninoff *Rhapsody on a Theme of Paganini* (1934)—were written more than fifty years ago. A few solo pieces written later, among them the Prokofiev Sonata no. 7 (1942) and the Barber Sonata (1949), have defied the odds to become part of the celebrity repertory. Among more or less recent concertos, only the Bartók Third (1945) manages to lead a fitful life in the concert hall.

Here, then, is the "romantic" piano repertory as it stands today, wildly successful and suffocatingly constricted. Played by young and old pianists alike, taught by young and old teachers alike, this is the repertory that wows audiences, beguiles critics, and wins contests. The ease young pianists thus find, through familiarity, in attracting and moving an audience is more than balanced by the inevitable comparisons so easily made between callow contemporary performances and the splendid musical conceptions preserved for all eternity on recordings. In this competition, it is difficult not to feel that youth, in its touching attempts at success through emulation, almost always loses.

From time to time, a new arrival attempts to break out of this rut of comparison and emulation. Such was the case with the much-trumpeted Carnegie Hall debut recital in November of the Soviet émigré Vladimir Feltsman. The struggles of this tough-minded and tenacious artist in his homeland are by now well known to readers of the world press; his release from what amounted to involuntary servitude in the Soviet Union can, I suppose, be interpreted as a welcome symbol of *glasnost*. It can also be interpreted as a long overdue recompense for the deprivation of the most basic human rights, not just of artistic freedom but of freely chosen residence and travel.

For his Carnegie Hall recital, Feltsman chose a curious program. It began traditionally with the best known (and most comfortable) of Schubert sonatas, that in A major, opus 120; it ended traditionally, too, after the intermission, with the hallowed (and often performed) Schumann *Symphonic Etudes*, a technically exacting work made even more challenging by the pianist's inclusion of the posthumously published sections, which are often left out.

In Feltsman's case, however, it wasn't the opening and the closing of his program that seemed out of the ordinary: it was the middle work, coming just before the intermission. This selection—actually three excerpts from a much larger composition—was the French composer Olivier Messiaen's *Vingt regards sur l'enfant Jesus* ("Twenty Aspects of the Infant Jesus") of 1944. It has always seemed a fascinating example, difficult to decipher and play, of extreme post-romantic piano writing, being pianistically flamboyant in its combination of clashing dissonances and almost saccharine harmonies. The work's stature, despite its undoubted interest, has always been affected by what was perceived as a palpable and paradoxical contradiction between Messiaen's pious Catholic devotion and an incompletely integrated modernist musical style.

But on this night last November, in Carnegie Hall, before as glittering and traditionally sophisticated an audience as a New York piano recital has seen since Horowitz's return in 1965 and Sviatoslav Richter's American debut in 1960, Messiaen's *Vingt regards* seemed not modernist, not dissonantal, not incompletely integrated, and not contradictory. Instead, the three excerpts Feltsman played—"*Nöel,*" "*Première communion de la Vierge*" ("First Communion of the Virgin"), and "*Regards des prophètes, des bergers, et des Mages*" ("Views by the Prophets, the Shepherds, and the Magi")—seemed a brilliant and triumphant culmination of twentieth-century French piano writing, including the *Préludes*, the *Images*, and the *Etudes* of Debussy, and *Gaspard de la nuit* (especially its final section, "*Scarbo*") of Ravel. Even more, Feltsman's playing of Messiaen managed to stake a claim for the composer in the not unrelated progression from the mystical Scriabin through that unappreciated Polish composer Karol Szymanowski. Indeed, this night, Messiaen's *Vingt regards*, for all the incomprehensibility they formerly seemed to enshrine, now stood as fulfilling the promise of *Masques* (1916), Szymanowski's great set of three piano pieces.

As Feltsman played Messiaen, one was no longer conscious of the immensely talented duty with which he had played Schubert and Schumann; one was no longer conscious of the immense technical mastery he brought to these classic works, so loaded with traps for the unwary and clumsy. In Feltsman's Messiaen, one heard and felt melody, color, sonorous resonance, sweep—and, above all, music. I can only add that in Feltsman's performance, Messiaen seemed not just music, not just beautiful music, but great music.

Now in fact Feltsman had managed this hitherto unaccomplished miracle not by playing the piano in a "new" way, or by being in any way a "modern" pianist. In order to play the Messiaen he did not abandon his past, he fulfilled it. His playing in the Messiaen, as in the

Schubert and Schumann, brought to the music the great virtues of the "romantic" pianist: depth of tone, fleetness of fingerwork, sureness of chord playing, rhythmic freedom across (rather than within) bar lines, lyrical melody rather than the clatter of millions of notes, and the suppression of the piano as a percussive instrument in favor of its ability to convey the richness and diversity of orchestral color.

Here, surely, was one answer, if only one, to the survival of "the romantic piano": new music, even unlikely new music, amalgamated into the tradition of the consensually validated great works of the past through the application of the best traditions of past performance. It would be heartwarming to report that Feltsman's achievement was recognized, both that night at Carnegie Hall and later in the critical press, for what it was. In the hall, filled as it was with piano cognoscenti, the reaction to the Messiaen seemed sadly lukewarm; the audience, quite plainly, had come for—and applauded—the old razzle-dazzle, not the new. The situation seemed the same with the critics. Though I haven't read all the press, it is my impression from the several major articles I have seen that, regardless of whether they raved over the pianist's Schubert and Schumann or not, Feltsman's vitalization of Messiaen was either quickly passed over (as in Donal Henahan's *Times* review the next morning), virtually ignored (as in Henahan's wrap-up piece about the concert in the following Sunday's paper), or roasted in comparison to the earlier performances of Messiaen's wife, Yvonne Loriod, and of Peter Serkin (as in Peter Davis's review in *New York* magazine).

And so the piano rut has been dug ever deeper. The message to young artists, as to old, is clear: play safe pieces, concentrate on the most marketable of these guaranteed successes, and, above all, leave the audiences where you found them, changed only by having given up a significant amount of money to hear you play. To presenters the message is clear, too: schedule the famous, program the hackneyed, count the crowds. Then everything will exist in the best of all possible worlds. Artists (and their managers and publicity agents) will be famous and rich; audiences will feel complimented; and presenters, all full of enthusiastic audiences, will be able to apply for grants to hold panels on the demise of "the romantic piano." Who could complain?

Vladimir Horowitz 1904–1989

THE DEATH of Vladimir Horowitz in November at the age of eighty-five was more than the passing of one of the greatest pianists the world has yet known. In a way that can only become clearer as the years pass, it also seems the end of the era of the piano. For if Horowitz in his maturity was the king of the pianists, the piano for close on two centuries was the king of the instruments. We have known for some years that we no longer can say, with Walter Pater, that "all art aspires to the condition of music." Horowitz's death tells us that, with the collapse of a living musical tradition, the piano, too, as the prime medium for the communication of that tradition, is now yet another candidate for the museum of civilization.

As long as Horowitz lived, it was possible for many to be beguiled by the idea that the piano still lived. It was his gift to seem to occupy fully every musical stage on which he deigned to appear. From the time of his much-heralded return to the concert life in 1965 to the very day of his death, Horowitz never ceased to be the cynosure of his colleagues and of the musical audience. His concert appearances, relatively few in number, and almost always in solo recital rather than with orchestra, were breathlessly awaited and invariably oversubscribed on their announcement. His many recordings, made from his young manhood to almost the close of his life, sold marvelously and had a way of becoming the reference point from which the performances by others of the same repertory were evaluated.

It is the very existence of Horowitz's recordings, extending as they do over some six decades, that now provides us with an opportunity to survey his great achievement. The purpose of this examination must finally be the measurement of this brilliant artist's playing against the work of his distinguished twentieth-century colleagues. But this altogether natural, proper, and indeed inevitable process of comparative judgment can hardly be made without a description and assessment of his playing in its own terms, so as to identify its salient attributes and the course of its development.[1]

At the core of Horowitz's playing was his characteristic sonority. He possessed perhaps the most distinctive piano tone of the age: big, gleaming, and penetrating. To make the Horowitz tone possible, the pianos he played were Steinways that he owned and took care to have prepared to suit his requirements; they were always louder, brighter, more aggressive in sound, and quicker in response than any his colleagues were likely to find comfortable. As a result, when Horowitz played, listeners always knew that the instrument he played was itself being tested to the limit.

Close in importance to Horowitz's tone—and intimately related to it—was the demonic energy of his playing. Not only did the individual notes he played crackle, but his characteristic rhythmic pulse was sharply etched, natural-seeming even at its most surprising, and attention-getting whether the tempo at which he was playing was fast or slow. He was known as a pianist who loved speed, and on occasion (as in his famous recorded performances of the Tchaikowsky First Concerto with his father-in-law Arturo Toscanini from 1941 and 1943) he chose blindingly fast tempos. But throughout his career the effect of speed came at least as much from the tautness of his rhythm as from his tempos in themselves. The result was the opposite of regular and metronomic: when Horowitz played slowly, which in fact he often did, his characteristic fluidity of pulse so bound the notes together that the listener had little choice but to hang on each sound and breathlessly await the next.

His technique was imposing in its power to articulate melodic lines, even at moments of great pianistic complexity; it was imposing too in its articulation—the amount of space he seemed to be able to put between the notes even when his fingers ran at their swiftest. His technique, combined with the force of his musical intellect, enabled him to be concerned with the smallest details of phrasing and touch. One must assume that his technique, though immense, was not universally applicable to every demand. He recorded curiously few

[1] For a fuller treatment of Horowitz's playing and life than is possible here, see my "Horowitz: King of Pianists," in *Music After Modernism* (1979) and "The Real Vladimir Horowitz?" in *The House of Music* (1984). The earlier article first appeared in *Commentary* in May 1977, the latter in the *New Criterion* in March 1983.

Chopin *Etudes*, for more than 150 years the truest test of a pianist's equipment; it must be said, though, that those he did record (and play in the concert hall) were spectacular.

His knowledge of the musical repertory—not just that written for the piano—was huge, though he was very selective about the works he chose to essay in public. His concerto repertory, for example, was sadly restricted. He only recorded five concertos: the Beethoven "Emperor," the Brahms B-flat, the Tchaikowsky First, the Rachmaninoff Third, and (at the very end of his life) the Mozart A major (K. 466).[2] Of these concerto recordings, the two Tchaikowsky recordings with Toscanini are unsurpassed. So too are his 1930 (with Albert Coates) and 1951 (with Fritz Reiner) Rachmaninoff Third recordings; his third and final recording of this stirring work, based on a 1978 live Carnegie Hall performance (with Eugene Ormandy) in which Horowitz was appearing with orchestra for the first time in more than twenty years, now seems stronger in passion than in pianistic command. Only the recent Mozart A major (with Carlo Maria Giulini), the only one of his concerto recordings to appear first as a CD, cannot be said to be in the musical class of the other Horowitz concerto recordings.

Horowitz's repertory was centered for many years on the solo music of Chopin, which he played with a unique rhythmic force and snap, and also with an often compelling tendency to waywardness; his performances and recordings of the *Mazurkas* have never been equaled. He was also a marvelous player of Mendelssohn and Liszt, where he brought to the former an unrivaled songfulness and to the latter an equally unrivaled brilliance and excitement.

Of music earlier than that of the great romantics, Horowitz performed almost no Bach in the original; some Bach, though, he performed memorably in the grand transcriptions of Busoni. He was an extraordinary Scarlatti player, finding wit and color in every measure of these small gems. His Haydn, going back at least as far as a 1932 recording of the imposing E-flat Sonata (Hoboken XVI: 52), was revelatory, though by contrast his Mozart always seemed vanquished

---

[2] There is, however, a live 1936 recording, presumably taken from a radio broadcast, of Horowitz playing the Brahms D-minor Concerto, with Bruno Walter conducting the Amsterdam Concertgebouw. It is newly available on a CD transfer, and it is marvelous.

by pianistic overkill. He played relatively few of the thirty-two Beethoven sonatas: the D major, opus 10, no. 3; the *Pathétique*; the "Moonlight"; the E-flat major, opus 31, no. 3; the "Waldstein"; the "Appassionata"; and the A major, opus 101. In his playing of the Beethoven sonatas he lacked a certain warmth and richness, always preferring hard-etched contrasts and stark colors; his early (1934) recording of the thirty-two Variations in C minor, however, is, in its perfect lightness and clarity, a classic of the phonograph.

Mention must be made of Horowitz's extraordinary performances of the sadly limited amount of contemporary music of his maturity that he chose to play. Only two such composers benefited from his immense talents—the Russian Sergei Prokofiev and the American Samuel Barber. The Horowitz recordings of the Prokofiev Sonata no. 7 (1942) and the Barber Sonata (1949) are not simply classic, but definitive. In their unlikely combination of hot lyricism and cold clarity, they define the very sound of these marvelous works. That he recorded no other great works written after World War I (and, save for the Prokofiev sonatas nos. 6 and 8, played none in concert either) must remain a comment both on what was available to him and on his own energy and curiosity. His Bartók, Copland, and Stravinsky, to name three very different kinds of music written for the piano, might well have equaled his Prokofiev and Barber.

Whereas in his youth and middle age Horowitz looked for novelties in the early romantic repertory—for example, in the music of Muzio Clementi (1752–1832) and Karl Czerny (1791–1857)—as he grew older he seemed to be searching for late romantic music that, although little known, would enable him to deploy his vast pianistic resources of sound and excitement. Thus in his last years he turned to the extended solo works of Scriabin and Rachmaninoff, the contemporary music, after all, of his early childhood in Russia. Both these composers were great pianists, and playing their music seemed to involve Horowitz totally; here, at least to my taste, Horowitz's performances ultimately failed to be persuasive, for these composers' more ambitious solo works lack the structural interest needed to support either their harmonic and melodic sweetness, or to justify their pianistic demands.

It is impossible, even in this early assessment of Horowitz's integral pianistic achievement, to avoid comment upon how his playing developed over the course of his life. Before the advent of recorded sound, such a survey had perforce to rely upon the more or less accurate memory of more or less qualified colleagues and critics. Now, of course, recordings provide a kind of hard evidence for description and comparison. With Horowitz such evidence seems even more reliable than it does with many of his colleagues, for his recordings—many of them, especially as he grew older, from live performances—seemed as if they were issued to match listeners' memories of the concerts they had recently heard from him, and to predict accurately what they would hear in the future.

The evidence of these records suggests, not surprisingly, that Horowitz's most virtuoso playing—in the sense of sheer athleticism—was done in his youth, and that this period of fleet brilliance was closed at the time of his marriage to Toscanini's daughter in 1933 and his resulting close musical relationship with the conductor. The influence of the powerful Toscanini on Horowitz hardly produced a carbon copy of the Italian maestro: Horowitz's lyrical freedom, like his choice of repertory, always remained his own. What did come from Toscanini, and what stayed with Horowitz even after Toscanini's death in 1954, was an increased depth of emotion and power of structural projection. Horowitz's vintage years, then, were from about 1933 until his retirement in 1953 from the concert stage, a retirement doubtless due to what in a gentler time would have been called unhappiness, and is today called severe psychological difficulties. It is in these years that we witness the great core of his art, the most serious repertory in the most masterful performances. It is these records, ranging from Haydn to Barber, that will remain in the pianist's enduring legacy.

Horowitz did some recording immediately after his 1953 retirement, and as part of a return to full activity he resumed large-scale recording in the early 1960s. But when he returned to live performance in 1965 with a triumphant Carnegie Hall recital, it was to present a musical image at once backward- and forward-looking. In one important sense, the 1965 Horowitz was the old Horowitz, electric, impulsive, and commanding; he played the same pieces in recognizably the same way as he had for three decades. But it was a new Horowitz, too, sometimes more heedless of the requirements that good taste imposes on scale, and often noticeably more wayward in matters of rhythm and pulse than he had ever been before.

As the years passed after 1965, it became clearer to seasoned Horowitz admirers that their idol was no more immune to the ravages of time than anyone else. To say this is not simply a matter of saying that he now was playing more wrong notes than he had played earlier; he had never been an immaculate or antiseptic executant, even in his days of glory—and mistakes, after all, can easily be cut out of recordings. It is also not to say that he shirked the most challenging part of the repertory; though he seemed to avoid some of his old specialties—the Tchaikowsky Concerto is a case in point—in general his late repertory remained, as it had always been, at the highest level of difficulty. What Horowitz lost as he grew older was his incredible pianistic refinement and *souplesse*, his ability effortlessly to convey the most minute levels and difference of phrasing, rhythm, and tonal shading. Now, as I listen to his last recordings, it is difficult to escape the conclusion that their greatest beauty comes from our awareness of how much he wanted to do, and how little he was able to accomplish. It is perhaps the highest compliment that can be paid to Horowitz as a pianist to recognize that it was only in noticing this inevitable loss of command that it became fully possible to honor the magic of what he had once possessed. Only hearing is believing: to witness this magic at its most magical, one must listen to his 1944 recording of the Czerny Variations on the aria *La Ricordanza*, opus 33.[3]

One can regret, as I do, that Horowitz did not choose to illuminate more of the most profound works of the piano repertory; one can regret, as I did earlier, that he did not play more of the music of his own maturity. But after the death of Rachmaninoff in 1943, Horowitz, as a pianist, had no rivals; as a musical eminence who played the piano, he had only one—Arthur Rubinstein, who died in 1982 at the age of ninety-five. Marvelous as Rubinstein's playing was, and large as his concert and recorded repertory was, by purely pianistic comparison with Horowitz he was merely remarkable, hardly a titan. But as what I have called an eminence—as a man commanding not just the concert stage but in some sense the world—Rubinstein, in love of music, love of people, and love of life, was incomparable.

[3] To the best of my knowledge, this performance was last available, at least in this country, on RCA LD 7021, along with other stunning performances of music by many composers. It will surely be reissued on a CD transfer.

It is a blessing for us in these glory-denuded times that the recordings of both Horowitz and Rubinstein convey their separate greatnesses. In the future we shall find it hard not to think of them together as encapsulating the last great age of the piano. Now our thoughts can only be with Vladimir Horowitz. It is not too much to say that in death he looms larger than those he has left behind.

18.

My first knowledge of the Polish violinist Josef Hassid came when I saw, in a record store, an LP reissue in the HMV Treasury series of the 78 RPM records this amazing and tragically short-lived artist made in London in 1938 and 1939. Out of curiosity—and out of a habit of respect for anything thought good enough in the old days to appear on the HMV Red Label Celebrity Series— I bought the disc, and put it on immediately when I returned home. I was astonished by the magnificence of the playing, and even more I was thrilled once again to hear virtuoso violinism that bore no resemblance to the saccharined sentimentalities of the currently ubiquitous Itzhak Perlman, Pinchas Zukerman, and Isaac Stern school of playing. My article appeared in the October 1987 New Criterion, *and the recording, I am glad to say, still seems to be available.*

The Violinist of the Age

THE VIOLIN is a curious instrument. When ill played, it is supremely ugly; when mastered, more than any other string instrument it approaches the human voice in its ability to communicate what I am afraid can only be called (even in this advanced and putatively rational age) soul states. It is for this reason, I suppose, that the violin has so often been seen as a favorite instrument of the devil. This association has entered literature and art (to name only two examples, the first now little known and the second relatively recent) in the German poet Lenau's drama *Faust* (1836–46) and in Stravinsky's music-*cum*-dance-*cum*-narration *L'Histoire du soldat* (1918). In the rather more public world of performance, the suggestion of satanic inspiration formed the largest part of the legends surrounding the Italian violinist and composer Niccolo Paganini (1782–1840).

As far as performers are concerned, in our own century the violin (in the proper hands) has seemed a benevolent voice, a speaker on behalf of the deepest yearnings of the individual, and, in the case of Jewish violinists, a representative of a whole people. It is in this light that most of the greatest violin careers of our time are to be seen. Unlike such intellectually sophisticated artists as Joseph Szigeti (1892–1973) and Adolf Busch (1891–1952), such famous artists as Fritz Kreisler (1875–1962), Efrem Zimbalist (1889–1985), Mischa Elman (1891–1967), Jascha Heifetz (b. 1901), and David Oistrakh (1908–1974), for all their natural musicality and grace, were content to play brilliantly and "with feeling"; they did not readily attempt to articulate musical structure and content.

Often vulgar and sometimes coarse (even the supposedly "aristocratic" Heifetz was not above a winking indulgence in questionable taste), these immensely gifted violinists of the heart aimed at, and found, a mass audience that reacted to their every throb. Their successor today, at least in terms of fame and box-office appeal, is, of course, Itzhak Perlman; but whereas his predecessors were at one with their art even in their excesses, Perlman, for all his violinistic flair and his daunting success, strikes many (including this writer) as both imitative and cynically distanced from the tradition and the emotions he so facilely exploits.

Until now, this demotic approach to violin playing seemed to be best expressed by the names listed above, along with their many well-known, albeit lesser, colleagues. Now, however, this landscape has been permanently changed by the rediscovery of the complete recordings of the Polish violinist Josef Hassid. Made for the great English record company HMV in 1939 and 1940, these nine 78 RPM record sides (less than thirty-four minutes of music in all) can tell us only briefly of a performing career that was tragically cut short by mental illness in 1940, when the artist was only sixteen. Hassid died in 1945 following brain surgery to correct a condition that the available information does little to specify.

Indeed, what I have called the available information on Hassid seems pretty much confined to the record jacket of this invaluable disc.[1] He is listed in none of the standard reference works, including the late Boris Schwartz's 1983 *Great Masters of the Violin*, the fifth and sixth editions of *Grove's Dictionary*, and the fifth, sixth, and seventh

[1] *Josef Hassid: The Complete Recordings*; EMI HMV Treasury EH 29 12301. The reverse side of this LP is devoted to relatively less significant, though still impressive, recordings made in Berlin in 1938 by the American violin virtuoso Ruggiero Ricci.

editions of the standard *Baker's Biographical Dictionary of Musicians*. His entry in the standard violin discography, James Creighton's 1974 *Discopaedia of the Violin*, gives his dates as 1924–1946 rather than 1923–1945, as given on the HMV record jacket, and contains no further information on his life and career. Exceptions to this rule of oblivion are brief mentions in the supplement to the memoirs of Hassid's teacher, the great Hungarian violinist and teacher Carl Flesch (1873–1944), written by Flesch's son, and in Dominic Gill's recent and sumptuous *The Book of the Violin*.[2]

The repertory played by Hassid on this record is hardly promising. It is in fact little more than a brief tour through the frayed and tattered world of violin encores. Here are short pieces by Elgar, Tchaikowsky, Massenet (the famous "Méditation" from *Thaïs*), Dvořák, Sarasate, Achron, and Kreisler (the famous *Caprice viennois*). We hear the Elgar work—*La Capricieuse*—in two versions, the earlier made as a test in September of 1939, the later made around a year after, and issued, as were all the discs Hassid made save the initial test, in the prestigious HMV Red Label series. In all the issued records, Hassid's pianist was the redoubtable accompanist Gerald Moore; in the test record, his pianist was the then well-known Ivor Newton.

Encore pieces, of course, have long been a staple of violinists, and have been a staple of the phonograph since its earliest and most primitive days. The greatest violinists of the pre-electrical recording era before 1925 are known to us essentially only in the crowd-pleasers which their faithful audiences most wanted to hear—and which had the advantage of being short enough to sit comfortably on a 78 RPM record side. Our knowledge of the playing of Zimbalist in his prime is almost completely confined to this repertory; a new reissue of all the Victor pre-electric records made by Fritz Kreisler, running to ten LP sides,[3] makes clear how an entire phonographic reputation could be sustained entirely by the recording of just such trifles.[4]

But what are trifles for Kreisler and for his marvelous colleagues are

[2] *The Book of the Violin*, edited by Dominic Gill, was published by Rizzoli in 1984. It gives Hassid's dates as 1923–1950.
[3] *The Art of Fritz Kreisler—The Acoustic Victor Recordings* (1910–1925); Strad LB1/5.
[4] With the coming of electrical recording, or course, Kreisler—and other great violinists—did record longer and vastly more serious works. In Kreisler's case, as recording technology improved, his playing grew less polished and secure.

quite otherwise for Hassid. Perhaps the highest honor that can be paid to these recordings made by a sixteen-year-old Polish boy is that when one listens to him play, one does not think in terms of trifles, but rather of a pure manifestation of music. Here, as Hassid indulges in superhuman flights of lightness, grace, and ease, one senses immediately that his playing is beyond style, beyond taste, beyond technique. Put another way, so fully formed and perfect is Hassid's style, taste, and technique that he directs our attention away from the earthly world of performance toward some metaphysical realm of tone.

Perhaps no critic ought to write in such an unguarded fashion. If the critic is doing his job, then even the highest genius ought to have some defining characteristic that a mere mortal might describe and mere mortals might understand. If this is so, then Hassid's divine center is the unequaled penetrating richness of his tone, and not just in the long notes played on the lower strings, where richness comes naturally to players of high ability; all the notes Hassid plays, whether fast or slow, short or long, *legato* or *spiccato*, are fully resonant, as if he has *imagined* them to the depth of his being. Not once does Hassid produce the thin, wiry tone so easy to confuse these days with brilliance; instead he plays every display passage with the same fullness other violinists reserve for the big tunes. And so all through the formidable technical traps of these pieces, traps that today's violinists solve in the fashion of so many callow Olympic hurdlers, Hassid plays melodies that dance and charm—and enter the listener's heart.

What would this mere boy have done with the real meat of the violinist's repertory, with the great concertos of Mozart, Beethoven, and Brahms and the equally great solo works of Bach, Beethoven, and Brahms? Would he have (to use the vogue word) "grown"? Though it is clear that his playing did ripen extraordinarily in the year between his test pressing of the Elgar *La Capricieuse* and the issued recording, for poor Hassid, alas, getting older meant ruin, as it does in one way or another for so many child prodigies.

One child prodigy who managed by force of will to remain violinistically more or less alive through (and after) this tortuous transition from youth to adulthood was, of course, Yehudi Menuhin. Indeed, in listening to Hassid one's responses time and again repeat those inspired by the ineffable records Menuhin made at the age of twelve, and continued to make for a very few years thereafter. Heard today these Menuhin records—unique in their beauty until the rediscovery of the Hassid discs—encapsulate an otherworldly purity. Though I hardly wish to make an argument for reincarnation, it is tempting to remark that Hassid, in a curious way, achieved in his playing of these small pieces what Menuhin's full and unforced maturity might have been, and was not.

On the overpowering evidence of his few records, it is difficult to avoid the conclusion that Josef Hassid was the greatest violinist of whose playing we can have any firm knowledge. About his early death, we can only echo the famous words of Grillparzer on the monument at Schubert's grave:

Die Tonkunst begrub hier einen reichen Besitz
Aber noch viel schönere Hoffnungen.

(Music has here entombed a rich treasure,
but much fairer hopes.)

19.

The entire Metropolitan Opera Ring, *of which the performance of* Die Walküre *I described in the following November 1986 article in the* New Criterion *was the first installment, is now a part of the company's annual repertory. Furthermore, the entire cycle will soon be available on CD, though in many cases the recorded singers will be superior to, or at least more celebrated than, those who might have been seen and heard on any given night at Lincoln Center; such was certainly the case in the* Walküre *I am writing about here, where only the Brünnhilde (Hildegard Behrens) was thought good enough to make the recording. I should add that Met broadcasts of* Die Walküre *in the years since I saw the opera on the Met stage suggest that the level of singing and conducting remains unchanged.*

The Met's Failed Walküre

A PALPABLE AIR of unease these days surrounds the Metropolitan Opera. There is, it is true, some good news: after a poor showing last season at the box office, ticket sales for the current season have picked up. Reportedly, Bruce Crawford, the Met's new general manager, is looking forward to a more than 90 percent sold-out year. But the good news doesn't go beyond ticket sales. The press seems lukewarm, albeit respectful. Opera fans complain of arbitrary casting policies and a general dearth of great singers. Except for James Levine, the Met engages curiously few conductors with large careers or even international reputations. And there is a noticeable absence of innovative—that is, avant-garde—stage direction, resulting in lack of controversy surrounding the Met's offerings of familiar works.

One does not know how far to go in blaming the Met for the vocal shortcomings of its casts. For many years it has hardly been a secret that singers' careers now seem to burn out more rapidly than they used to. All too frequently the collapse of highly ballyhooed young voices reminds one of the glib and venomous remarks (attributed to Georges Clemenceau) about America's being the only society that went from barbarism to decadence without passing through civilization. There is indeed a shortage of conductors of overwhelming musical personality. The result is that there is a dearth of excellent but routine conductors working in the geniuses' musical wake, following the patterns they have established.

The Met's problems are clearly not financial. The company has not been unwilling to spend money on its productions; indeed, it has undertaken expensive and complicated stagings. The Zeffirelli staging of Puccini's *La Bohème* involved a financial and technical effort that would have bankrupted almost any other company. The Met's costumes are lavish, the orchestra is generously staffed, and the chorus is full and well rehearsed. In general, the Met gives every impression of honestly trying to do its best to provide New York—and the United States— with the best opera company in the world. It is even possible, though hardly reassuring, that in this goal the Met has largely succeeded.

But despite the Metropolitan Opera's undoubted virtues, the unease remains. One important source of this unease is the Met's equivocal approach to doing the most serious works of the repertory. And yet even here the problem is fairly subtle. It is not that the Met performs trash: it is a rare occasion when the company performs a really second-rate opera. Nor has the Met failed to perform great works: it has regularly presented such masterpieces as Mozart's *Die Zauberflöte*, *Le Nozze di Figaro*, and *Così fan tutte*; Beethoven's *Fidelio*; Wagner's *Parsifal*; Verdi's *Aida* and *Otello*; Strauss's *Salome*, *Elektra,* and *Der Rosenkavalier*; and Berg's *Wozzeck* and *Lulu*. And there are on occasion worthwhile novelties, like the French and Stravinsky triple-bills of recent seasons. All this takes place, as it should, in a general context of the Met's attempting to please large audiences through the exhibition of celebrated voices singing works of proven appeal.

And yet the problem of the Met's contribution to a serious operatic culture remains. It has even intensified as recent highly publicized administrative changes have begun to communicate an organizational and financial solidity which must be the envy of all other American companies. Much of this problem has been due to the Met's settled unwillingness to schedule the most musically demanding twentieth-century works. Some of these works, such as Pfitzner's *Palestrina* and

Hindemith's *Mathis der Maler*, only promise to bore the supposedly sophisticated New York audience silly; others, such as Schoenberg's much-feared *Moses und Aron*, offer the possibility of actively offending the sensibilities of a public always tempted to see Puccini as high culture. Then too there is the problem of the Met's nonexistent relation to American opera; with the exception of Gershwin's *Porgy and Bess*, the Met has not done an American opera since the late 1960s, when it put on Marvin David Levy's *Mourning Becomes Electra*. It is not just new American operas, one must hasten to add, that have fallen under the Met's ban; with the exception of the works of the musically safe Benjamin Britten, no new European works have been done since Stravinsky's *The Rake's Progress* in 1953. There seems little likelihood that this situation will change any time soon: even the Met's much-trumpeted new commissions from Jacob Druckman and John Corigliano hold out little promise of producing works of lasting musical importance.

But it would be wrong to assume that the Met's problems of musical seriousness are entirely confined to an unwillingness to produce new, or even relatively recent, operatic compositions. There is clearly something wrong with the Met's approach to the universally accepted cornerstones of the repertory, to those works whose purely musical stature marks them as both symphonic and operatic masterpieces. At no time have the Met's failings in this regard seemed clearer, or more disconcerting, than at the beginning of its current season, with its performances of *Die Walküre*, the second part of Wagner's *Der Ring des Nibelungen*.

There can be little doubt that those responsible for the Met's administration, Messrs. Levine and Crawford, attempted to meet the challenge head-on. They scheduled the four-hour work for opening night, in a new production by Otto Schenk. Neither Mr. Levine nor Mr. Schenk had ever before done the *Ring*, or any of its four constituents, and that only seemed to emphasize the Met's desire to break new ground. There was a further reason, too, that doing *Die Walküre* at this time seemed to throw down the gauntlet to the company's critics: it was announced at the end of last season that the Met will be recording all four operas of the *Ring* over the course of the next several years for Deutsche Grammophon, and that this will be the first

Ring made specifically for compact discs.

Because good news in music is nowadays in short supply, it would be pleasant indeed to report that this production of *Die Walküre* marked an auspicious beginning to the Met's great project. Unfortunately, I cannot, for I have seen *Die Walküre* several times before, and I have an extensive acquaintance with its recorded literature. Measured against the evidence of the past on stage and on record, this production failed both scenically and musically; measured in its own terms, the Met's new *Walküre* failed to convince, and in the process failed to give the kind of satisfaction that is to be expected from a major performance of a great work.

Critical attention, both before the event and after, has tended to concentrate on the staging. There can be no doubt that Mr. Schenk's direction, complemented by Günther Schneider-Siemssen's sets, did mark the kind of radical break with the past that this production was designed to accomplish. In *Die Walküre*, Mr. Schenk employed the romantic naturalism so applauded in his 1977 production of *Tannhäuser* at the Met. The company's 1986–87 souvenir booklet praises that production for "its evocative beauty, shrewd exploitation of the Met's physical plant and its artful return to a representational style after the long reign of Wieland Wagner-inspired mythic starkness."

What the Met booklet referred to as "the long reign of Wieland Wagner-inspired mythic starkness" had meant, at the Met, the 1967 Herbert von Karajan *Ring* production, which was created originally for the Easter Festivals at Salzburg. Very much in the Wieland Wagner tradition (which dates back to the first post–World War II Bayreuth productions of the *Ring* in 1951), Karajan's stage was dim and virtually empty, with a few platforms set at different heights and distances from the front; dark and hulking shapes filled in for palpable rocks and trees. The backdrops were simple projections of semi-abstract clouds and forms drawn from the cosmos. Like Wieland Wagner, Karajan put his characters in conflict with each other. The resultant instinctual forces of greed, treachery, and murder were played out against a background of what Matthew Arnold calls (in "Dover Beach") ". . . the vast edges drear/And naked shingles of the world."

By contrast, in the Met's new production the lights were turned up, and there were real trees. The sets took up much of the available stage area, with massive rock formations closing off approximately one quarter of the stage on the (audience) right. Much notice has been taken of the fact that in the new production the rear doors of Hunding's hut actually opened to reveal the fluorescently lit, leafy beauties of a spring night, as Siegmund sang his aria-like "*Winterstürme wichen dem Wonnemond*" ("Winter storms made way for the month of May"). There was general applause too for all the jagged rocks in Act II, and for the very realistic fire in which Wotan, with the fire-god Loge's help, wrapped his daughter Brünnhilde as she lay sleeping on the rocks at the end of the opera. And with the lights up, it was easy to see other features of the production: a giant tree trunk in Act I with what looked to be a very bad complexion, the dimestore weapons and helmets, the clothing made out of what appeared in some cases to be pieced rags, and the charming visage of Wotan's hectoring wife Fricka, gotten up with two pigtails in front to look like Pocahontas.

Not only did this production manage to restore all the ghostly tinsel which Wieland Wagner (and his brother Wolfgang also) had relegated to the musty museum of operatic horrors. Even worse was the way in which the bright lights, the realistic sets and costumes, and the enclosing of the stage area combined to render Wagner's gods and goddesses less than life-size. Here were all-too-human beings, shown in bright light for all the world to see just how impossible it is to act convincingly while singing difficult music at the full volume necessary to fill the enormous space of the Metropolitan Opera House. One wonders whether Mr. Schenk and his lighting director Gil Wechsler realize just how well they have filled the role of a none-too-friendly radiologist.

While it is difficult not to have sympathy for the impossible position singers are put in when they must act Wagner as well as sing his music, two enormities in particular must be mentioned. The first came perilously close to exciting laughter, and the second actually did. In Act I, as the handsome and youthful Siegmund (tenor Peter Hofmann) and the extremely beautiful Sieglinde (soprano Jeannine Altmeyer) went about discovering both that they were brother and sister and that they were passionately in love, I kept thinking that they really acted like small-town high-school students bent on exchanging valentines. The second risible moment came in Act II when Wotan (baritone Simon Estes), enraged at his inability to protect Siegmund from Hunding (bass Aage Haugland), Sieglinde's outraged husband, struck Hunding dead with a wave of his hand. Here the artificiality of Wotan's motions, combined with Hunding's hokey stage fall, actually produced guffaws from several persons around me in the audience. Of the acting of the Brünnhilde and her sister Valkyries, it is enough to say that at their most clumsy they recalled Anna Russell's parodies of the *Ring*.

And then there was the singing. As vocalism *qua* vocalism, I found it undistinguished, and frequently only barely acceptable. The weakest member of the cast was Peter Hofmann as Siegmund. His voice has a marked wobble, of which he must be aware, for he often failed to hold long notes long enough. As Sieglinde, Jeannine Altmeyer displayed an attractive voice, though one without a particularly distinctive quality. I did not like the singing of mezzo-soprano Brigitte Fassbänder as Fricka. She seemed to lack an even vocal production, and her chest register sounded particularly strident. The Brünnhilde, Hildegard Behrens, was noticeably cautious in her traversal of the famous *Hojotoho* whoops at the beginning of Act II; elsewhere, her voice often wobbled. Simon Estes, as Wotan, seemed comfortable with the notes, and often produced a singular melodious and sometimes even powerful tone. I thought that the Valkyries in Act III sang on a level embarrassing in a great opera house; one difficult passage toward the end of the long Valkyrie scene seemed to have strayed in from a rehearsal of twelve-tone music.

But there is more to singing than vocalism, important as pure sound is. There are the problems of the dramatic comprehension of the text and the musical comprehension of the notes. Dramatic comprehension is not simply a matter of good diction; as a matter of fact, I thought that on the whole the words were well articulated on this occasion. Dramatic comprehension involves singing the words as if they were one's own. Here the requirement is total immersion in the character being portrayed. With the fortunate exception of Simon Estes's Wotan, I thought the vocal characterization was poor and even at times completely lacking. Musical comprehension can go a long way toward making up for inability to penetrate an operatic character, but in this production the vocal surge and flow—in a single word, the passion—of Wagner's music was in short supply.

But other performances, containing all the weak elements I have described above, have turned out to be absorbing experiences in the opera house. The reason, of course, was the quality of the musical direction coming from the podium. In the end, great opera, no matter how important the voices might be, no matter how interesting the production might be, rests on the shoulders of one individual: the conductor. And here the Met's new *Walküre* was an abject failure. Much of this failure must be chalked up simply to Mr. Levine's not having conducted the work before. But he has done other Wagner, including *Tannhäuser, Lohengrin, Tristan und Isolde*, and *Parsifal*, the last not just for many years at the Met, but also in Bayreuth in 1982, on the hundredth anniversary of the work's premiere. Clearly, he feels confident enough in his own conception of *Die Walküre* to be conducting it in the Deutsche Grammophon recording this coming spring.

Mr. Levine has a reputation for being a nervous, often aggressive, operatic conductor. I have never found these qualities to appear in his Wagner. On the contrary, I find his Wagner conducting to be pale and static, as if he were paralyzed by respect for the Master. In *Parsifal*, such an approach can easily seem like reverence for the solemnity of the score and the stage action, but in *Die Walküre* such reserve—if that is what it is—can only eviscerate the opera's content. So it was on this occasion. From the opening musical description of the storm beating on Siegmund as he comes exhausted into Hunding's hut, everything seemed heavy and passionless. Rather than being given individual meaning and weight, the rapidly moving quarter notes of the Prelude were accented in groups of two, giving the impression of plodding rather than running. The beautiful themes associated with Sieglinde's growing excitement were played dutifully and even flaccidly. By the end of Act I, the lovers seemed to be having such a difficult time getting around on the stage that one fervently wished them better luck as they ran out of the hut to embrace under the spring moonlight.

Act II is a difficult act for all concerned because of the long stretches of narrative, taking place first between Wotan and Fricka, then between Wotan and Brünnhilde, then between Siegmund and Sieglinde, and finally between Siegmund and Brünnhilde. Here there are many short silences, meant to be pregnant pauses; when these silences are seemingly of random length, as they were in this production, when they lack a musical presence in their very silence, then all action—musical and dramatic—comes to a dead halt. In the final act, with its immensely touching scene of Brünnhilde's exalted acceptance of her future as Siegfried's bride, and Wotan's farewell to her, Mr. Levine's conducting produced only a kind of stately indulgence in lush harmonies and cushioned orchestral playing. On this occasion, Mr. Levine's tempos were very slow, and the total performance was almost a half-hour longer than in the Met's exciting and vocally impressive 1975–76 performances under Sixten Ehrling. The great sweep necessary to carry off a long opera was missing, and the result was simply boredom.

There will be more performances at the Met of *Die Walküre* this spring, and then the recording will be made. The cast will in all probability be quite different from the fall's, though Hildegard Behrens will remain as Brünnhilde. Of the others to be in the recording, only James Morris, as Wotan, has been announced. Mr. Levine, it goes without saying, will be the conductor.

There will be formidable competition for this new recording. Even the recording's technological newness may not be an advantage, for older *Ring* recordings are now being remastered for release on compact disc. These two- to three-decade-old complete *Ring* performances by Karajan, Böhm, Solti, and Furtwängler remain summits of the Wagnerian conductor's art; the singing they contain is on a level apparently unreachable today, as the recent Boulez recording of the 1976 Bayreuth *Ring* production suggests. Also in existence are so-called "pirate" recordings, taken from radio broadcasts, of all the Bayreuth *Ring*s from the early 1950s through 1960. On these reasonably good-sounding recordings there are such great conductors as Clemens Krauss and Hans Knappertsbusch, and such great singers as Hans Hotter and the still undervalued Astrid Varnay.

And then there are the recordings of a half-century ago, of the golden age of Wagnerian singing. Here, in a discussion of *Die Walküre*, it suffices to mention the 1935 Lauritz Melchior–Lotte Lehmann recording of Act I, with the Vienna Philharmonic conducted by Bruno Walter.[1] Act II is available in a brilliant recording which uses, for the Siegmund-Sieglinde section of the act, the same singers,

---

[1] This fiery performance is available in an excellent LP transfer on EMI Référence (France) 2C 051-03023. There can be little doubt that it will soon be available as a compact disc.

orchestra, and conductor; those parts of the act solely involving Wotan, Fricka, and Brünnhilde are done by Hotter, Margarete Klose, and Marta Fuchs, with Bruno Seidler-Winkler conducting the Berlin State Opera Orchestra.[2] So far as Act III is concerned, I am partial to a 1945 recording by the great American Wagnerian soprano Helen Traubel and Herbert Janssen, a commanding even if not vocally splendid Wotan; this recording has the New York Philharmonic in its best days, conducted by the excellent Artur Rodzinski.[3]

One hates always to be driven back to the recordings of the past, into what must seem to those who know not its riches as nostalgia and nothing more. For those who do know these riches, a better *Walküre* and a better *Ring* exist than can now be seen at the Met. Till matters change, one piece of advice can suffice to conjure a stage picture to go with the wonderful sound which can still be heard on records: use your imagination.

[2] This recording is a good deal harder to get than the Vienna Act I mentioned above. The Walter sections alone are still available on Vox Turnabout THS65163. The complete Act II is available in the wonderful French EMI set 2902123, *Les Introuvables du Chant Wagnérien*; it is also available on Volume IV of the Danacord (Denmark) collection of the complete recordings of Lauritz Melchior.

[3] This recording is still available, electronically enhanced for stereo, on CBS Odyssey 32260018E.

20.

By now, television ought to have proven a boon for opera, doing for it what the radio did for music in the 1930s and 1940s. Yet despite the really quite remarkable technological developments that have made televised opera sound— at least on decent playback equipment—so good, and despite all the work that has gone into engineering ever smaller cameras and ever more flexible image editing capabilities, one sad fact remains: televised opera can be no better than the live performances of which the broadcasts are presumably faithful replicas. So when the fault in contemporary operatic performance lies, as I believe it now does, with the artists—the singers and especially the conductor—one can only expect television to reveal and even magnify the problem. In this May 1987 Commentary *article, my targets were the superstar singers Joan Sutherland and Luciano Pavarotti, along with Miss Sutherland's husband, conductor Richard Bonynge. In my opinion, they are only symptoms, albeit famous symptoms, of an endemic problem.*

Dead from Lincoln Center

EVIDENCE that a massive expansion of the American opera public might be possible has been gathering since the beginning of the twentieth century. The first great expansion took place with the popularity of acoustic recordings of opera excerpts shortly after 1900. This era, closely associated with the tenor Enrico Caruso (1873–1921), brought the hit tunes of the great operatic composers into every home aspiring to culture. After 1925, with electrical recording, came the presentation of famous operas in essentially complete form. More important, the advent of radio brought live performances, free to anyone with a cheap set, by the reigning opera stars of the day under commercial sponsorship; listeners with the desire and the patience to sit through an afternoon were able, from the mid-1930s on, to hear weekly Metropolitan Opera broadcasts featuring international casts.

After World War II, the LP made possible the recording of the entire known operatic repertory, and the exploration of sizeable parts of the forgotten repertory; thanks to the LP's low price and improved reproduction, listening in the home became a viable economic and artistic substitute for attendance at live performances. Television, too, seemed to promise much for the cause of opera, including even contemporary opera; the NBC Opera Theater, a project much beloved of RCA's (and thus NBC's) then-czar David Sarnoff, presented new works specially written for the screen. This particular promise, however, unfortunately petered out after the 1950s with the increasingly total abdication by commercial television of any responsibility for the life of serious culture in the United States.

From the mid-1970s on, the future of opera on the highest level for a mass audience clearly lay with public television and the Public Broadcasting Service (PBS). Indeed, one of the great hopes of public television, advanced sincerely by some of its backers and cynically by others, was that opera "at its best" could thereby be made available to an American audience otherwise limited by low income, poor education, or geographical location away from the great cities. Because nothing but the best—or at least the most famous—was thought to be good enough for this projected new audience, PBS began to broadcast Metropolitan Opera productions, bathed and overbathed in the kind of glitter associated with opera for the past century and more.

But watching long operas on television, after all, requires a rather greater attention span from the audience than anyone in television might reasonably expect. And so it was soon realized that even Met offerings, restricted as they were to presenting complete works, failed to capitalize sufficiently on the stars in their casts. Now was born the celebrity recital, in which short excerpts highlighting the vocal strengths of these stars could be sold as delivering not just the best of opera, but the best of the best.

The chief beneficiary of this process on public television during the past decade has undoubtedly been the Italian tenor Luciano Pavarotti, born in Modena in 1935. Pavarotti's career has risen spectacularly since the mid-1960s. Every success (save for a film career) has been his: roles with every major opera company, widely publicized song recitals before huge audiences, and innumerable recordings for Decca/London, capped by triumphant appearances on public television, not just in opera but in recitals of varied material including Christmas carols and those staples of the popular tenor's repertory, Italian folk songs. Through a combination of vocal strength, a teddy-bear personality on and off the stage, vastly astute commercial management, and real popular appeal, Pavarotti bids fair to join Caruso and Beniamino Gigli (1890–1957) in the ranks of the most commercially successful tenors of the Italian tradition.

One of Pavarotti's closest associates on the stage has been the Australian soprano Joan Sutherland. Born in Sydney in 1926, she came to London in 1951, where she studied at the Royal College of Music and soon gained a contract with the Covent Garden opera company. Beginning without a specialty in any particular repertory, under the tutelage of the young Australian conductor and pianist Richard Bonynge (whom she married in 1954) Sutherland turned to florid eighteenth-century compositions and to the Italian and French dramatic coloratura repertory of the nineteenth century, and therein found her métier. After her 1959 Covent Garden appearance in the title role of Donizetti's *Lucia di Lammermoor*, Sutherland embarked upon a conquest of the most brilliant and difficult works—always, however, excluding the great German operas of Wagner and Strauss—written for the female voice. From Handel through Bellini to Massenet, the singing of Sutherland in performance and on records (again, as with Pavarotti, for Decca/London) has made operatic history.

The first joint appearance of Sutherland and Pavarotti seems to have been in *Lucia di Lammermoor* at the Greater Miami Opera in March 1965. In the same year they sang together in Bellini's *La Sonnambula* at Covent Garden, and then in these two operas, along with Verdi's *La Traviata*, in the performances, promoted and directed by the soprano and her husband throughout Australia, of the Sutherland Williamson International Grand Opera Company. Since then they have often collaborated in the opera house, on records, and on television: not only do they work comfortably together as singers, but Pavarotti's height and imposing stature make him a suitable partner for the tall and equally imposing Sutherland. All this is photographically documented, together with many pictures of them at work and *en famille*, in two large and glossy books published last year, *The Joan Sutherland Album*,[1]

---

[1] *The Joan Sutherland Album*, by Joan Sutherland and Richard Bonynge; Simon & Schuster, 1986. Full biographical material on Sutherland may be found in *La Stupenda*, by Brian Adams; Hutchinson of Australia, 1980.

compiled by Sutherland and her husband (along with a short tribute by Pavarotti) and in Martin Mayer's *Grandissimo Pavarotti.*[2]

And so it must have seemed natural for PBS—and the Met, its favorite (and almost sole) operatic presenter—to bring these two artists together this winter in a "gala" appearance, taped in the Metropolitan Opera on January 11, and televised across the nation on March 4. There was, not surprisingly, the usual discovery of an "anniversary" to celebrate. In this case, indeed, there were, according to the honeyed but frenetic patter of host Joanne Woodward, actually two: the twenty-fifth anniversaries of Sutherland's debut at the Met and of Pavarotti's operatic debut at a little theater in Italy.

Instead of simply singing single arias and duets, Sutherland and Pavarotti this time presented three fairly substantial stage excerpts, conducted by Richard Bonynge, from operas in which they have often collaborated: *Lucia di Lammermoor,* Verdi's *Rigoletto,* and the same composer's *La Traviata.* These passages, all imperishable moments of the high tragedy of doomed love central to grand opera, provide famous singers with every opportunity for the kind of vocal and theatrical acting that goes beyond the striking of rhetorical attitudes to the creation of personality: not the familiar personality of the singer, not the formulaic personality of a character out of literary history, but rather the amalgam which results from a great actor's total penetration of, and immersion in, the character being portrayed.

Perhaps it is enough of a verdict on the Sutherland-Pavarotti performances of these stirring scenes to remark that the most distinguished feature of the telecast was the evidence provided of the enormous improvement recently made in the television transmission of music. Heard on reasonably good equipment rather than through a standard home television set, the sound now approaches in fullness and lack of distortion that available on the FM stereo simulcasts which often accompany the original, though not the repeat, television broadcasts.

The trouble, however, is that the basic sound of broadcast opera

[2] *Grandissimo Pavarotti*, by Martin Mayer; Doubleday, 1986. This book, though clearly an authorized effort of adulation, also includes much solid biographical material in addition to many pictures, and even some interesting comments on the art of singing.

today, whether heard via television or radio, unfortunately resembles all too closely the slick electronic packaging of pop singers. This sound is the master confection of multitrack recording, constant and intrusive variations in the mixing of these tracks, and musical decisions made by engineers and directors sitting in a control truck, not by musicians satisfying their own ears as they go about the business of performing. All this fiddling at the controls produces an artificial and unmusical loudness and nearness, in place of the natural variation of balances which conductors must employ to suggest not only dramatic atmosphere but even musical structure itself. Thus the stars, when they are singing, always sound brash and close; when they are not singing, the orchestra—even when playing minor introductory accompaniment figures—is quite literally flung in the listener's ears. The result is a spurious glossiness, with the aesthetic tension created and sustained by the sheer level of decibels rather than by artistic intelligence and the evocation of authentic emotion.

Electronics aside, the Sutherland–Pavarotti telecast had precious little to contribute to the experience of great opera. There is, I suppose, plenty of virtuosity in their work, if by virtuosity one means accurate, dependable, forceful, and generally pleasant singing. But the fact is that when isolated, virtuosity in singing, as in all other branches of musical performance, all too easily becomes *mere* virtuosity, the cultivation of display for its own sake.

In the case of Sutherland's performances as Lucia, as Gilda in *Rigoletto*, and as Violetta in *Traviata*, it was impossible to escape the impression that the singer brought no more to her work than a pretty, phenomenally agile—though essentially impersonal and, at least to my ears, often unfocused—voice and a generalized musicality. Of differentiation among the contrasting characters of the unstable and vulnerable Lucia, the ultimately heroic Gilda, and the febrile yet passionate Violetta, there was almost no grace either in voice or in stage deportment. As she sang in an all-purpose voice, there was an all-purpose look on her face, as if an expression of worried and matronly concern—rarely even rising to agitation—could be a substitute for the creation of tragic character. Nor was there anything authentic or moving in her rendering of the characteristic sound of the Italian vowels and consonants, so flavorful in themselves and so necessary, not just for conveying the story but for giving an appropriately Italianate ring to the singer's voice and to the music.

Considered solely in terms of vocalism (but excepting, of course, the problem of poor diction), Sutherland's voice retains, at sixty, much of its youthful bloom and ease in both melodic and ornamented passages;[3] it is this bloom and ease which have been responsible for her position as the queen of twentieth-century bel canto—of the virtuoso repertory of Handel, the pre-Verdi Italians, and the French composers of the second half of the nineteenth century.

It is often said that Sutherland, with the vital help of Bonynge, has resuscitated this repertory, which had languished in our time for lack of competent performers. This way of putting the matter, so assiduously fostered by publicists, does scant justice to Maria Callas (1923–1977), whose commanding performances of the operas of Bellini and Donizetti—in addition to many staples of the later repertory— awakened new dramatic and especially musical interest in once-familiar works. Indeed, the recorded evidence suggests that Sutherland's mere virtuosity falls far short of Callas's phenomenal musical and dramatic achievement. Like Sutherland, Callas made many recordings; her numerous commercial recordings compete with a seemingly endless stream of "pirate" versions taken from radio broadcasts. In the case of the three operas performed by Sutherland on the telecast with Pavarotti, the Callas recordings, whether commercial or "pirate," are quite sufficient in every case—despite what must be called undeniable technical vocal flaws—to convey an unparalleled force of dramatic character in a voice of haunting and plangent quality.[4] As a singing

---

[3] Documentation of the state of Sutherland's voice at the beginning of her international career is currently available, in up-to-date remasterings of the three operas excerpted on the telecast. Her 1961 *Lucia* may be found on London 411622-1 LJ3; her 1962 *Rigoletto* is on London 42012; her 1963 *La Traviata* is on London JL 42010. Comparison of these recordings of a quarter-century ago with her most recent singing makes clear that, though her voice has suffered remarkably little from the passage of time, her ability to create dramatic character has grown scarcely at all.

[4] Callas's recordings of these operas, dating from a time before her final tragic vocal decline, are also available: her 1955 Berlin *Lucia*, conducted by Herbert von Karajan, is available in a "pirate" version on Replica 23; her commercial recordings of the same opera, dating from 1953 and 1959 and both conducted by Tullio Serafin, are available, respectively, on Seraphim 1B 6032 and on the even more deeply characterized EMI/ Angel AVB-34066 (remastered); her remastered 1955 *Rigoletto*, again conducted by Serafin, is available on EMI/Angel AVB-34069; her 1955 "pirate" *La Traviata,* conducted by Carlo Maria Giulini, is (or was) available on Paragon 78-157 F.

actress Callas is at her greatest—and Sutherland is at her weakest— in *Lucia*, where every note must suggest the heroine's impending doom. To put it simply, Callas, here as elsewhere, uses her voice to create unforgettable character; Sutherland uses hers merely to convince the listener that she possesses a great voice.

I am not sure that even this much can be said of Luciano Pavarotti. Like a tennis player who is used to getting all his first serves in, Pavarotti has always seemed to belt all his notes out with the confidence of a supreme professional. And though hardly a flattering verb, "belt" is, I am afraid, the right one to describe Pavarotti's physically (though not emotionally) jaunty method of delivery. Always brilliant rather than warm and resonant, Pavarotti's voice, unlike Sutherland's, *has* lost its youthful bloom and ease;[5] in place of these qualities, so estimable in an Italian tenor, Pavarotti today puts a kind of breathless determination, as if physical effort and concentration might just possibly serve to get the notes out in a winning way.

Of differentiated character in his vocal and dramatic portrayals, Pavarotti conveys surprisingly little more than Sutherland— surprisingly, that is, considering the distance which separates the libidinous Duke in *Rigoletto* from the tormented Edgardo in *Lucia* and the serious Alfredo in *La Traviata*. It is true that the great Italian tenors with whom Pavarotti is often compared, namely Caruso and his successor, Gigli, were not great actors either. But judging from the recorded evidence, they hardly needed to be.

Caruso, even in our digitalized age, remains the touchstone by which tenors in this music are judged. His discs, all made by the primitive acoustic process, have now been remarkably improved through a method of computer restoration.[6] This technique removes

---

[5] Pavarotti's recordings—all with Sutherland—of the three operas excerpted on the telecast are the 1971 *Lucia*, on London OSA-13103, the 1971 *Rigoletto*, on London OSA-13105, and the 1981 *La Traviata*, on London LDR-73002. The change over the years in Pavarotti's voice is easily demonstrated by comparing the youthful freshness of his singing in the famous aria *La donna è mobile* from *Rigoletto* and the subsequent introduction to the equally famous quartet *Bella figlia dell'amore* on the 1971 recording with the stentorian bleating of the same passages on the current telecast.
[6] At the present time, Volumes 4 through 16 (with the exception of volumes 9, 12, and 13) of *The Complete Caruso*, covering the years 1906 through 1919, are available from RCA.

the spurious resonances added to the recording by the wooden horn which, in lieu of a microphone, mechanically focused the sound onto the wax discs as they were being cut. The result of the reworking is astonishingly lifelike so far as the voice is concerned; even the weak accompanying instruments, always a problem in acoustic recording, are strengthened. Two excerpts from Act IV of *Rigoletto*—*La donna è mobile* and the quartet *Bella figlia dell'amore*—made in the first months of 1908, show Caruso in what can only be called juicy voice, with a rich middle and upper register and brilliant and free top.[7] There is in the quality of Caruso's voice what can only be called joy in singing; there is also a marvelously Mediterranean joy in music and life.

This same joy colors Gigli's art. Lighter in timbre than Caruso's, and even warmer, his voice can perhaps best be described as the musical equivalent of Italian sunlight and the very best olive oil. Perhaps Gigli made some special use of these national elements of weather and food; unlike Pavarotti, who now seems to have lost the musical quality of his sound, Gigli kept his voice well into his fifties and sixties,[8] singing with seemingly vast reserves of color and breath.

As heard in records from the prime of his career in the 1920s, Gigli's combination of finesse and ardor now seems overwhelming. In the opening of the *Rigoletto* quartet, sung coarsely and brazenly by Pavarotti, Gigli uses his undoubted vocal sensuality to flatter, not to taunt.[9] Whereas Pavarotti was both strained and restrained in the closing scene of *Lucia* on the telecast, Gigli's recording of this extended passage, made in 1927 with the excellent bass Ezio Pinza and the equally excellent Metropolitan Opera Chorus, is youthful and impulsive.[10]

---

[7] *The Complete Caruso, 1908–9*, Volume 5, RCA ARMI-2767.

[8] This remarkable vocal survival is documented in the many performances recorded between Gigli's fifty-seventh and sixty-fifth years. They have recently been available in an HMV Treasury album, EMI RLS 732.

[9] The *Rigoletto* quartet, with the great singers Amelita Galli-Curci, Louise Homer (composer Samuel Barber's aunt!), and Giuseppe de Luca, in addition to Gigli, was recently available on Seraphim 60054, and also on Seraphim 1C-6136, mentioned below in note 10.

[10] This performance, along with numerous other gems, was available on LP as Seraphim 1C-6136. It is still available on cassette tape as Seraphim 4XG-60054.

The decline of singing in our time is, I know, an old story. The situation was well put by the English music critic Alan Blyth in his introduction to *Opera on Record*, the indispensable book of annotated discographies he edited in 1979:

> There can be no doubt that artists in the early part of the century took a more liberal view of the score in hand and justified such liberties by giving a more personal view of the music, enhanced by a greater care over, and love for, words. Their techniques in most cases being more secure, they could devote themselves more fully to thoughts about vocal interpretation. Today, singers are more musically respectable but, as a result, often more dull.

Because Blyth's focus was on singing, one element in the present state of opera performance was left out. The missing element is the role of the conductor. The very greatest singers can work—or at least they think they can—without a great conductor; for these superstars a conductor is, and must always be, nothing more than a facilitator, a gentle and complaisant traffic cop who keeps everyone and everything, often including the drama of the music, out of the superstar's way. Therefore, conductors of decided opinions and forceful personality are rarely chosen as collaborators by celebrity singers. (In fairness, it must also be said that, for their part, great conductors rarely choose to work with superstar soloists.) However, there is more to being an opera conductor than keeping the orchestra down, following the singers, and taking tempos famous soloists are comfortable with. If the conductor's conception of the opera being performed is not a gripping one, the audience in its turn will not be gripped by the opera, and instead will be captured, if it is captured at all, by the individual singers on stage. Delightful as this prospect may be for great singers, it is dismal for anyone hoping to witness the total art work that a great opera can be.

For Joan Sutherland, the ideal of a perfect conductor is her husband and musical guide, Richard Bonynge. As a singer she seems truly happy only when he is in the pit accompanying her. To judge by the number of recordings and performances Sutherland and Bonynge have done with Luciano Pavarotti, the tenor too is happy with Bonynge. Unfortunately, however valuable Bonynge is to Sutherland as a vocal coach and musical influence, he is, on the evidence of a career going back more than thirty years, an undistinguished and uninteresting conductor. Although Sutherland—and others—may be happy with this arrangement, the ultimate loser is the musical integrity of the operatic work being performed.

And so it turned out on the Sutherland–Pavarotti telecast. The orchestral playing in general, and *pizzicato* playing in particular, was ragged throughout, as if at crucial moments the musicians were not quite sure when to play. Tempos were bouncy rather than taut, and the relationship of the tempos to each other seemed more accidental and random than necessary. Loudness was substituted for drama, and lush, heavy tone for emotion. A listener coming to these works for the first time might be forgiven for thinking himself in a world of popular music, of overblown tunefulness and sweeping melodies going nowhere.

But once again, recorded evidence proves, if such proof be needed, that great conductors can make all the difference in opera. Tullio Serafin's engrossing performances of *Lucia* with Callas, mentioned above, bring a kind of rhythmic weight and seriousness to Donizetti's music that lifts the opera from the level of a star vehicle to the level of tragedy. Carlo Maria Giulini's conducting, in the last act of the "pirate" *La Traviata* with Callas, despite its poor recorded quality, is incredibly delicate and poignant, sounding at times almost like an anticipation of Debussy's *Pélleas et Mélisande*.

Not surprisingly, the most purposeful conducting on records of two of the telecast operas has been done by Arturo Toscanini, undoubtedly the greatest of all Italian conductors, and perhaps the greatest conductor of the twentieth century.[11] It was Toscanini's achievement to purge *Rigoletto* and *La Traviata*—and much other music besides—of the accumulated sentimentality foisted upon them by generations of weak-willed but opportunistic interpreters. Though he uses many first-class singers—among them such native Americans as Leonard Warren, Jan Peerce, Nan Merriman, and Robert Merrill— the animating intelligence in these performances was the conductor's own; the result, in terms of orchestral playing, is a firmness and

[11] Toscanini's recording of the final act of *Rigoletto*, taken from a 1944 Red Cross benefit concert in Madison Square Garden, was available on RCA Victrola VIC-1314. My copy of his *La Traviata*, taken from an NBC broadcast in December 1946, is on RCA (Germany) 26.35008 DP.

certainty of execution not possible when the vagaries of singers rule the musical roost. Because Toscanini, as was his wont, kept the tempos strict and the prevailing texture of the orchestra lean, both *Rigoletto* and *La Traviata* emerge as masterworks of ennobling emotional directness. In listening to these records, it is difficult indeed not to feel that here is the ultimate justification for all the egotisms of famous conductors: at their best, they truly know how the music goes.

Today, more than thirty years after his death, Toscanini is as controversial as he was during his long life. He is currently the subject of an indignant and often unfair attack (though one containing much fascinating material about American musical life in the first half of the twentieth century) by the music critic Joseph Horowitz.[12] Curiously, this blistering attack is not aimed at Toscanini's real or alleged musical shortcomings, though Horowitz's taste does tend to run to less tense and more thoughtful Germanic music making. Toscanini's real crime, for Horowitz, lay in his celebrity appeal to a large and unsophisticated audience, an appeal he quite willingly accepted and even cannily encouraged. Horowitz, in his zeal to confront the very idea of the marketing of musical reputations, criticizes even such renowned associates of Toscanini as the violinist Jascha Heifetz and the pianist Vladimir Horowitz.

Certainly it is tempting, as one looks at today's crop of musical celebrities, to work backward as Joseph Horowitz does to the conclusion that any artist who becomes the object of ballyhoo must somehow be undeserving of respect. The taste left in the mouth by all the many "Live from Lincoln Center" concerts and their ilk is an unpleasant one; the constant selling of not-quite-first-rate artists as historically great figures, and as entrancing human beings into the bargain, is indeed hard to stomach.

But there is a world of difference between a Caruso, a Gigli, a Callas, or a Toscanini, on the one hand, and a Sutherland, a Pavarotti, an Itzhak Perlman, or a Zubin Mehta, on the other. However great our disgust at the musical antics and the electronic gimcrackery on television, there is nothing wrong with selling a truly great artist.

---

[12] *Understanding Toscanini: How He Became an American Culture-God and Helped Create a New Audience for Old Music* by Joseph Horowitz; Knopf, 1987.

Indeed, music needs celebrity performers not just because they bring new audiences to art but also because, when they are the real thing, they permanently shape our ideas of how great music sounds.

It has been clear for many years that we are living on the inherited capital of the great music of the past. Despite the present critical vogue for performances of old music and despite the original-instrument boom, it is now becoming increasingly plain that we are also living on the capital of the great recorded performers of the past. For the time being, we are largely dependent upon these performers, both for a convincing account of the works themselves and for a true standard by which to measure musical life today. One hopes that soon we will once again have a few new celebrities worthy of being sold, and worthy even of being oversold. One hopes, too, that these new celebrities will be encouraged to use the immense possibilities of television to bring serious musical culture to the largest possible audience.

But whatever the future may hold, the recent Sutherland–Pavarotti telecast demonstrates once again that our current celebrities just do not measure up.

21.

It was a great satisfaction to write so warmly about the great Marian Anderson. Great artist and remarkable person as she is, the public perception of her artistic achievement has always seemed to lag behind the perception of her symbolic importance as a representative of her people; the reissue of many of her recordings on CD allows us to pay her proper tribute as a singer and a musician. Now, when so many black leaders, especially in entertainment and the electronic media, are highly visible and outspoken, even her quiet human force and immense dignity can so easily be made to seem out-of-date; in this article, written for the October 1989 New Criterion, *I attempted to correct this false view of history. It seemed natural, in the* New Criterion *issue (November) immediately following the one containing my Anderson piece, to discuss the vocal riches similar to hers to be found on various new CD reissues of famous early electrical recordings. In this latter article, it also seemed natural to invoke T. S. Eliot on the artist's proper abnegation of personality, as I had earlier invoked him (see Chapter 3) on the place of new work within the tradition.*

Marian Anderson: The Diva from Philadelphia

As ELECTRONIC technology advances from 78s, LPs, and audio cassettes to CDs, the lovers of song hold onto their memories, cherishing the great performances of the past as they continue to reappear in ever newer, and on the whole better, sonic manifestations. The new RCA CD reissue of performances by the American contralto Marian Anderson,[1] in documenting an important part of this remarkable artist's career, can only arouse our deepest gratitude for the miracle of sound recording, even as it confirms our present propensity to look to the past for vocal splendor and beauty.

Born in Philadelphia in 1902, the daughter of poor parents, Marian

[1] RCA CD 7911-2-RG.

Anderson was what used to be called a Negro and what is today called a black. That is not the most important fact about her, though reasons of fate and the ill will of many people, past and present, conspire to make any account of her life incomplete without mention of the "race question" as it affected her and her audience. *Ars longa, vita brevis*: the most important fact about Marian Anderson is that in her prime she was one of the greatest singing artists of the century.

First, a few facts about her career. She studied singing in Philadelphia, financed by a small education fund from her church. In 1925, she won first prize in a New York Philharmonic competition, and duly sang with the orchestra at an outdoor concert in Lewisohn Stadium in August of that year. Though the appearance was successful, her American career languished, and at the end of the 1920s she decided to go to Europe, to undertake further study in German *Lieder* and, one must assume, to try to succeed in a less color-conscious musical environment. In the early 1930s she proved triumphant in Scandinavia, and soon thereafter sang in Salzburg, where Arturo Toscanini, hearing her at the Mozarteum, is said to have remarked, "A voice like yours is heard only once in a hundred years."

But clearly the turning point for Miss Anderson (she always was called Miss Anderson, and there seems to be no good reason today to do otherwise) was her discovery in 1935 by the mythical Russian–Jewish–American impresario Sol Hurok at a Paris recital in the Salle Gaveau. Hurok immediately signed her to an American contract and presented her at the end of that year in a rapturously received New York recital at Town Hall.[2] The concert was covered by Howard Taubman of the *New York Times*, who would go on to become the paper's chief critic but who was at the time only an assistant; Taubman was joined later in the evening by the *Times*'s chief critic, Olin Downes. Their reviews were ecstatic, and two Carnegie Hall recitals followed in the same season. The young singer, still in her early thirties, was launched as a star.

Her European successes continued, and here in America national

---

[2] Hurok's account of his discovery and management of Miss Anderson is contained in *Impresario*, a memoir by Sol Hurok in collaboration with Ruth Goode, published in 1946. Though romanticized, wooly, and factually elusive, it effectively conveys the atmosphere of a lost time when high art was seen as contributing to the achievement of world understanding and unity.

tour followed national tour. More was still to come: Miss Anderson broke out into extra-artistic fame when, in 1939, the Daughters of the American Revolution blindly refused to let her sing a Washington, D. C., recital in Constitution Hall, which they owned and from which they excluded Negroes. With the patronage of Eleanor Roosevelt, Hurok arranged that the concert take place at the Lincoln Memorial. Seventy-five thousand people were present, and the event became a milestone in the Negro battle for civic equality.

Miss Anderson's career flourished throughout the 1940s, and a great wrong was righted when she finally was invited by Rudolf Bing to appear at the Metropolitan Opera in 1955. She sang in a performance of Verdi's *Un ballo in maschera* with tenor Jan Peerce. Though her Met debut occurred late in her career, it signified better than words what had been lost to the operatic public through prejudice and obscurantism. In 1957 she made a much-publicized tour under State Department auspices to the Far East, singing for American troops in South Korea and for local audiences in Vietnam and Japan. Everywhere she was recognized as an artist-heroine, and by her Carnegie Hall farewell recital in 1965 she had become an American institution.

Marian Anderson's career lasted into the LP era, and post-78 RPM transfers, along with original LPs, have made it possible to study all the stages of her artistic development. Fortunately, the proper documentation is to be found on a 1986 HMV (England) Treasury LP,[3] a Pearl (England) LP,[4] and a 1956 RCA collection devoted to Negro spirituals,[5] in addition to the new RCA CD. The RCA CD effectively brackets her career: it contains a 1924 recording of a spiritual as well as an impressive excerpt from *Un ballo in maschera* made at the time of her Metropolitan appearance in 1955, along with performances from Miss Anderson's American years. The HMV Treasury LP covers Miss

[3] EMI EG 29 0016 1.
[4] Pearl GEMM 193. Unlike the HMV and RCA reissues, sonically resplendent as they are in their filtering out of noises characteristic of the 78 RPM recording process, Pearl transfers are characterized by a minimum amount of processing, thus conveying to the listener a reasonably accurate account of how the original discs sounded.
[5] RCA LM 2032. A further collection of spirituals, recorded in stereo and including titles not on the 1956 disc, was issued by RCA in 1962 on LSC-2592.

Anderson's decade abroad from 1928 to 1938, and the Pearl LP presents in detail her European recordings from the years 1927 to 1930.

The artistic achievement that emerges from all these performances is consistent, full of developing vocal splendor, and musically unforgettable. In the 1924 performance of "Go Down, Moses," her voice, as heard in the RCA transfer from the primitive, acoustically recorded original, is not altogether pleasing in its tight focus and unvarying color. Yet her youthful sound, one year before winning the New York Philharmonic appearance, is extraordinary, for it achieves a pure stream of silvery tone, free from flutter and wobble, as Miss Anderson's sound always was; remarkable too is her clarity and elegance of diction.

By the end of the 1920s Miss Anderson seems to have reached full vocal and artistic maturity. In two recordings from the second act of Saint-Saëns's *Samson et Dalila* (including the famous aria *Mon coeur s'ouvre a ta voix*), made in English in 1928 and 1930, we hear a great voice, more soprano than contralto, at once full and swordlike; in this combination of opulence and cutting power, the best comparison seems to be with the young Ljuba Welitsch in her performance, forty and more years ago, of the closing scene of Richard Strauss's *Salome*.[6] The rest of Miss Anderson's prewar recordings, ranging from impeccable Handel through deeply felt and projected Schubert *Lieder* to familiar spirituals, are stunning, too, and clearly justify her enormous impact on the international concert stage.

As Miss Anderson grew into full maturity, her voice gained in a typically alto warmth what it slowly lost in soprano brilliance. For me, the high point of her recordings made in the 1940s is her gripping and vocally glorious 1945 performance on the RCA CD of Brahms's *Alto Rhapsody* (a setting of the eloquent Goethe poem *Harzreise im Winter*) with Pierre Monteux and the San Francisco Symphony Orchestra; this beautiful work has the reputation of being an ugly duckling among

---

[6] Three remarkable documentations of the Welitsch performance exist, and all, in their powerful security of voice and passionate intensity, are classics of the phonograph. The first, from 1944, was available on Seraphim 60202; the second, from 1949 and conducted by Fritz Reiner, was made after her sensational Metropolitan Opera debut in *Salome*, and was available on CBS-Odyssey 32 16 0078; the third is a pirate recording of a Met *Salome* broadcast with Welitsch and Reiner slightly later in 1949 and was available on discs cryptically described only as MRF-1.

Brahms's many swans, but on this occasion, through the miracle of performance, it is haunting and startling in its evocation of loneliness redeemed by hope.[7]

Throughout Miss Anderson's career she was the leading interpreter of Negro spirituals, that strange phenomenon of church singing transformed by a people's sadness. Her simple and noble singing of these songs moved millions, of every color, to tears. More than that, the spirituals suggested that the vicissitudes of history could be redeemed by the fulfillment of the ethical imperatives of the American founding. It seems irrelevant whether or not these spirituals were authentic expressions of her people's folk music; what is significant about them is that in Miss Anderson's performances, admirably preserved on the 1956 RCA LP, they became universal rather than particular, and in so becoming they achieved the status of high art. It is marvelous indeed that in a 1966 LP of Schubert and Brahms *Lieder*,[8] sung with diminished voice well after the end of her public career, this American singer took these gems of German culture and made of them as well something universal.

Finally, there is Marian Anderson the human being. Edward R. Murrow called his 1957 "See It Now" television program about her, focusing on a State Department-sponsored trip to the Orient, "The Lady from Philadelphia." With poise and grace she represented, abroad as at home, an evolving America, an America with problems, to be sure, but with a deep underlying sense of purpose and direction. She did so as an artist and as the holder of a deeply felt religious position. As Sol Hurok convincingly tells the story, when Miss Anderson asked her mother what gift she might want from her successful daughter, the reply, coming after much provocation from a sometimes hostile world, was simple: "All she wanted was that God would hold Marian Anderson 'in the hollow of his hand and raise up the people to be kind.'"

[7] A later and much less taut performance by Miss Anderson of the Brahms, conducted by Fritz Reiner, was issued in the early 1950s on the long-disappeared RCA LM-1146. It was coupled on this disc with Miss Anderson's affecting singing of the Mahler *Kindertotenlieder*, with Pierre Monteux and the San Francisco Symphony Orchestra.

[8] RCA ARL1-3022, released in 1978. Mention should be made here of Franz Rupp, the splendid pianist on Miss Anderson's American recordings; her European recordings benefit from the collaboration of the equally splendid Kosti Vehanen.

Marian Anderson was both an artist and an American leader. It is sad that the artists who have succeeded her have not been her equals as singers; it is tragic that the leaders who have succeeded her have not possessed her immense dignity.

New Life from Old Records

WRITING ABOUT the renowned contralto Marian Anderson in last month's issue of the *New Criterion*, I described how musical beauty can be communicated through the art of a single great singer, one who combines an extraordinarily beautiful voice and a touchingly restrained musical personality. It is my intention here to shift the focus from the singer to the music sung, and to discuss some examples of the fate of the greatest masterworks at the hands—or more precisely at the vocal cords—of artists in the present and the past.

As an example of the present, my text will be Jessye Norman's recent "Live from Lincoln Center" telecast on PBS, with Zubin Mehta conducting the New York Philharmonic, of the concluding *"Liebestod"* from Richard Wagner's *Tristan und Isolde*. Miss Norman, born in Georgia in 1945, is perhaps the reigning diva of the day. Now (one must assume) in the prime of her vocal estate, she is the toast of continental Europe, Great Britain, and the United States; her schedule is full, her fees are astronomical, and her press coverage is both copious and reverent. At the Metropolitan Opera last season she was granted the rare honor of what might be called a one-woman evening: twin productions of Béla Bartók's *Bluebeard's Castle*, in which she shared the stage with bass Samuel Ramey, and Arnold Schoenberg's monodrama *Erwartung*, in which she occupied the stage alone. She is also a much admired Straussian and Wagnerian, singing the lead role in James Levine's Vienna Philharmonic recording of Strauss's *Ariadne auf Naxos* and Sieglinde in the Metropolitan recording (also with Levine) of Wagner's *Die Walküre*.

Miss Norman's fame thus established, much interest attached to her singing on the General Motors-sponsored Philharmonic broadcast, a gala event opening the orchestra's 1989–90 season (the last but one of music director Zubin Mehta) in Avery Fisher Hall. Mr. Mehta began with a heavy-handed and plodding rendition of the Overture to Wagner's *Tannhäuser*; after the intermission, he led the orchestra in a loveless version of the much-played Mozart Symphony no. 40 in G minor, K. 550. Miss Norman made her first appearance of the evening in the *Five Rückert Songs* of Gustav Mahler. This music, as always in Mahler's vocal writing, emphasizes the sound of the voice as a quasi-orchestral instrument rather than as a means for limning character and personality; Miss Norman met this challenge admirably.

It was different with the music from *Tristan und Isolde* that concluded the program. It must be admitted that matters were hardly helped along by Mr. Mehta's wayward yet rigid, distorted yet predictable performance of the Prelude to the opera that preceded the *"Liebestod."* So concerned was he with mooning over the impassioned aspects of the Prelude that vital ensemble was ragged, and composer-indicated nuances, often calling for soft playing from the orchestra, were engulfed in a flood tide of what seemed, at least to me, vulgar and wearyingly constant self-expression.

Matters hardly improved when Miss Norman entered upon the *"Liebestod,"* with its musical evocation of the magically rapt and supremely inward opening words:

Mild und leise wie er lächelt,/wie das Auge hold er öffnet—/seht ihr's, Freunde? seht ihr's nicht?/Immer lichter wie er leuchtet,/sternumstrahlet hoch sich hebt?

(Softly and gently he smiles,/how sweetly he opens his eyes—/do you see him, friends? don't you see him?/Always brighter he glows,/raised high, enwrapped in star-rays?)

For Miss Norman, the mood of the *"Liebestod"* was not to be taken from its words, or from the argument of the opera, or even from a more refined and elevated conception of the Prelude than Mr. Mehta offered. Individual words were given exaggerated weight; everything was external, effortful, and frenetic, with even Miss Norman's powerful (often consciously too powerful) voice overtaxed, her last notes suggesting nothing so much as a giant sail flapping in a high wind.

Miss Norman seemed concerned at every moment to thrust herself, every inch the careful and calculating *prima donna assoluta*, into the place of the composer's poetic conception, to substitute for Isolde's transfiguration her own personal self-assertion.

All in all, the impression the performance gave was that she had decided to confront personally, and deny, a self-effacing attitude toward art. This was the attitude that T. S. Eliot gave powerful expression to in "Tradition and the Individual Talent" when he wrote that for the artist,

> [w]hat happens is a continual surrender of himself as he is at the moment to something which is more valuable. The progress of an artist is a continual self-sacrifice, a continual extinction of personality.

The lesson of Eliot's counsel of perfection is surely that the artist must look to the art, not to himself. Such self-abnegation is more difficult today than ever, when art—especially the art of the past—seems dead, while the artist's managers, press agents, and fans are very much alive. We will be told that it was ever thus, and doubtless to some extent this thought, at once comforting and ultimately dispiriting, contains a bit of truth. Singers, like actors, have little choice but to point their lives toward their relatively few and brief moments on the stage; the Latin phrase *carpe diem* has, after all, a special meaning for these larger-than-life-size creatures.

But the evidence of phonograph records—and it is their chief value, in addition, of course, to the pleasure they give us—shows that, at least in the case of the greatest works of the German operatic stage, times once were better. It has long been known that the two decades from 1920 to 1940 were a golden age of Wagnerian singing in Europe, and here in America as well, at the Metropolitan Opera. This golden age fortunately coincided with the introduction in 1925 of the electrical recording process, a remarkable improvement in the fidelity and amplitude of both vocal and orchestral reproduction. Though the recordings actually made were initially limited to excerpts, the foresight of the legendary producer Fred Gaisberg and his associates at His Master's Voice in England (or at its German affiliate) ensured that the great singers of the age, and some remarkable conductors as well, were captured for posterity.

These recordings, though originally made in the scratchy 78 RPM format and destined to be played *faute de mieux* on the primitive playback equipment of the time, have proved to have a remarkable afterlife. As reproducing technology advanced from recording on wax and pressing on swiftly revolving shellac to recording on tape and pressing on slow-spinning vinyl, concomitant developments in electronics enabled an ever larger amount of the information contained in the original 78 RPM grooves to be reclaimed and made available inexpensively to listeners. In the last years of the LP record, the techniques of Direct Metal Mastering made possible a hitherto unknown dynamic range, at minimal distortion, to be incised on the vinyl disc;[1] more to the point here, in the last five years the CD has become a prime medium for making available old recorded performances reclaimed by state-of-the-art techniques.

Several of these important CD reissues have now appeared, and they have much to tell us about the way things once were in Wagnerian performance. Perhaps the most interesting of these reissues—because the original discs on which they are based are currently for the most part quite forgotten—are those of major excerpts from *Tristan und Isolde*[2] and the slightly later *Die Meistersinger*.[3] There are also new CDs of excerpts from three components of *Der Ring des Nibelungen: Die Walküre*,[4] *Siegfried*,[5] and *Götterdämmerung*.[6]

The *Tristan* excerpts come from discs made between 1926 and 1929, and present to our lethargic age the remarkable Albert Coates's enthralling conducting of this music. Coates (1882–1953) was an Anglo-Russian, very active in recording for HMV in the 1920s both before and after the advent of electrical recording; by the 1930s,

---

[1] For an account of the situation of these old Wagner discs as it appeared at the end of the LP era, and for a memoir of my own experience with the phonograph, see "Growing Up with Old Records" in the April 1984 issue of the *New Criterion*.
[2] Claremont/GSE CD GSE 78-50-26.
[3] Pearl GEMM CD 9340.
[4] Pearl GEMM CD 9357.
[5] Danacord DACO CD 319/21. This material first appeared several years ago on LP as Danacord DACO 171-76.
[6] Pearl GEMM CD 9331.

inexplicably, he had quite disappeared from the musical scene. His hundreds of 78 RPM discs are characterized by what can only be called blazing intensity. Nowhere is this more true than in the *Tristan* Prelude with which this CD begins. But there are other riches here, including the Love Duet from Act II, sung by the legendary tenor Lauritz Melchior and the soprano Frida Leider, both of them artists unequaled today and for many years past. So searing is this performance that one can well believe Leider's account (cited in the notes to the CD) of the making of the recording: she was so excited while singing that she became dizzy and had to hold on to Melchior for support.[7]

The *Tristan* CD ends with a large chunk of Act III, like the Act I Prelude never before transferred, I believe, from the 78 RPM original; this material, beginning with the Prelude and ending with the "*Liebestod*," is marvelously—and unaffectedly—sung by three artists now unremembered: the English tenor Walter Widdop, the Swedish soprano Göta Ljungberg, and the English baritone Howard Fry. The conductors, rare as their like are today, include Coates, the equally splendid (though less intense) German Leo Blech (1871–1958), and Lawrance Collingwood, one of HMV's highly competent house conductors. Despite all the changes in personnel in these performances, the overall musical conception seems remarkably integrated in its straightforwardness and simplicity; everywhere the music (and the story) is left to take its own hair-raising course.

The very welcome *Meistersinger* excerpts come from an actual performance in 1928 at Berlin's Theater unter den Linden; its only previous transfer from the 78 RPM originals was on poorly engineered and little-circulated LPs. They represent our only knowledge of a live Berlin opera performance in the 1920s, and present a cast headed by baritone Friedrich Schorr, by all accounts the greatest Hans Sachs who ever lived, and conducted by Blech. The touching young lovers Eva and Walther are Elfriede Marherr and Robert Hutt, singers unknown today; they combine, in an exemplary fashion, the great vocal qualities of security—no flutter, no wobble—and freshness of tone. Pogner, Eva's father, is movingly sung by the great bass Emanuel List. It is a

[7] Further and indispensable Leider performances from *Tristan*, including the 1928 "Narrative and Curse" from Act I and the concluding 1931 "*Liebestod*," are included on the Pearl *Götterdämmerung* mentioned above, and discussed below.

pity that no more than seventy-two minutes has survived of what was evidently a performance recorded in its entirety; what we do have on this CD conveys a stunning impression of a freely flowing ensemble, of singers effortlessly *being*, not premeditatedly acting, their roles.

The *Ring* excerpts are of scarcely less interest. Almost all of the *Walküre* material comes from a 1927 abridgment conducted by Blech and sung by Leider (Brünnhilde), Schorr (Wotan), and Ljungberg (Sieglinde). Wisely, the present CD has filled in the missing but vital Wotan–Fricka dialogue from Act II, from the 1932 discs conducted by John Barbirolli, with Schorr as Wotan and the wonderful contralto Emmi Leisner as his shrewish but nonetheless rich-voiced wife Fricka. Unfortunately (doubtless to avoid going to a second CD), a significant part of the 1927 set, the Siegmund–Sieglinde passages from Act I (sung by Widdop and Ljungberg), have been omitted from the present collection,[8] along with equally important material from the second half of Act II (sung by Widdop and the excellent English Brünnhilde, Florence Austral). But what there is on this CD, so marvelous in musical power and vocal strength, approaches perfection; taken together with the 1930s Vienna recordings, starring the conductor Bruno Walter, the soprano Lotte Lehmann, and Melchior,[9] this CD makes clear the travesty represented by present-day Wagner performances, in and out of the opera house.

The *Siegfried* material also has much to tell us. Here is most of the pieced-together abridgment made in the late 1920s, conducted by the unappreciated German *Kapellmeister* Robert Heger (1886–1978), Coates, and Karl Alwin (then the husband of the renowned *Lieder* singer Elisabeth Schumann). The star-studded cast includes Melchior (Siegfried), Schorr (Wanderer), the sumptuous (but tremulous) contralto Maria Olszewska (Erda), and the brilliant English soprano Florence Easton (Brünnhilde); it also includes the wonderful character singer Heinrich Tessmer (Mime) and Eduard Habich (Alberich and Fafner). Amidst all these riches it is the virility of Melchior's Siegfried, so different in its heedless exuberance from the strangled musicality

[8] A major part of this material, however, may be found on Pearl GEMM 218, an LP transfer devoted to Walter Widdop.

[9] These extraordinary performances, documenting Viennese Wagner performance on the eve of the *Anschluss* in 1938, may now be most easily found together in one set on Danacord DACO CD 317/318.

of today's leading Heldentenors, that immediately compels attention. But despite the excellence of all the vocal performances, one thing must not be forgotten: it is the directness of the conducting that makes the overpowering dramatic effect possible, and indeed ineluctable.

Finally, in discussing these new releases, there remains the *Götterdämmerung* CD. Here is a live recording of two conflict-ridden scenes from Act II taken "off the air" from a performance of June 7, 1938, at Covent Garden in London, conducted by the now mythic Wilhelm Furtwängler and sung by Leider (Brünnhilde) and Melchior (Siegfried); here too is an excellent transfer of Leider's classic 1928 commercial discs of the Immolation Scene that closes the opera, and with it the entire *Ring* cycle.[10] By now we are tempted to take Leider's and Melchior's excellence for granted. What cannot be taken for granted, however, is the musical leadership of the live performance. As a conductor Furtwängler is now celebrated as a "mellow" conductor, an enthusiast for mystical draggings-out of the rhythmic pulse so constitutive of nineteenth-century music.[11] But here at least, as in Furtwängler's two recorded post–World War II *Ring* cycles,[12] his conducting, taut and energetic, is the very soul of sinister and propulsive drama.

As this article is in proof, news comes of the arrival of a CD transfer on the Opal label (England) of all the *Parsifal* recordings made at the 1927 Bayreuth festival, and at about the same time in Berlin, by the

[10] It is sad that Leider's discs of the Immolation Scene end not with the actual orchestral finale of *Götterdämmerung* but rather several minutes too soon, with an absurd "concert ending" tacked on to Brünnhilde's last sung notes.

[11] Indeed, to return for a moment to the unfortunate Zubin Mehta, it is difficult not to feel that the single most harmful influence on Mehta and his generation of musicians was the examples of Furtwängler's late-career self-indulgences; nowhere were these indulgences to be so noticed, and therefore so slavishly copied, as in his much-worshipped 1952 *Tristan* recording with soprano Kirsten Flagstad. It must be said, too, that Flagstad's effortless ability to spin out endless volumes of creamy vocal tone has induced many without her supreme endowments to sing, like Jessye Norman, slower than slow.

[12] The 1950 La Scala *Ring*, with Flagstad as Brünnhilde throughout, was available for some years on various LP transfers of varying quality; the 1953 Rome RIA *Ring*, with a less stellar cast but better sonics, was long available on Seraphim LPs. Both performances are wonderful, and will doubtless soon be available on CD; they are musts for every true Wagnerian.

great conductor Karl Muck. Together with the related 1927 Bayreuth recordings conducted by Siegfried Wagner (the composer's son), these unique performances convey the exaltation of Wagner's summation in *Parsifal* of the romantic myth of the artist-savior. But important Wagner recordings of the 1920s still remain unavailable on CD. Among them are many Albert Coates recordings of vocal and orchestral excerpts, including electrically recorded passages from *Das Rheingold, Götterdämmerung,* and *Parsifal,* as well as acoustically recorded material from *Götterdämmerung.*

Cui bono? I don't think performances on old records can be copied, for imitation readily results in exaggeration and even corruption. But there is more to be learned from them than is comprehended by a slavish reworking of the successes of others. The key to the value of these records is what they can teach about the artistic process in general, and in this case about the way a performer must approach the re-creation of a dramatic masterpiece. Earlier I quoted T. S. Eliot's words from "Tradition and the Individual Talent" about the artist's necessary extinction of personality. A passage near the end of that great essay shows that Eliot, in his extraordinary balancing of opposites, also did justice to the importance of personality. Indeed, this passage seems to me to encapsulate the lesson about art to be learned not just from Wagner's music and Eliot's poetry but from the very ideal of tradition itself:

> Poetry is not a turning loose of emotion, but an escape from emotion; it is not the expression of personality, but an escape from personality. But, of course, only those with personality and emotions know what it means to want to escape from these things.... The emotion of art is impersonal. And the poet cannot reach this impersonality without surrendering himself wholly to the work to be done. And he is not likely to know what is to be done unless he lives in what is not merely the present, but the present moment of the past, unless he is conscious, not of what is dead, but of what is already living.

Here, then, is the point of these great old records. The lesson is not easily learned, for learning depends, after all, on both learner and teacher. Still, the lesson is clear: the goal of beauty and meaning in musical performance—what is usually referred to as "expression" and "feeling"—cannot be achieved as an end in itself; it can only be indirectly approached, and then only by the most gifted, through the satisfaction of the most immediate and most compelling demands of the music. As Eliot well knew, only the greatest personalities need apply.

22.

In recent years, the appearances with the New York Philharmonic of such guest conductors as Erich Leinsdorf have served to show just how much the problems of this orchestra transcend those of Zubin Mehta, and just how general the problems of symphonic music making are in our time. There is a great lesson to be learned, not just from the Leinsdorf concerts I have described below in a May 1985 Commentary *article, but from this esteemed conductor's entire career, spanning as it does more than a half-century: how empty musical leadership finally is when it does not arise out of, and communicate, a sense of passion and commitment. For many years now, the Philharmonic, and our other great orchestras, have lacked this kind of dedicated direction. In Leinsdorf's case, it is a particular pity that he doesn't care, when he more than most musicians knows just how much there is to care about.*

Leinsdorf at the Philharmonic

FOR THE ERSTWHILE—and would-be—fans of the New York Philharmonic, the issue of Zubin Mehta, the orchestra's present music director, now seems closed. Summary rejection by the critical press, culminating in a blistering attack by Peter Davis in *New York* magazine at the beginning of January, has left little doubt that Mehta (whose contract, at least in theory, runs until 1990) is now the lamest of lame ducks. For reviewers, as for sophisticated music lovers and record buyers—and New York's professional musical community—the question is not whether but when Mehta will leave and who will replace him as the leader of this once proud and great orchestra.

Finding a successor to Mehta will not be easy for the Philharmonic. The problem, obviously, is not that Mehta's is a hard act to follow; it is rather that the pool of possible replacements, for reasons both real and illusory, is neither large nor widely viewed as richly stocked. In recent years, American conductors, no matter how talented, have failed to follow Leonard Bernstein's road to musical glory and box-office riches. And European *maestri*, though increasingly willing to accept American engagements paid for in our strong dollars, still seem resistant (despite the laudable example of Christoph von Dohnányi in Cleveland) to making anything like a full-time commitment even to the most important of American orchestras.

Because Mehta has so little to offer, and because the future direction of the Philharmonic seems so murky, whatever musical interest there is these days at the orchestra's concerts in Avery Fisher Hall lies in the guest conductors who are now, as for many years, a ubiquitous feature of the season. Since September, for example, the Philharmonic has been conducted by—in addition to Mehta—Myung-Whun Chung (Korean), Andrew Davis (English), Klaus Tennstedt and Kurt Masur (both German), and Erich Leinsdorf (Austrian-born but resident in America now for almost a half-century); still to come before the season closes is the English baroque and classical specialist Raymond Leppard. Missing from this roster has been an American guest conductor—an omission all the more curious at a time when a new course for this leading American orchestra has become urgent.

Particular significance, it seems to me, attached to the recent concerts of Erich Leinsdorf with the Philharmonic. He is the oldest of the guest conductors this season, and the only one whose roots go back to the great days of such hallowed names as Arturo Toscanini and Bruno Walter; he was particularly close to Toscanini, as whose assistant he worked at Salzburg prior to the German takeover of Austria in 1938. Almost immediately upon his arrival in New York in the late 1930s Leinsdorf became a major factor in the musical leadership of the Metropolitan Opera, specializing in Wagner. In 1943 he succeeded Artur Rodzinski at the head of the Cleveland Orchestra, but lost the position after he was drafted into the army. From 1947 to 1955, he was the conductor of the Rochester Philharmonic Orchestra, and then in 1956 he was music director of the New York City Opera. Though he returned to the Met in 1957 as a conductor and musical consultant, his heart lay with symphonic rather than operatic work, and in 1962 he replaced Charles Munch as music director of the Boston Symphony. Here he remained, amid mounting and mutual dissatisfactions, until 1969. Since that date, he has been a roving figure, serving somewhat as (to paraphrase Herbert von Karajan's sobriquet, General Music Director of Europe) General Guest Conductor of America.

Wherever Leinsdorf has conducted, he has impressed thoughtful music lovers as a maker of interesting programs, representing a wide historical variety of music and musical styles. He has never been afraid to take on the challenges of large choral works, unfamiliar versions of familiar pieces, or the most difficult contemporary compositions. Furthermore, he is the fortunate possessor of a large repertory, encompassing all the major achievements of the great composers; he has a healthy interest in, and happily performs, worthy works by such unfamiliar composers as Peter Cornelius (the nineteenth-century disciple of Wagner and Liszt) and the twentieth-century opera composer Erich Wolfgang Korngold (the prodigy who wrote his first opera at the age of eighteen). If he has rarely been a fiery performer, he has never been less than a serious one.

Of all the major conductors in the world today, Leinsdorf is also perhaps the most intellectual. Widely read, and a particular devotee of the works of Goethe, Leinsdorf is himself the author, in fluent and literate English, of two books: his memoirs, *Cadenza* (1976), and the primer for conductors *The Composer's Advocate* (1981). Both books serve to reinforce the impression Leinsdorf made in Boston as a conductor, that of a stern and often cruelly witty taskmaster intolerant in the dedicated service of his beloved musical art. Here at last, one thinks, as one reads Leinsdorf's scathing comments about colleagues and competitors and dismissive reflections on the present state of his profession, is a conductor who will be satisfied with no less than the best from himself and from the musicians whose fortune it is to play under him.

Thus, if anyone might have been expected to begin the task of correcting the playing of the Philharmonic and the taste of its audience, both prime casualties of the Mehta years, it was Leinsdorf. Unhappily, however, Leinsdorf's first two weeks of concerts with the Philharmonic, at the end of February and the beginning of March, served as a savage rebuke to those expectations. Though the results of these three hours of music making were hailed by two different critics of the *New York Times*, to my ears they sounded like a routine going-through of the motions, with the only musical purpose in mind a performance without gross error and palpable breakdown.

This was immediately apparent in the opening work of the concert I attended on March 1, Aaron Copland's *Music for the Theater* (1925), the first of the composer's attempts to write a self-consciously American music through the use of jazz. For Copland, as for the jolly French *provocateur* Darius Milhaud, jazz was the vinegar needed to spice up the academicism which, in the 1920s, was so widely seen as the accursed remnant of the nineteenth century. For Erich Leinsdorf and the Philharmonic, alas, the vinegar of jazz might as well have been *crème anglaise*, otherwise known as boiled custard. From the opening trumpet solo to the end of the work some twenty tired minutes later, the prevailing mood was gentility, caution, and boredom. Completely absent from the performance was the raucous spirit, combined with a certain animal warmth, which Leonard Bernstein brought to his 1958 Philharmonic recording of the piece.[1] Where Bernstein's rhythm had been tight and mean, Leinsdorf's was flabby. In part the trouble inhered in his decision to play what is after all a small orchestra piece in the acoustically glacial spaces of Fisher Hall. Still more trouble came from his conducting the work with broad, flowing, cornerless beats. On the other hand, despite the total failure of the orchestra to bring the Copland piece off, at least its playing here reached a level of correctness and accuracy I did not hear in any of its performances of other works under Leinsdorf.

The next item on the March 1 program was the Third Piano Concerto of Béla Bartók. This tuneful and affecting piece, a further step in the retreat from an assertive modernism which had marked the composer's Concerto for Orchestra (1943), was Bartók's last work; its concluding bars were still not orchestrated at the time of his death in 1945. Where the genius of Copland's *Music for the Theater* lies in the harnessing of its jazz component to a symphonic orchestra, the greatness of Bartók's Third Concerto—so different from the motoric dissonances of his earlier two piano concertos—resides in the subtilization of the basic Hungarian folk element in the context of the relatively orthodox musical structure he uses.

The soloist in the Bartók was the American pianist Malcolm Frager, described by Leinsdorf in a recent *Times* article as a "consummate

[1] CBS MS 6698.

musician." Since winning the 1959 Leventritt Award, Frager has been known as a careful player, an artist who makes up in musical dedication what he lacks in personal magnetism. For this performance of the Bartók Concerto, Frager chose to play on a Bösendorfer piano rather than the more commonly used Steinway. The Bösendorfer is one of Vienna's nineteenth-century glories; more than any other piano it is capable—at least when heard close up—of conveying an aura of what the Germans call *Hausmusik*, home music making. But the Bösendorfer is hardly suited to very large halls, let alone a hall with the weak and coarse tone projection of the much-altered space in which the Philharmonic now plays.

In this case the instrument's weak tone only complemented the pianist's own lack of projection. The soloist's entrance at the beginning of the first movement, though it was played against a properly subservient orchestral background, failed, for reasons of dull sonority and stolid rhythm, to take command. Throughout the piece, the listener was conscious not of a soloist asserting himself alongside of and against the orchestra, but of a general pianistic rumble, with only isolated and none too attractive accentuations breaking the prevailing level of sound. The concerto's most difficult keyboard passage, an excruciatingly demanding section in fast double notes in the first movement, was indistinct at the crucial moments.

In the very beautiful music of the second movement, both soloist and conductor seemed so determined to observe Bartók's curiously fast metronome indications that they quite lost sight—or rather sound—of the clear intent of the composer's mood as conveyed by the Italian tempo marking (*Adagio religioso*). And in the jaunty final movement Frager made little attempt to communicate the rhythmic bite inherent in the music; at the end, where the composer directs the musicians to play *Presto*, Frager quite plainly chose a deliberate tempo, thus condemning the whole movement, and therefore the entire piece, to end in something of a slow-motion heap. (I should add, in fairness to the audience, that the applause was lukewarm, and remarkably so for what is, after all, a virtuoso and very accessible concerto.)

After intermission, there was only one work: the glorious Second Symphony (1877) of Johannes Brahms. Unhurried, supremely self-confident, this masterpiece seems now, more than a century after its first appearance, to be bathed in an autumnal glow. The autumn is of German and Austrian greatness, of Viennese culture, of the heroic age of the nineteenth-century bourgeoisie, and not least that of symphonic form itself. But in Fisher Hall, this autumnal glow was replaced by the light, at once wan and harsh, of a gray winter's day. Nothing in the orchestra gleamed, nothing shone; there was no richness, no comfort of sound or of phrasing. As I sat watching Leinsdorf's large, flaccid beat, I thought that here was a conductor who, for all his magnificent experience and undoubted good taste, was now at this moment in his career just content, in the disreputable catch phrase of the 1960s, to "go with the flow."

For if Leinsdorf had really cared, he might at least have been able to clean up the orchestra's playing (as he had in fact done with the Copland). The brass, for example, essayed the difficult beginning of the first movement well, but almost immediately, upon being presented with out-of-tune string playing, lost their confidence and themselves began to have problems with intonation.

Indeed, throughout the Brahms, the strings played with that kind of intonation which, without being wrong, is not yet right. This dubious intonation—caused as much by lack of ensemble *within* the string section as by the whole section's getting the pitch slightly wrong—may be hard for the average music lover to identify, but it makes the orchestra sound harsh, strident, and vulgar, instead of properly sweet, pure, true, and clear. (I was reminded here of what one of my piano teachers used to say about my technically dubious playing of difficult passages: it was, he said, like yesterday's shirt, not noticeably dirty, but also not noticeably clean.)

Leinsdorf's second concert, which I heard on the evening of March 7, was to have begun with the Schoenberg Concerto for String Quartet and Orchestra (after the Concerto Grosso opus 6, no. 7, of Handel); to have continued with the three Nocturnes for orchestra of Debussy and the Love Scene from Berlioz's *Romeo and Juliet*; and to have concluded with Tchaikowsky's very different Overture-Fantasy bearing the same name. But when I arrived at the concert that night, I found an insert in my program deleting the Tchaikowsky, and substituting for it the Copland *Music for the Theater* of the previous week. The program order thus now went Copland, Schoenberg, Berlioz, and Debussy. No reason was given for the change; it seemed clear to me then (and was confirmed in the press the next morning) that the problem was insufficient rehearsal time for the Schoenberg, a state of affairs that evidently could only be met by replacing the Tchaikowsky, which needed rehearsal, with the Copland, which supposedly did not. Yet as it turned out, the Copland certainly could have used more rehearsal. The accuracy of the orchestra's performance the week before now gave way to a certain rickety quality; the trumpet playing in particular seemed uncomfortable.

The Schoenberg Concerto for String Quartet and Orchestra which followed the Copland on the revised program presented a rarely played item of major interest. One of the least-known works in the Schoenberg canon, it is a massive expansion and transformation of a rather unassuming Handel Concerto Grosso.

Schoenberg's music, from such early and appealing tonal pieces as *Verklärte Nacht* (1899) and the *Gurrelieder* (1901–11) to the harsh and knotty twelve-tone compositions of his maturity, is always difficult to play. Unusual harmonies and sequences, hard-to-hear dissonances, dense textures, novel instrumental effects, and rhythmic complexity require that his compositions, to be appreciated at all, be given performances of the highest technical virtuosity, combined with a lyrical, rhapsodic musical approach not often vouchsafed to mere virtuosos.

The Concerto for String Quartet and Orchestra is no exception to this rule of difficulty, in which Schoenberg so delighted. The special problems here are intonation and bowing for the string-quartet soloists, and clear, buoyant, and comfortable playing for the orchestra. Rather than ask the Philharmonic's own first-chair string players to do the demanding solo parts, the orchestra management and (one assumes) Leinsdorf engaged the Juilliard Quartet, a group famed as long ago as the early 1950s (with different personnel, except for Robert Mann, the founding and present first violinist) for its playing of the contemporary literature in general and the Schoenberg string quartets in particular.[2] The best guarantee of proper orchestral playing was of

---

[2] The early Juilliard recordings of the Schoenberg quartets, still classics for their passion and cohesion, were last available in the 1970s on special order as Columbia CML 4735-7.

course the vast experience of the Philharmonic, not just under Pierre Boulez but also under such even earlier music directors as Leonard Bernstein and Dimitri Mitropoulos, in quickly preparing and performing the most difficult contemporary scores.

Sadly, the effect of the Schoenberg concerto in this Philharmonic performance under Leinsdorf was just another black eye for the cause of unfamiliar and demanding music. Wherever I looked—or rather listened—I heard out-of-tune playing from the string quartet, and in particular from the first violinist; bar after bar in the orchestra was shaky, labored, and unmusical. The Handelian elements which remain audible in Schoenberg's reworking were played almost unrecognizably, as if Handel too had written wrong notes. The general disorder in the dissonantal passages made it impossible without recourse to the printed score to reach an informed judgment as to which were Schoenberg's written notes and which were the performers' failures to play them properly. In fact I had a score with me, and I found in the performance all too little correspondence between Schoenberg's notated intentions and the sounds coming from the stage.

After the Schoenberg botch came the excerpt from Berlioz's *Romeo and Juliet*. Here what should have been full of song became a dense harmonic impasto. Everything was thick and slow-moving and once again ultimately lifeless.

And so Leinsdorf's second concert arrived at its last work, the Debussy *Nocturnes*. The three pieces which make up this composition, *Nuages, Fêtes,* and *Sirènes*, are tone paintings, clad in Debussy's most brilliant and haunting orchestral colors; to the evocations of clouds and the festivals of the first two pieces, the composer adds the haunting voices of a women's chorus to serve as the very incarnation of his sirens. So attractive is all this gorgeous scoring that every musician who performs the *Nocturnes* must bear in mind that beyond the sounds of the music there is its sense. The sense of Debussy is its formal structure, its marvelously exact representation of the composer's aural image. For contrary to its general reputation as an impressionist— i.e., vague—art, Debussy's music is precise, clear, and in this way classical. Therefore, if the very evocative qualities present in the music are to have their full effect, it is especially important for the performer to guard against self-indulgence and to be *correct* and neat, in the manner of the fabled 1954–55 Pierre Monteux recording of the *Nocturnes* with the Boston Symphony.[3]

The outstanding impression of the Leinsdorf–Philharmonic performance of the Debussy *Nocturnes* was one of lackadaisical sloppiness. During the open rehearsal I attended the morning of the concert, the conductor seemed hardly interested in correcting what seemed to me relatively elementary mistakes of rhythm and intonation; in the directions he gave from the podium while the orchestra was playing he seemed concerned in the music's many tempo changes to keep a steady beat rather than making the sometimes drastic alterations demanded by the composer.

Nor was the evening performance any improvement on the rehearsal. Melodic upbeats were left unarticulated, plain tempo shifts were ignored, and a common rhythmic error by the chorus—the singing of the last two notes of a triplet figure after a tied and therefore silent first note as if the sung triplet notes were a pair of much faster sixteenth notes—was allowed to be incessantly repeated. Once again, as so often at these Leinsdorf concerts, the end result was boredom: boredom with the conductor, with the orchestra, and, alas, with the music itself.

The poor quality of Leinsdorf's conducting is puzzling. How could a conductor with (to judge from his books) so many good ideas, so many firmly held and laudable musical convictions, manage to elicit so little from the orchestra and communicate so little to the audience?

The answer, I am afraid, is that he took the easy way out. It is quite plain from his writings that he decided, when he left Boston in 1968, that he wanted no more of the onerous and dictatorial responsibilities of a music director; he wanted only to come into a city, do his rehearsals and concerts, and quietly leave. Now, in Fisher Hall, he found himself faced by a demoralized and fractious orchestra, an orchestra in severe need of the kind of discipline which only a brilliantly equipped musician-conductor can achieve. Rather than embarking on what must have seemed a hopeless task, he simply chose to get through the concert, no less and no more.

Remarkably, Leinsdorf has written (in *The Composer's Advocate*) about just such a dilemma in the course of distinguishing between two

---

[3] This performance is now available on RCA (France) GM 43366.

kinds of conductors. One is exemplified by Gennaro Papi, who was at the Metropolitan Opera for many years. According to Leinsdorf, he

> maintained a singularly calm manner as he piloted his usually unrehearsed performances through to the end. . . . When Papi finished, no one would have learned anything new about the works he had played. The performance would have been unexceptionable but routine. Papi had been conditioned by circumstance and his own personality to confine his own great knowledge of music to solving the dire practical problems of repertory opera.

The second type of conductor is exemplified by Serge Koussevitsky, one of Leinsdorf's predecessors in Boston. Koussevitsky, says Leinsdorf,

> was not gifted with an easy conducting arm; he needed help on the musical side to prepare himself; he performed by the standards of some observers superlatively, for others only intermittently so. Yet he has been welcomed into the halls of fame, having been a figure of musical importance. . . . Koussevitsky, whatever his shortcomings, brought his own personal insights and emotional response to the music. If Papi possessed the "technique of conducting" that the other lacked, Koussevitsky, whatever his shortcomings, was nonetheless the musician of consequence. In the bluntest of terms, one handled traffic, the other made music.

It is not very difficult to guess that in Leinsdorf's mind, he himself resembles Koussevitsky; it is ironic and unfortunate that after his recent concerts, he seems more to resemble Papi.

Guest conductors come, and guest conductors go; the New York Philharmonic remains. It is not now, either on its own or under any of its conductors, a great orchestra. I very much doubt that the problems of the Philharmonic derive in any significant measure from the inadequacies of its players. Even though Zubin Mehta has by now replaced more than thirty of the musicians who were in the orchestra when he came in 1978, the Philharmonic is still staffed by many members who played under Boulez and Bernstein, and even under Mitropoulos. The new members, too, are of first quality, representing a cross-section of the best younger orchestra players in America today.

As individuals, clearly, the Philharmonic musicians are vastly more than adequate.

Why, then, does the Philharmonic not play up to its potential? The explanations abound. Many critics, notable among them Donal Henahan of the *New York Times*, have pointed to a hostile attitude on the part of the orchestra to musical authority and to the very act of music making itself; on this analysis the Philharmonic could be a great orchestra if its members would only apply their talents to the job at hand. Critics have pointed as well to the difficult situation in which the Philharmonic is placed simply by being in New York, where great visiting orchestras make a point of bringing their best-played and best-rehearsed programs for specially arranged presentations, thereby putting the city's resident orchestra in an unfair competitive position. It has also frequently been said that the Philharmonic's management is both inefficient in its conduct of business and unnecessarily patronizing in its treatment of orchestra members.

Less often mentioned, but perhaps still a significant factor, is the great number of concerts and rehearsals the Philharmonic schedules each year; this consummation, devoutly wished for by its members and their labor union, undoubtedly asks more from the orchestra than it can comfortably give. And some musicians, it must be said, even blame the critics for the orchestra's plight: the first oboist of the orchestra, in responding in *New York* magazine to Peter Davis's strictures on Mehta, called this fair and even generous critic the "worst lesion" at the present time in the "severe case of critical shingles" which is responsible for the "sickness affecting the New York Philharmonic."

But to blame the employees of an organization for bad results, or to blame the critical messengers for bringing the bad news, is surely to ignore the larger and more important truth: an orchestra plays as well as its music director demands that it play. Here is the secret (though it is hardly a well-kept secret) of the greatness in recent years of the Berlin Philharmonic under Herbert von Karajan or of the NBC Symphony in the late 1930s and throughout the 1940s under Arturo Toscanini; here too is the secret of the magnificent results Pierre Monteux produced under debilitating union conditions with an essentially local orchestra in San Francisco over more than a decade beginning before World War II; here too is the real achievement of the late Eugene Ormandy in maintaining the richness and precision, over more than forty years, that Leopold Stokowski had established as the norm for the Philadelphia Orchestra. And the list could go on, with Cleveland under George Szell, Boston under Koussevitsky, Chicago under Fritz Reiner, and many more—including, as anyone listening to old recordings and broadcasts can attest, the New York Philharmonic under several of its former conductors. The lesson is plain: it is leadership that makes great orchestras.

So in the end, the problem of the New York Philharmonic cannot be solved by guest conductors, even when they are more energetic and committed than Erich Leinsdorf; it cannot be solved by manipulation of the orchestra members; it most assuredly cannot be solved by complaints and extravagant metaphors about the proper behavior of critics. The problem is the present music director, a musician who substitutes a presumed show-business glamour for musical interest, who shows his respect, affection, and care for the orchestra by blaming the players for the ensemble's lack of success, and who continues to blame the players when he himself is responsible for having chosen a third of the orchestra, including most of the solo players, and who in any case conducts less than half the orchestra's concerts and gives the orchestra less than half his time.

It is, then, high time that a new music director were brought in to begin the urgent task of rebuilding the New York Philharmonic, not in new personnel, but in the fundamentals of what it means for gifted musicians to play together as a group. This means finding a conductor willing to give something like his or her full time to the Philharmonic, and it certainly means finding a conductor with the kind of ear for orchestral sonority which can tell the difference between playing with feeling and playing correctly. Zubin Mehta has failed the test. The task of the board and the administration of the Philharmonic is to find a successor who will restore the New York Philharmonic to its rightful position at the head of New York musical life.

23.

The Karajan problem has now become a subject for the history of musical performance. Undoubtedly the greatest conductor to emerge on the international scene since World War II, he combined complete dedication to his work, total knowledge of the European classical music tradition, and unrivaled technical control of the orchestra. Where he suffered—at least by comparison with such past greats as Arturo Toscanini, Wilhelm Furtwängler, and Bruno Walter— was in his inability to convince sophisticated listeners that he could impose any personal stamp on his performances other than a characteristic Olympian standard of execution. Because Karajan's greatest achievement was the building of the Berlin Philharmonic into the finest orchestra in the world, his infrequent appearances with this ensemble were must events for music lovers. When he was obliged because of illness to withdraw from the 1986 Berlin tour, I was interested in just how the level of the orchestra would be maintained with someone else—in this case James Levine—on the podium; I described my impression of just what happened in this December 1986 New Criterion *article. When Karajan actually was able to conduct the Vienna Philharmonic in New York, just six months before his death, I attended the concert with the feeling that I was witnessing the end of a chapter in concert life; my account of what happened appeared in the April 1989* New Criterion.

The Berlin Philharmonic Without Karajan

I T H A S S E E M E D for some years now that the Berlin Philharmonic is the nonpareil of orchestras playing today. Whether on its innumerable recordings or in the quite limited number of concerts it has played here over the past three decades, the Berlin Philharmonic has set the kind of standard in performance that we in America used to associate with the Boston Symphony Orchestra under Serge Koussevitsky, or with the Philadelphia Orchestra under both Leopold Stokowski and, later, Eugene Ormandy.

So it was a matter of extraordinary interest when several months ago a new visit of the Berlin Philharmonic to these shores was announced. The tour wasn't scheduled to be anything like a full traversal of the continent; it was to include only a few concerts, including appearances in Boston, New York, Chicago, and cities on the Pacific Coast. Indeed, people on the inside of the music business widely expressed the opinion that the Berlin's American concerts were only throwaway events, done, as it were, *en passant* as the orchestra traveled to Japan, its "real" destination.

The excitement caused by the announcement of these concerts, few as they were, was of course not solely a matter of the Berlin's great reputation. The tour would provide audiences with one more chance, perhaps the last, to hear Herbert von Karajan, the orchestra's great conductor (and music director since 1955).[1] Not surprisingly, tickets to the concerts vanished immediately upon their being put up for sale.

As it turned out, American audiences were not to get this chance to hear Mr. Karajan. At the beginning of October, Columbia Artists Management, the organizers of the orchestra's American concerts, notified the newspapers that Mr. Karajan had been bitten by an insect and had come down with the rare (and serious) Lyme disease. As a result, he would not be able to do the tour. The orchestra was to come in any case, and Mr. Karajan's place was to be shared by Seiji Ozawa and James Levine, two conductors now very active on the American concert scene. Mr. Ozawa, the music director of the Boston Symphony, and Mr. Levine, the artistic director of the Metropolitan Opera, are both favorites of Mr. Karajan's. At one time it had been rumored that Mr. Ozawa was Mr. Karajan's choice to succeed him in Berlin, and Mr. Levine is currently active each summer at the Salzburg Festival, perhaps Mr. Karajan's chief musical fiefdom.

The New York concert at the Metropolitan Opera House on Sunday afternoon, October 19, was assigned to Mr. Levine. Mr. Karajan's program—which was to have consisted of the Ninth Symphony of Bruckner and a short piece by Mozart—was changed to a rather more "popular" program for Mr. Levine. His program was to begin with the

[1] For a discussion of Karajan and the recent biography of him by Roger Vaughan, see my article "Zeroing in on Karajan" in the *New Criterion*, October 1986; for a discussion of the Berlin Philharmonic's 1982 American tour under Karajan, see my article "Berlin on Two Coasts" in the *New Criterion*, December 1982.

Siegfried Idyll of Wagner, which would be followed by the *Four Last Songs* of Strauss (with the Bulgarian soprano Anna Tomowa-Sintow as soloist) and the Seventh Symphony of Beethoven. What had been a sold-out concert for Mr. Karajan quickly became anything but a sold-out concert for Mr. Levine. Advertisements for the concert appeared in the *New York Times* until the very day of the concert, and it seems that many tickets were given for distribution to members of the Metropolitan Opera Orchestra. Indeed, several minutes before the concert began both the most expensive tickets and the cheapest were still available.

In the event, the great hall, holding almost four thousand people, was full, and the audience responded to the orchestra's entrance onstage—just before the music began—with a hearty wave of applause. A word is perhaps in order about late stage appearance: not for the Berlin Philharmonic is the wretched practice, so common among American orchestras, of appearing before the incoming audience a half-hour before the concert starts and warming up at full force with excerpts from the evening's program as well as favorite selections from the solo concerto repertory. On the occasion of its New York concert, the Berlin Philharmonic was represented onstage before the concert only by the double-bass section, which made practically no sound at all, and by the tympanist, who tuned his instruments with great reserve and delicacy. The lovely result was that the first real sound heard by the audience at the concert was music, not aimless fiddling and tootling.

I must say at the outset that the decision—one must assume it was made by Mr. Levine—to combine on the first half of the program the Wagner *Siegfried Idyll* with the Strauss *Four Last Songs* seemed both interesting and fraught with difficulty. These two masterworks, in some ways so similar in their prevailingly mellow and gentle mood, are in fact at opposite ends of the emotional spectrum.

The *Siegfried Idyll* celebrates what may well have been the high point of Wagner's personal life: the birth and infancy of Siegfried, his only son. The story of the work's first performance has often been told. Siegfried had been born to Wagner and his wife Cosima in June of 1869, and in November of 1870 Wagner composed a serenade for his wife's birthday, which fell on Christmas Day. The work, scored for fifteen players, was secretly rehearsed and then, with Wagner conducting, performed for the surprised Cosima as she awakened in her bedroom at the Villa Triebschen on Lake Lucerne. Except for an old German cradle song, the material of the serenade came from the last act of *Siegfried*, the writing of which Wagner had finished (all but the last few pages) the previous year shortly after the birth of his son. And so the music of the *Siegfried Idyll*, drawn from Wagner's immersion in the opera, including the ecstasy Siegfried feels upon freeing Brünnhilde from her fire-girt rock and Brünnhilde's passionate surrender to her lover's entreaties, represents Wagner's own fervent involvement with both his wife and his infant son. After writing the *Siegfried Idyll*, Wagner went on to finish *Götterdämmerung*, oversee the first performance of the *Ring* at Bayreuth in 1876, write *Parsifal*, and oversee its first performance at Bayreuth in 1882, the year before his death in Venice at the age of almost seventy.

In contrast to the inner vitality of the *Siegfried Idyll*, the *Four Last Songs* of Strauss represent a very old man's farewell to life and to music. They were written in 1948, when the composer was eighty-four. The two works are thus very different. The *Siegfried Idyll* is dominated near its end by the melody which in Siegfried accompanies the hero's words to Brünnhilde:

Sie ist mir ewig,
ist mir immer,
Erb' und Eigen,
Ein und All'

(She is ever mine,
Is always mine,
My heritage and own,
One and all!)

But how different is the Strauss! *Im Abendrot* ("In the Sunset Glow"), which is set to a poem by Joseph von Eichendorff (1788–1857), closes the *Four Last Songs*. It ends with the words *"Ist dies etwa der Tod?"* ("Can this perhaps be death?") as the orchestra mournfully invokes the closing theme from Strauss's hugely successful early tone poem *Death and Transfiguration*. And the valedictory nature of the Strauss songs is not limited to the finale. Everywhere the mood is somber, even in the opening poem by Hermann Hesse, *Frühling* ("Spring"); Strauss's (and Hesse's) spring is filled with suspended life and nostalgic ecstasy rather than the coursing vitality of which composers and poets love to speak in their youth. And in the two middle songs, *September* and *Beim Schlafengehn* ("Upon Going to Sleep"), again set to poems by Hesse, the mood has all the sadness of a long life come to its end, a sadness mitigated only by the faith that for an artist there is an eternal existence beyond the physical world.

Hesse's words in *Beim Schlafengehn* deserve quoting, both for their own lyrical beauty and for the insight they give into Strauss's musical treatment:

Nun der Tag mich müd' gemacht,
Soll mein sehnliches Verlangen
Freundlich die gestirnte Nacht
Wie ein müdes Kind empfangen.

(Now the day has made me tired,
My passionate yearning shall
The starry night receive in friendship
Like a tired child.)

These words follow a magical passage for solo violin, in which the instrument, in itself a surrogate for the soprano voice—Strauss's lifelong representation of the eternal feminine—prepares the way for the artist's hope of disembodied eternal life:

Und die Seele unbewacht
Will in freien Flügen schweben
Um im Zauberkreis der Nacht
Tief und tausendfach zu leben.

(The Soul, unguarded,
Will hover in free flight
About the enchanted circle of night
To live deeply, a thousandfold.)

If the juxtaposition of the Wagner and the Strauss in the concert had seemed problematical, no such worries could attach to the choice of the Seventh Symphony of Beethoven. This work, of powerful rhythm and with countenance at once sunny and serious, has nothing to do with the world of tired or even fecund old men. Wagner himself was right on the mark when he called the finale of the Seventh Symphony the "apotheosis of the dance." To hear the work now is to receive an antidote to the apathy and despair so characteristic of today's thinking classes.

I must confess that it seems a kind of overkill to subject the program of the Berlin concert to such analysis, for in the event it was a tired-sounding and boring affair. Great as the Berlin Philharmonic undoubtedly is as an ensemble, it is difficult to avoid the conclusion that the most interesting part of its performance at the Metropolitan Opera House was the period of relative silence before the music started. The silence was audacious; the concert was merely dull.

Indeed, I am tempted to apply to the program as played a variation of a classificatory scheme once used in mail-order catalogues. They ranked their merchandise as good, better, and best; in the case of the Levine concert, the appropriate terms are dull, duller, and dullest. The Beethoven Symphony was dull, with often ragged ensemble (perhaps due, it must be said, to the orchestra's insufficient rehearsal time with Mr. Levine), and a deadening preponderance of brass and tympani. The work did not end with any sense of implied progression and gathering momentum; instead, the usually exciting last movement just got faster and then suddenly stopped, the orchestra having run out of notes to play and the conductor of bars to beat.

The distinction of being duller belonged to the Strauss songs. Though Anna Tomowa-Sintow is certainly a world-class performer if judged in terms of the engagements she fills, her voice seems to me often unfocused and wobbly; her delivery, too, seems marked by the opera singer's theatricality of gesture and movement rather than by the *Lieder* singer's self-effacing involvement with mood. But the major problem of the performance did not come from her. The problem lay rather in the musical inspiration—or the lack thereof—coming from the podium. Everything seemed so spun out and so drawn out, so cautious and so reserved, that it put one in mind of a particularly somnolent traversal of Debussy's *Pelléas et Mélisande*.

Dullest, alas, was the Wagner. Here too there were signs of inadequate rehearsal preparation. The ensemble in the opening octave leap in the violins, for example, was not precise, and neither was the answering entrance on the next beat of the violas and the cellos. Totally missing was any sense of what must have been the gaiety, the heartiness, and the good feeling of the work's birth and first performance. Everything was so hushed and breathless as to be tentative and even insubstantial. The parts in the score marked *forte* by the composer shared in the general apathy, and even the horn call at the end, so revelatory of Wagner's passionate feelings about his wife, seemed to belong to the category of "pipedreams," the kind of easy-to-listen-to organ music now becoming increasingly popular on WNYC, New York's city-owned public radio station.

It would be unfair not to make clear that even on this dismal occasion there were many wonderful things in the playing of the Berlin Philharmonic. Wonderful soft brass playing, silky strings (especially in soft passages), and a total absence of the grainy sound quality now sadly so characteristic of American orchestras—all these splendid virtues seemed to lack only a great leader making use of them. What an orchestra can do serves musical purposes only when the orchestra is given musical purposes to serve. In the concerts I have heard of the Berlin Philharmonic under Herbert von Karajan, there were musical purposes to serve; it has been in the services of Mr. Karajan's musical purposes that the orchestra has gained its present reputation.

But on this particular Sunday afternoon, in the neo-1890s red-and-gold plush splendor of the Metropolitan Opera House, there did not seem to be anything of musical value going on, unless one counts a fancy audience witnessing the work of a rudderless ensemble as musically valuable. Here, in the heartland repertory of German romantic music, it was only possible for this listener to appreciate these undoubted masterpieces of the repertory, and this undoubtedly great orchestra, by filling in all that was lacking on the podium with the formative artistic experiences of a lifetime of professional musical activity, concertgoing, and record listening.

For those of mature years, the necessity of engaging in this kind of divided listening is unpleasant enough. I do not know what the present shortfall in contemporary musical experiences—and it must be remembered that I am talking here not about musical composition but about the vastly less problematic area of performance—means for a new generation of audiences, a generation which come to concerts and to serious music without the golden memories of the past. But I suspect the worst. I suspect that all the folderol over international celebrities, promoted by powerful management and publicity apparatuses, all the musicological blather about putatively original performances on putatively original instruments, all the hype about great new art and the glorious institutions which are giving it birth— the whole barrage of words only obscures a simple fact: little of interest is now going on in music, and that little is but a pale imitation of the past.

There was a curious moment in the Berlin Philharmonic concert just before the music was to resume after the intermission. From somewhere upstairs in the cavernous auditorium came a disembodied voice, yelling something which sounded very much like: "This concert does not evoke the memory of Wilhelm Furtwängler!" To disturb a concert with such a remark is surely to carry the practice of speaking one's mind too far. But however addled he may be, the heckler had a point: the only musical event going on at the Metropolitan Opera House on the afternoon of October 19, 1986, was the sketchy and inadequate evocation of a better and a richer musical time. That one is tired of restating this simple truth doesn't make the truth any less true.

Karajan: The Last Time?

FOR GREAT CONDUCTORS—at least for those who make it that far—their ninth decade is often their most magnificent; it is also, alas, their last in which to perform. Toscanini, Monteux, Walter, Stokowski, Böhm: whatever their differences, these legendary conductors share the bittersweet distinction of attaining the heights of their careers at the very ends of their lives.

Now, at eighty-one, Herbert von Karajan is entering this rewarding and treacherous decade. By all odds the most important conductor to emerge on the international scene since World War II, Karajan is the last of an all but vanished breed, that of the *Generalmusikdirektor*: master at one and the same time of orchestral and operatic conducting and musical administration, discoverer and promoter of new talent, captain of musical industry, platform idol, and final arbiter of musical taste. There have been few indeed of this breed; of these few, only Karajan has managed to be a veritable Weberian ideal-type of the species, the *ne plus ultra* of everything a conductor can aspire to in the modern world.

This past winter the Vienna Philharmonic, the great orchestra with which Karajan has been closely associated, in concert and opera and on recordings, since the late 1940s, made an American tour.[1] Despite a long history of serious injury and illness and what we are told is now a life of constant pain, Karajan came here with them. At the end of February, the orchestra and the famous conductor arrived in New York for two programs in Carnegie Hall. On the first program was the Schubert Eighth Symphony (the "Unfinished") and a group of waltzes and polkas by the two Strauss brothers, Josef and Johann II; on the second was Bruckner's Eighth Symphony.

I attended the first program. Even before the concert began, the occasion was special; unlike our American orchestras' wretched habit of tuning and tootling onstage for what seems like hours before the music starts, the Vienna Philharmonic, as I have remarked of the Berlin, walks out in a body and begins to play with a minimum of preliminary noise. But something still more extraordinary was to come. I had known for a long time about Karajan's physical debilities, which have caused him to cancel many appearances; I had also read about his continuing difficulties with the Berlin Philharmonic, the orchestra of which he is music director for life but which has grown increasingly restless under his autocratic sway. But I was unprepared for the shock I felt when a gray creature, wizened and lamed, appeared at the side of the stage, leaning for what seemed like life itself on the arm of a young and tall companion. The great conductor thus accompanied made his way, at once dragging and hurtling, to the podium, effortfully climbed on it, sat down with his back to the

[1] Some six years ago, as part of the celebration of Karajan's seventy-fifth birthday, EMI issued three LP sets containing his early recordings with, in chronological order, the Vienna Philharmonic, the Philharmonia (London), and the Berlin Philharmonic. The Vienna volume (1C 137-54 3070/3), containing extraordinary performances of music by, among others, Mozart, Beethoven, Brahms, and Richard Strauss, is of great interest to those concerned with developments in musical execution immediately following World War II.

audience on the specially built-in bench, and with no flourishes at all began the Schubert.

The result was the culmination of Karajan's lifetime quest to achieve music through the refinement and clarification of orchestral sound. As he now conducted this thrice-familiar Schubert symphony, it did not begin; it suddenly *was*. The whispered opening phrase in the cellos and double basses, never so whispered before, seemed (like the opening sustained low E-flat of Wagner's opera *Das Rheingold*) an antecedent state of affairs, not a musical phenomenon but a fact of physical reality. And with these few notes, the mood for the entire symphony was set. The conductor's legs and feet, of necessity I was afraid, were perfectly still; his arms moved in flowing and graceful motions perfectly paralleling the sounds coming out of the orchestra.

These sounds were wholly passionless, without sudden attack or evident release, with everything bathed in what can only be called rapt refinement. All the notes were clear, but there was no brilliance; even the big chords, loud and forceful in every other performance of the piece, were here disembodied, as if conductor and players, composer and composition, had all gone beyond our earthly life. There was no thought here of the mortal Schubert or even of the immortal Schubert, of a Viennese Schubert style or of any other Schubert style; instead there was only a suggestion of what a pure music might be.

The strain on the orchestra in this kind of disembodied performance surely must have been immense. It seemed to me that the strain told in some momentary lapses in intonation in the solo winds and in some tentative string playing; even a great orchestra cannot be comfortable playing a long symphonic work without once digging into the sounds it is producing. But no matter: the perfection of Karajan's "Unfinished" Symphony was one not of performance but of *idea*. What was heard in Carnegie Hall on this cold Saturday evening was (at least for me) a transcendent musical conception—and execution—of a masterpiece, a conception of such personal delicacy and restraint, such accumulated wisdom and maturity, that it has never been heard before and perhaps will never be heard again.

The contribution of the brothers Strauss which followed the intermission changed the mood completely. Here, with Josef Strauss's *Sphären-Klange* and *Delirien* waltzes, and Johann Strauss's *Zigeuner-*

Baron Overture, *Annen-Polka, Perpetuum mobile,* and *Kaiser-Walzer,* Karajan exchanged his role of messenger-from-the-hereafter for that of an entertainer playing to his public. Priggish as it may be to say so, I must admit that I did not enjoy the conductor's return to the here and now. In this less-than-profound music, I felt the presence of Karajan's infirmities, and I found myself thinking back on just how many times, in blossoming health and in the fullness of youth, he had brought to these works the glitter and vitality which alone can make them great art.[2] What had seemed ethereal in the Schubert was now, in the music of the Strausses, flat; what had earlier seemed revelation was now mere lethargy.

When the audience, which had been bewildered at the end of the Schubert (these days New York audiences are hardly used to being on the receiving end of revelations), cheered lustily after the waltzes and polkas, Karajan rewarded them with an encore—the *Radetzky* March of Johann Strauss the elder. Now the audience really had a great time clapping with the beats, and matters only got more boisterous when the conductor turned to them and gave a half-smiling, half-mocking cue for the final round of claps.

How are we to understand the metamorphosis that took place in this concert, this descent (or so it seemed to me) from the sublime to the faintly ridiculous? Several thousand people were privileged to witness an unforgettable moment in musical history—the manifestation of a great musician's highest vision at the very end of his career; then a few minutes later, the very same audience—and the very same great musician, along with his collaborators—happily joined in what can only be called a clap-along. How, I repeat, are we to understand this?

The answer is simple. Musical performance, like every other kind of performance, means pleasing an audience. Performers—even, or perhaps especially, the greatest—live to give pleasure to an audience; the more the pleasure, and the larger the audience, the better. In this pleasure is the audience's satisfaction; in this satisfaction, indeed, is the performer's pleasure. That there is the capacity, in the very greatest

---

[2] Karajan's recordings of the *Perpetuum mobile* (1948) and the *Delirien* waltz (1949), both properly brimming with vitality, are contained in the EMI Vienna set I mentioned above.

musical performers, to convey an insight into matters beyond mere pleasure and satisfaction, into the ultimate nature of art and perhaps even of life, is something extra, and miraculous. That the glorious talent of Herbert von Karajan was able to convey, through the medium of his pain-wracked body, this insight in the Schubert symphony was more than we have a right to expect; that he shortly thereafter reverted to the entertainer he has always prided himself on being—well, that's just life. *Carpe diem*, and all that.

24.

I first read of Ernest Fleischmann's now renowned, if not notorious, speech on the future of the symphony orchestra in a short summary, clearly taken from a publicity release, in a high-fidelity equipment magazine. I immediately knew that he had touched a raw nerve in musical life, and I thought that his position deserved to be answered. I did so in this September 1987 New Criterion article. Mr. Fleischmann replied to me, and I in turn to him; our exchange was printed in the December 1987 New Criterion (not reprinted here). In early 1989, there was a panel discussion at the Cleveland Institute of Music (with both of us attending) based on Mr. Fleischmann's article, and to some extent on my response. This discussion demonstrated (I think conclusively) that while there was no interest in reforming orchestral organization on the lines Mr. Fleischmann had suggested, there was major concern with the low quality of musical leadership prevalent in our orchestras; I could hardly expect Mr. Fleischmann to have agreed, here or anywhere else, with my strictures concerning administrators.

Is the Symphony Orchestra Dead?

IN MATTERS affecting the future of high culture, it is often difficult to tell the friends of art from its enemies. Art is a shibboleth, an unexamined good in whose service—and in the solving of whose problems—many can prosper. Whether what is good for art's advocates is in fact also good for art is a murky matter.

These days, the attention of the well-wishers of art is beginning to fasten on the plight of serious music. There are many elements in this plight: a decline in audience sophistication, at once caused by and resulting in an increased concentration on already-known and crowd-pleasing repertory; the complete failure over the past half-century of avant-garde composition, both acoustic and electronic, to win a place in the minds of musicians and in the ears of serious music lovers; the almost total loss of confidence in the idea that the writing of music is a craft requiring fundamental and structured training; a shortage of new performing celebrities perceived to be of historical importance; the continuing encroachment of academic musicology on the standard repertory, an encroachment (in the manner of the killer bees) now progressing into Beethoven and moving forward in time at the rate of a decade every five years or so; a management revolution in which administrators are replacing practicing musicians as artistic policy makers; and finally the weakening of any future audience through the inability of our society to prescribe a serious course of education for the young in the humanities, including the study of great music.

All of these circumstances are now focused on the symphony orchestra, the most successful, visible, and vulnerable of our musical institutions. The success, the visibility, and the vulnerability alike stem from the massive expansion orchestras have enjoyed over the past few decades. In a process that began as long ago as the late 1930s, American orchestras have grown in numbers to the point where there is now hardly an area anywhere in the country not served by a locally supported symphonic ensemble. The statistics are indeed impressive. According to the American Symphony Orchestra League, in the 1984–85 concert season 19,969 symphony concerts took place in this country. These concerts were attended by 23.7 million people, with an average attendance per concert of 1,187. As the number of concerts has increased, so have the budgets for orchestras large and small. Our greatest orchestras are now projecting annual expenditures approaching twenty million dollars and more. In order to fund these large sums, increased ticket sales have become the object of strenuous marketing efforts, and orchestra development directors have built fund-raising networks stretching from government and corporations down to a vast number of small individual contributors.

But symphony orchestras are not just about institutional success. Even in the most cynical analysis, they are also—and even primarily— about the communication of great music. And despite their gains in frequency of activity and scale of operation, American orchestras are now widely seen to be beset by troubles. Overall, the playing of our best ensembles seems rather less tonally integrated and refined than in the past; in the most rosy assessment, a general gain in reliability has been offset by the tendency for different orchestras to sound alike rather than artistically distinct. But the most immediate troubles have been financial, usually triggered by difficult labor negotiations in which management cannot meet union demands or finds it necessary to ask for substantial concessions from the players. In recent years, regionally significant orchestras in Dallas, Denver, Kansas City, Phoenix, and San Diego either have threatened to suspend operations for a time or have actually done do; in the case of the Oakland (California) Symphony Orchestra, this suspension remains in force at the present time. Even so important a major orchestra as St. Louis, led by the popular and vital music director Leonard Slatkin, has not been immune to the threat of financial disaster.

For the large majority of orchestras not as yet in parlous financial straits (though even here high wage costs and restrictive work rules exert strong pressures on balance sheets), profound and nagging questions about artistic purpose can no longer be hidden in the clouds of self-congratulation and local boosterism. Like most basic questions, those that affect orchestras are simple to formulate, albeit difficult to answer: What do orchestras do? For whom do they exist? Why should they be supported? Each of these questions, and all of them together, must be answered in the context of the plight of serious music today.

A significant contribution to this debate has recently been made by no less a figure than Ernest Fleischmann, since 1969 the respected and eminent executive director of the Los Angeles Philharmonic Orchestra and general director of the Hollywood Bowl. Born in Germany in 1924, Mr. Fleischmann grew up in South Africa, where he was both a music critic and a conductor. In 1956, he was named director of music and drama for the Johannesburg Festival. From 1959 to 1967 he was general manager of the London Symphony Orchestra, and in the two years before coming to Los Angeles he served as the director of the classical division in Europe of Columbia Records. Energetic and outspoken, Mr. Fleischmann has been active in bringing new European conductors and soloists to the United States, and he was a major force in securing Carlo Maria Giulini and André Previn for the Los Angeles Philharmonic; he has also been associated with the practice of bringing enormous audiences into the Hollywood Bowl through the programming of blockbuster film scores and the staging of lavish light shows.

Mr. Fleischmann's thoughts on the orchestral situation are contained in a widely circulated address he delivered on May 16 of this year at the commencement exercises of the Cleveland Institute of Music. It must be said that the positions taken in this speech gain added weight from their having been delivered from the platform of such a prestigious institution, an institution closely associated throughout its history with the great Cleveland Orchestra of George Szell, Lorin Maazel, and now Christoph von Dohnányi.

Mr. Fleischmann's position certainly has the virtues of simplicity and directness. Calling his speech "The Orchestra Is Dead. Long Live the Community of Musicians," he begins by agreeing with Pierre Boulez's call more than two decades ago to burn the opera houses, and with Gunther Schuller's harsh characterization, in a 1980 speech at Tanglewood, of the life of the orchestral musician. In Schuller's words, as quoted by Mr. Fleischmann, orchestral musicians are "embittered, disgruntled, and bored. They've come to hate music, are apathetic and cynical. They have no spiritual identification with the scores they play."

Going beyond this verdict, Mr. Fleischmann finds that with the rise of union consciousness among the musicians the conflict between players and management has become a "them and us" situation. Even worse, he finds players everywhere frustrated by uninteresting repertory, poor conductors, inadequate halls, insufficient remuneration, and excessive tension. "No life for a real musician this," he says, "with little opportunity to develop as an artist, let alone as a human being." He notes that the situation in Europe is little better. "Why the hell," he asks, "should anyone then contemplate an orchestral career?"

He answers his own question by noting that with goodwill and cooperation on everyone's part, life can be made "truly stimulating for the musicians and richly rewarding for our audiences"—if we acknowledge that "the orchestra as we know it is dead," and begin to change its shape, structure, schedules, duties, and repertory. After remarking once again on the shortage of inspiring and knowledgeable conductors—and adding to the list a shortage of similarly equipped administrators—he gives a cogent analysis of the dull, routine, but always pressure-ridden process by which every year orchestra programs all across the country achieve their predictable and homogenized repetitions of the familiar and banal. He points, too, at a little-admitted fact: many subscribers, despite their willingness to buy tickets, often end up unwilling to attend the concerts for which they have paid.

Mr. Fleischmann again asks what can be done to remedy the situation. His answer is to turn "the rather rigid structure of the symphony orchestra . . . into a more flexible Community of Musicians." This new grouping would no longer be a band of approximately a hundred musicians, divided in traditional ways among strings, winds, brass, and percussion. Now in place would be a complement of around 150 musicians, with extra players for each instrument. He interrupts his recommendations to explain how this larger group would be funded: by consolidating the number of orchestras in each metropolitan area, and in particular by "eliminating one or more of the best ensembles [in the area] and merging them into a pool of 140–150 musicians under one expert administration, that will reduce administrative costs and rationalize fundraising and marketing activities."

As examples of the proposed consolidation, Mr. Fleischmann mentions "hypothetically, or better still, metaphorically" the merging of the Orchestra of St. Luke's with the New York Philharmonic, or, closer to (Mr. Fleischmann's) home, the Los Angeles Chamber Orchestra with the Los Angeles Philharmonic. These combinations would, of course, still need a music director, but they would also need a conductor to oversee new-music programs and still another to direct chamber-orchestra concerts. What he calls this "golden pond" of musicians could then be divided and re-divided to form a full symphony orchestra, a chamber orchestra, and a new-music ensemble, in addition to various string quartets, wind quintets, and brass ensembles.

In Mr. Fleischmann's vision, the full orchestra would play only twelve programs a year rather than twenty-four to thirty, with each program rehearsed from four to eight times, rather than the present maximum of four. Because of the drastic cut in number of different programs, each concert would be sold out to eager, enthusiastic audiences, grateful to hear perfectly prepared performances under such conditions of scarcity. There would also be approximately eight new-music concerts per season, each rehearsed eight or ten times, using an ensemble of as many as forty players. These programs, too, Mr. Fleischmann envisions as treats, composed as they would be of exhaustively rehearsed performances "conveying all the excitement, the stimulation, the surprises, the adventure that truly convincing performances of new music can create. And what a great job they'll do for our living composers, for the scintillating, disturbing, challenging, thrilling music of our time!"

For Mr. Fleischmann, the marvelous tasks waiting to be accomplished by his Community of Musicians go on and on. These include the provision of opera and ballet orchestras as well as "at least one and probably two" chamber orchestras. The chamber orchestras would present at least twelve programs a year, each program repeated two or three times. And then there would be any number of string quartets, wind quintets, and brass ensembles, all performing regularly and administered by the Community's highly competent staff. Finally, two or three times a year all the players would get together "to play a Mahler 8 or a Berlioz Requiem!"

Mr. Fleischmann has education in mind as well, for all his groups would be available in the schools, with "everyone of them . . . able to provide its own special kind of performance/demonstration services." Musicians would participate in adult-education activities to prepare audiences for concerts. For those who like to teach, there would be the possibility of "enlightened, well-planned and well-organized teaching activities, all developed in collaborative efforts between the pool's musicians, their management team and the relevant education authorities." Mr. Fleischmann's last suggestion is that the Community include performers of ethnic music, folk music, and jazz, so that

> every single member of our Community of Musicians . . . [might] practice those forms of musical and ancillary activity which allow each and every one of them to express themselves [*sic*] fully.

Returning to the incendiary exhortation of Pierre Boulez with which he began, Mr. Fleischmann ends with nothing less than a resounding call to arms:

> I really need to ask you to commit a crime. I want you to become arsonists, yes, arsonists, to join me and lots of musicians, administrators and trustees in setting the symphony orchestra ablaze. If the music we care about so deeply is to survive, we must accept that the orchestra is burnt out, but from its ashes

something infinitely richer, more varied, more satisfying can arise if we all work together to create it—ladies and gentlemen, the symphony orchestra is dead—long live the Community of Musicians!

We should, I assume, pass over the curious rhetorical formulation in which Mr. Fleischmann asks us to burn down something which (according to his account) is already, presumably through the previous incendiary actions of others, "burnt out" and in a state of "ashes." We should perhaps pass over, too, Mr. Fleischmann's easy, though rather late-occurring, assumption that "the music we care about" is indeed all truly valuable music, and that an institution rooted in the classics has a necessary commitment to every form of musical expression.

It is rather more difficult to ignore the arrogant utopianism in which Mr. Fleischmann clothes what are rather unpleasant proposals. In many ways, this idea of a perfect music-performance community resembles radical nineteenth-century schemes of a liberated life in which there is a proper place for each person and in which each person finds that place through the rationally contrived arrangements of a beneficent social order. The adversary of these schemes of true community—whether they are based on sexual, spiritual, or economic premises—is individualism: the free and rationally determined choice, bound and shaped by our human need to live in society, to bear private responsibility for our thoughts and actions.

Whatever his motives, Mr. Fleischmann, like all utopian advocates, bases a conception so opposed to individual responsibility on the promise of a hitherto unachieved fulfillment of the individual. In the last century, utopianism was engendered by the erosion of socially shared values, values derived from religion, philosophy, and economics. This erosion provided an increased scope for individual action at the same time as it rendered the individual ever more alone in the cosmos. Some may find it a far cry from the last century's loss of faith in a transcendent being to our present musical situation, but there can be little doubt that the contemporary musical life of which Mr. Fleischmann speaks displays many of the same characteristics of the collapse of belief which, in mid-nineteenth-century England, gave rise to agnosticism, relativism, and the poignant attempt to recapture through ritual the essence of religion.

Almost within recent memory the sea of musical faith, to adapt Matthew Arnold's phrase in "Dover Beach" (c. 1855), was at the full; for most of those today deeply touched by great music, that artistic tide has now run out. Musical developments of the last half-century— and perhaps more—bear an uncanny resemblance to the wider developments associated with nineteenth-century rationalism: I am here referring to the present loss of faith by the most musically creative in a usable past, to the widespread equivalence of high art and popular culture, and to the passionate attempts now being made by performers and audiences alike to find a musical salvation based upon academically sanctioned "authentic" performances of compositions from the beginning of the classic repertory.

This musical condition of creative exhaustion at the core is accompanied, curiously enough, by an appearance of the most floridly prosperous performing activity at the periphery. Like a fevered patient whose flush is mistaken for rosy health, the true state of music is almost impossible to diagnose—because of the sheer amount of activity taking place, because of the numerous celebrity careers being urged upon the audience, and because of the vested interest of those in musical power in justifying their perquisites and emoluments. And it is here that Mr. Fleischmann, acting as a powerful spokesman for the musical establishment, emerges not as a utopian at all, but rather as the hardest-headed of businessmen—or perhaps, one should say, of labor leaders.

For quite clearly Mr. Fleischmann is not suggesting the creation of a free community of musical saints, working in a condition of subsidized concentration on the creation of artistic truth. What he is urging upon us can only have the effect of saving a richly rewarding, though shaky, market for its present suppliers through the time-honored means of eliminating competition. Both the creators of the great nineteenth-century trusts and the captains of craft unions understood this process exceedingly well; they did not, however, describe what they were doing as necessary to the future of art and beauty.

In advancing his position, Mr. Fleischmann is only carrying further the explicit policies of our great orchestras over recent decades. It is known to all observers of the musical scene that these orchestras are territorially aggrandizing institutions whose primary concern, as fund-raising and image-creating organisms, is to preserve their positions as the first and only true orchestras in their communities. This is true in Boston, in New York, and certainly in Los Angeles; it is the reason why in the United States we have only one-orchestra towns. Everywhere in Europe, the great cities have more than one orchestra performing the symphonic repertory, in both live concerts and broadcasts. Here in the United States, major orchestral life is already deeply noncompetitive, not just in each city, but even in the nation as a whole, a condition made more efficient by the close relations among the senior administrators of our major orchestras, and between these administrators and commercial managers operating out of New York. The extent of Mr. Fleischmann's concern for the preservation of this status quo is demonstrated by his proposals—advanced, it is true, only "hypothetically, or better still, metaphorically"—to merge into the great orchestras of their cities groups offering as little competition (for funds or audience) as New York's Orchestra of St. Luke's and the Los Angeles Chamber Orchestra.

Clearly, the centerpiece of Mr. Fleischmann's new order is not the concentration of musicians; it is the concentration of administration. At its highest level, the world of musical administration today is a tight little place; if anyone should doubt this fact of institutional life, he need only be aware that recently the Boston Symphony Orchestra and the Cleveland Orchestra have dealt with their need for bold new policies and fresh administrative blood by the simple expedient of exchanging top administrators—Thomas Morris leaving Boston for Cleveland and Kenneth Haas leaving Cleveland for Boston.

There can be little doubt that a few powerful administrators would indeed stand to benefit from the enactment of Mr. Fleischmann's proposal. There would be higher budgets to allocate, more money for the surviving organizations to raise, more employees, bigger and more powerful boards to support administrative policies, and an even greater tilting of the balance of power from artistic concerns to those of business management.

What would be the fate of the musicians if Mr. Fleischmann were to have his way? Even more than is true now, there would be only one employer in town. Competition with that one employer would be even more difficult to carry off successfully than is the case today; labor negotiations would find musicians pitted against much more powerful management negotiating teams than now; most important, the power of the individual, self-concerned musician would be vastly reduced. All in all, insofar as musicians are concerned, the situation which Mr. Fleischmann envisions could only have the effect of replacing one-orchestra towns with company towns.

What about the music-loving audience under this new dispensation? Doubtless the administrative skills which Mr. Fleischmann and his colleagues possess would provide better-run—and perhaps even better-prepared—concerts, though their number would be fewer and the choice available to listeners inevitably smaller. Mr. Fleischmann is, after all, suggesting the scheduling of no new activities, only the better presentation and organization of what is now being done. But even this better presentation would of necessity be centrally determined, with musical decision making divided between an absentee music director with no interest in new music, a new-music director with a limited or even nonexistent public, and a chamber-orchestra conductor with no access to the major symphonic repertory. Only strong administrative control, in the hands of one individual, would have any hope of making sense out of such a chaotic situation.

Above all, there is no reason whatsoever to believe that Mr. Fleischmann's proposal would bring any musical benefits at all. It is idle to suppose that increased rehearsal time under the direction of what Mr. Fleischmann himself states are inadequate conductors would bring any benefits; it is unreasonable to assume that cutting down the number of available concerts would produce more, rather than less, musical knowledge; it is illusory to think that the problems of new music can be helped by providing a golden ghetto for contemporary composition. The small size of the ensemble Mr. Fleischmann desires for new-music performance—no more than forty players—would, under the monopoly conditions inherent in his scheme, practically guarantee that composers would give up the attempt to write truly symphonic music. The same celebrities would be playing much the same repertory in the same way. And why should ethnic music or folk music and jazz benefit from performance under the aegis of an institution devoted primarily to classical music? As to the ultimate artistic value of Mr. Fleischmann's suggestion that there should be one or two jamborees each season in which all the musicians, of whatever interests and goals, get together to give extra-loud performances of much-played sonic spectaculars of the literature—I leave it to the reader to judge for himself.

I cannot end without returning directly to the title of this article: Is the symphony orchestra dead? The answer to this question must be no. The symphony orchestra is very much alive, if by "alive" one refers to the interpretation of some of the greatest works of art for audiences composed of sophisticated listeners and new cadres coming to beautiful music more or less for the first time. By performing this task, the orchestra is accomplishing the vital function of preserving and extending civilization. Because it performs this task it is worthy of support by all those responsible for the future of our society.

The fact that the symphony orchestra is alive and is performing a vital cultural function does not mean that its present condition is either healthy or happy. The problems with orchestral life, and with musical life as a whole, are great. As I have tried to make clear, they stem from internal difficulties in the musical creativity of our time, and from the way the resultant artistic vacuum has been filled by extraneous economic and social forces. The scale of universal public success on which symphony orchestras are expected to operate is too large; the quasi-commercial success they must achieve in order to be perceived as legitimate is unrealistic. To restrict the scale of orchestral life through a process of further concentration provides no solution. It is time for musicians to take their futures in their own hands, by demanding that conductors be chosen for their musical skills rather than for their European celebrity status. They must also take seriously the problem of contemporary composition; this can only be done by performers demanding new music that they, as musicians, can love. There is nothing wrong with musical life that serious conductors in charge of great orchestras, playing new compositions of permanent value, cannot cure. In any case, there is little likelihood that our salvation will some from administrators whose skills lie entirely in the merchandising of that which has already become famous somewhere else.

IV

MAKING CULTURE POSSIBLE

25.

I wrote this October 1983 New Criterion *article in an attempt to defend the role of private decision making in private philanthropy. As the reader of the article will soon notice, the book I was concerned to attack seemed to me a prime example of the "just leave everything to us social scientists" school of public policy analysis. Following upon the publication of this book, restrictions were introduced, in the Tax Reform Act of 1986, on the deductibility of gifts to museums of appreciated property, i.e., art works whose cost to the donor was lower than market value at the time of the giving. Though I do not in fact think that these restrictions, in light of the present hypertrophied state of the art market, are unfair, their effect in cutting down new gifts has already been marked and may well increase. As I look back at this article, I now think that what is most important in it is the use of the word* decides *in the title. The issue in high culture and its patronage, and it is one that will occupy the rest of this book, is both "who decides" and "what is decided."*

Funding the Arts: Who Decides?

THE BURNING QUESTION in the cultural world today is not the creation of art, but its funding. In Washington, the Reagan administration's halfhearted attempts to bring the budget of the National Endowment for the Arts into line had been opposed by a solid phalanx of advocates passionately convinced that more money means more beauty. The very health of our national soul, we are told, is a simple function of just how generously the federal government supports cultural activity.

Among the several states, the scurrying for the arts dollar goes on as well. Oregon now has a simple checkoff provision on its income-tax returns, painless in its execution, which has been welcomed by Joan Mondale—America's erstwhile "Joan of Art"—as a milestone in paying for culture. Massachusetts prides itself on an arts lottery, in which purchasers of inexpensive tickets can pursue fortune and the sustenance of art at one and the same time. State legislatures are almost everywhere appropriating more money for the arts, and cities too are increasing their own commitments to art.

Public appropriations for the arts, whether from cities, states, or the federal government, are of course fairly new in the United States. The backbone of cultural support now as before is the private patron, a category which has for many years included charitable foundations and which has now been widened to include corporations eager to improve their own images. The White House, eager to repair the damage caused by its widely advertised NEA budget cuts, has laid much stress on the role of private contributions, and has marshaled the prestige of the presidency on behalf of increased nongovernmental backing of the arts.

For many years it has been clear that a major factor encouraging our undoubtedly high level of private patronage in culture has been the preferential treatment accorded charitable contributions as a whole by our tax laws. Every sophisticated fund-raising appeal for a worthy cause, whether that cause is religious, educational, medical, social, or cultural, emphasizes without let that a contribution is "tax deductible to the full extent permitted by law." That extent, under a system of progressive marginal tax rates, is sizeable, and increases in rough but direct proportion to the income of the individual making the gift. There are other tax breaks, too. Localities, for instance, are often generous with property-tax exemptions for charitably funded institutions, thus enabling them to enjoy the advantages of real-estate ownership without having to pay the accompanying public costs.

So attractive has this use of tax incentives seemed, and so successful has it been in raising money, that the advocates of philanthropy, with the powerful participation of arts advocates, have turned their attention to increasing the possible use of these measures, making them easier, more widespread, and above all more profitable to the individuals or businesses making the gift. Indeed, such improvements in the system are a particular task of two Reagan initiatives, the Presidential Task Force on the Arts and Humanities and the President's Committee on the Arts and the Humanities.

Until recently, this peculiarly American practice of private arts support encouraged by tax preferences was a widely accepted national achievement. But now the entire system has come under attack at its most vulnerable point, that of the charitable deduction itself. In a study sponsored by the Twentieth Century Fund, Alan L. Feld, Michael O'Hare, and J. Mark Davidson Schuster have written a detailed analysis of present tax policy and the arts.[1] Their verdict is clear: present practices are undemocratic, inefficient, corrupt, and damaging to the very arts whose cause they purport to advance.

It would be tempting to attack this study by pointing to the authors' evident lack of feeling for art and culture. Indeed, Messrs. Feld, O'Hare, and Schuster were not chosen for their aesthetic sensibilities; the report's foreword (written by M. J. Rossant, the director of the Twentieth Century Fund) states proudly:

> Their range of knowledge—in public policy, taxation, and not-for-profit institutions—seemed suited to an investigation of indirect subsidies and the implications of changes in the tax laws on institutions and artists who were the recipients of subsidies.

To reject this report merely because of its insensitivity to art, however, would be to miss not only its main thrust but its very *raison d'être. Patrons Despite Themselves* is in fact a peculiar blend of populism and statism. And its political implications are no less dangerous for being presented in a tone of injured intellectual virtue.

Throwing scholarly caution to the winds, the authors begin their study with these words:

> The present study originated a decade ago in a chance remark by a trustee of the Boston Museum of Fine Arts to Michael O'Hare (during his employment as a planning consultant to the museum): " . . . but, Mr. O'Hare, if you do all those things, they'll all just come here in droves and be all over the place!" This attitude toward the public was not universal among the museum staff or trustees, but it is certainly not an unknown opinion for someone in that environment to hold. How is this possible in a public institution heavily subsidized by government aid?

A rather more clearly worked out statement of this attitude is presented two pages later:

[1] *Patrons Despite Themselves: Taxpayers and Arts Policy.* A Twentieth Century Fund Report. New York University Press, 1983.

We are enthusiastic advocates for the arts. We think the government should play a significant role in funding culture, and we think more people should enjoy more and better presentations of the fine arts. But we are democrats before we are art enthusiasts. . . . We think much of the failure in expanding the arts audience in the past decade has resulted from ambivalent commitment to this goal on the part of arts institutions (partly due to the funding structure we describe in this book).

With the requisite ideological superstructure in place, the authors set about demonstrating the facts they deem essential to making their case. In the first chapter they present a representative museum budget, first organized along conventional lines and then organized in a way they feel better expresses the reality of government aid. The conventional budget credits to public sources only those subsidies directly paid out by government agencies. The revised budget counts taxes forgone by government as a direct subsidy. The difference between the two budgets is striking. In the conventional budget, public funds constitute a mere 9.16 percent of income; in the revised budget, public funds account for 30.65 percent.

Here—in what the authors call "indirect aid"—lies the heart of the matter. What appears in the revised museum budget, they generalize to all of cultural support, and indeed to philanthropic enterprises in general. Tax forgiveness, in the form of relief from income, estate, gift, or property taxes, makes up between two and three times more aid than direct programs. This tax forgiveness, for Messrs. Feld, O'Hare, and Schuster, is a tax expenditure, a term used by Harvard Law School professor Stanley Surrey to describe revenues which would be collectible by government were it not for tax exclusions, credits, and deductions. The thesis of this book is that tax expenditures in the field of culture are flawed for two reasons: they allow these so-called government funds to be directed by private citizens, and they allow the wealthy a greater share of this direction, because progressive tax rates guarantee that the charitable deduction will be more valuable to the rich than to the poor.

After a qualified rejection of the idea that the present tax policy is unfair to artists, the authors go on to discuss "indirect aid" to institutions in detail. Their discussion is limited by their inability to cite data more recent than the mid-1970s. In 1973, for example, the total estimated tax expenditures for the arts amounted to $458 million, of which the federal component made up 75 percent, the states' 3 percent, and the localities' (via property-tax exemptions) 22 percent. Of the total indirect contribution from federal and state government, slightly more than four-fifths resulted from corporate and individual charitable deductions on income tax and from the forgoing of capital gains taxes on gifts of appreciated property. Another 7 percent was the result of gifts made through private foundations (funded with contributions subject to the charitable deduction). The remaining 13 percent came directly through charitable deductions on estate and gift tax returns.

It is clear to the authors that while the arts do benefit from tax incentives, they also benefit because the wealthy, who generate the largest tax expenditures per dollar of their contributions (because of progressive tax rates), are more heavily represented in the support of culture than in any other philanthropic area. The figures are impressive. The authors show that individuals with yearly incomes of $50,000, while giving 4 percent of the gifts to religion, 31 percent to non-health social welfare, 33 percent to health, and 60 percent to education, contributed no less than 77 percent of the total charitable gifts to culture.

Given the philanthropic preferences of the wealthy—and progressive tax rates—it is hardly surprising that the lion's share of tax expenditures goes to culture. Of the total federal funding going to religion as a result of private giving, only 11 percent was the result of contributions from individuals with yearly incomes over $50,000; for non-health social welfare the figure rose to 50 percent, for health it was 60 percent, for education 76 percent, and for culture a whopping 84 percent.

Not only do those with money support culture disproportionately and control unequally the direction of tax-expenditure funds. They also enjoy a lopsided share of the benefits created by the institutions their dollars support. According to the authors, statistics for 1974–75 show that though individuals with an adjusted gross income of more than $30,000 annually made up no more than 8 percent of the population, they were responsible for 18 percent of visits to museums, theater, classical-music concerts and opera, and dance. The well-to-do thus encountered art more often than the less affluent: whereas the

average number of visits to artistic events for all income brackets was
4.46, for those earning more than $30,000, it was 10.44, or well over
twice as many.

Nonetheless, the authors do conclude that there is some redistributive
effect in the support of art by the wealthy, that it is not a matter of "all
of society [paying] to support an entertainment for the rich." Indeed,
their statistics show that benefits from arts support are greater than
payments for every income group below the highest. But they draw
cold comfort from this modest fact of democratic life. Dourly, they
explain that

> subsidies to the arts, including those financed through the tax
> system, flow from the very wealthy to the moderately wealthy
> and the well-educated. Notwithstanding the stated goals of
> government support, such as, for example, through the National
> Endowment for the Arts, poor and moderate-income people
> apparently do not benefit much.

Messrs. Feld, O'Hare, and Schuster are aware that a widely
appreciated virtue of our present system of arts support via tax
incentives is that it encourages diffusion of decision making. But they
do not find a mere criterion of numbers sufficient. Decision makers,
they argue, should reflect expertise in their spending of public money;
there should be diversity of opinion; there should be no exercise of
"narrow partisan politics or self-serving interests." The authors don't
discuss party politics, but they do find the status quo lacking on every
other count.

For our authors, the wealthy—despite their relatively better
education—have little to recommend them save their money. They
cite no recent patron with an artistic sensibility except when his
actions can be presented, as in the rumored case of Arthur Sackler (and
the Fogg Museum at Harvard), in an unfavorable light. Instead, the
patron is presented as a buffoon:

> Cornelius Starr, a New York insurance executive, commissioned
> a new production of *Madame Butterfly*, citing his impatience with
> the old production's unforgivable anachronism: cherry blossoms
> (a spring flower) and chrysanthemums (an autumn flower) side
> by side on the stage. (The Met does turn down some gifts: the

bequest of McNair Ilgenfritz, a Metropolitan Opera box-holder and amateur composer, which was to be used to produce one of his own one-act operas, was refused.)

As it goes with the expertise of patrons, so it goes with meaningful diversity. For the authors, "board-level decision-making within cultural institutions usually rests in the hands of the socially prominent wealthy." According to several surveys cited, these worthies are overwhelmingly white, mostly male, usually at least sixty years old, frequently Episcopalian, often businessmen and lawyers, and even, 7 percent of them, bankers. The conclusion is simple:

> In most cases, trustees of arts institutions resemble donors more closely than the general public; the trustees' allocation of tax expenditure funds thus is likely to be closer to donors' preferences than those of the general public. The problem is not that the allocation decisions necessarily are bad, but that diversity is more likely to suffer than would be the case if the trustees were more representative of the public at large.

Perhaps the gravest allegation made by this report against the present system is that it harms the arts in two ways: it distorts the artistic outcome by encouraging institutions to do certain things rather than others, and it involves administrators in professional and ethical compromises brought about by donor pressures. The first kind of compromise—letting standards sag in order to cater to patrons' whims—is an inevitable result of having patrons at all:

> Arts administrators often modify their programs in the presence or absence of financial support. Generally, any input or output distortion will affect arts administrators' plans and may leave them with a sense of having made a professional compromise.

Messrs. Feld, O'Hare, and Schuster are indeed quick to admit that government aid might be thought to be just as flawed as private support. But they are equally quick in finding a saving grace for the flaw:

> Presumably, if direct [i.e., government aid in lieu of the indirect tax expenditure] aid programs were well formulated and efficiently administered, changes in the operation of arts institutions would

be applauded as working in the public interest even though arts professionals might have been forced to change their plans, "lower" their standards, or aim toward a different audience.

However complex a matter professional compromise might be, ethical compromise is just plain cheating. Here the authors cite numerous examples of possible tax dodges, with the plain implication that these frauds are frequent and practiced on a large scale. In principle, such illegalities involve the collusive overvaluation of donations, resulting in larger tax savings to the donor which then turn up as tax-expenditure aid to the institution. The authors' verdict on the whole process is severe:

> The tradition of public philanthropy disguised in private garments has produced a generation of art museum professionals so conditioned to play the role of courtiers and toadies in their relationships with wealthy donors that they apparently have lost hope for any other possibility.

The authors' case against the present organization of private philanthropy is more than a matter of allegations of unfairness and sometimes illegality. Even in the intended operation of the tax laws, the authors find deleterious consequences for art. The particular offenders here are the property-tax exemption and the generous treatment given to gifts of appreciated art works. The property-tax exemption encourages the flow of charitable funds into grandiose building projects; these projects would not have been undertaken, so the authors believe, had their economic cost been calculated without the benefit of tax forgiveness. And had the appreciation of art works been taxable to the donor as a capital gain, there might not be the present tendency on the part of museums to possess vastly more works of art than they can possibly display.

Thus the authors attack museums simultaneously for overbuilding and for having too much art. When one wishes to know from this report just what kind of ideal museum the authors have in mind, the answer is in fact available; they seem to admire institutions which have

> elected instead to acquire a small collection nearly all on display, or no collection at all, with extensive, temporary exhibitions, a lecture program, slide tapes, art classes, and field trips. Similarly,

a museum might mount a special exhibition that depended on a few borrowed works and others from its own collection combined with an extensive catalog or lecture program, or it might borrow dozens of objects from around the world for a blockbuster exhibition.

The report ends with suggestions for improving the efficiency and equity of the system. The first suggestion is for improved data collection, through tax returns, by the Internal Revenue Service. Here the authors display a telling faith in the virtue of such governmental initiatives:

> Historically, the Internal Revenue Service has resisted collecting information other than that required to administer the tax code. We believe it should view its mission more broadly and include among its responsibilities reporting to the public not only where tax monies come from but also how efficiently the tax system as a whole is working.

As alternatives to the present charitable deduction, they suggest various matching-grant proposals, which would have the effect of restricting the amount of tax savings to donors. Because it would apply to all charitable contributions, one proposal involving a flat tax credit would seriously cut (by 20 percent) contributions to both educational and cultural institutions. Another proposal, establishing a government contribution to each charity based on private contributions, would avoid the problem of decreasing cultural funds; it would also avoid "the problem of the charitable institution perceiving the public contribution as private." A third proposal would have the government allocate an amount to the donor's preferred charities based on the percentage of the donor's income given to charity each year. The authors' preference lies with a flat tax credit of approximately 30 percent. Any shortfall to the arts could be made up, they feel, by direct government aid. They also feel that the amount of such aid would have to be determined through increased and more responsive record keeping and data collection.

It should be clear by now that the ever-prevailing bias of the authors is away from the private sector and toward government. Their opinion of direct governmental aid is indeed high:

As regards the direct system, several points should be noted in its favor. The government authority empowered to distribute funds, even in the simplest description of the direct aid system, should not be viewed as a usurper of rights that legitimately reside with the governed. A more appropriate view is of a willing exchange by the decisionmakers of their individual responsibility for the greater efficiency and expertise found in a centralized agency.

Evidence of such a voluntary exchange also is found outside government in the existence of United Funds and, say, the March of Dimes. (In fact, some communities are now witnessing the birth of United Arts Funds.) Individuals, of course, give their money directly to hospitals and laboratories, but most elect to make their contributions more effective by delegating to a centralized bureaucracy power to make the allocation. . . . The establishment and funding of government charitable agencies like the National Endowment for the Arts operate similarly.

The praise that follows makes quite plain just what specific direction arts funding should take:

The National Endowment for the Arts displays considerable diversity as well as insulation against political influence—in addition to the expertise we should expect to find in a centralized agency. The basic statute that established the NEA, as well as the agency's internal policy, provides for varying levels of expert decision making. For example, there is no "arts czar" within the NEA: no one person can veto a particular project or reject a specific artist. Applications to the NEA go through a variety of review stages, the most important of which is the advisory panel review. NEA grants most often go indirectly to arts institutions and arts projects through state arts councils or arts service organizations. The NEA imposes no guidelines on substance. Thus, diversity is protected both geographically and by the wide range of people and projects receiving money.

The sole reference cited by the authors for this extraordinary collection of misinformation on and misevaluation of the NEA is Michael Straight's trivial account of his days as number two man at the agency during the Nixon and Ford administrations. But in fact the NEA during the Carter years (the period immediately preceding the authors' project) was deeply susceptible to a wide range of political influences and even control, exercised not just by Vice President Mondale's wife but also by Chairman Livingston Biddle (a close associate and protégé of Democratic Senator Claiborne Pell), Deputy Chairman Mary Ann Tighe, who came to her job directly from the vice president's staff, and assorted ethnic and interest groups in Congress. Despite relatively superficial circulation among staff and panels, there has been a steady revolving-door relationship between the NEA and the arts advocacy organizations. Panels have historically shown the same key names popping up again and again. Not only does major power at the NEA reside with the staff rather than with the panels, who only see applications after they have been winnowed through staff-inspired guidelines and staff review; staff recommendations are virtually the only factor in determining who is asked to serve on panels. There is an "arts czar" at the NEA. He is called the chairman, and he chooses his staff as well as having final power of veto on grants. He also has the power to make grants in his own name and on his own authority. NEA grants do not go most often indirectly to institutions and projects through state arts councils and service organizations; the majority of them, both in number and in dollar value, go directly to institutions and individuals.

Few observers of art would credit the NEA with having had other than a marginal effect on the development of American culture during the nearly two decades of its existence. In music, for example, America's best years were in the period from the mid-thirties to the mid-fifties, well before the NEA's founding. The same would seem to hold true for literature, and for the visual arts as well. The NEA has poured large sums into performance and exhibition; this largesse has seemed to have had little effect on artistic creation itself. If the changes advocated by the authors of this report were to be put into law, there is no doubt that the vastly increased amount of government funding required to take up the slack would be administered by the NEA. There is no reason to think this added burden would be either fruitfully or efficiently borne.

It hardly seems fair to expect Messrs. Feld, O'Hare, and Schuster, who care so little about art, to know very much more about the NEA.

But the issue is not whether they know either about art or about the NEA. The issue here is their ideological commitment to government as something to be preferred to the world of private individuals. In this connection, the authors go beyond a mere critique of the power of wealth and seem—at least by indirection—to be attacking all non-expert opinion. Thus, they quote Monroe Price, writing in the *Hastings Law Journal*:

> The present condition is that museums characteristically represent a context in which a public trust, largely publicly supported, is vested in individuals over whom the public has virtually no control. Wealth and status, independent of other characteristics, can find their place. While there is nothing wrong with those characteristics, it is wrong to have a system of museums dependent on wealth. . . . By relying on tax induced contributions, we place the center of strength for our arts institutions with the rich. It is their taste that becomes the museum's taste, and thence the community's. As a nation we have always depended on the bounty of the rich and the powerful to build our cultural institutions, but in this century we have rewarded such gifts with general tax savings. Perhaps it is time that we review our method of building public collections to determine whether more democratic means would yield institutions that are freer of idiosyncratic and individual taste.

Significantly, the argument immediately passes on to another subject.

The authors thus appear to the reader as veritable worshippers of Big Brother. Whether that powerful creature wears the mask of the IRS or the NEA seems less important to them than that he wears the cloak of the democratic community. Not only have voters—as shown by the election of Ronald Reagan—rejected this vision of the proper organization of society, increasing numbers of intellectuals too (including many of the authors' social-scientist colleagues) are coming to the conclusion that the genius of America is not housed in the Capitol in Washington.

To speak against the role of government in culture or in any other of our philanthropic pursuits, though it is unavoidably to advocate the participation of those who are best able to contribute, is not to bless everything the private sector or its members do. Of course patrons are often foolish; of course they are often willful and capricious; of course they are often ignorant. They too are sometimes venal, and a few are even criminal. The chief justification for a private system of cultural patronage—and for the use of tax provisions to direct "government" funds to the objects of private choice—is not just that it has worked well for our artistic life. It is not even that many nonliberals properly object to the whole tax-expenditure argument because it seems to presume that all the fruits of society belong to the state. Vastly more significant is that our reliance on the private sector, in all its richness, its power, and even its arrogance, is a manifestation of liberty. Because of the *private* patrons' power, this liberty extends even to the rights of artists to resist, criticize, and even replace supporters as the artists themselves see fit.

All these tributes to the private patron hardly mean that patronage cannot be improved. Arts supporters are greatly responsible for the intrusion of government into the funding of culture. The demand for government aid has not come from the private sector because of any real unwillingness on the part of patrons to contribute; rather it has resulted from a loss of willingness by the private sector to take responsibility for its own taste and its own decisions. The result of this loss of nerve has been a desire for government endorsement of private actions. Here is the origin of the need for the famous "governmental Good Housekeeping Seal of Approval" so often mentioned by high corporate executives. Here is the reason for the vast success of NEA Challenge Grant programs in raising several private dollars for every one offered by the government as bait.

This loss of confidence by the private sector can be broken down into two parts. The first is a widespread loss of willingness to rely on individual intellectual and artistic judgment. There is, unfortunately, a solid basis for this feeling of weakness: the rich, no less than every other economic group in American society, have been the victims of a slack and meretricious educational system. As a result the knowledge necessary to make intelligent decisions in culture is all too often lacking. The cure for this state of affairs is hardly an increased role for government in making up people's minds; it is better and more serious education, in the arts and in every other area, not just for the rich, but for all Americans.

The second part of this pervasive loss of confidence by the private sector is a consequence of the powerful virus of the welfare state and its notion that only government, not the individual, can take responsibility for human life. Private wealth has, at least until recently, seemed a dubious possession, a relic of the primitive individualism of a bygone era. Foremost among the believers in this socialist doctrine, oddly enough, have been those Americans rich enough and well-educated enough to form and execute decisions in cultural philanthropy. The rich too have believed that socialism is coming; what better way to accommodate the inevitable than to take shelter in the shadow of government?

A further comment must be made. Many will find it curious indeed that the authors of this report, with the backing of the prestigious Twentieth Century Fund, have taken the trouble to attack the entire charitable deduction, extending as it does across the enormous fields of religion, education, social welfare, and health, merely for the purpose of adjusting perceived inequities in cultural funding. Though culture accounts for only 2 percent of charitable contributions, it is plain that the real destination of this report's attack is not just cultural funding but rather the dependence of the entire philanthropic sector of American life on private funding and private decision making. Culture and education, health and social welfare, are now the recipients of the largesse of affluent Americans; as our prosperity increases, religion too will increasingly be supported by those groups able to take advantage of the present charitable deduction. Plainly there is now common cause, in attacking the idea that decisions are best made by the government, to be made by groups ranging from the richest lovers of Beethoven quartets to the poorest worshippers in small churches. What is at stake is nothing less than the preservation of our historical diversity against the artificial diversity provided by governments capable only of programmed and imposed representation.

26.

The original form of this November 1984 New Criterion *article was a speech I delivered to the annual meeting that year of the National Association of Schools of Art and Design. In both article and speech I was at this time concerned to make two points: that direct federal support of the arts had not made a favorable difference in the artistic life of this country, and that the proper reason for the existence of such support was not principally the bettering of art but of fulfilling the necessary interest of the state in transmitting the highest values of the society to posterity. Toward this end I adumbrated an educational role for the National Endowment for the Arts. As will be seen from the account I give late in this book of my work at the NEA, this remained one of my primary concerns throughout the 1980s.*

Cultural Policy: Whither America, Whither Government?

W E A L L K N O W that the life of art is perhaps more than ever before determined not just by the encounter between the artist and the art public but also by the interplay between the art work and the social, economic, and political matrix in which art is inspired, funded, produced, and experienced. As modern life becomes more complex and at the same time more centralized, the process by which art exists increasingly becomes the object of rational analysis and calculation. This manifestation of what the French call *planification*—the institutionalizing of the making of goals and projections—goes by the name of cultural policy, a phrase whose inevitable associations with the Third Reich of Hitler and Goebbels seem to have done little to render moot.

Though it is perhaps unfair to prejudice a discussion of cultural policy by reference to the monstrous regime of Nazism, even in this unfairness there is a grain of truth: cultural policy is, and has been, a settled part of European life, and not just under totalitarianism. Among Europe's many cultural policies, it is those directed toward high culture that have played the leading part. Admittedly, the phrase *high culture* is often problematical. About the only sure thing one can say about high culture is that everything belongs to its domain and at the same time nothing does. My own, no doubt incomplete, definition is this: high culture is concerned with, though not strictly limited to, art, literature, and learning that is either created to endure or that at some point after its creation is widely recognized to have become a permanent part of the civilization that is transmitted by the settled institutions of society.

In Europe—in what so touchingly used to be referred to as the old country—this high culture was the province of established elites who drew their legitimacy not from the marketplace but from their participation in the state or, in premodern times, in the institutions that eventually gave birth to the state. To say this is hardly to deny the role of the people in building the great Romanesque and Gothic cathedrals or in creating the folk music upon which Western art music has so gloriously built. The point is not that the great notables of traditional societies created art, but that they organized its production, paid for it, and provided for its preservation in their homes, their courts, and their established churches.

When these ruling elements of society, casualties of industrialism and egalitarianism, were replaced after many hundreds of years by the more or less modern governments that today rule from the Atlantic Ocean all the way east to the Pacific Ocean, matters were different. Responsibility for the direction of high culture was now assumed by all-powerful central state apparatuses. Interestingly, this generalization is as true for the democratic and still largely capitalist countries of Western Europe as it is for the monolithic Communist states of the East. Indeed, it is difficult to avoid the conclusion that the difference between the French government's attitude to culture and that of truly socialist governments is a difference—one to be cherished, I hasten to add—of quantity and efficiency of control rather than quality and ambition.

Before we jump to defend European practice on the basis of its high-mindedness or to attack it for its capitulation to arrant statism, we might pause for a moment to see what real issues are involved. I would suggest that Europe is reacting in a rational way to two peculiar developments that mark and even distort modern political life: the modern state's loss of legitimacy in the hearts and minds of its citizens, and the ascendancy of high culture over religion as the means of carrying and articulating the spirit of the nation. Sad to say, this loss of legitimacy, though of course vastly more pervasive on the other side of the Iron Curtain, has even begun to eat into the political life of such former bastions of public spiritedness as Great Britain. The role of high culture in filling this awful vacuum can be seen all the way from the all-Beethoven concerts at London's Royal Festival Hall to the Bolshoi Ballet's position in the Soviet Union as a national shrine. Neither politicians nor more altruistic representatives of national communities have been slow to notice the political disease or the cultural cure. It can all be put rather simply: as the people lose faith in God and in the state, appropriations for culture and the rhetoric of its advocacy go up like the hottest of hot-air balloons. Although dictators of left and right have been the quickest to take advantage of this high cultural road to political survival, it must be noted that even democratic groups across the water increasingly see their future in art.

How much of this poignant story is relevant to our blessed America? The answer is: more than you might think, and less than you might fear. But before we can attempt to understand the present state of affairs here at home, we should first consider briefly the history of cultural policy in this country.

As Americans we live in a uniquely free country. We all have known about our political and economic liberty; we have relied on, and exploited to the hilt, the autonomy and diversity America has enjoyed since its founding two hundred and more years ago. We have exalted pluralism wherever we have found it and even tried to encourage diverse and sometimes bizarre behavior where we have fancied too little existed. The slogan "Don't tread on me" could well stand as the rubric in whose name the good—that is, the free—life in America has been lived.

From our free society to our free culture is but a small step; culture, after all, is what the sociologists tell us society does. Mirroring our social melting pot, American culture over the years has been a kaleidoscopic whirl of dippy trends, stairways to nowhere, herd-like self-indulgence, and calls to repentance. To put it another way: we have reaped the advantages, as well as the penalties, of living in a world of private freedom and public limits. The lesson of America, let me repeat, has been the lesson of liberty.

Has this liberty, so fretted about by observers of the American scene since Mrs. Trollope, been deleterious to the pursuit of high culture? If we look, for example, at a whole line of popular entrepreneurs from P. T. Barnum to Hugh Hefner, the answer might seem to be yes. But when we look at the great American private universities founded in the last century and even before, with their art departments and their dedication to the humanities; when we look at the great private art collections, such as those of Gardner, Frick, Morgan, and Mellon, that have been given over to public use; when we look at New York's Metropolitan Museum, founded in the last century, and the Museum of Modern Art, founded more than fifty years ago; when we look at our greatest musical institutions, from the Metropolitan Opera in New York to the San Francisco Opera, from the New York Philharmonic (founded in 1842 by its own musicians) to the Boston Symphony (founded in 1881 by the banker Henry Lee Higginson and personally maintained by him until the end of World War I)—when we look at these magnificent achievements of high culture, extending from the purses of the rich to the inquiring minds of the poor, we see that America has lacked neither high culture nor a rational way of preserving that culture. Comparing these achievements to those of Europe suggests no difference in quality or scope; what is remarkable is that these triumphs, though undeniably for the benefit of the public at large, were private in conception, planning, funding, and direction.

It is true that these achievements constitute examples not of the creation of high culture but rather of its preservation and presentation through institutions. But when we look at the American record in the *creation* of art over the last century we can surely be proud of the record of this young (in comparison to the nations of Europe) country. In nineteenth-century painting, for instance, we can claim such notable artists as Homer, Eakins, Whistler, and Sargent; from a somewhat later time we can mention Marin, Hartley, Dove, Macdonald-Wright, and O'Keeffe, all of them born between 1870 and 1890. In twentieth-century painting, we know that the School of Paris was succeeded after

World War II by the New York School. In early modern architecture Americans, led by Louis Sullivan and later Frank Lloyd Wright, assumed world influence; in photography the names of Stieglitz, Steichen, Weston, and later Ansel Adams come immediately to mind. In nineteenth-century literature Hawthorne, Whitman, Melville, Poe, and Henry James were world figures; in the present century, I need hardly list the mighty procession of American authors who have changed the way the modern world sees itself. In dance, Isadora Duncan, Martha Graham, Agnes de Mille, and George Balanchine, together with his creation the New York City Ballet, have led the way. In music there is Copland and Sessions and Carter and even (though hardly to my own taste) Cage; in music performance the important American singers and instrumentalists are too numerous to mention.

It would be unfair to leave this account of the place of America in the creation of high culture without mentioning our colossal achievements in that most democratic of areas, the audience. Millions of people have gone to museums, concert halls, opera houses, bookstores, libraries, and private schools, institutions supported almost entirely by private funds with the wise encouragement of blanket tax exemptions and deductions. Nor, in this context, should we ignore the achievements of the commercial radio networks (and, in their early years, the television networks also) in expanding and satisfying an enormous audience for the good things of the mind.

It should be stressed that these triumphs took place *without* our possessing an articulate, planned, and enforced cultural policy. The same glorious anarchy that made Mencken, to mention only one of our brilliant homegrown critics, feel that he was living in a zoo also produced the achievements of high culture. There are those who say that this expansion of high culture was enforced upon a witless rabble by a pack of exploiting capitalists determined to use art and learning as the opiate of the masses and a goad for them to become good bourgeoisie. But these salesmen of Marxist cant love neither art nor the masses whose "primitive" culture they profess to adore. Of course America's enlightened patrons and savants had a "cultural policy"; of course immigrant and native parents alike had in mind a "cultural policy" when they sent their children to school, to concerts, operas, and art exhibitions. But their "policy" was decided individually and in small groups, and its goal was to enlighten, not to exploit.

There is one other myth that needs to be dispelled, this one regularly retailed by the present guardians of the arts establishment: the myth that the arts in America somehow began just a little less than twenty years ago, with the inception of *federal* funding and *federal* cultural policy. According to this mistaken reading, 1965 is the *annus mirabilis* of American art because it marks the first year of the National Endowment for the Arts, the central organization for federal arts funding (and of whose advisory board I have been a member for the past two years).

The idea that before the existence of federal funding there was no healthy growth of high culture in the United States is easily rejected. The evidence is simply overwhelming that high culture has been a major and well-supported activity in America for more than the last century. But at the same time it can hardly be denied that the very existence of federal involvement in the arts has meant that for the first time in our history we do indeed have a cultural policy, backed by money collected from the American people in taxes and spent according to the legislative intent of the Congress and the administrative direction of the executive branch.

Because we have had a cultural policy in the recent past, we must ask ourselves about its effect. But before we can talk about results, we must ask just what this cultural policy has been. It is not an easy task to describe this policy in any exact way, of course; however intrusive our federal government can on occasion be, we hardly have the kind of *dirigiste* tradition in this country that makes the imposition of the will of the state so prominent in France. In America governmental cultural policy, like the federal apparatus in general, is not fully integrated and coherent, or even rigorously enforced when it is capable of such enforcement. It must be remarked, too, that this cultural policy has not been absolutely consistent from year to year or from administration to administration.

These caveats notwithstanding, it is possible to describe the overall character—and effect—of official cultural policy as it has been reflected in the rhetoric and actions of the National Endowment for the Arts. When I attempted such a description for the Heritage Foundation just prior to the 1980 presidential election, I found a tendency on the part of officeholders and their clients to receive criticism first with scorn and then with rage. I trust that whatever else the past four years of uneasy relations between the Reagan administration and arts advocates may have proven, it now can be accepted that the arts will survive in America even when the actions of its advocates are held up to the same kind of public scrutiny we accord to art itself.

What, then, has our cultural policy been? At its heart, it has been the support of institutions, not individuals. These institutions have been of two kinds: the great presenters (museums and symphony orchestras, opera, dance, and theater companies) and the organized advocates—in music, for example, the American Symphony Orchestra League, Chamber Music America, Opera America, and the National Institute for Music Theater. These latter organizations, often funded by the very government whose funds they then solicit, exist to represent their membership, largely re-creative institutions rather than creative artists. It is true that there has been support available, through the medium of individual fellowship grants, to individual creative artists. This support, however, has over the history of the NEA amounted to only a small fraction of total federal arts funding.

At no time has the federal government—or for that matter any other level of government—attempted to take a predominant role in *financing* the arts in America. On the contrary, along with the constant exhortations for increased official support, backers of government's role in the arts have made clear that at no time should public subsidy assume the major responsibility for footing the arts bill. But at the same time it must be stressed that official cultural policy has from the beginning concerned itself with maximizing official *influence* on how private arts dollars are to be spent.

This policy goal has been accomplished by means of what is called at the Endowment *leadership* and *presence*. In this context, leadership means the NEA imprimatur, the "governmental Good Housekeeping Seal of Approval." (I might add that I heard this exact phrase used by a responsible and respected executive at a congressional dog-and-pony show whose purpose was to round up public opposition to proposed cuts in the NEA budget.) The need for this official endorsement, of course, suggests a lack of confidence by the arts-advocacy establishment in the intelligence, artistic sophistication, and will of private and (most especially) corporate patrons.

If NEA *leadership* desires to direct private funds toward those projects the NEA considers qualified, NEA *presence* represents an effort to proclaim the involvement of the federal government in every meritorious arts activity. The intended effect has been the reflection of glory *from* the art back *to* the NEA, rather than vice versa. The message going out to the American people no less than to artists has been quite clear: government legitimizes art, and art legitimizes government.

If this notion of reciprocal blessing has been the general policy, the *specific* policy has been to use federal funds in a matching-grant program in order to "leverage" private contributions toward arts organizations. In this way, one federal dollar, whether awarded as a regular or a challenge grant, entails the contribution of several private dollars. Thus public funds are made available only when much larger private funds are allocated to purposes deemed worthy of support by the federal government.

It would be a mistake to think that this governmental role has been achieved only through the spending of public monies. Politicians, ranging from the president and vice president and their families to senators and congressmen, have gained extensive publicity from their enthusiastic demonstrations of love for the arts. During the Carter administration matters went so far that to the presidential testimony for beauty was added the labor of the vice president's wife, otherwise known, as I have said before, as "Joan of Art."

A hallmark of all this support of culture has been a pronounced tendency to turn art into entertainment, to advocate those kinds of art that are already attractive to a large and expanding audience or can be packaged so as to appeal to such an audience. Thus the most proudly proclaimed fruits of official support of the arts have been blockbuster museum exhibitions sponsored by the National Endowment for the Humanities and public television programs, of which "Great Performances" and the "Live from . . . " offerings are the most prominent. Loudly trumpeted, too, has been NEA support of the year-round activities of symphony orchestras and opera companies, support that has been justified on grounds of audience numbers, as if the only justification for high culture in a democracy is the size of the body count made after the event. Time and time again the emphasis has been not on what art *teaches* to its audience but on the *pleasures* and *satisfactions* that may be obtained from what is now so nicely called "the arts experience."

Flowing naturally from this idea of art as a consumer—and consumable—good has been the idea that art is for everyone in every situation. This conception received perhaps its most lapidary formulation in John D. Rockefeller 3rd's injunction for arts education: "We need to expose *all* of the children in our schools to *all* of the arts." A similar approach, though one couched in less Olympian terms, may be found in the words delivered by football star Joe Namath in two 1983 spots prepared for television distribution by the Oklahoma Arts Council:

> When I played football for the New York Jets, the good guys didn't always win. But now that I'm an actor, I've learned that with the arts, everybody wins.
>
> Whether it's a child's first drawing or a wonderful symphony, art makes our lives richer and more enjoyable.

Added to this conception of art for everyone have been the ideas that everything is art and that art can improve everything. From the idea that everything is art has developed an unwillingness to make necessary distinctions between arts and crafts, and between high and popular culture; from the idea that art can improve everything has developed a willingness to see art as improving the amenities of everyday life and reclaiming whole neighborhoods from the blight of urban decay.

It cannot be denied that much thought and effort have been given to two areas that would seem irreconcilable with the goal of presenting high culture as entertainment: the participation of minorities and other disadvantaged groups in the cultural expansion, and the presentation of an avant-garde—or at least new—art to an audience that wants none of it. Both areas are similar in that their spokesmen represent active and troublesome constituencies: the minorities and related groups because they speak for large blocs of voters, and the avant-gardists because they occupy a position of strength in the media disproportionate to their representation in the world of the arts. Fittingly, both problems have been similarly "solved": while the main business of marketing arts circuses has been allowed to continue unopposed, protesting groups have been bought off by being accorded special programs in which they only compete with themselves and by being allowed prominent figurehead representation elsewhere.

Another important component of our present cultural policy is budgetary. Two easy-to-grasp adages are at all times urged upon those who would consider themselves cultured: More money for the arts is better, and No amount of money is enough. The implications of this kind of thinking are simple; the standard of quality is the size of the budget, and the measure of rate of artistic progress is the rate of budgetary increase.

Finally, mention must be made of the fact that our cultural policy relies, for both the formulation and implementation of its goals, on a formidable bureaucratic class of administrators and advocates. Indeed, it is this class, and most assuredly not the artists or the present amorphous and unsophisticated audience, that is charged with making decisions about what the contemporary image of art shall be and what part of even that confected product will be brought to the attention of the public. It is this governing class too that is seen to be responsible for fund raising, now euphemistically called "development." Furthermore, the possibility of raising money for an arts organization is seen as the surest sign of that organization's *artistic* viability. I should add that crucial to gaining large contributions from generous patrons now is the perception by these donors of the organization's financial stability. Thus the arts "development" circle is made complete: money can be raised because the institution is financially solid, and the institution is financially solid because money can be raised.

The cultural policy that I have polemically described above is not just a matter of *government* fiat. There is now no conspiracy on the banks of the Potomac to direct American culture. What does exist is a happy cooperation between the private sector, which personally used to contribute money and now is content to contribute its time, and government officials, who wish both private-sector endorsement and future career possibilities. In this regard, another salient difference between European (at least Western European) cultural policies and ours must be noted: in Europe the Edward Heaths and the François Mitterrands are themselves cultural leaders and representatives of the educated and prosperous classes; in the United States, political leaders fear any identification with elite cultural attitudes and tastes.

With this summary of current cultural policy in mind, we may perhaps be ready to describe where in our cultural life this policy has brought us. Unfortunately, just because such exaggerated claims have been made by its backers for the transforming role of the National Endowment for the Arts, any negative appraisal will be taken as a criticism of the NEA itself. While I cannot deny that I am criticizing the agency, I do not see the agency in particular or government in general as the sole architect of our problems. The responsibility, as is only proper in a democratic society, is both public *and* private, and deserves to be treated as such.

As we look around us at the life of high culture in America at present, I am afraid that there is little in blossoming health. The last great era of American painting was in the 1950s; in architecture we are confronted with a congeries of styles whose greatest recommendation is that they are truly artless. In literature, the general run of fiction seems dismal, with few acknowledged masters to offer leadership; in poetry, despite the vaunted explosion of activity for which present policies are held responsible, the little being written that is first-rate hardly seems new, and of that which is new very little seems first-rate. In music composition, though we are told that creativity is taking wing on every side, what one hears of the postmodern "revolution" sounds either like the 1960s avant-garde writ tame or like the amateur musings of half-trained sound fanciers. In opera, there are no works being written today that can engage the attention of the greatest American opera houses or of dedicated opera audiences. We are being told, it is true, that great art is now being created on the "cutting edge" of multimedia and performance art; thus far, the only real achievement of these genres has been to *épater le bourgeois*.

What about the performing arts, the repository of such a large percentage of cultural funds from government and the corporate sector? Here the result is a triumph not of art but of merchandising. Of all the disciplines, dance—largely because it is the immediate inheritor of the great work of Graham and Balanchine—seems in the best shape. But even here the last few years have seen a disturbing contraction in the flourishing of modern dance so proudly associated with official cultural policy; the result has been a tilt in both funding and audience attendance toward traditional ballet and away from the new. In theater, we are witnessing the collapse of the historically great Broadway theater as an artistic force; the nonprofit theater sector, despite flashes of creativity, is mired in the production of crowd pleasers, golden oldies, and trivial novelties. In music performance, American orchestras no longer occupy the preeminent world role they once did; American orchestras, moreover, will go to any conceivable length, and then some, to avoid a music director whose career bears a native stamp.

Having been so critical of the way things are going, and so pessimistic about the creative value of what is now so praised, I must hasten to state my fundamental faith in the essential vitality and interest of American art, and in the existence of a sophisticated and mature American audience willing and able to support new art. Without doubt, there is art in America beyond what we now so easily call "the arts," just as there are art lovers in great numbers who act as individuals rather than as objects of mass marketing. Yes, there is art being created in America; yes, there is art being loved in America. But it is being made by artists, and loved by—and that means supported by—art lovers. It is being neither created nor facilitated by the kind of bureaucratic advocacy we now see all around us.

And so we have come to what is perhaps the most difficult problem: the future of official cultural policy, of its proper nature and desirable direction. One question must be gotten out of the way immediately. Can we go back to our former ways, to private support and a guidance of high culture assisted only by indirect and unorganized mechanisms of government support? There was certainly value in the way we used to do things, in the days when artists went only to patrons, not to government, when to be rejected by one patron meant only that one had to find someone else. Today, in the case of a government turndown, the very future of the cultural enterprise itself is called into question.

Can we, then, turn back the clock? Of course the answer is no. The present state of mutual public-private cooptation came into being because of fundamental changes in the 1950s and 1960s in American society. The combination of widening economic affluence and degenerative changes in the quality of American education ensured both a clamor for popular culture and the erosion of the base for private patronage. Furthermore, in these matters mere existence in the present is the best guarantee of continued existence in the future. Because our present system of arts advocacy and support is now at least twenty years old, it has acquired a formidable bureaucratic and economic inertia, in which arts institutions directly and artists indirectly are everywhere dependent on the status quo. I count myself, after all, a conservative, and the purpose of conservatism is not revolution but conservation, not of the perfect but of the best.

There is still another important point to be made here. Even—perhaps especially—for conservatives, the state is a necessary organ of society, a vital component of the process whereby individuals can live in society, and whereby society transmits its highest values from history to posterity. Precisely because it is clear from even a cursory study of Western cultural, social, and political life that art can legitimize the state under whose wing it takes shelter, the American state, no less than its European counterparts, will find itself forced in its own interest to have a cultural policy. To say this is not to say that this cultural policy should, as it does today in Europe, rule, predominate, or even direct, or that the present hand-in-glove relation between the private and public sectors, in which private arts advocates use government to manipulate private activities, is either necessary or proper.

If government, then, will inevitably have a cultural policy, what kind of cultural policy should it have? Because the state is unavoidably so important in our lives, because the state has duties to society which go so far beyond the satisfaction of immediate desires, it is clear that the state should never support entertainment. Woe to the citizenry when the state, in addition to providing bread as it now does, provides circuses. Instead, the state should support art, construed not as amusement but as one of the chief carriers of civilization. Here in America this mission can be seen as having a particular relevance to our national mission of making one people out of many, of building social unity out of a pluralistic culture. Whatever the future of our society, we can hardly doubt that Western civilization can and must serve as a binding force, using the best that has been felt and thought and accepting, it goes without saying, the contributions of other great civilizations and cultures. The goals must be what it has so proudly been throughout American history: cultural uplift for all.

And so I think we come to some idea of a proper role for the National Endowment for the Arts. It should be *educational*, an attempt to teach rather than to beguile. I am aware that art diverts and amuses; I am aware that people can have a good time making and experiencing art. But these laudable *personal* goals seem to me, as I have stated above, false goals for government. Instead, the NEA should concern itself with communicating to our citizens the particular kind of knowledge about ourselves, our world, and most especially the civilized heritage that art enshrines.

In the area of scholarship and learning, I am happy to say that under the chairmanship of William J. Bennett, the National Endowment for the Humanities has made great progress toward finding a noble role for government in communicating our civilized heritage. At the NEA, despite recent attempts to restore administrative integrity and a sense of quality, interest-group pressures and bureaucratic foot-dragging have all too frequently meant business as usual; in particular, it has proven amazingly difficult to improve NEA arts-education programs, those happy hunting grounds for "arts experiences," studies, conferences, and position papers without number or end. Beyond the confines of specifically instructional programs themselves, any serious attempt to educate for civilization through art to the highest levels of culture has all too often been viewed at the NEA as improperly elitist and unresponsive to presumed—and usually encouraged—constituency demands.

What can be said about how the NEA might go about its proper role of education? Though we have no model in our official arts policy for such an effort, and though policy is not forwarded by talking but by action, I do think several suggestions can be advanced. To begin with, the tyranny of the number of bodies served and of the celebrities that serve them must be ended, so that artistic content and not audience reaction will be the chief criterion for support. I would also suggest that thought be given to ending the separation between the support of what is popular and old and what is unpopular and new. This can only be done by stressing not the revolutionary nature of new art but its development out of, and continuity with, the past. Furthermore, a sincere try must be made at bringing into the work of the NEA two hitherto underused resources: creative artists and teachers. In particular, the NEA must make peace with the educational establishment, which it has historically outflanked, devalued, and even ignored. Art is too important to be left to administrators.

Will the Congress, and back of the Congress the American people, support what will immediately be characterized as a program both quixotic and arrogantly elitist? It is difficult for me not to believe that once the citizens of America understand that it is the purpose of government to inspire individual and local aspirations to and activity in high culture, a truly educational NEA would not be welcomed and backed. Allow me to give just one example of what I mean: surely art and official cultural policy alike are better served by encouraging a local pianist in a small, isolated town to give an all-Beethoven recital than by bringing in, for one night only, an over-touted touring celebrity to do the same thing. If we can make this clear, I have faith that the people and their elected representatives will understand.

We have heard much in recent years about public-private "partnership." I confess that, understandable as this desire to lessen conflict between these spheres and lessen governmental budgetary outlays is, such talk seems confusing and even misleading. In cultural life and in public life both, our pressing need is not for a muddying of the distinctions between that which belongs to individuals and that which belongs to government. The need is rather for an exact understanding of proper government functions and the invigoration of private action in everything else. In the arts, this suggests the importance of efforts to strengthen the private sector of American life in its ability to make educated, sophisticated decisions about cultural matters, decisions which are based not upon the public relations imperatives of advocacy or the mindless praise for all art, any art, and every art. What is needed is a private sector that will do more than pay for art, a private sector that will treat art, because it is a carrier of civilization, as a cornerstone of its own liberty. Here too is an educational task, and this one not the least important. It is time to begin teaching.

27.

Like its immediate predecessor in this book, this May 1986 New Criterion article had its origin in a speech, in this case one I delivered to the annual meeting that year of the National Art Education Association. Here my concern was to show the essential, and malign, congruence between the motives and the practices of corporate and public patronage. Once again, I laid this situation to the weaknesses of our educational system, in this case that part of it concerned with arts education. As a measure of the importance with which these matters are viewed in the arts community, I should mention that I delivered the speech in a New Orleans hotel ballroom, the largest room of its kind I have ever seen, with a capacity of perhaps three thousand; my audience, however, on the most upbeat estimate, numbered no more than a hundred.

Art and Patronage Today

AS FAR AS PATRONAGE is concerned, it seems difficult to avoid the conclusion that all the arts are in pretty much the same condition today regardless of their separate developments and relative prosperities. This condition may be characterized as an inversion of John Kenneth Galbraith's famous (if not notorious) formulation about the state of American society in the late 1950s. For Professor Galbraith, America was then a land of private opulence and public squalor. For us today the arts in America are in a condition of public opulence and private decrepitude.

Clearly such a position does not represent the received wisdom. According to this quintessential distillation of past error, present self-service, and future illusion, the United States is the last haven of the private sector in culture. This supposed reality is pointed to with pride by conservative partisans of our democratic capitalistic society, but scorned by those who admire the glitter of European state culture. The proud cite the high level of private contributions to our arts institutions—made possible under a beneficent tax system—and the scornful lust after the cornucopia abroad of government largesse for such disparate artistic activities as the Berlin Philharmonic and the operas (if they can be called that) of the perennial avant-gardist Karlheinz Stockhausen.

There is no point in quoting statistics. Those available are, to put it most kindly, imperfect. But their burden is clear. In this country the preponderance of support for the arts comes from the private sector; in Europe, it comes from government. Because everywhere the role of education in making artistic activity possible is so downplayed, it must be added that both here and abroad a substantial amount of money for the arts comes in the form of school budgets; in Europe these budgets come almost totally from government sources, and here largely so. In any case, our national per capita arts expenditures, combining private and public contributions, stack up well against the figures for most of the major European countries. It should therefore be understood that when people extol the European state arts systems as a model for our country, what they desire is not a switch from private support to public, but rather an increase in total support produced by an increase in public spending.

But the issue is not just money. The issue is rather the relationship of money to art. From this perspective, our present means of supporting art is little different from that in Europe, for arts support increasingly means the same thing, whether here or abroad: support of public, not private, culture. Or put another way, the support of art, whatever the source, is not the support of the individual tastes of the givers; rather it is the support of the tastes which are held widely in the society as a whole. This formulation may be obscure; it certainly is difficult.

To understand the present relation between art and patronage, it is necessary first to describe something of the historic shift in the place of the arts in society during the four decades since World War II. In 1945, the greatest art was seen as belonging to high culture, which was the historical possession of a cultivated minority. This minority was usually of fortunate birth, mostly of economic privilege, and almost always of refined education. Whatever the art under discussion, whether visual arts, literature, music, or dance, the natural audience for it was small, self-selecting, and self-defining.

It goes without saying that although the culture favored by so restricted an audience was the leading intellectual and artistic force in society, it was not the only source of entertainment or art for the larger public. By 1945, popular culture was already carried by radio, recordings, and film (though not yet by television). It was widely seen by both its own audience and the smaller audience for high culture as an entirely separate activity, influencing more sophisticated pursuits and being influenced by them but nonetheless existing in its own world of creation and mass consumption. To use an up-to-date term, it could be said that while there was "crossover" between popular and high culture, there was very little confusion between them.

To be sure, this idea of a separate audience for an elite culture was deeply affected by the progress of what we might call the democratic ideal. European opera houses, after all, were built with many cheap seats and even with large areas for standing room, and the operas of Verdi did provide tunes for organ grinders on the streets. The emergence of public museums and public concerts in Europe occurred along with the coming of public education and universal literacy. But despite the democratic spread of culture, in the upper strata of many European societies there was deep satisfaction with the continuing reality of distinct cultures: one for the millions and another for those with the millions. These pre-industrial attitudes may be found today in the rigorously selective character of French higher education and in the impregnable career status of its graduates. An analogous phenomenon is evident in the position of Oxford and Cambridge (and their graduates) in English life. Indeed, only in the most recent years can it be said that wherever one looks in Europe—take France and England as examples—one sees enormous and troubled concern on the part of government with what in the United States is called "outreach."

In America, the situation of elite culture has always been different. This country was founded, after all, as a reaction against the continuation of those aristocratic social attitudes which bordered on the feudal. Such aristocracy as we have had—one thinks immediately of the Adams family—either made its peace with democracy or found itself in external or internal exile. The new monied elite of the nineteenth century was deeply affected by the gospel of wealth, which itself was the product of the many leveling influences, both religious and secular, at work in the expansion of the original colonies into a continental nation. The watchword, of course, was education, which meant education for the masses as well as education for the elite. Indeed, all of us are beneficiaries of the strength of our national educative impulse.

The effect of American attitudes toward education was not restricted to McGuffey's Reader and the one-room schoolhouse. There was the great growth of our public schools, the founding of our public-library system, the development of land-grant colleges, and the provision (well back in the nineteenth century) of facilities for what is now called adult education. In this connection, it is also important not to forget the extraordinary flowering in this country of privately financed and controlled education; it is equally important to remember that this private education often assumed denominational forms.

But beyond—although not *above* and beyond—education in its specialized sense of teachers, classes, and students, and beyond the provision of facilities for scientific and scholarly investigations such as the Rockefeller Institute for Medical Research in New York and the Institute for Advanced Study in Princeton, culture for the masses included hefty doses of high artistic culture, regularly administered as a part of the social responsibilities of the leading figures of the community. The principle was the same whether the particular benefaction was the Metropolitan Museum or the Art Institute of Chicago in the second half of the nineteenth century or the Museum of Modern Art and the National Gallery in the first half of the twentieth; whether it was the Juilliard School in New York or the Curtis Institute in Philadelphia; the Metropolitan Opera in the East or the San Francisco Opera in the West. The duty of the lovers of high art was to provide that art in undefiled form as an *educational service* to those who by reason of birth, social position, economic status, and educational background did not, to put it in the vernacular, "know what they were missing." Both the governing taste and the money necessary to communicate that taste belonged to the rich, the cultured, and the powerful; only the bodies on the receiving end belonged to the masses.

Curiously, despite the comfortable patrician assumption that the rich would stay rich and the poor poor, it was never questioned that the culture the masses really wanted was exactly the high art that their betters wanted for themselves. And curiously, too, this upper-class self-confidence remained in operation well into the recent past. To cite just one example, many opera fans alive today remember the haughty yet eagerly ingratiating tones of Mrs. August Belmont as she raised funds on the air for the Metropolitan Opera Guild from the millions of Saturday radio listeners across the United States and Canada.

But after 1945 something changed. With the death of Franklin Roosevelt and his replacement by Harry Truman, the age of political leaders drawn from the patriciate came to an end. The passage by Congress of the G.I. Bill and the Fulbright awards program opened up college study in this country to most Americans and, for many of the brightest, even the prospect of graduate study abroad. A very few years later *Brown v. Board of Education*, along with the increasing entry of women into higher education, began the long-delayed process of making "most Americans" into "all Americans." About 1950 the CIA discovered that judicious covert aid to culture and ideas abroad might influence intellectuals, and after 1953 the Eisenhower administration realized that cultural-exchange programs could be a valuable tool in foreign policy.

In the 1960s, forces within the Kennedy administration, led nominally by the president's wife but perhaps more effectively by Arthur Schlesinger, Jr., Richard Goodwin, and Michael Straight, argued for open federal support to the arts and the humanities.This support, in violation of a longtime taboo against American government interference with culture, was to be undertaken not for the purposes of foreign policy, or of social welfare (as had been the case in the 1930s with the WPA), or of ideological democratization. The arts and the humanities were to be supported for themselves, with *quality* as the sole criterion.

Yet there can be little doubt that another, and rather more complicated, reason for support was lurking in the background, surrounded by all the scrimshaw and the decorator rooms which have become a part of the cultural mythology of the Kennedy White House. This was the nagging idea that the existence in the United States of purely private culture—of a cultural life, that is, that did not receive the imprimatur of the state—robbed the state and its leaders of the legitimacy and the glory which in the great European countries was conferred by a rooted association with the imperishable monuments of civilization. There is evidence for the power of this nagging idea over Michael Straight, who later became deputy chairman of the National Endowment for the Arts during the Nixon administration. In his 1982 memoirs, *After Long Silence*, Mr. Straight wrote that his much-postponed decision to tell the FBI about his involvement with the Anthony Blunt espionage ring was forced by one fear: the exposure of his past might alter the fact that in 1963 "the United States Government accepted a limited but continuing responsibility for the advancement of the arts in America."

The legislation finally creating the National Endowment for the Arts (and the National Endowment for the Humanities) was not passed until the Johnson administration, where it took its place in the blizzard of Great Society legislation promulgated in the years following Kennedy's assassination. Small at first, the NEA grew rapidly under President Nixon and his NEA chairman, Nancy Hanks; this growth continued under President Carter and his chairman Livingston Biddle. It was not until the coming of Ronald Reagan in 1981 that the NEA budget leveled off, and indeed there are no signs today that the immediate future will see any increases for the agency. But regardless of the fact that NEA budgets are now on something of a plateau, one simple fact remains: no major arts event in the United States, and hardly a minor one either, takes place without the appearance of the telltale legend, printed in the material which accompanies the art: "This event is supported by a grant from the National Endowment for the Arts, a Federal agency."

It is the proud claim of partisans of the NEA that the increase in government arts funding, coming not just from the federal treasury but increasingly from state and local entities as well, has meant an enormous increase in private funding. It is no secret that this increase has hardly come from individual contributions or even from foundation grants; in recent years these have remained constant, and in some cases have shown signs of decreasing, as many private foundations have decided to turn their agendas toward social welfare programs and related social action. The great increase in private funding has instead come from corporate sources, from those profit-making enterprises which have become convinced that the arts are good for business.

There is little need to remind the reader who these corporate Maecenases are. The largest corporate patrons have by now firmly established themselves in our minds. If one watches public television, one will immediately recognize the role of Exxon, Mobil, and ARCO; if one follows the museum world in New York, one will immediately think of Philip Morris and Equitable; if one is interested in orchestras on tour, one will think of AT&T and perhaps Citibank; if one listens to opera on radio, one's mind will turn to Texaco. And so it goes. So great has been the success of corporate sponsorship of art that long after the art presented has been forgotten the corporate logo on the screen remains firmly fixed in our minds.

It may be taken for granted that money is a good thing. No one would like to do without it. Furthermore, no one would dispute the proposition that if more money in general is a good thing, more money for the arts is a wonderful thing. And yet one may surely be pardoned for quietly asking: "More money for what?" Just what has all this money from new forms of patronage, both governmental and nongovernmental, brought us in the way of art?

In my own opinion, it has brought us very little, and what it has brought has been often harmful to the true cause of art and its lovers. It must be said at the outset that this new money has on many occasions gone to worthwhile artists, and has brought much worthwhile art to millions who might never have become part of what is now so nicely called the arts audience. It must be said, too, that under this new financial dispensation, more people than ever before are calling themselves artists—well over one million by the census bureau's last reckoning. And there are vastly more arts institutions, too, run by vastly more arts professionals working in marketing, development, publicity, community relations, personnel, accounting, and generalized mass advocacy.

More people in the audience, more people calling themselves artists, more institutions and people working in them, and everybody spreading the gospel: what, in God's name, could be bad about all these virtues existing in such a state of plenty? The answer is that all this activity is not about the creation of art, or arts education. Rather, it signifies the transformation of the art of the past into consumables for the present, along with the trivialization of what has been, and is being, created.

Let us begin with public television, the flagship of all this new patronage. Here, on the tens of millions of television sets in American homes, may be found just what in the arts governmental and corporate patrons think should be watched. In the theater, Shakespeare and schlock, both archly delivered, from England; in music, the warhorses of the European classics and American pop, both in routinized performances; in opera, the safest repertory imaginable, handled with kid gloves; in dance, only a smattering of the new developments which have made America the capital of the dance world; in the visual arts, blockbuster programs rich in glib judgments and expensive travel shots. Of the history of the modern arts in America there is almost nothing; of the history of our great literature nothing; of the arts and the humanities for small but highly educated audiences nothing; of arts education, nothing. Of the meretricious personalities in the performing arts of our day there is, however, everything.

As with public television, so with a broad range of arts today. In all too many cases the prime criterion for giving and getting help, in both government and corporate support, is not the particular character of the art being done, nor the need. It is purely and simply high visibility, or the possibility of such visibility soon. In vanishingly few cases is the criterion for support the pleasing of the taste of the patron. In the vast majority of cases the criterion is that the grantee, now or in the near future, bring the grantor favorable publicity.

Just because this requirement of favorable image recognition is so widely observed, it is foolish indeed to talk of a governmental or a corporate taste in culture and art. The architecture of Lincoln Center, so wrongly called "Mussolini modern" by some critics, does not represent corporate taste. It represents what the powerful in business and government believe their fellow New Yorkers and Americans of a certain substance will like. Similarly, the art in the Whitney Museum branches at the Philip Morris building and the new Equitable Life Assurance Society building in New York does not represent the artistic taste of corporate bureaucracy, any more than the grants made by the National Endowment for the Arts represent what governmental leaders think art is or should be. All these efforts represent an attempt to please important economic, social, and political constituencies. When artists are consulted, it is because a judgment has been made that they will produce or select well-liked work; when the avant-garde is supported it is out of a desire on the part of various funders to be thought up-to-date and "with it." The struggle everywhere is not so much to do substantive good in any particular art as to be seen to be doing good for the arts as a whole.

Even when corporate and governmental support is directed toward the needs of the grantee rather than the grantor, the funds are often not directed at covering the basic operating costs of the institution or at supporting the art. Instead, the money must be used to expand programming or fund raising. Programming must be expanded to bring in audiences regardless of the artistic or financial cost, and money must be raised in ever-increasing amounts regardless of how much it costs to raise or of how much programming must be changed in order to appeal to a broader base of funders. The reality of support for the arts in this country at the present time is well described in the words of an arts-contribution officer of a major corporation who was addressing the head of a very distinguished arts institution: "We don't give anyone fish, we give a fishing rod." This oracular saying can be translated in a way every grant applicant in the arts knows only too well. Money is given primarily for the purpose of enabling more money to be raised from others. The key to such expanded fund raising is increased visibility; such visibility is only obtained by expanded programming and activities—far-flung orchestral touring and highly publicized blockbuster museum exhibitions, to mention only two examples—which please the largest possible audience.

As the reader will have noticed, throughout my description of contemporary patronage I have yoked business and government. I have not done so because I think that the responsibility for the present situation in arts patronage falls equally on both. The pressures beating on government are pressures which arise out of our political system, out of the day-to-day legislative and administrative process which guarantees our liberties. Government personnel, after all, must be at least as much representatives as leaders. Private patrons, however, have a greater freedom and a much greater responsibility to choose their course of action.

I have yoked government and business because, despite the very real difference which should separate them, there is an intimate, and I believe deeply mistaken, link between the decision-making processes which govern their support for the arts. This link can be simply described. Government, in order to demonstrate maximum impact for its grants, finds it most convenient to support that to which corporations have been contributing; at the same time corporations, in order to avoid artistic responsibility for their decisions, rely increasingly on the "governmental Good Housekeeping Seal of Approval" as the necessary condition for their own grant-making.

It is this linkage between government and business patronage of the arts which constitutes the public opulence mentioned earlier. The private decrepitude is simply the other side of the opulence. Board members who go to the concerts or the operas which their boards oversee are scarce, as are volunteers willing to contribute their own money rather than just work endlessly to get others to give. Patrons who make individual, artistically competent, and committed decisions about what their own money—not the taxpayers' money, not the shareholders' money, not the community foundation donors' money—will support are in short supply. Above all, knowing, discriminating, core audiences—and here I speak authoritatively about music, but I fear that what I am saying can easily be matched in other artistic fields—are getting smaller and less sure of themselves year by year. They are being replaced by casual and even fickle audiences who are less and less capable of understanding the art being offered to them and who demand more and more celebrity performances and a cheapened repertory as a price for their continued presence.

Despite all the negative aspects of this story, in fairness it must be stated that the present situation is not a conspiracy, not the result of evil intentions, not even the result of political and economic opportunism, but rather the result of an educational failure in the arts. The problem is not bad motives; those responsible for our present system of public patronage, whether governmental or corporate, mean well. They like art. They have a general perception that art is a good thing. They are responsible citizens. They want to help. But in all too many cases they do not themselves know what to do. Their problem, like that of the audience, is insufficient knowledge. Insufficient knowledge of art, of the high culture of which we should be so proud, of the connections which civilization makes possible between a known past and an unknown future.

It must be repeated yet once more that this insufficient knowledge is responsible not just for the kind of patronage we see today but also for the behavior of the public this patronage is attempting to reach.

This situation is merely the adult equivalent of the lowered scores we see everywhere in students' general comprehension of and knowledge about the arts. The scores themselves, it need hardly be stressed, are but the symptom of the state of arts education in our nation today.

What is the way out of this depressing situation? The way out can only be found through education. Perhaps now that the climate for education has changed so much in so many subjects we are ready for a new look at education in the arts. Perhaps we are now ready to understand that art, like every other intellectual activity, is composed of skills and knowledge; that art can be taught and learned; that beauty, no matter how difficult it is to define, is not merely a matter of the feelings, but partakes of the nature of objective reality.

We cannot go back, in arts patronage, to a pre-democratic era of rule by an elite few. Whatever the mix of private individuals, corporations, and government is to be—and it is very much to be hoped that individual patronage will increasingly constitute our predominant mode of support—only education can promise that informed citizens, in art as in politics, will be able to make wise choices. This will hardly be the first time in the life of democracy that education has become the saving hope: more than a century ago, the English liberal politician Robert Lowe advised those who wished to extend the franchise that "it will be absolutely necessary that you should prevail on our future masters to learn their letters." We know that these letters include literature, mathematics, and the sciences. It is now our job to convince our society that these letters include a serious and high art as well.

28.

What follows appeared as my contribution to a Summer 1986 New Criterion
*Special Issue symposium called "New York in the Eighties." In it I wanted to
make clear that in my opinion the cultural predominance of New York in the
United States, and indeed, in the world, remained a fact of life. I was also
concerned to get across the point, using music as an example, that the problems
of art came from within art, and not from developments in the real-estate
market. Now, as the 1980s slide into the 1990s, I have still not lost my faith
in New York. Its provision of what I referred to in this article as "the critical
mass necessary for intellectual life" remains unparalleled in the world.
Despite—and even a bit because of—its continuing political and social
instabilities, the city continues to be an exciting, albeit tough, place to live and
especially to work, for young and old alike.*

New York and Its Future

A NEW ELEMENT has now been added to the accusations against
New York: the charge that culture itself, the longest lived if also the
least tangible expression of a city's power, is in a serious and perhaps
terminal condition because of the direction New York real estate has
taken over the last decades. On this reading, the enmity shown by the
city fathers is not directed simply at the poor and the minorities, or
even at an exploited working class; it is directed at the arts and at their
creators and custodians, the artists. Thus the *Village Voice* blossomed
in the middle of May with the catchy cover headline, in two-inch-high
caps: "NEW YORK TO THE ARTS: DROP DEAD." The better-
mannered *New York Times* had gotten in on the act too, by coming out
a bit earlier with a lead "Arts and Leisure" section article on the
pressures a booming real-estate market was putting on New York
theater. I might add that both publications, following their custom of
keeping news columns and advertising practices separate, carried,

along with these articles about the plight of the arts, their customary bounty of ads for posh condominiums in arty neighborhoods.

For many years now it has been possible to write whole symphonies from the assorted taps and death knells being sounded each minute of the writing day for every aspect of New York's future. For those of an impeccably agrarian orientation, New York has always been one of the Cities of the Plain, imminently subject to God's condemnatory edict; for the apocalyptic Left, New York has been at once the running sore of capitalism and the pot in which the future of progressive mankind will be cooked.

The genealogy of the doomsayers goes back at least to the reformers of the Gilded Age and the muckrakers of Progressivism. The malefactors held responsible for the mess in Gotham have always been corrupt politicians and newly enriched real-estate interests; more recently the symbol of the triumphant union of these nefarious beings has become the automobile, the very center of the American dream.

The spate of news in the last few months about what appears to be the involvement of much of the elected and appointed leadership of New York City in massive graft shows that corruption is still very much with us. The real-estate industry is as always the target of those whose self-appointed task it is to preserve their own idea of the metropolis. The charge of speculative and unplanned overbuilding leveled against the real-estate industry in New York is a constant theme, running from Daniel M. Friedenberg's piece in the 1961 "New York, N.Y." issue of the socialist journal *Dissent* to the current populist campaign against gentrification and new luxury condominiums. Similarly, the past twenty-five years have been full of the demand for the elimination of private driving from Manhattan; there is a straight line connecting Percival and Paul Goodman's impassioned plea for such a ban in the very same issue of *Dissent* with the now successful fight against the Westway super-highway project.

One would hardly say that life in New York these days is comfortable. The sheer pressure of numbers is indeed often intolerable. Furthermore, we should not be surprised that along with the desire of many people to live in what can never be more than a finite amount of space go all the other afflictions of city life: traffic, social tensions, and everywhere an underclass, sometimes merely apathetic and sometimes actively hostile to what they see as the privileged life going on around them.

There is no way of being sure that the dire prophecies about New York will not, in the absence of the various radical nostrums being urged, one day be proven right. Still, all the evidence till now suggests that, far from being moribund, New York is at the height of its attractiveness as a place for the brightest, for the richest, and for the most energetic of the world's most mobile inhabitants to live. Surely this is the meaning of the prolonged real-estate boom which has seen living space in Manhattan, as always New York's commercial and intellectual center, continue to be unaffordable for all except older residents protected by rent control and those successful newcomers willing and able to put up with high rents for cramped quarters.

All this is merely the story throughout history of the rise of cities and the response to that rise of those who were, or felt themselves to be, dispossessed, or who anyway always wanted to live somewhere else. In any case, as perhaps the preeminent world city of the twentieth century, New York can hardly be expected to be safe from those for whom the very idea of a cosmopolis is repugnant.

New York has always been frightfully expensive, for artists as for everyone else. A glance at two American novels, the first set in the early 1890s and the second at the turn of the century, demonstrates how little matters have changed in this regard: both William Dean Howells's *The Coast of Bohemia* (1893) and James Huneker's *Painted Veils* (1920) show their heroines, one a painter and the other a singer, coming from the provinces to New York in search of art and finding the cost of food and lodging exorbitant. When I came to New York in 1959 to study at Juilliard, I found housing almost unobtainable and, even when located, available only at something more than double the going rate I had known in San Francisco. I have heard the same story from those who came to the city just after World War II.

The memories of a New York cheap for artists and intellectuals to live and work in, like so much else in our cultural pipedreams, come from the sordid era of the Great Depression when, though prices were cheap, people had no money whatsoever. The test of survival for artists in the 1930s was a few coins for a meal; today the test is a stable income, adequate housing, and even health benefits and pension plans. To note this is not to disparage the desirability or the justice of these newer expectations; it is merely to point out that rather more is being demanded today in the way of hospitality from the urban environment than was dreamt of fifty years ago.

But whether or not their demands are immediately answered, the artists and writers—and those thinkers too independent for the padded cells of academe—still come. Along with the yuppies and what the *Voice* (with its customary decency toward its targets of abuse) refers to as "Eurotrash," creative figures realize all too well that only New York, of all the cities in America and perhaps of all the great cities in the world, provides what must be called the critical mass necessary for intellectual life.

In my own field of music, I know that the pull of New York remains as powerful as ever for Americans, if not indeed more powerful. Successful New York recitals and orchestral appearances are still, for instrumentalists, the *sine qua non* for a career in the rest of the United States; well-received engagements at the Metropolitan Opera are still the *fons et origo* of operatic fame everywhere else in the country. The same, moreover, is true for such compositional success as is available to anyone these days; a New York performance is a model to be repeated other places, whereas a performance in Boston or Philadelphia or San Francisco is just that—a performance in Boston or Philadelphia or San Francisco. On the top level of professional training, Juilliard, despite the uncertainty of its course over the past decade, remains the school of choice for the most talented young musicians in America and perhaps everywhere else this side of the Soviet Union. Employment opportunities for free-lance orchestral musicians, though under pressure from the competition of synthesizer-produced artificial music, remains the envy of the rest of the country.

It would be nice for me, confirmed New Yorker that I now am, to be able to say that all this activity and preeminence stems from the simple fact that the performance and composition of serious music are in wonderful shape here, and that music education is in a golden age. But I cannot say this. In fact, the performance level of major New York musical institutions seems to me low, both absolutely and relative to what goes on outside the city.

Nowhere is this more clear than in the orchestral field, where the New York Philharmonic, despite the unwillingness of those responsible for its fate to open their ears, is now the sick man of the American orchestral world. The Metropolitan Opera combines boring repertory with variable casting and mostly indifferent conductorial leadership, while the City Opera, under the cult of Beverly Sills's personality, serves up a mix of dollar-opera and middle-of-the-road avant-garde trifles. The future of Juilliard, under a new president, is at the present time unclear; whatever its exact direction, it would seem that the Juilliard of tomorrow will resemble more an elite college school of music than the distinctively New York trainer of putative geniuses it was in the past. The new music menu being served uptown these days seems about the same as is available in other places; the far-out new-music scene downtown, for me at least the domain of lost causes, is said by those who know—among them John Rockwell, the *Times*'s expert in such matters—to be of less interest than is such activity in other parts of the United States.

The result of all this busyness without corresponding excellence of achievement is that New York's musical influence on the United States as a whole is a function not of its quality but of its size. Because both the electronic and print media are so powerfully concentrated here, what New York wants to sell is perforce bought, more or less irrespective of its content. This operation of a cultural Gresham's law may be seen at its most potent in the prominence of Lincoln Center institutions and personalities in the musical presentations of public television. It is not simply a matter of the overexposure on PBS of the now sadly second-rate Philharmonic, or of the carte blanche given the Metropolitan Opera's James Levine to be America's television *primo maestro assoluto*. The Lincoln Center mystique also travels: as I write these words PBS is presenting a lifelessly performed John Philip Sousa program emanating from Wolf Trap (the overballyhooed and mediocre performing-arts facility just outside Washington, D.C.) with—surprise—Beverly Sills as the uncomprehending hostess.

The result of this stranglehold is that we have little if any chance to see on television such great orchestras as the Cleveland and the Chicago, or such important opera companies as San Francisco or, in the summer, Santa Fe. Similarly, the continuing fact of the *New York Times*'s complaisant treatment of major New York City musical institutions only assists in selling to a national audience the vicious circle of local shortcomings.

I don't think that much can be done to take from New York the national cultural primacy it has had since the decline of Boston well back in the nineteenth century; it has that primacy not because of specific achievements but because of its size and economic power. The power of New York, contrary to its critics, comes from the brute economic strength they despise. But because of that strength, there is talent here, and the money to back it, to burn. The pity of it all is that the real resources of the city, so much greater than anything in the imagining of its present detractors, could be used to lead with excellence rather than level with mediocrity. But mediocrity, I suppose, sells in a way excellence does not; at the very least it makes fewer enemies. So once again, it comes down to something simple: what is lacking in New York musical life is courage.

29.

The following four short pieces appeared in, respectively, the New Criterion
(December 1983), Connections Quarterly *(January 1988),* Vantage Point
(October 1987), and Arts Review *(Summer 1987). They discuss several areas
I find of importance in today's world of the arts and its advocacy: the prevalence
of uncultured cultural administrators, the tendency to market for an audience
rather than build one, the takeover of individual grants and patronage
decisions by institutional subsidies and committee decision making, and the
paucity of solid arguments for supporting the arts at all. The first piece was
prompted by a particularly telling example of arts-administration rhetoric; the
second is a review of a highly interesting book on selling tickets for arts
attractions while at the same time educating audiences for the future; the third
is excerpted from a discussion with Alberta Arthurs, the director of the
Rockefeller Foundation's Arts and Humanities Program; the fourth and last
is a speech I made, shortly after a visit to the American Academy in Rome, to
a group of New Jersey foundation executives.*

To Teach the Administrators Art

J A M E S B U R N H A M'S famous *Managerial Revolution* (1941), by detailing the transfer of power over society from capitalists to managers,
ought to have prepared even the arts public for the inevitable. What
makes the arts go today isn't art and it isn't artists; it isn't (socialists
and other all-knowing types to the contrary) the financial power of
patrons or even the pressures of a boorish mass audience. It is rather
a thriving, confident, well-paid—and well-expense-accounted—class
of administrators.

Whether these administrators work in opera companies, symphony
orchestras, museums, foundations, government agencies, or the
numerous powerful advocacy groups funded by all these institutions,
it is they who bring us the art we see and hear, and they who mediate

the encounter between artists and patrons, artists and audience, and audience and patrons. In music, these administrators choose composers, conductors, and soloists. In the visual arts, they choose the exhibitions that make small reputations big and great reputations greater. In foundations and government, administrators establish which programs are to be supported, and then select the experts who bear the putative responsibility for what is to be done.

Given the very real shift in power toward administrators so apparent today, art lovers are quite justified in wondering about the aesthetic basis on which decisions about our cultural agenda are being made. Fortunately, an article in the August 1983 issue of the *Research & Information Bulletin* of the National Council of Art Administrators provides some light on this hitherto murky subject. In this article, James Hutchens, who teaches arts administration and arts education at Ohio State University, addresses the problem of educating those who are responsible for arranging the supply of beauty to a trusting public. Professor Hutchens deplores the fact that our cultural bureaucrats have other than aesthetic priorities in school:

> A review of current programs in arts administration points out the glaring deficiency of aesthetic education for students in these programs. The emphasis on business management practices and the omission of the aesthetic orientation in the education of our future arts administrators is especially clear in a recent survey published by the Center for Arts Administration at the University of Wisconsin (Spisto, Leslie & Prieve, 1979). Sixty percent of the existing arts administration programs surveyed in that publication were in schools or colleges of business administration. Another survey of 128 arts organizations on the question of how students should be prepared for positions in arts administration revealed even more discouraging results. Study in the following areas was ranked very important by the indicated percentage of respondents for that study: accounting (63%), marketing (63%), human relations (61%), public relations (47%), promotional strategy (44%), and political science (13%). On the question of the necessity of specific knowledge of the arts and aesthetics for future arts administrators, respondents indicated this was less important for students seeking a graduate degree. For the

student seeking an undergraduate degree in arts administration, specific knowledge in arts and aesthetics was rated as *unnecessary*. [Emphasis in the original.]

One can only applaud Professor Hutchens's attempt to point out that, even in marketing, the nature of what is sold is more important than the process of putting it over on the buyer. But to recognize this truth is not enough; one must then have some idea of just what the *art* that administrators deal in should be. Here, unfortunately, Professor Hutchens occupies highly dubious ground. This is what he thinks ought to be at the heart of an attempt to "place equal focus on the aesthetic needs of people (artists and audiences) served by arts organizations as well as on managerial processes":

Ursula Meyer, in her introduction to *Conceptual Art*, remarks: "The physicist J. Robert Oppenheimer's comment on science applies as well to art: There have been more discoveries during the past few decades than during all the preceding centuries" (1972, p. xv). Since the seminal work of Marcel Duchamp at the turn of the century there have been numerous attacks on the art object—both the traditional aesthetics associated with the production of art objects and the sale and distribution of art as a valuable commodity for the elite classes of society. Conceptual art appears to be the logical heir to this tradition, and the ideas associated with it have influenced artists working in many of the areas referenced above—concrete art, environmental art, happenings, performance art, et al. In addition, cross-fertilization with other fields and the exploration of the aesthetic dimensions of science have been encouraged by conceptual artists. Recognition by future arts administrators that an information explosion has occurred in the arts is a necessary first step in understanding the work of artists whose appeal is often limited to a relatively small audience.

Perhaps Professor Hutchens's problem could be simply solved. For example, lectureships for Christo and Laurie Anderson at graduate programs in arts administration might go a long way toward uniting the warring realms of commerce and culture. Considered more seriously, however, Professor Hutchens's potted history of anti-art art, extending as it does from a misdated account of Duchamp's work in the second and third decades of this century to today's "Next Wave" posturings, cannot possibly provide administrators with what they now (on Professor Hutchens's own testimony) so sorely lack: knowledge of the great works of the past, discrimination in separating the wheat of contemporary creation from the chaff of media-made reputations, and courage in defending the idea of art as an autonomous realm of human intellectual activity. Professor Hutchens would seem to be telling administrators to embrace the fads of our time. The problem, on the contrary, is not to embrace these fads, but to resist them.

How, then, can arts administrators be given the solid core of culture and spirit they badly need? It is clear that this necessary task will not be accomplished by treating administration and management according to the curricula of prestigious graduate schools of business, as a universally applicable body of learning to be applied by faceless and interchangeable whiz kids. The proper training for arts administrators is not in the first instance administration and the allied skills of marketing and fund raising. The proper training of arts administrators is first *art*—in its practice, its history, and its particularity. Doubtless it will be said that such a course would amount to putting arts administration into the hands of artists, who, by definition, don't know anything about money. A silly response indeed. No one who knows anything about art and its history could possibly think anything so foolish.

New Thoughts on the Great Audience Hunt

THOUGH the American arts millennium is hardly just around the corner, a faint but still heartening glow may now be discerned on the horizon. The American Council for the Arts has just published a book about audience development by arts management consultants Bradley G. Morison and Julie Gordon Dalgleish, which calmly says the recently unsayable, and says it with aplomb, *panache*, and just plain guts. Liberally sprinkled through *Waiting in the Wings*[1] is such wisdom as:

The enthusiasm in the 1980s among arts trustees and arts administrators appears to be leading to an undiscriminating application of marketing principles, endangering the very objectives of audience development.

In the commercial world, the goal of marketing is to produce a profit—the accumulation of money. . . . To reach this goal, practitioners of marketing *manipulate people and products* [all emphasis in the original]. . . . In the arts, the objective and the means of achieving it are quite different. In fact they are exactly reversed. *The goal is to build a long-term relationship between people and the product—art.*

The real danger, of course, is that, in pursuit of funding, arts organizations may begin to create programs to appeal to corporations or to suit the needs of foundations and government agencies—with only passing concern for whether those programs are artistically valid or relate to the institution's primary purpose. Said one knowledgeable arts executive, "When my colleagues discuss programming for their organizations these days, I hear them talking more and more about what kinds of things are being funded this year rather than what kinds of programs are needed."

Tough as these sentiments are, they are matched by the authors' basic premise—that Dynamic Subscription Promotion, Danny Newman's extravagantly praised (and extravagantly practiced) method for building arts audiences and insuring an organization's financial stability, has failed. The authors have come to the conclusion that because it concentrates marketing activities on subscriptions rather than individual ticket sales, DSP is unable—after its apparent initial successes—to increase the percentage of the population attending arts events.

Waiting in the Wings is candid about the failure of Dynamic Subscription Promotion: because DSP is based on the idea "that the

---

[1] *Waiting in the Wings: A Larger Audience for the Arts and How to Develop It,* by Bradley G. Morison and Julie Gordon Dalgleish; ACA Books, 1987.

right package of benefits coupled with a strong sales pitch can make a subscriber out of almost anyone, *whether or not they have ever attended or even heard of the arts organization involved*" (emphasis in the original), it is successful only with those people the authors call "Yeses." Put another way, DSP has failed to motivate reluctant box-office patrons—the authors call them "Maybes"—to undertake long-term commitments to arts institutions based on increasing knowledge and curiosity. The consumer is, as it were, used. In the words of Morison and Dalgleish, "The arts are trying to force a new breed of Maybe audience into a ticket selling system that primarily benefits the organization rather than the potential customer. And the new customers aren't buying." It must be added, too, that Morison and Dalgleish are quite aware that the DSP's relentless concentration on selling out on subscription produces an inevitable cheapening of artistic offerings, as all the organization's attentions become focused on advertising the most attractive package possible.

Waiting in the Wings offers an alternative to DSP: SELL—Strategy to Encourage Lifelong Learning. While I can't say I find the new acronym either tasteful or particularly just to the authors' lofty goals, the content of what they are proposing strikes me as the first worthwhile initiative in audience development in the last three decades. The authors' own words say it well:

> Audience development strategy . . . should be a system of events and activities that provide *stepping stones* for people to increase gradually their interest, understanding and adventurousness. And in that system, the attendance at artistic events needs to be layered with participation in learning experiences. It should provide opportunities for increased *commitment* to the organization along the way and include a communications and promotional strategy that encourages people to take the steps that lead toward full commitment.

Morison and Dalgleish recognize that what they call "Points-of-Entry" are necessary to begin the process of attracting the "Maybes." They also recognize that such an initial attraction for a new audience may well be a Broadway musical (in the case of a theater) or a Pops concert (in the case of a symphony orchestra). These promotions are indeed useful, as long ago those responsible for the Boston Pops concerts realized. But the authors are to be praised for their forthrightness in recognizing that such crowd-pleasing events must lead the audience into the real work and the true artistic mission of the organization:

> But it is important to remember that promotions can contribute to the long-term development of audiences only if they [the promotions] do not stray too far from the vision of the organization and do not overwhelm its artistic program. The goal is to make Points-of-Entry more comfortable for new people, to help create excitement, to intensify, not to distort or misrepresent, the artistic experience.

I fervently hope that this warming will be taken to heart by all those boards of directors and administrators who think that ballyhooed superstar benefits and concerts of pop and blockbuster film music are acceptable ways of killing the two birds of box office profit and audience development with one trashy and vulgar stone.

In the end, SELL comes down to education, not just by schools but by arts institutions as well. Morison and Dalgleish are deeply aware of just what a poor job has been done in arts education since World War II; they are also aware of the prejudice against education held by many involved in the arts. But they know that the anti-education position is a dead-end road for the arts, and they know that such a nihilistic position does not satisfy those who experience art. And so they talk about a "thirst for knowledge among audience and potential audience," and they go on to quote some comments made in a discussion group at the Guthrie Theater:

> The biggest thing the theater can do for us is to give us information.
>
> The Guthrie is more than entertainment. It is continuing education. We must try to understand what they are doing.

Morison and Dalgleish are to be praised for repeatedly stressing that education is a long-term goal, not one to be measured in terms of immediate commercial results. They demonstrate a commendable and fervent orientation toward what they call cultural democracy. By this they mean the widest possible diffusion of cultural goods in a democratic society. Because of this orientation *Waiting in the Wings* concentrates on the "Maybes" and perhaps gives less than sufficient attention to the gathering and widely recognized loss of sophistication and commitment on the part of the very "Yeses" who have been the object of so much marketing attention in recent years. The tragedy of Dynamic Subscription Promotion, in my opinion, is not simply that it does not increase the outreach of the arts; at the same time as it fails to bring in new members of the audience, DSP, through its hyped rhetoric and absence of educational mission, impoverishes the relationship of subscribers toward the arts they are supporting.

All in all, Bradley G. Morison and Julie Gordon Dalgleish have written a splendid book. Despite all the authors' virtue, it is comforting to report that they are human: they spell the name of George Balanchine with two "l"s rather than one. This trifling error will, of course, be corrected in the many reprintings *Waiting in the Wings* is certain to receive; it is must reading for boards and arts administrators, good for the soul as well as for the body. Congratulations, too, to the American Council for the Arts for publishing it, and to the Shell Companies Foundation for paying for it. Such courage should be rewarded.

The Buck Goes Where?

BECAUSE INSTITUTIONS accomplish the financially onerous and publicly successful tasks of presenting, performing, and exhibiting art, most grants in the arts—especially large grants—will always go to them. So the issue in grants policy today is not eliminating institutional grants, but rather preserving an important place for grants to individuals.

At first glance, deciding on the weight to be given to individual grants would seem to be a question of mere administrative prudence, not one of artistic principle. Money for the arts, after all, ends up in every case with individuals, whether or not it passes first through institutional hands. Similarly, institutional money, whether paid through government, foundations, or corporations, comes originally from individuals as taxpayers, donors, or shareholders. Thus it is possible to view the entire process of arts support as composed of individual-to-individual transactions, mediated in most cases by benevolent nonprofit institutions.

If the issue is to be posed in this way, the only discussion—since we all agree that art is a good—can be over the extent of institutional participation in the making of grants. This discussion would seem to involve only questions of efficiency. Should the making of grants be separated from the appropriation of money which makes the grants possible? Who should choose the recipients? Who should choose who chooses the recipients? Who should decide the purposes for which money is given? How restrictive should these purposes be? How can, and by whom should, grant performance be evaluated?

Questions of efficiency undoubtedly are important: No one in a position of fiduciary responsibility could feel happy allowing money to be scattered like so much confetti. But we do not live in a world in which the gospel of efficiency suffices either to choose our goals or to analyze our predicament; the support of art can hardly be reduced to the orderly following of recipes in a cookbook. In art as in the most important activities of life, beneath discussions of procedure lie vital (and often unarticulated) questions of ends—in this case, the kind of art we want, the extent of the responsibility we wish to take for our patronage decisions, and the kind of society in which we wish to live. In this connection, it is clear that the question of individual grants to artists cannot be separated from the patrons who make these grants.

Let us treat these questions in the order I have posed them. We should not be surprised to find that the partisans of grants to institutions accept the corpus of existing art as a fully realized achievement and are profoundly unhappy with the newest art being produced. In most cases this unhappiness extends to the entire cultural creation of the twentieth century and even to modernity itself. Those who share this reaction against the undoubted excesses, trivialities, and provocations of much of the contemporary cultural scene hope to direct future artistic activity into the familiar paths of the hallowed past, and by their patronage of established and sanctioned institutions ensure the continuation of the taste with which they feel comfortable.

The question of individual responsibility for patronage decisions is also important. An individual's gift to an individual, unmediated by institutions, is marked by total responsibility on both sides. As the numbers of institutions between giver and recipient proliferate, individual responsibility and commitment is lessened. Indeed, in situations where foundations, corporations, and governments give to foundations who then give to arts institutions who finally employ artists, so many boards, committees, panels, arts marketers, and administrators have a hand in the outcome that responsibility and commitment for the expenditure of funds—indeed, the very intensity of the relationship between artist and patron—ceases to exist. It must be added that this outcome, much encouraged by our tax laws, is to many donors' tastes, for a potentially chancy and difficult-to-make gift to an artist is replaced by a widely approved and simply accomplished gift to a prestigious institution.

Then there is the final issue: what kind of society do we want to live in? If art is a mirror at once perceptive about our lives and influential on the way we live, then it behooves us to treat the future of art as we would treat the future of society. So the issue then becomes, by whom should artistic decisions be made? Do we want cultural policy to be made by the boards, committees, panels, and administrators, to whom I referred above? How large a role do we wish to preserve for the lone individual, whether as artist or as patron?

The answers to these questions can hardly be formulated according to considerations of efficiency. Such grants, it is true, offer no guarantee of producing the greatest art. We should not be under any illusion that grants to individual artists—and grants by individual patrons—will in themselves usher in some kind of artistic paradise; once again, it must be stated that art cannot be accomplished by following recipes.

But what is the alternative to a healthy role for individual grants? In my opinion, the present trend toward making "organization men" out of both artists and patrons is a vote for the unreasoned worship of past taste, the abdication of responsibility and commitment by patrons, and an increase in the bureaucratization of our lives. Grants to individual artists, made in many cases by sophisticated and consistent individual patrons, offer the possibility of placing the burden of artistic decisions where it belongs—on independent minds and spirits. In this case at least, what is good for our art also seems good for our society.

Why Give to the Arts?

MANY OF THE THOUGHTS I want to share with you have emerged out of the crucible of personal experience. The experience which has sparked my current thoughts involves having a teenage son about to go off to college. As I thought about this prospect, I realized how difficult it was for me to make any rationally founded—that is, defensible—arguments about what one should get out of an education. I knew I could say that I wanted my son to get an education that was rich in the arts and the humanities, in what Matthew Arnold called (in *Culture and Anarchy*) "the study and pursuit of perfection" and "the best that has been thought and known."

But I soon became aware just how hard it was, in a world increasingly ruled by considerations of career success, to justify such an elevated position. Most of the children of my son's age I knew would be going to college for professional training. Whether they would gain admission to the best colleges or have to settle for something less, they were still insistent on going to college for professional training, achieved at the cost of ignoring the permanent values of civilization.

Such certainly wasn't what I meant by an education. It became equally clear to me that this educational devaluation of the truly important was a widespread, systemic problem. And to my chagrin I realized all the more that the arguments for the arts and the humanities, whether in education or outside in the great world, are very, very difficult to make.

I want to talk briefly about where we stand in the making of these arguments. All of us here are involved, in one way or another, in raising money for the arts and humanities. We know that the first question from a prospective donor that we must be able to answer is "Why should I give to this cause?" There are those who will say that whatever answer we can give that gets money is a good enough answer. There are those who will tell us that the only test of an argument on behalf of culture is whether it is successful. A friend of mine who has devoted much of her life to working for the arts on the nonfederal level said to me that, in her experience, no arguments save those of direct economic relevance are possible with legislators. When I asked her what she will do at a future time when she is faced with competing arguments—or even when she wants her legislators to attend and enjoy that which they support—she replied, "I don't care what happens as long as we get the money now."

What I have just said is, I am afraid, an epitome of the present situation. This, it seems to me, is the prevailing line of discussion in cultural boards and executive committees and in contacts between boards and staff. We see everywhere an increasingly strong emphasis on earned income; the arts must be positioned so as to generate ever-larger percentages of earned income. I needn't tell you what this means: marketing plans, ticket sales, shops, and the owning of what are, in effect even if not in name, profit-making businesses. Everywhere we turn we find the attention of arts organizations going off into how they can increase their publics, increase income, and thus reduce their dependence on contributed funds. All in all, everything comes down to audiences and dollars: the only justification for cultural activities that can now be proudly made is that we have more people experiencing the arts—and supporting the arts through user fees—than ever before.

Let us look at another part of the present situation. There is a dirty little secret among those who live and work in nonprofit arts institutions. This secret is the scarcity of good board members. It is very difficult—if not impossible—to explain to prospective board members just why they should come on, and what their duties must be. Board members today, it seems to me, increasingly see themselves as economic consultants, voluntary experts brought in because of their success in business life, so that they might enable arts institutions to be run like businesses and at least break even. Of cultural sophistication amongst the pool of prospective board members there is sadly little; that the primary duty of a board member is to give money so that the artistic direction of the institution might continue seems to be an idea whose time has come—and gone.

Today in the world of cultural funding we have very little money available for education, that cornerstone of any solid future for art and civilization. Here I would say that the current record of the great foundations is not good; indeed, several great foundations have taken the position that they are only interested in the creation of new art and that they are not going to worry about the transmission of the art of the past.

There is, too, the increasingly powerful conception of culture as an entertainment experience—as an activity which is legitimized by whether or not it is liked by the audience. This idea is not new to me: I've been a pianist all my life, and I can tell you that a pianist lives or dies by whether or not the audience responds. On the other hand—and the other hand here is very large indeed—if audience response is the only reason an artist makes art, and if that is our only reason for making the artist's work possible, then the arts are in direct, and losing, competition with the most powerful and even triumphant trends in mass society and popular culture.

Let me recapitulate all the arguments for culture we hear today: entertainment, tourism, real estate, jobs, and all the spinoffs therefrom. Of the arguments for the culture and the arts in themselves, we hear almost nothing. The result of all this is a general cheapening of the whole discussion. To read the *New York Times* these days, for example, is to see more and more articles relating the arts to the smart and fashionable worlds of trendy society and go-go business. I am sure many of you saw the article (March 20, 1987) on Washington parties, with their use of the arts to provide corporate access to the movers and shakers in Washington; I am sure, too, that many of you saw the *Times* article (May 7, 1987) on the Rockefeller University Founders Ball, with its sheeplike parading of Nobel Prize winners before the glamorous patrons. And now, widely urged as a panacea for arts deficits, we have the rise of cause-related marketing, in which we are beginning to see the greatest masterworks of Western civilization merchandised in the demeaning way the Statue of Liberty was sold last summer.

What has gone wrong? I want to suggest that we have lost sight of supporting the arts and the humanities as indeed the great repository of the best that has been thought and known, as the best repository of our history, as the best secular repository of that which makes us aware that we are not alone in time here on this planet.

In this regard, just one week ago I had an extraordinary experience. I was in Italy—in Ravenna, to be precise—and I went to the tomb of Dante. I must tell you that I'm not Italian, I'm not Catholic, and I'm not even a Christian. My grandparents, in the little Russian towns where they grew up, would have been scared to death of what Dante represented, of what he meant for them as Jews, or rather of what they thought he meant for them. But I can tell you that standing with my son and wife before Dante's tomb, I realized that Dante is mine and that he is ours. I realized that the last two thousand and more years of history—the legacy of Athens, Rome, and Jerusalem—belong to all of us. This inheritance must be taught, via the arts and the humanities, to every child, and made available to every citizen of our democracy.

It is just this ability of the arts and the humanities, when allowed to speak for themselves and in their own terms, to bind us together as a people in the past, the present, and the future, that makes them so important for us all as a nation. The United States of America is unique for its glorious record, now extending over more than three hundred years, of making one indivisible nation out of many disparate peoples. Our nation has never been, and is not now, a completed act. We are always engaged in the process of creating a nation through the expansion of our body of citizens. One of the most important elements in this process is bringing new peoples into the legacy of our past, in making it possible for them to share the legacy, to participate in transmitting it to their children, and to help add to that legacy for the future. It cannot be repeated too often that this legacy lies in our civilization and in the arts and the humanities that make up so much of our civilization.

I want to close by speaking against the idea that there is not enough money available to support culture. I must tell you that it is only necessary to read about the prices in the art market these days to know that the argument of poverty is perfect nonsense. It is possible now to spend $2 million for a Klimt painting, and $40 million for a van Gogh. Some poverty! Patrons make choices about what they wish to spend money on. It is our job, whether we are artists, foundation executives, or government officials, to persuade them to support the communication of the world's greatest goods to all the inhabitants of this great country. We are the advocates of the world's greatest goods; only through making arguments for them in ways which enhance rather than destroy the integrity of that which we love can we fulfill our responsibilities.

30.

For many of the older members of the arts-advocacy establishment—the long-time leaders of and workers in arts-service organizations and lobbying groups, and a few NEA veterans—the memory of Nancy Hanks, a Nelson Rockefeller protégée and a Richard Nixon appointment as NEA chairman, remains something uniquely pure, an example of all public arts leadership once was, and hasn't been since. I never met Nancy Hanks, and until recently I could know of her only through the praises of her friends. The Hanks biography by Michael Straight that I discuss in the following November 1988 article from the New Criterion *suggests that despite her warm human qualities and her marvelous fortitude throughout a long and painful illness, not all of the praises of her work as a cultural administrator are accurate; it is my impression that the persistence of nostalgia for her lost glory serves only to forestall an assessment of her work and to confuse discussion about our present predicament. Still, I count myself an admirer of the energy and tenacity with which she attempted to deal with the problems of culture in a democracy; as I reread my own words about her, I am painfully aware of my own difficulties in reconciling the need to transmit civilization with the imperatives of democratic political arrangements, and the American context in which this reconciliation must be managed.*

The Case of Nancy Hanks

IN THE PREFACE to his new and fascinating memoir of Nancy Hanks,[1] the much-admired second chairman (1969–77) of the National Endowment for the Arts, Michael Straight, her deputy during her years in office, makes a proud claim for their joint place in the history of our republic: "We had worked together," he writes, "to create a democratic culture at a high level in America." While one would hardly want to claim felicity for the use of the word *create* in a context

---

[1] *Nancy Hanks: An Intimate Portrait*, by Michael Straight; Duke University Press, 1988.

of bureaucratic policy making, fulfilling the role of cultural leadership on behalf of a proud nation is a goal neither trivial nor ignoble. To render productive the inevitable tension between a mass democracy flexible enough to accommodate the pressures of necessary change and a high culture based upon enduring standards of content and form is a task only the greatest leaders can accomplish.

It can hardly be said that the ideal of cultural leadership is as yet widely accepted in this country. Whenever the subject is raised, from the political and social Left are heard accusations of imperialist hegemony and social exploitation; from the Right come well-founded fears of official contumely and the stifling of individualism. In the sadly half-educated and apathetic center of American life, the ideal of leadership in art and learning bids fair to become at best the advocacy of genteel diversions and at worst the provision of fodder for the voracious maw of a debased popular culture.

And yet the need for "a democratic culture at a high level" goes on, for us as it does for all societies that would call themselves at once free and great. In the achievement of this freedom and greatness, the state, as the nominee of the nation, may choose or may fail to choose to bear some of this responsibility. Two centuries ago, the oft-quoted words of Edmund Burke put it well:

> [T]he state ought not to be considered as nothing better than a partnership agreement in a trade of pepper and coffee, calico or tobacco, or some other such low concern, to be taken up for a little temporary interest, and to be dissolved by the fancy of the parties. It is to be looked on with other reverence; because it is not a partnership in things subservient only to the gross animal existence of a temporary and perishable nature. It is a partnership in all science, a partnership in all art, a partnership in every virtue and in all perfection. As the ends of such a partnership cannot be obtained in many generations, it becomes a partnership not only between those who are living, but between those who are living, those who are dead, and those who are to be born.[2]

High standards, surely, by which to judge anyone attempting to live in the maelstrom of Washington politics. Yet here as elsewhere these

---

[2] From *Reflections on the Revolution in France*, quoted in *Selected Writings and Speeches of Edmund Burke*, edited by Peter J. Stanlis; Doubleday Anchor Books, 1963.

standards cry out to be applied to our elected and appointed leaders, and it speaks well for Mr. Straight that he himself has raised the issue of leadership in the context of federal cultural policy, and has devoted so much of his book to recounting how Nancy Hanks, with his devoted cooperation, accomplished her tasks.

Viewed solely in human terms, the story of Nancy Hanks is often touching and, in the end, deeply moving. Born in 1927 in Florida, the daughter of prosperous parents curiously unsure in social standing, she attended then-fashionable Duke University. She seems to have devoted little attention or interest to the arts and the humanities, but she did take courses in botany, economics, political science, and philosophy. Personable and attractive (she was once elected a May Queen), albeit hardly much of a scholar, she seemed destined for the kind of comfortable marriage that was so much the goal of well-brought-up young coeds in the mid-1940s.

But there was another side to this seeming belle. While the young Nancy Hanks had little interest in what for Mr. Straight were the burning issues of the day facing her because she was Southern, white, female, and American,[3] she was active in campus politics, becoming successively freshman representative to and then treasurer of the student government, house president, and finally, as a senior, president of the student government. All in all, despite her success in college life, she wasn't much of an opinion shaper, remaining (in the words of her roommate) "more a tool of the establishment than a member of the establishment."

Upon her graduation from Duke in 1949, Nancy Hanks seemed at loose ends and unable to make up her mind about the future, though she did want to go to Washington. The death of her brother the next year, shortly after his graduation from high school, concentrated her parents' attention on her, inspiring in her father dreams of a brilliant career and in her mother a concentration on marriage and childbearing.

---

[3] In this regard, it must be remembered that while Nancy Hanks was a young student at Duke, Mr. Straight, then in his forties, was, as of 1946, the publisher of the family-owned *New Republic*, a left-leaning magazine edited by Henry Wallace, vice president of the United States from 1941 to 1945 and secretary of commerce in the Truman administration until his pro-Stalin speeches on foreign policy caused him to be fired after one year in office.

Despite many suitors, the young woman decided on a career. Washington continued to beckon, and a letter from her father to his friend Charles E. Wilson, them working for Harry Truman as chairman of the Office of Defense Mobilization, secured her a job interview. When it immediately became plain that she couldn't "cook, type, or sew," she was offered a job as a receptionist. Knowing at the outset what she was always to understand, she chose to do what was asked of her rather than demand immediate preferment.

On February 3, 1953, her life changed. On that day, she met Nelson Rockefeller, the new chairman of Dwight Eisenhower's Advisory Committee on Government Organization. Rockefeller was then in his mid-forties, innovative, energetic, charming, and sympathetic. Determined to make his mark in American political life, he spewed forth ideas and plans; one of these ideas called for the establishment of a cabinet-level Department of Health, Education, and Welfare. President Eisenhower and the Congress agreed, and Rockefeller was chosen as the department's second in command. Nancy Hanks became his tireless confidential secretary, "ready to work from dawn until darkness." In the words of a woman friend:

> She was glued to Nelson. He would head for Capitol Hill; she would accompany him. That was when she learned to deal with congressmen and senators—he was so persuasive, in his relentless way. She listened as he argued. She didn't say much, but she didn't forget anything. She kept tabs on everything that was going on. She attended all of the conferences and all of the strategy sessions. She came to know everyone, and they came to respect her.

When Rockefeller left HEW (as it soon became known in acronym-loving Washington) to become a special assistant to the president for Cold War strategy, he took Nancy Hanks along. She did more than assist in his government tasks; as Mr. Straight strongly suggests (and as was long rumored in capital gossip), the young woman from the South and the married multimillionaire politician, then living apart from his first wife, seem to have become lovers. She appears to have saved only one letter from him; it reads in part, "Nancy, there is nothing more beautiful . . . than our love." The gentlemanly Mr. Straight's comment is telling: "What more can and should be said on this score?"

Despite Rockefeller's willingness to leave his wife, it appears from Mr. Straight's account that Nancy Hanks refused to marry him, thereby earning the enduring respect of the Rockefeller family. By 1955 their relationship cooled, and he went back to New York and his wife. She continued to work for him, spending much time acting as liaison with Henry Kissinger on the national-security inquiries Rockefeller had commissioned as part of his first drive for the White House. By 1959 she was working with Nelson's brother Laurence on an ecological study; more important, somewhere around 1963 she began to work with eldest brother John D. Rockefeller 3rd on what was to prove her niche for her final twenty years, the advocacy and support first of the performing arts and then of the arts in general.

It is indeed curious, given Nancy Hanks's intense association with the arts during the last and most consequential period of her life, that nothing in her past presaged such an outcome. As a young person, she seems to have had no ability or interest in the arts; in her work with Nelson Rockefeller, the arts—despite his own passionate interest in painting and sculpture—don't seem to have come up at all. She described her first encounter with John D. about the arts in an almost deadpan manner:

> John D. Rockefeller 3rd said to me, "If the techniques that my brothers Nelson and Laurence have used . . . are applicable to areas of public policy like education or health, why shouldn't we apply those same methods to an area which, I believe, relates to public policy—the arts?"
>
> Well, I said yes. I said it too quickly. I really did not have any understanding of what I meant.
>
> What we found out was this: while it was exactly right that the performing arts should be looked at as a matter of public policy . . . we did not realize how difficult it would be.

It will be remembered that in 1965 the Rockefeller Brothers Fund published its influential Panel Report on the Performing Arts; while stopping short of recommending substantial and direct federal funding, the Rockefeller report attempted to make a powerful case for the value of the arts and of increased national attention to their support. This case, like all those that have been made by influential personalities and reports in the years since the Rockefeller report was published, was based on a calculus of pleasure for the consumer rather than of centrality to the expression and preservation of the values of civilized society.[4]

Nancy Hanks's name is on the report as a member of the Rockefeller Brothers Fund Arts Planning Committee, and as the head of the staff responsible for the report. With Rockefeller sponsorship, she soon became active in the burgeoning community-arts-council movement. In 1968 she became the president of the Associated Councils for the Arts,[5] the umbrella organization of groups responsible for the administration of local public funding. In her work across the country on behalf of arts support, she was as always careful to eschew the high road of intellectual conviction and rhetorical grandeur. An associate described her approach to public speaking in these terms:

> She had a very interesting technique. She defused criticism. She'd always start out by saying, "I'm just a poor little country girl, and here I am in my housecoat and curlers, and all I want to do is to make something nice happen."

Mr. Straight's comment on the above quotation—with all the abdication of responsibility it suggests—is laconic and (at least to me) sadly accurate: "It worked."

As Nancy Hanks's career began increasingly to take on a wider aspect, two dramas which were mightily to affect her life, one private and the other public, were being played out. In 1962, she suffered her first brush with the cancer which was to kill her twenty-one years later. Her initial mastectomy was followed the next year by a hysterectomy, and as the cancer recurred, she was often hospitalized and laid low by the effects of intensive chemotherapy. Throughout this lengthy ordeal, she behaved with exemplary courage and self-control, concealing the extent of her illness and often even the fact of the illness itself from her closest friends and co-workers.

As her health became increasingly problematic, the public progress

---

[4] In the preface, signed by John D. Rockefeller 3rd, to the Rockefeller report, this ultimate rationale for the arts is succinctly stated: "The arts today are more fully appreciated as one means by which man can achieve the satisfactions he seeks, and therefore are important, even essential, to the human mind and spirit."

[5] Now the American Council for the Arts, a leading national arts-advocacy and governmental lobbying organization.

of federal arts support was gathering force. In the early 1960s costs associated with producing the performing arts were fast outstripping box office income; such large-scale foundation help as was available— in particular the Ford Foundation orchestra grants in the late 1960s— only raised budgets without providing a long-term commitment. Individual patronage, though often available for bricks and mortar, seemed increasingly unwilling and unable to cover the dreary succession of yearly operating deficits always characteristic of arts institutions. Into this void stepped the federal government, at first, in the Kennedy administration, only with words and personalities, and then, in 1965, with the signing by Lyndon Johnson of the enabling legislation for the National Endowment for the Arts and the Humanities.

The early federal funds appropriated were small: in fiscal 1966, the first arts-programming subsidies amounted to no more than 2.5 million dollars. Under the NEA's first chairman, Roger Stevens, patronage was scattered, and, judging by a new and dismaying book written by Livingston Biddle, Stevens's deputy and the agency's chairman in the Carter administration, unduly subject to personal whim and caprice.[6] But the appropriations continued to increase, and, by fiscal 1970, as Richard Nixon took office, the amount available to the NEA for programming had risen to 8.25 million dollars. It is here that Mr. Straight's story of the rise of his heroine becomes particularly interesting, for he describes in hitherto unknown detail the labyrinthine and indeed Byzantine process by which, with the savvy assistance of presidential advisor Leonard Garment, the Rockefeller family retainer Nancy Hanks became the chairman of the NEA under the decidedly Rockefeller-hating Richard Nixon.

At the NEA she devoted her life to the task of running the agency. She was very much of a hands-on administrator, delegating no ultimate responsibility for anything and attempting to oversee everything, down to the physical condition of the offices in which her staff worked. During her years as chairman, she had little personal life, taking work home and coming in to the office on weekends—and expecting others to do the same. In return for her demands, she treated her staff as a large family, showing great concern for them as well as

[6] *Our Government and the Arts: A Perspective from the Inside*, by Livingston Biddle; ACA Books, 1988.

a consuming interest in whatever lives they managed to live outside the agency. She earned the deep loyalty of her associates, a loyalty which for most of them has lasted through the years since her death.

She did more than earn the title of "matriarch." She showed an intuitive understanding of the essential difference between administrative control and staff advice. Doubtless many were uncomfortable with her rigorous making of this distinction, but despite Mr. Straight's criticism of her administrative style, it is evident from his own testimony that he too profited from her courage and grip:

> As Nancy's deputy . . . I was never entrusted with any administrative authority. At times my colleagues wondered if I was wise in allowing myself to be demeaned. To me, it wasn't a matter of wisdom. I was happy carrying out my assignments, armed as I was with Nancy's reflected power. At the same time, I was free of the burdens of final responsibility. Had I held the responsibility, I would have had to act upon my convictions, firing staff members who I felt were unproductive and abolishing programs which I believed were inappropriate and wasteful. For me it was easier to take my stands; to see my recommendations accepted or rejected, to wait until events proved me right or wrong.

As subservient as Nancy Hanks had been in working for the Rockefellers, with Nixon she pursued a different tack entirely. From the outset she demanded a large NEA budget; her argument fell on unpredictably sympathetic ears, for despite Nixon's overall commitment to cutting the federal budget, he had been convinced by his advisors that support for the arts and for culture was an inexpensive way of repairing the political damage done to his presidency, first by cuts in social programs and later by his intermittently vigorous prosecution of the Vietnam War.

The winning "terms" (as Mr. Straight calls them) on which Nancy Hanks served were simple: "immediate, rapid, and continuous growth." The result of Nixon's political needs and her immensely skillful lobbying within the White House and with Congress was a total victory for budget expansion. The first Hanks NEA budget provided 15.09 million dollars for programming; her final budget, eight years later, provided 94 million. So great was the Hanks budgetary momentum, and so total was her victory in convincing both the executive and legislative branches that the arts were good things for grantor as well as grantee, that even when she left the agency, it continued to grow. The NEA budget in fiscal 1978 (the first year of Livingston Biddle's term) reached $123.85 million.

What did all this spending amount to in terms of the creation, to use Mr. Straight's prefatory words once again, of "a democratic culture at a high level in America"? At almost the end of his book, he comes close to answering his own question: her legacy, he writes, "lies in the arts themselves rather than in any concept of the role of government in relation to the arts." In saying that her effect was "in the arts themselves," it is unclear whether Mr. Straight means that she actually affected the *nature* of the artworks created during her tenure or only that she changed the *volume* of arts-related activity.

There can be little cause for arguing that Nancy Hanks had a direct influence on the art that was created while she was in office. Only the foolish would have expected her—or, for that matter, any other public official—to create culture itself. Artistic creation is, as always, the primary responsibility of artists; the actual creation of the component works of civilization is no more a responsibility of political leaders than is the living of citizens' lives for them.

Insofar as she influenced art, it seems to me she did so by propagating the idea that the vitality of artistic life was to be judged by considerations of quantity rather than quality. In general, she was at pains not to separate the idea of "more" from that of "better"; to put it another way, she failed to distinguish quantity from quality. By Mr. Straight's own testimony, when Nancy Hanks campaigned strenuously in 1976 for her reappointment by the newly arrived Carter administration to a third term, she signed a memorandum (over staff objection) to the president understating the volume of arts activity before she took office, and overstating it after her chairmanship.[7]

---

[7] It must be said that Mr. Straight is so honest in these matters as to recognize that the conservative criticism of federal cultural support which surfaced in 1980 had a point, at least insofar as it applied to the Carter administration: the conservatives, he writes, "pressed too hard . . . to cut the Endowment back, yet they were right in arguing that quantitative data, reliable or unreliable, was [*sic*] a poor measure of the value and vitality of the arts."

In general, her goal was the fact of large-scale funding in itself, rather than what was done with the funds. In this connection, Mr. Straight tells a story that would merely be funny if it did not so perfectly catch the way the public business in a democracy—not just in cultural matters—is so often done. It seems that Nancy Hanks decided early on that the NEA should fund projects—requiring yearly applications and agency determinations—rather than ongoing operating support formulaically determined on the basis of institutional budget size and need. The symphony orchestra field violently objected, feeling that project support forced them to undertake programs they neither desired nor needed, and in effect drained support from day-to-day activities. She persevered, requiring that orchestras justify their requests on the basis of their public outreach services rather than their continuing artistic needs. Mr. Straight explains how a modus vivendi was reached:

> In time to come, the Chicago Symphony Orchestra, the Los Angeles Philharmonic, and other great institutions dutifully lined up, requesting $100,000 a year in order to provide youth concerts and educational services for their communities. Then, as these services became embedded in the schedules of the orchestras, the contrast between project funding and formula funding was blurred. The orchestra managers found it easy to shuffle their financial accounts; the Endowment's panels, year after year, granted to the great orchestras the maximum sums which were available to them, and so the program, which began as project funding, turned into formula funding. As the Dodo said to Alice, "*Everyone* has won and *all* must have prizes!"

In reading the thousands and thousands of words Mr. Straight devotes to Nancy Hanks's labors, one searches in vain for any sort of an overarching understanding as to why the arts, and the civilization of which they form so constitutive a part, should be supported, not just by governments but by society as a whole and by its individual members. Her emphasis seems always to have been on the growth of the NEA, and on a kind of simple arts boosterism best demonstrated in her constantly employed technique of convincing resistant congressmen to support her requests by publicly reminding them of the grants the agency made in their constituencies. These crass arguments aside, one cannot help coming away from this book discomfited by just how little evidence there is that Nancy Hanks knew about—and by implication cared for—the living corpus of greatness whose support she advocated.

What evidence Mr. Straight provides in fact goes the other way. Thus he notes that "Nancy was ill at ease in dealing with literature. She had been trained by the Rockefellers to deal with institutions and with the performing arts. She had no background in literature and no sense of what she wanted to accomplish in supporting it." Just a few pages later, he states that "in architecture and design, as in literature, Nancy had no notion of what she wanted to accomplish when she took over the Arts Endowment." This lack of personal knowledge, experience, and interest in the matters with which she had to work sometimes caused permanent harm: thus, when dealing with the problem of arts education, she took an anti-teacher and anti-classroom position which still haunts the relations between the NEA and the world of arts education. As Mr. Straight tells the story:

> She settled . . . for advocacy films which were mediocre and for rhetoric which served only to heighten the tensions which existed between teachers and artists at the classroom level. Thus in her speeches Nancy was fond of quoting children who spoke of their loathing for their teachers.

Above all, in her advocacy of government support for the arts, Nancy Hanks left a legacy of defensiveness and overreaction in the face of legitimate criticism. All too often she responded, as she did in defending a grant the NEA had made to an artist who spent the money to drop crepe-paper streamers from a light plane, by

> . . . in effect . . . saying, you cannot criticize any grant which I make unless you are prepared to condemn the entire structure of the Arts Endowment. It was as if, in a game of poker, she was saying to all of the players, I'll raise you, I'll bet every chip I hold in my hand. Fair enough, if her hand consisted of four aces. But, supposing she was holding a pair of deuces?

This short-sighted attitude became intensified during the succeeding and highly politicized Biddle regime at the NEA, and continues to affect relations between the Endowment and members of Congress, who find they cannot criticize particular actions of the Endowment without being branded as anti-art. In responding this way to criticism of individual grants and general policies, those responsible for the fortunes of the NEA have regularly missed opportunities not just to build a stronger and more efficient agency but to educate everyone, supporters and opponents alike, about the relationship between the health of art and civilization and the health of the nation.

Here, then, is the ultimate criterion for judging the success or failure of Nancy Hanks at the NEA. Her proper task was not to create art but to influence, in a profound way, the regnant conception of the place of art in the life of the republic. Lacking as we do a prescriptive aristocracy and an established church, such influence must often come from duly constituted political leadership. In determining that she did not leave a legacy in the "role of government in relation to the arts," Mr. Straight clearly suggests that she failed in this, her highest function.

It is not possible to read Mr. Straight's memoir of his friend without a feeling of sympathy for Nancy Hanks's character and her labors, and without a sense of loss occasioned by our awareness of the disparity between what had to be done and what she was to leave behind. And so one cannot leave this subject without asking the most important question of all: just why did a person so bright, courageous, energetic, and warm-hearted, so willing to work and so at home in the American social and political establishment, fail in this way? The answer must go to the core not only or even primarily of Nancy Hanks but of our own condition as a people. We, as she, have always tended to value scale over substance; we are, as she was, half-educated in the life of the mind and the world of our civilization; we are, as she was, all too willing to see political life and governmental service as the achievement of short-term, easily quantifiable objectives, rather than as the binding of a nation, through the furtherance of its cultural inheritance, to its highest political expression; as much as we are, as she was, willing to work, we spend too little time in reflection about our ultimate purposes and ends. Nowhere is the correction of these, our lacks, so important as it is now in the question of leadership in democratic culture.

31.

The following article is based on a speech I gave in Washington, D. C., in June of 1988 to Chorus America, the service organization for choruses in the United States. At that time, the great issue at the NEA was the failed attempt by the then chairman to alter certain procedural elements of the peer-panel process by which the agency makes its grants. In my article (and the earlier speech), I attempted to combine a discussion of the NEA's then-current problem with a discussion of the place of arts education in federal arts support, and to place both these matters in the context of a thumbnail sketch of what had happened to the NEA during the Reagan administration. The tone and concentration of this September 1988 New Criterion article is very much a product of my own service in Washington. In this, it stands in some contrast to the tone and concentration of the Epilogue, which immediately follows it.

The NEA: Looking Back, and Looking Ahead

SIX YEARS AGO, I heard, via telephone call from the White House, that I was being nominated by the president for a term on the National Council on the Arts, the advisory board of the National Endowment for the Arts. This month my term officially comes to an end, and questions of what has happened, and even more of what has been accomplished, lie heavy on my mind.

I am afraid that I am hardly able to keep a certain valedictory air from suffusing my thoughts. Valediction is the right of the young and of the old; it may accord less well with those who are, as I am, in what might be called the full steam of middle age. And yet in the present context, I do have something to look back on. I have spent most of my life playing the piano, performing music from Bach and Scarlatti to Olivier Messiaen and Elliott Carter. For over a decade now I have been writing about music as a critic. Recently, somewhat to my own surprise, I have begun a kind of third career, as the artistic director of a small but ambitious summer music festival and school.

There is no point in recounting here the fears and reservations which my appointment seems to have aroused in the arts community. I came to the Endowment not just as a critic of American cultural life but as a critic of the role the agency was playing in our artistic life; I also came to the agency with the strongly held belief that what is done must be done well. In any case, despite the hullabaloo over my appointment, the arts, and certainly their advocates, are still very much in evidence six years later; I hope I may be pardoned for saying that I, too, have survived.

As we look forward to the 1990s and to the prospect of a new administration in Washington, the time seems ripe to attempt some consideration of just where matters stand in the public world of the American arts, and some consideration as well of the role the National Endowment for the Arts has played—or has failed to play—in the complex filiation that always obtains between our recent past and our present.

Let me begin with some thoughts on how things looked some years ago, although not *in toto*, for to sketch the entire picture of the arts in America at any given time would require a very large book rather than a mere article. Two issues in particular seem worth focusing on: our working description of arts activity and the arts, and our working description of arts education.

The best place to start is with arts activity and the arts. By the early 1980s, the arts in America had reached a pinnacle of expansion and development unprecedented in our history. There is no need to cite statistics. It is enough to say that the operative word was *more*—more museums, more ballet companies, more modern-dance companies, more theater companies, more creative writing, more poetry, more symphony orchestras, more opera companies, more chamber-music ensembles, more avant-garde groups, more exhibitions, more performances, more artists, more audiences, more patrons, more administrators, more press, more arts-conscious politicians. Everywhere— more, more, more.

With more, of course, went bigger. Bigger groups, bigger companies, bigger institutions, bigger staffs, bigger earned income, bigger budgets, bigger subsidies, bigger commitments, and, of course, bigger deficits. Perhaps the crowning confirmation of all this bigness was the happy news from the Census Bureau that in 1980 our artists, taken together as a class, amounted to at least one million souls, all struggling to create what at least some people some of the time might be open-minded enough to call art.

Much of this emphasis on more and bigger came from factors powerful in our history for many years, and in some cases going back to the founding of the republic. We Americans have always been a people with continental ambitions, and our goals in the arts have been little different in form from our goals in agriculture and industry. To feed a continent, to industrialize a continent, and, lest we forget, to school a continent—all this has required monumental labors to guarantee the production of monumental results. The American urge to provide culture was already evident in the nineteenth century in the very different successes of Ralph Waldo Emerson and Walt Whitman, of Jenny Lind and the Metropolitan Opera, of the Metropolitan Museum and the *Little Blue Books* of the Kansan E. Haldeman Julius. We have often seemed to have a hard time separating quality from quantity; indeed, when faced with a choice between the two, it has been our national bent, and often our national virtue, to choose quantity.

Clearly, quantity in itself is not the whole story of our artistic development. In literature, for example, we have had a powerful national art since the days of Washington Irving. In the visual arts of the past century we have nothing to be ashamed of, and much of which to be proud; modern American painting is admired the world over and, *mirabile dictu*, even here at home. Our twentieth-century dance, helped along in the early years by the likes of Ruth St. Denis, Martha Graham, and Agnes de Mille—and, of course, by the immigrant George Balanchine—is properly our joy.

In the field of music, the situation has been a good bit more complicated, for here we have had to contend at one and the same time with the great achievement of the eighteenth and nineteenth centuries in Europe, and with the contemporary European failure to inspire us by extending its own triumphant creations into the present. Our own disappointment in musical composition is perhaps no more than the local manifestation of a condition to be found throughout the Western world; even in this case, however, we happily possess many composers of the past fifty years and more who have written beautiful and enduring music. Of our orchestras, there is little that needs to be said:

for the whole of this century, they have been universally accepted as the standard of the world; our choruses, too, like our singers and instrumentalists, have won worldwide recognition.

All in all, the great expansion in American artistic life which took place from the Great Depression to the end of the 1950s, aided by the great post–World War II expansion of college education, strikes me as a remarkable democratic achievement. By the 1960s, however, much had begun to change. Commercial television, so beguiling and full of hope when it transmitted shows like "Omnibus" in the fifties, quickly showed that sitcom characters and late-night talk-show hosts were to be the new cultural celebrities of our time; by the 1970s, educational television, once thought of as a university of the air, had become what it is today, an upscale vendor of semi-cultivated pabulum for the prosperous. Such general publications of intellectual quality as still existed began increasingly to devote themselves to discussions of politics and "life styles"; the new trend in periodical journalism toward single-subject magazines guaranteed that the reader's prior educational achievement would become an ever less important requirement for his comprehension. In the media as a whole, the inflation of publicity and glamour had begun to make the arts in America into another branch of Broadway and Hollywood. Led by the sexual revolution of the 1960s, the cry of pleasure was everywhere in the air, and the forces of seriousness and reflection were in full flight. The consequence of these society-wide developments was a gathering tendency to see the arts as entertainment and artists as entertainers, lavishly paid to sing for their suppers.

As the 1980s succeeded the 1970s, and in particular as the quasi-populist administration of Jimmy Carter came to its end, these developments in art and culture seemed to impinge with particular force on the National Endowment for the Arts, charged as it was with dissolving all our long-accumulated guilt about being the only country in the civilized world without a tradition of direct governmental support for culture. By the end of the seventies, this agency had been so successful at accomplishing its mission that it seemed to many as if all of America's artistic excellence could be laid at its door. All the activity and all the art, all the employment for artists and all the enjoyment for audiences, all the momentum of artistic civilization in the country—everything seemed to depend for its existence and continuation on the work of a federal agency delivering rather less than a $150 million each year in subsidies doled out to thousands and thousands of grant applicants.

Such was not the case then, and is not the case now; the NEA makes up only a small part of the funding for the arts in this country. It seems to me that the credit for the propagation of this myth of the NEA's necessary centrality belongs not to artists but to politicians who have manipulated the electronic media and the press.

It is now history that the Reagan administration walked into this situation with scarcely a thought in its collective head. At David Stockman's Office of Management and Budget the determining word in arts and humanities matters was *cut*: cut not to improve, cut not to alter in any thought-out way the endowments' policies, cut not simply to save money, but cut to destroy. This is not the place to go through the long and tedious arguments for and against government support of the arts and the humanities. My confidence in the intellectual probity of all the participants in this debate would be greater if the pro-government-support arguments came more often from those who wish to give their own money to the arts, and if the anti-government-support arguments came more often from those who believe that the arts and humanities require support—of any kind whatsoever.

In the end, of course, the president, aided by a blue-ribbon task force that gave federal art subsidies a clean bill of health, was able to reach agreement with a Congress strongly sympathetic to such support. The NEA budget was cut by only a small amount, and Frank Hodsoll, a career government official well placed in the administration and sympathetic to the idea of arts subsidies, was appointed the agency's chairman.

What was so unfortunate about all the ruckus over abolishing the endowments was that it tended to obscure the very real problems in the fields they served. We must never forget that in our society, government reflects what is going on in the country at large. At the NEA our systemic, debased idea of the marketability of art as entertainment affected the discussion of public policy in a thousand ways, large and small, gross and subtle.

Perhaps a personal recollection will be of some use here in describing just how far this putatively artistic gospel of consumer satisfaction had gone by the early 1980s. In one of the first meetings of the National

Council I attended, I interrupted the usual discussion about the poverty-stricken state of American orchestras to ask why some of our great ensembles were paying (with NEA support) second-rank celebrity conductors hundreds of thousands of dollars for rather less than a half-year's work. In answer, I was told by an NEA staff member that the employment of such stars was the only way audiences could be inveigled into coming to hear the music.

As it was in music, so it was in the other arts. Institutions were measured by their turnstile count; museum exhibitions were evaluated in terms of drawing power (with the word *drawing* referring not to draughtsmanship but to box office); even the various avant-gardes, once thought to be hermetic, were praised as the coming inheritors of the salable mainstream. Administrators were praised, and large challenge grants awarded, on the basis of a continuing record of budget increases. Agency grants were continually described to the council by staff members in terms of the "impact" they would have on the artistic field in question or even on the cause of the arts as a whole; it was proudly proclaimed that the major purpose of bringing interns from all over the country to Washington to work at the agency was to spread knowledge of the Endowment and enlarge its reputation. A major concern of the agency two years before the celebration of its twentieth anniversary in 1985 was how to arrange a prime-time television spectacular using the entertainment services of stars from the world of commercial culture to salute the Endowment. Everywhere the goal was to expand and enhance the arts' image as a bringer of pleasure. Everywhere the enemy was the dull image of the status quo. An artistic task well and repeatedly done was invariably seen as evidence that the responsible institution was in a rut—and whatever might be said in favor of old ruts, they certainly weren't as sexy as new waves.

It is not too difficult to see that turning art into amusement is an integral part of what the English poet and critic C. H. Sisson has called "the conversion of religion as well as political events, the 'arts,' and all particular knowledge to the purposes of a power-ridden entertainment world." But beyond the redefinition of the idea of art, this trivialization-through-expansion had a devastating effect on what had once been seen as a civilized glory: I refer here to the calamitous drop in the level of general arts education in America during the 1960s and 1970s. Under the influence of the doctrine that to feel good is to be good, a two-tier system of the arts was established: professional glamour merchandised to the adult millions on the one hand, and the encouragement of the most aimless self-gratification by children on the other. The monument to the triumph of artistic glamour is, of course, public television, with its incongruous mating of movie stars serving as hosts to the hackneyed tragedies of the operatic stage.

The monument to the destruction of the idea of serious general arts education was *Coming to Our Senses*, the 1977 Arts, Education, and Americans Panel Report which summed up where general arts education stood after the triumph of progressive education.[1] For *Coming to Our Senses,* the arts—or rather the cultivation of the senses—were seen as a necessary counterweight to reason, or the life of the mind. This whole approach was well put in a quotation from *Synaesthetic Education,* a 1971 book by Michael E. Andrews which *Coming to Our Senses* placed in a position reserved for approved insights:

> To most persons majoring in Art Education, the term is interpreted to mean a preparation for becoming a teacher who is to train individuals from the observation of nature and the ability to record accurately the socially agreed upon symbolic conventions and facts by a process of drawing and painting. . . . The term Art Education in this sense, then, merely confuses the issue, which is not to teach teachers to teach the making of artists; but to free the individual so that he may discover his inner-self and nurture his individual ability to search for, find and apply truths in relation to himself.

Of course, there was nothing in *Coming to Our Senses* about general arts education having as its goal the training of young people in the skills and content of great civilization. The definition of art this 1977 report recommended was, at bottom, to be student-determined:

> Existing standardized material [should] be reevaluated constantly in order to meet the needs of particular student populations. Materials should be changed or amplified if they do not illuminate

[1] *Coming to Our Senses: The Significance of the Arts for American Children*, the 1977 Arts, Education, and Americans Panel Report; ACA Books, 1977 (revised edition 1988).

the students' life experiences or if they condition students to a narrow definition of acceptable forms of art.

At the Endowment, this new approach to arts education was expressed by a policy of supporting not *art* in education but *artists* in education. There were plausible reasons for this policy: school performances given by artists rather than school classes given by teachers nicely avoided conflict with school bureaucracies for control of funds and curriculums; and the provision of performances in schools seemed a massive and welcome employment opportunity for unemployed artists.

Unfortunately, by the time I came to the Endowment in the early 1980s, the deleterious consequences of this policy, which in so many cases resulted in entertainment rather than teaching, were clear. Little arts education of any substantive kind was going on; teachers were sullen and hostile toward what was perceived as an unwanted invasion by artists; and the very idea of arts education, just because it was seen to depend upon the casual and irregular appearances of outsiders, increasingly seemed irrelevant, frivolous, and totally dispensable.

The time was ripe for a change in educational policy. Under Frank Hodsoll's energetic and patient leadership, several changes were made. The name of the program itself, which had been "Artists in Education," was changed to "Arts in Education." On the level of the allocation of funds, an attempt was made to change what was essentially an artist-residency program into one which also allowed for the support of basic education. Furthermore, a strong attempt was made to bring arts teachers, and their representatives, back into Endowment planning, from which they had previously (and with good reason) felt excluded.

Public evidence of what had taken place at the Endowment has now been provided by yet another report, but this time (at least in my opinion) an excellent one. I have in mind *Toward Civilization*, which was prepared by the NEA over a period of about two years and submitted to Congress last May. This report documented the unhappy state of arts education in this country and made substantive suggestions for its amelioration. What seems to me special about this report—so well conveyed by its title—is that it takes a position on just what basic arts education is. Here are the report's opening words:

Basic arts education aims to provide all students, not only the gifted and talented, with knowledge of, and skills in, the arts. Basic arts education must give students the essence of our civilization, the civilizations which have contributed to ours, and the more distant civilizations which enrich world civilization as a whole. It must also give students tools for creating, for communicating and understanding others' communications, and for making informed and critical choices.

And, a bit later, the report goes on:

The first purpose of arts education is to give our young people a sense of civilization. American civilization includes many cultures—from Europe, Africa, the Far East, and our own hemisphere. The great works of art of these parent civilizations, and of our own, provide the guideposts to cultural literacy. Knowing them, our young people will be better able to understand, and therefore build on, the achievements of the past; they will also be better able to understand themselves. Great works of art illuminate the constancy of the human condition . . . . Without knowledge of such supreme achievements, we are "culturally illiterate."

If this is to be the wave of the future, then this is one wave we can look forward to.

The reader will have noticed that, in devoting myself to developments in NEA arts-education policy, I have not as yet had anything to say about the problem I raised earlier: the conversion of art into entertainment. If in arts education I am proud of what has been accomplished at the NEA and moderately optimistic about the effect of its new policy, in the rather more difficult area of our fidelity to the very idea of the arts we serve I am unhappy with the role the Endowment has played in recent years, and I am in no way sanguine about the future.

To illustrate the present situation, allow me to cite a letter I recently received from a person deeply committed to the field of choral music. Here is my paraphrase of what he wrote:

For many among us, choral performance is especially valuable because, combining as it does significant literature with affecting music, it speaks directly to an audience. It is often an irrational concern of ours that we are unable to secure a public for chorus of an equivalent size to that for operas, ballets, and orchestras.

Curiously enough, this sentiment is not restricted to artistic fields which have traditionally enjoyed small audiences: it is widespread throughout the arts today. Yet there is no reason to think that the primary blame for the current direction of the arts in America rests with the people who share these sentiments. As I pointed out earlier, we have always thought of collective activities in terms of quantity and size, and in this country perhaps more than abroad, government has a remarkable record of reflecting the wishes of its citizenry. The problems of the arts are not at heart problems for government to solve; even so, the government does have a role: to inform and educate, and to provide a desired leadership.

In recent years as well as over its entire history, the National Endowment for the Arts has not adequately served to make clear the present over-expanded and over-hyped state of the arts in America. The Endowment has not sufficiently encouraged—and explained the reasons for encouraging—either public or private arts funding based on artistic commitment, taste, and knowledge. Too often the Endowment has accepted the mere existence of funding, both public and private, as a good in itself, without asking the reasons behind this funding and its effect on the education of the public. Too often the Endowment has treated the arts as a matter of the financial and social prestige of its backers rather than as a common inheritance of all. Too often the Endowment has failed to press the general case that the arts are a vital part of the civilization which binds our people to each other in the present and binds our past to our future. Above all, too often the Endowment has treated success in numbers as the criterion not just for funding but for the pride it takes in accomplishing its mission. The effect of all this has been to shake the confidence of artists, patrons, and the public alike, whose faith in art is vital to everything we do.

The most interesting presentations I have heard at the National Council on the Arts have centered on how marvelously successful organizations have grown, and how others might follow in their footsteps. By contrast, the artistic presentations which have been made to the council have usually been of a very drab and second-rate, show-and-tell nature. The discussion of the council, a group of intelligent people reasonably representative of artists, arts institutions, and state arts agencies, have all too often focused on success by numbers, as if all that can be talked about in the arts is marketing strategy. State arts agencies are routinely complimented by council members not for the quality of their grants—or even for the high quality of the activity going on in their jurisdictions—but rather for the year-to-year increases in their budgets; the same criterion of size is used when the discussion turns to local arts agencies. It is significant that when the council focuses on the one Endowment program in which numbers are very difficult to adduce—the Literature Program, which supports individual writers and poets, and small presses—the amount of discussion and interest seems to dwindle to the vanishing point.

There has recently been an important controversy which suggests that this habit of judging art by numbers has now come close to becoming a codified part of the way grants are to be awarded. I have in mind here the policy, proposed by Frank Hodsoll more than a year ago, of determining grant amounts by directly relating an institution's artistic ranking to its budget size. The announced goal of this new policy was to correct various inconsistencies resulting from the present system, whereby institutions of lower artistic ranking and lower budgets from time to time received a greater percentage of their budget support from the Endowment than institutions of higher artistic ranking and higher budgets.

The new policy would involve a major change in the functioning of the Endowment's peer panels, the groups of artists and administrators charged with making the primary decisions about grants. Hitherto, panels had based their judgments first upon artistic ranking, and then adjusted the resulting grant amounts—on an ad hoc basis—so that questions of scale might be taken into account. According to the new policy, panels were to use the scale of applicants' activities, along with their artistic ranking, as a necessary factor in determining grant amounts. The change in the outcome of this new panel process would be great: if budgets were to be a required factor in determining amounts, larger-budget applicants, in a time of flat Endowment appropriations, would receive increased funding, while smaller-budget applicants would receive less. The signal sent to the world of art would be clear: henceforth, artistic achievement would properly be judged by money, not art.

The battle over the chairman's proposed new policy has raged for many months. The possibility of obtaining a more consistent set of grants seemed, at first, reason enough for many, including me, to support the new process. But as an attempt was made to put the new policy into practice, it became clear that the effect would be to make scale of activity the determining factor, and a factor furthermore that would unduly reward large applicants. From various artistic fields came an almost unanimous defense of the present ad hoc process; the chairman, in turn, made a spirited defense of his position that fairness requires the explicit factoring of budget size into grant decisions.

I am happy to say that the National Council on the Arts was drawn into the controversy, and for the first time in my memory there were sustained discussions at the council which explicitly recognized that big budgets and high levels of activity do not necessarily bring with them art of permanent value. These discussions took an often militant "art first, budgets second" position. At the National Council meeting in St. Louis in May, a compromise between the chairman, intent on changing panel procedure, and the council, united in opposition to the idea of grant-making by budget size, was arranged. According to this compromise, information about an applicant's budget size would be made available to panels, which they might use to provide consistency in their grant making; without such consistency, the panels would have to provide explanations for any anomalies that might thus result.

It is difficult to say where we stand now. The primary importance of the artistic judgments made by peer panels, the very heart of the Endowment's traditional way of making grants, has come under attack. The chairman has been widely accused of wishing to impose some kind of formulaic funding. Furthermore, there have been indications that the Congress, under severe pressure in an election year from the artistic fields, might go so far as to use the upcoming Endowment appropriation bill to prohibit any change in the status quo. Should the Congress ever take this matter into its own hands, a questionable precedent would be established whereby the legislature would determine Endowment guidelines.

Unwisely, the defenders of the present system have seen fit to oppose *any* use of budget data in panel deliberations. Moreover, there has been much extravagant talk, from people who are highly capable of rational decision making, about the need to make grants on the basis of intuitiveness and subjectivity. Equally unwisely, the chairman pushed ahead too fast at the beginning with the imposition of his initiative, without waiting for a consensus to be reached outside Washington. What is more, he did not make clear the implications of his new policy—who would get more money, and who would get less.

My own position in this matter is that panels should employ all available data in reaching their decisions; an applicant's budget size should always be taken into consideration, so that the amount of money granted might be in reasonable relation to the quality, activity, and need of the applicant. But just as important, there is no *necessary* correlation between budget size and the artistic needs and aspirations of an artist or of an institution. In awarding grants, it is always vital to be sure that artistic ranking is based on talent and aspiration, not on the advantages money can buy.

So important is all this for the future of the relations between the applicants and the Endowment, and indeed for the future status and working of the Endowment itself, that it behooves use to stand back and look dispassionately at the core of the controversy. This core is our old national problem of the supposed virtue of size. Size of audience, it goes without saying, is closely related to size of budget; within any given artistic field, institutions with larger audiences almost always have larger budgets. More expensive productions draw larger audiences; larger audiences cost more to satisfy (I almost wrote "to entertain"). Artistic ranking itself, properly the primary concern of panels, is often closely related to budget size; bigger budgets, after all, mean more money for artists, more money for productions and exhibitions, more money for administrators to arrange better presentations, more money for development personnel to raise more money for better presentations—and for bigger budgets.

None of this is necessarily wrong. It is all just a fact of life: the race is often to the large as well as to the swift. But to put matters this way is once again to load the discussion in favor of big budgets, big audiences, and the performance of entertainments that allow audiences to grow. Alas, it is no secret that today it is not the biggest and the busiest arts organizations that are under the strongest economic pressure; it is rather the medium-sized institutions, deeply rooted in medium-sized communities, that are beginning to feel the threat of financial failure. A quick glance at our marvelous symphony orchestras of intermediate budget size will show an increasing and unacceptable attrition rate over the recent past; the salvation of these institutions does not lie in the expansion of budgets, even if such expansion might bring larger government grants; it lies in the stabilization of their costs and, at the same time, the artistic education of their audiences and private contributors.

Above all, there is no way in which the concentration on largeness of budget per se as a criterion for support can do anything but further degrade the image of the arts and the civilization which we all wish to further. It is high time that we recognize the primary artistic contribution made by serious institutions and artists who cultivate neither the celebrity glamour of big budgets nor the artificially controversial hype of the so-called avant-garde "cutting edge."

This position can be summed up in a credo: The greatest art, just as the greatest civilization, is the heritage of all. Therefore, education in art is the noblest function of the artist, just as education in the humanities is the noblest function of the humanist. To accomplish this function, the idea of art must be kept as something shining, golden—and serious. To cherish this elevated idea of art cannot be the task of artists alone; it also must be the task of all, politicians, patrons, and public alike, who cherish the future of civilization in a democratic and capitalist society.

Epilogue

At this point, little needs to be said, other than to remark that this article appeared in the December 1989 New Criterion—*and to thank the reader.*

Redefining Culture and Democracy

CULTURE AND DEMOCRACY: these two words are central, separately and in association, both to the discussion of art in our society and to the larger debate about the meaning and the organization of life that has so occupied intellectuals in our time. The current definitions of these crucial terms have proven to be unstable and subject to the changing pressures of politics and the moral upheavals of the present day. As a result, the words *culture* and *democracy* themselves are now in danger of becoming unusable if they cannot be rigorously redefined in a way that makes them relevant both to the life of art and to the vitality of our democratic institutions.

It is this making of distinctions in an area so given to their blurring that I shall attempt here, in full consciousness of the hazards involved in redefining terms that so many have used and through which so many vested interests have been created. Culture, in the form of music, has been the work of my life; democracy is the political system under which we live, as well as the political system under which we, in view of the alternatives, would certainly choose to live. For many of us, our lives are in some way dedicated to culture; for us all, our lives are perforce dedicated to democracy. Ours is not the first historical period to notice the standing tension between the existence of culture and the extension of democracy, but ours may well be the first period in which free men feel it necessary to choose between them.

"Culture" and "democracy" are, of course, ideals. As ideals they sum up and embrace a multitude of our thoughts, our hopes, and, not least, our confusions. As ideals they also raise questions of ultimate meaning; unfortunately our own time is, as perhaps never before, uncomfortable with "ultimate" questions. Indeed, what is perhaps most distinctive about our spiritual life is our inability to deal with these most fundamental questions, even though we have hardly lost the need to ask them. In this regard, we are all children of the age; for us, merely to entertain the possibility of such questions is to hear the chill voice of skepticism and doubt.

Any attempt at redefining words like *culture* and *democracy* can hardly escape the charge of quixotry, if not a charge of something worse. We all know that the idiosyncratic use of words is the most foolish of lost causes: it lends itself first to miscommunication and finally, if kept up long enough, to the charge of madness. Yet the attempt must be made. Definitions are fundamental to normative social thought; in the very act of defining our terms we go a long way toward defining goals. So central are the issues involved in this case that when we talk about culture and democracy we are doing more than talking about mind and the polity. We are proclaiming, both by commission and by omission, how we want to live—or, more precisely, how we want our children to live; we are, in other words, offering a vision of the future.

The best way, then, to begin to offer this vision is, I believe, to remind ourselves how these two words, *culture* and *democracy*, have been related to each other since the Enlightenment. In the eighteenth century, the chief threat to culture—if by culture is meant the life of the mind—seemed to come from the once monolithic structures of church and state. Even before the French Revolution, and for long after, the enemies of culture were seen to be the holders of established power. These included the inheritors of ascribed status, landed wealth, and spiritual office. Culture, accordingly, was thought to be achieved not through cooperation with the status quo, but in resistance to it— resistance in the name of democracy. In music, for example, this was the significance of the careers of Beethoven and Wagner, two eminent heroes of nineteenth-century culture: Beethoven's visions of human brotherhood in the Ninth Symphony and of freedom in *Fidelio*, like Wagner's combination of revolutionary politics and revolutionary music, symbolized the Enlightenment and post-Enlightenment linkage of culture and democracy.

The twentieth century has taught the world things about political evil that the nineteenth century was incapable even of imagining. Nevertheless, in the present time this received idea about the union of culture and democracy has remained an unquestioned truth. When the autocracies of Prussianized Germany and Tsarist Russia gave way to the bloody tyrannies of Hitler's Nazism and Lenin's and Stalin's Bolshevism, the correlation between cultural barbarism and political dictatorship was made perfect. Two world wars served to vindicate the claims of culture against tyranny; merely to mention all those groups in the 1930s, 1940s, and 1950s devoted to the defense of culture is to recall that the struggle against Hitler, Mussolini, Stalin, and Mao was carried on in a significant and effective way in the name of culture.

The lesson that was drawn from this struggle for culture was plain. If autocracy and tyranny were the enemies of the life of the mind, the only possible friend of culture was (and is) democracy, now understood in wider and wider terms as the bearer of equally distributed political, social, and economic power. For intellectuals everywhere, the freedom necessary for the future of culture would then, and can now, only be assured through the universal victory of democracy in its most expanded definition.

Once democracy and its accompanying political, social, and economic freedoms had become the essential preconditions guaranteeing the health of culture, it was only a short step to seeing democracy itself as congruent with cultural vitality and integrity. As democracy was increasingly identified with the health of culture, it became increasingly convenient to equate democracy with culture; precisely because democracy was taken to mean unfettered cultural expression, culture came to be understood not in terms of its specific content, but as an expression of unfettered democratic freedom. It is this merging of culture and democracy that so confounds us today, and that, as we now see, is spreading to societies other than our own.

Thus, in our attempt to understand the fate of culture under our democratic system, more is involved than an effort to comprehend our own condition; for we are living in a world increasingly concerned to imitate, at least superficially, both the Western political model and the role it accords to culture. It is not clear whether the end of the twentieth century is witnessing the kind of global triumph of liberal democracy that Francis Fukuyama has envisioned in a much-debated article in the *National Interest*, the American foreign-policy journal.[1] Nor is it clear whether the recent fitful and tentative dismantlings of tyranny in the USSR and Communist China represent anything more than the beginnings of new autocracies; recent Chinese events are hardly reassuring. But whether or not the prospects for democracy in these hitherto unfortunate societies are bright, it cannot be doubted that much is going on in them that is conceived in the Western image; much that happens will be judged, to some extent at least, by the criteria and the rhetoric the West has developed in the name of democracy.

What, then, are the salient characteristics of this democratic model in our society? Ours is a form of government that seems to provide the largest measure of political stability. It is a form of government that has made possible (or has at least presided over) a hitherto unimagined prosperity in material life, unparalleled social mobility, and sweeping intellectual change. Another side to these usually admired developments cannot be ignored; this other side of liberal democracy is the hitherto unimagined, and unimaginably rapid, destruction of traditional ways of life, disciplined social structures, cherished habits of faith, and inherited moral values.

There is no need to dwell either on Western material prosperity or on the social price being paid for this prosperity. Whether the shift of population from country to city, the reformulation of sexual roles, supersonic travel, the benefits of consumer electronics, and the new information technologies—whether these and other related developments counterbalance, for example, the destruction of the family and the gutting of organized religious belief, cannot now be known; it does seem likely that the West's new prosperity and new freedoms are inextricably linked to the anomie, to the emptiness and the nihilism so many witness in daily life, and feel inside themselves.

The discussion of liberal democracy and its future thus ineluctably leads us back to the question of culture. What is the state of culture in the lands known as the liberal democracies? One is tempted to answer that, in one sense at least, culture is thriving. Indeed, never before in human history have so many people created so much culture,

[1] Francis Fukuyama's "The End of History" appeared in the *National Interest*'s Summer 1989 issue.

and been so richly rewarded for doing so. As we go down our mean Walkmanned streets, as we shop in tawdry malls and order from mawkish catalogues, as we watch trivial television programs and go to coarse movies, as bloated new careers continue to be made in mass entertainment, the fact is inescapable: we are veritably drowning in culture.

The question, of course, is what precisely is now meant by this word *culture*. To begin to answer this question is to confront the conundrums of definition, for the immediate and obvious reply to this question is simple: culture now includes everything, because as a term it now means little more than how people behave. If culture means behavior, there is indeed a lot of behaving—and misbehaving—going on.

To take comfort in this catchall definition of culture as behavior is surely to delude ourselves, for such acquiescence only invites a further question: if culture is to be defined merely as behavior, what place is there for the life of the mind? And here, as we start to address the present state of the life of the mind in our democracies, we find ourselves not only despondent in the present but pessimistic about the future. For those of us who have dedicated our lives to culture construed as the life of the mind, it is hardly too much to say that the word *culture* now hardly belongs to us at all.

Our loss is documented in the shifting definitions over time of the word *culture* itself. Of course, this word is notoriously difficult to define; not only has it been subject to a continuous process of redefinition by its friends, but it has proven all too easy for its enemies to define away. It is obvious to all that in its general usage the word *culture* has undergone a major shift in meaning and use over the last century and more.

A century ago, culture meant an ideal of intellectual and spiritual aspiration—the "study of perfection," as Matthew Arnold put it in *Culture and Anarchy* (1869). The Germans meant something very similar when they talked early in the nineteenth century of *Kultur*. In our own time, culture has come to mean no more than a description of observed behavior, as in Ruth Benedict's influential *Patterns of Culture* (1934). This shift is nothing less than a constitutive movement of thought and belief away from culture conceived of as the pursuit of what the Germans called *Bildung*, to culture conceived of in purely anthropological terms; as a shift, in other words, away from the formation of mind and character to the description of how individuals and peoples actually live. Put another way, this anthropologizing of culture quickly became in practice a mere rationalization of an often repellent social reality, rather than a constantly developing realization of the best and most hopeful features of that reality.

The loss of the older meaning of culture has been keenly felt. An attempt has been made by those who remain attached to the concept of culture as an ideal to reappropriate it via the use of a qualifying adjective. And so *high* has gotten itself attached to *culture*, and the combination—high culture, as we say—is in wide use. Though it has seemed natural to employ the phrase *high culture,* and though its use now can hardly be avoided, one cannot overlook the fact that the result of this semantic jiggery-pokery has been unsatisfactory. The understandable and even excusable addition of *high* has hardly managed to save *culture* in its former sense; the very need to distinguish high culture has done little more than make it one culture among many "taste cultures," to use sociologist Herbert Gans's rather untasty phrase. If in modern usage *culture* is taken to describe the behavior of primitive peoples and of the industrialized masses, *high culture* is increasingly used to describe the tastes of a putatively social elite. The life of the mind has thus come to be seen as little more than a battle between what might be called nobs and mobs, or as what might better be called, now that Marxist economics has been so badly discredited, an updated version of the class struggle.

Not only is culture now split into high and low, elite and popular, refined and vulgar; the simpler expressions *a culture* and *cultures* are now used only to sum up and organize anthropo-sociological descriptions of behavior. Of the former conception of culture as an aspiration to accomplishment and as the achievement of that aspiration, there now remains precious little. Of respect for culture existing outside the marketplace, for culture existing beyond the techniques of marketing, there is little more than a memory existing in the minds of the old. In its place we have what can only be called an entertainment industry, the matching of vulgar offerings with popular tastes through the agency of publicity and manufactured glamour. It can be simply put: increasingly, what counts is commercial success, nothing less and nothing more.

How much of this present situation of culture—construed, it must be stressed, as the life of the mind—is the inevitable and irreversible result of democracy? An answer to this question must begin, as in the case of culture, with a definition of the word. *Democracy*, even more than *culture*, is a word whose definition changes with its proponents; it would be idle to expect a word that grew strong in revolution, and has for so many years formed the centerpiece of revolutionary rhetoric, to have suffered a different fate.

How, then, is *democracy* to be defined? There is, of course, a simple definition of democracy: the organization of political consent through frequent and free elections, in which representatives are chosen for fixed terms to perform defined executive and legislative tasks. On this definition, democracy is no more than a convenience—a blessed and necessary convenience, to be sure—that makes possible the orderly and predictable conduct of official business and the peaceful transfer of political power from and to individuals and groups.

But it is not this simple definition of democracy that is most compelling in liberal democracies today. Democracy is now taken to suggest a metaphysical structure, a means of explaining the human personality and even more of forming it. Anything anyone wants, and everything everyone wants, is found to have its place in democratic theory and practice. Indeed, today democracy has only friends—but with such friends, who needs enemies?

As a result, *democracy*, like *culture*, hardly seems to exist any longer as a word without another word qualifying it. The necessity of this addition of various adjectives only marks the change that has overtaken the idea of democracy from its origins as a mechanism for arranging the social division of political power to its present function as a principle for organizing all of life. And so we have what might be called the hyphenated democracies: economic democracy, social democracy, capitalist democracy, people's democracy, participatory democracy, sexual democracy, cultural democracy, even liberal democracy.

What must be questioned is what these compound terms mean, and what they say about democracy. It is clear that on the whole they use the immense prestige, the philosophical rhetoric, and the political trappings of democracy to advance particular social visions that are not necessarily democratic. A few explanations tell the story: economic democracy now means the achievement of socialism; social democracy means egalitarianism; capitalist democracy, free market economics; people's democracy, Stalinism; participatory democracy, the rule of a mob led by intellectuals; sexual democracy, libertinism; cultural democracy, the farther shores of behavioral relativism; even our own liberal democracy increasingly uses the appearances of tradition and conservatism to camouflage and make palatable a relentlessly secular and socially dynamic society.

These visions most often have their origins not in any historical understanding of a merely political democracy or in any sympathy with it, but rather in hostile attempts at the conquest of social power; the Marxist–Bolshevist transformation of democracy into dictatorship is a supreme example of this alchemy. But at least gross phenomena, by their very brutality, make resistance to them possible. Such now hardly seems the case in the relatively humane environments of the liberal democracies. Here expansive democracy sings a siren song, a song attractive to those whose yearnings stretch into the future rather than back into the past.

America in particular has been populated with those for whom a limited political definition of democracy has not been enough. Foremost among these evangelists in the name of a supra-political democratic ethos was, of course, Walt Whitman. For Whitman, writing in 1867 in *Democratic Vistas*, democracy was "the best, perhaps only, fit and full means, formulator, general caller-forth, trainer, for the millions, not for grand material personalities only, but for immortal souls." Democracy's task in culture was to conquer, and in its victory it was to take no prisoners:

> I say that democracy can never prove itself beyond cavil, until it founds and luxuriantly grows its own forms of art, poems, schools, theology, displacing all that exists, or that has been produced anywhere in the past, under opposite influences.

So radical was democracy in Whitman's formulation that its culture was to be based, just as our contemporary definition would have it, on equal participation by, and equal contributions from, all. Consider the following lines from "I Hear America Singing," of which only the title is usually quoted:

I hear America singing, the varied carols I hear,
Those of mechanics, each one singing his as it should be blithe
    and strong,
The carpenter singing his as he measures his plank or beam . . .

The delicious singing of the mother, or of the young wife at
    work, or of the girl sewing or washing,
Each singing what belongs to him or her and to none else,
The day what belongs to the day—at night the party of young
    fellows, robust, friendly,
Singing with open mouths their strong melodious songs.

Here surely is Whitman's definitive statement, not simply of democratic culture, but of cultural democracy, the equalizing of all expression.

Thus Whitman's unfettered ejaculation of raw emotion, what he called his "barbaric yawp," now seems thoroughly modern in going beyond poetry to the imperatives of ideology; it is just as modern in the way his ideology ends up replacing the poetry with which it began. The result is surely not a statement of aesthetics, but of a world-encompassing and world-delivering crusade, a proclamation of democratic ideology as a way of life and in every sphere of life.

Here, already existing full-blown more than a century ago, is the definitive opposition to the Arnoldian idea of culture. Whitman's very title—*Democratic Vistas*—could not stand in greater contrast to Arnold's contemporaneous *Culture and Anarchy*. Whereas Whitman saw democracy not only as properly driving out everything past and present but as containing within itself every provision for the living of life, Arnold saw democracy as what he called "machinery," a mere set of contingent arrangements, among them a large population, abundant natural resources, an efficient transportation system, wealth, religious organization, and even freedom itself, providing a way to accomplish ends but not constituting any idea of the ends themselves. Because democracy, in Arnold's view, failed to provide transcendent values, its exercise without the external provision of values led inevitably to a collapse of social purpose and cohesion.

Because Arnold despised the organization of English society, in which he saw a hateful "spectacle of an upper class materialised, a middle class vulgarised, [and] a lower class brutalised," he was able to admire the achievement of American democracy in creating a very nearly classless society. But though Arnold was a friend of democracy, he did not confuse democracy with culture; he did not confuse political arrangements—even the best political arrangements—with the ends of man and society. For Arnold, it must be stressed, democracy was "machinery," and culture was the pursuit of the ends of life.

The evidence of the past century suggests that Arnold was indeed right in finding democracy incapable in itself of providing the ends of life, of generating the values by which a society and its citizens can live. And it is a measure of just how right Arnold was in this matter that the advocates of democracy have everywhere found it necessary to engage in the task of hyphenating, and thus transforming, a simple notion of democracy.

History has shown us the folly of making democracy the handmaiden of egalitarian and distributivist economics; it may well now be demonstrating the folly of making democracy and its freedoms the facilitator of pan-sexuality. In the area of culture, it is as yet little noticed how it is our practice of using democratic political arrangements in order to accomplish wider social goals that now exerts a terrible pressure on culture—defined, it must be stressed yet again, as the life of the mind. For example, it is the economic success achieved under democratic political arrangements that has created a market for mass entertainment that dwarfs other, more profound achievements of mind and spirit. Above all, it is the triumphant egalitarianism of democracy that under the pretext of equal access to culture alters, lowers, and finally destroys its content.

If culture—defined, it must be stressed, as the life of the mind— is thus to be inextricably tied to the ideology of democracy, then the implications for the relationship between culture and democracy are clear: culture and democracy cannot coexist, for democracy by its nature represents the many, and culture, by its nature, is created by the few. What the many cannot immediately comprehend, they destroy; what the few cannot directly control, they reject. In sum, it is very difficult these days to resist the idea that, whereas the principal threat to culture was once perceived to come from the established order of status, wealth, and office, it now comes from another establishment— a demagogic establishment that demands the unthinking and uncritical extension of democratic ideology into every area of intellectual and social life.

It is very tempting to derive from this analysis a wholesale condemnation of mass society, by which is meant the social life characteristic of modernity itself. This is a temptation we must resist. We must be clear that such a condemnation signifies nothing less than a rejection of the value of all social life from the beginnings of what is so quaintly called the Age of Reason to today. Unfortunately, as powerful and accurate as such a condemnation of modernity is in many of its diagnoses, it fails to take necessary account of the gains in the physical quality of human life (made possible by the achievements of the natural sciences and technology and made available through capitalism) and of the continuing ability of countless millions— despite the stresses of modernity—to carry on private life in a public maelstrom, to find personal meaning amidst the social chaos.

There is no need to remark here that mass society and modernity together represent an epochal movement in human history. They daunt any Canute to dares to stand in their way. And yet, powerful as they are, they cannot be more than what we—all of us—make of them. Our present-day ideas of culture and democracy are prime fruits of modern thought; it can hardly be doubted that, insofar as society is concerned, the current, confused usage of the words *culture* and *democracy* expresses, in the most exact way, what the nineteenth century chose to call the *Zeitgeist*—the spirit of the age.

Still, there is every reason to question the current degraded definitions of culture and democracy and reflect on what culture and democracy might mean as words and as ideas. This questioning, in producing a redefinition of these key terms, can suggest what must be done in individual thought and individual action. Surely it is not quixotry to cite, in support of this necessary going it alone, the famous passage on such putatively lost causes from Arnold's *Culture and Anarchy*, a passage that powerfully encourages our seemingly foredoomed twentieth-century advocacy of an older idea of culture:

> Oxford, the Oxford of the past, has many faults, and she has heavily paid for them in defeat, in isolation, in want of hold upon the modern world. Yet we in Oxford, brought up amidst the beauty and sweetness of that beautiful place, have not failed to

seize one truth,—the truth that beauty and sweetness are essential characters of a complete human perfection . . . [a]nd the sentiment is true, and has never been wholly defeated, and has shown its power even in its defeat. We have not won our political battles, we have not carried our main points, we have not stopped our adversaries' advance, we have not marched victoriously with the modern world; but we have told silently upon the mind of the country, we have prepared currents of feeling which sap our adversaries' position when it seems gained, we have kept up our own communications with the future.

Once we have made up our mind that there is purpose and grandeur in backing the right lost causes—not least because not all lost causes are, in the long run, truly lost—we must ask what, then, these great words might come to mean to us. What is necessary are definitions of culture and democracy based less on the muddling of definitions and more on their clarification, less on inclusions and more on exclusions, less of finding similarities between conflicting realities, concepts, and goals and more on recognizing the differences between them. Put another way, these two great words, *culture* and *democracy*, deserve to be defined by what they can accurately represent, rather than by what they can be made, through rhetoric and compromise, to accommodate.

Before we can begin to find a proper definition of culture, we must be clear about one thing: despite the fact that *culture*, as a word suggesting the finer things of life, still moves us, we can no longer expect its mere invocation to manage the necessary revivification. There will be those who will say that what Emerson wrote in the middle of the nineteenth century is still true: "The word of ambition at the present day is Culture." But just how much times have changed is shown by the words Emerson added: "Whilst all the world is in pursuit of power, and of wealth as a means of power, culture corrects the theory of success." Unfortunately, the only aspect of *culture* as a word that has remained constant to the present day is its prestige— and it is in the nature of culture's prestige today that it is no longer a way of correcting what is in fact the worship of success; it is instead in the hands of its boosters a capitulation to the notion of success that for Emerson culture was destined to combat. We all, it seems, stand to attention for culture; but the culture we salute is not the arduous acquisition of the knowledge of greatness, but rather an easy way of occupying our lives without getting our hands dirty.

The time has come, then, to stop using the word *culture* to describe the totality of our past and present social experience. The time has also come to stop using *culture* to embrace and dignify every product of our own minds, no matter how ephemeral or how trivial, how vulgar or how coarse. Instead, let us consider an alternative to this debased idea of culture, the alternative to be found, for example, in Arnold. It is necessary to go against the stream and use this simple, lonely word to mean what it meant in what now seems the last hopeful period of Western civilization, the second half of the nineteenth century: the aspiration (in Arnold's formulation) to possess and live "the best that has been thought and known." This is not just a call for a return to Arnold; it is more important that it is a call for a return to hope.

In this definition, culture consists of the masterpieces of intellectual and aesthetic activity made transmissible in written words or in images possessing corporeal existence. The corpus of culture is ongoing and permanent. It is continuously subject to distillation and selection. It is in the short term fragile, but in the end it is all that remains of what we have done. Though culture may originate in any past of a society, its perpetuation is usually of necessity in the hands of a self-selecting and self-sacrificing remnant, Arnold's term for the guardians of righteousness; it is the function of this remnant to preserve culture, even when, as it all too often seems today, it seems so difficult to create.

Why, it may be asked, should we aspire to live the life of culture? Why this unremitting labor, this sacrifice of immediate and assured pleasures, this eternal pursuit of an unattainable perfection? Because culture, in an age when it is so hard to embrace the divine, when pursued in itself and on its own terms, represents our best secular means of transcendence; because of all worldly activity culture comes closest to revealing, and conserving, the best of which we are capable.

But there is yet more in the way of an answer to the question, "Why culture?" Culture encapsulates the most abstract and distilled achievements of what Arnold called "the humanisation of man in society." It is the genius of culture to use beauty—the beauty of words, sounds, images—to carry and transmit the most profound truths about our human lives. These truths, often though not always religious in origin, not only describe what we are; they describe what we should be. They are, in short, the highest values—of knowledge of good and evil, of liberty and discipline, of joy and sorrow, of righteousness, work, understanding, courage, loyalty, friendship, pity, love—values that we recognize and that we try to live. Because the verdict of history is that living a life of culture leads to the living of life itself; because culture, by enduring, can make us comprehend that life—not the lives of men, but the life of man—endures; because the life of culture embodies the values of life, it can teach us that all our lives are worth living.

Against this definition, it has often been noted that horrifying crimes have been committed in this century in the name of *Kultur* by those whose proud boast it was to speak for civilization. These crimes have cast a pall over the very possibility of the humanizing power of art and learning. With this tragic failure in mind, it would be all too easy for us to turn upon the very notion of civilization itself, and think that by giving up the heights of civilization we might trade culture for life. But to make such a choice would be to charge culture with the duty of transforming the instinctual core of man, and then to find culture guilty of failing to effect this transformation. To have this expectation of what can be no more than a fallible human process is to forsake the possible in favor of the impossible, the realizable in favor of the utopian. Culture, it cannot be repeated too often, is not a guarantee; it is a goal.

What of *democracy?* What might constitute a viable definition for this other great word of the age? A realistic definition of democracy makes one thing clear: *democracy* is a term describing a legal process through which political power is allocated through electoral means. In a functioning political democracy, politics is only a part, albeit a necessary part, of human life; politics is not the governing principle of life or its *raison d'être.* Neither politics nor democracy is to be construed as the end of life. By providing liberty, democracy makes the exercise of freedom possible; by providing a widely agreed-upon set of procedures, the pursuit of permanent values concerning the ends of life is made possible with a lessened danger of internecine conflict and slaughter.

Viewed in this way, extra-political values are not immanent in democracy. Democracy cannot properly impose any other values than those that regulate the conduct of public business. Democracy, taken by and in itself, has little or nothing to say either about how we should live or about how we should die; still less does democracy provide us, outside the world of political process, with "a way of life." Democracy does not provide the answer to the most important questions of life; it gives us the space, the time, the freedom, and above all the social peace in which to try to find these answers—elsewhere, in our personal lives, and in that realm of spirit we call culture.

Historically religion has been the primary source of mankind's highest values, and to say that a return to culture (as properly understood) is our hope is not to state that a culture of this world can replace a religion of the next. To place our hope in culture is merely to note that, as we speculate about possible new sources of transcendent values, we have no choice but to conserve and extend in art, in learning, in every realm of the spirit that which we have received from thousands of years of civilization and thus from religion itself.

We live in a time of big government, of big corporations, of big foundations, and of an immense and highly developed mass market. In recent years government, in response to both the power and the weakness of the private sphere, has assumed ever more of a leading role in culture. Just because government in the United States is responsive to political constituencies, there will inevitably be increasing pressures to use public power to make culture serve the needs of what I have called an all-encompassing definition of democracy. To capitulate to these pressures would be to reduce culture to a mere expression of the democratic impulse. To do so would mean both the end of culture and the triumph of politics over life.

Our need today is not for a forced unification of culture and democracy, but for their amicable separation, based upon a careful definition of, and respect for, what each can accomplish. When we speak—as we inevitably do in a political democracy—of democratic culture, we must be clear that we mean not, as Whitman demanded, a life of the mind coming equally from all and appealing equally to all, but a life of the mind available to all. We must always be careful to remember that while it is the task of democracy to govern, it is the task of culture to make the best sense we can, this side of eternity, of life itself.

Index

Abel, Lionel, 120n
Abraham, F. Murray, 235
Academy of Ancient Music, 38
Achron, Joseph, 256
Adams, Ansel, 349
Adams, Brian, *La Stupenda*, 270n
Adams, John, 32, 64, 104, 110, 122,127;
   Grand Pianola Music, 82, 83; *Nixon in*
   China, 107, 110, 125, 131, 213
Adkins, Paul Spenser, 196
Adler, Kurt Herbert, 32, 146, 152,152n
Adler, Mortimer J., *The Paideia Proposal*,
   13
Altmeyer, Jeannine, 263, 264
Alwin, Karl, 290
Amadeus (film), 235
American Academy in Rome, 377
American Council for the Arts, 1, 380,
   384, 396n
American Guitar Institute, 103
American String Quartet, 63, 74
American Symphony Orchestra, 52, 103
American Symphony Orchestra League,
   135, 319, 351
American Theatre, 168
Amsterdam Concertgebouw, 249n
Anderson, Laurie, 30, 128, 169, 179, 379
Anderson, Marian, 280-285
Andrews, Michael E., *Synaesthetic*
   Education, 409
Annals, 67n
Argento, Dominick, 156; *Casanova*, 33,
   105, 106, 106n, 131, 181-187,198, 208
Arnold, Malcolm, 60
Arnold, Matthew, 387, 421, 425-426, 427,
   429; *Culture and Anarchy*, 387, 421, 425,
   427; "Dover Beach," 262, 325; *Stanzas*
   from the Grande Chartreuse, 126

Arthurs, Alberta, 377
Art Institute of Chicago, 363
Arts Review, 210, 377
Ashkenazy, Vladimir, 227
Ashley, Robert, *Private Lives*, 149
Aspen Music Festival, 50, 51, 52, 57, 73
Austral, Florence, 290

Babbitt, Milton, 30, 69, 72, 79;
Bach, Johann Sebastian, 36, 37, 38, 45, 60,
   66, 70, 87, 104, 219-225, 233, 243, 249,
   257, 403; *The Art of Fugue*, 61, 219-220;
   Chromatic Fantasy, 83, 231; *Musical*
   Offering, 220
Bain, Wilfred, 26
Baker's Biographical Dictionary of
   Musicians, 255
Balaban, Emanuel, 204n
Balanchine, George, 349, 355, 384, 405
Balassa, Sandor, *Lupercalia*, 82, 83
Bales, Richard, 49
Barber, Samuel, 56, 59, 69n, 70, 156, 251;
   Adagio for Strings, 21, 69n; *Antony and*
   Cleopatra, 48, 156, 189, 197, 198; Sonata,
   46, 243, 250; Violin Concerto, 59, 61
Barbirolli, John, 290
Barnes, Edward, 133
Barnett, John, 48
Barnum, P. T., 348
Barrett, Michael, 160n
Bartók, Béla, 45, 60, 67, 69n, 79, 81, 153,
   243, 250; *Bluebeard's Castle*, 155, 285;
   Concerto for Orchestra, 20, 78; Piano
   Concerto no. 3, 46, 244, 264, 297-298
Barzun, Jacques, *Romanticism and the*
   Modern Ego, 78
Baudelaire, Charles, 86
Bayreuth Festival, 266, 291, 292

Beaumarchais, Pierre-Augustin Caron de, 110
Beckett, Samuel, 87
Beecham, Sir Thomas, 24, 111
Beethoven, Ludwig van, 37, 45, 50, 63, 66, 67, 73, 74, 87, 104, 126, 219, 231, 240, 243, 250, 257, 314*n*, 319, 344, 347, 418; "Emperor" Concerto, 83, 249; *Fidelio*, 142, 260, 418; Symphony no. 7, 308, 310, 311
Behrens, Hildegard, 108, 259, 264, 266
Bellini, Vincenzo, 270, 273
Belmont, Mrs. August, 364
Benedict, Ruth, *Patterns of Culture*, 421
Bennett, William J., 358
Bentham, Jeremy, 59
Berg, Alban, 31, 81, 137; *Lulu*, 110, 211, 260; *Wozzeck*, 77, 77*n*, 110, 260
Bergsma, William, 29, 72, 72*n*
Berio, Luciano, 90; *Sinfonia*, 86, 87
Berlin Philharmonic, 304, 306-313, 314, 314*n*, 361
Berlin State Opera Orchestra, 267
Berlioz, Hector, 190, 323; *Romeo and Juliet*, 299, 301
Bernstein, Leonard, 22, 25, 29, 33, 48, 77, 92, 100, 111, 112, 113, 116, 117, 156, 157, 295, 297, 301, 303; *Candide*, 134, 144
Bianconi, Philippe, 234
Biddle, Livingston, 341, 365, 397, 399
Bilson, Malcolm, 126
Bing, Sir Rudolf, 152, 189, 282
Bizet, Georges, *Carmen*, 199, 212
Blacher, Boris, 60
Black, Robert, 79
Blair Quartet, 73
Blech, Leo, 111, 289, 290
Bliss, Anthony, 98, 99, 146, 147,148, 152
Blitzstein, Marc, 22, 157-158; *The Cradle Will Rock*, 22, 157-163; *Regina*, 133, 153
Bloch, Ernest, 59-60, 71; *America: an Epic Rhapsody*, 60, 61

Bloom, Allan, *The Closing of the American Mind*, 65
Blunt, Anthony, 365
Blyth, Alan, 65, 276
Bodanzky, Artur, 111
Böhm, Karl, 266, 313
Bolshoi Ballet, 347
Bolshoi Opera, 153
Bonynge, Richard, 268, 270, 273, 276, 277
Borges, Jorge Luis, 116
Boston Pops, 382-383
Boston Symphony Orchestra, 23, 24, 26, 37, 49, 295, 302, 305, 306, 326, 348
Boucher, Gene, 146
Boulanger, Nadia, 21, 158, 166
Boulez, Pierre, 30, 31, 48, 53-54, 77, 79, 83, 87, 92, 93, 97, 111, 112, 266, 301, 303, 321, 323
Boult, Adrian, 111
Bradley, Gwendolyn, 84
Brahms, Johannes, 63, 67, 232, 233, 240, 249, 257, 284, 314*n*; *Alto Rhapsody*, 283-284, 284*n*; Concerto in D minor, 234, 249*n*; Symphony no. 2, 298-299
Brecht, Bertolt, 158, 159, 162
Brenner, Janet, 136, 137, 139, 140, 141*n*
Brinkmann, Reinhold, 118, 122
Britten, Benjamin, 99, 133, 137, 211, 214, 261; *Billy Budd*, 110, 134, 210; *Peter Grimes*, 110, 134, 210
Brooklyn Academy of Music, 125, 170; "Next Wave" festival, 164-165, 178, 180
Brown, Earle, 30
Brown, Trisha, 165
Bruckner, Anton, 307, 314
Bryden, Jane, 82
Bryn-Julson, Phyllis, 79
Budapest Quartet, 23, 68
Bülow, Hans von, 112
Burke, Edmund, *Reflections on the Revolution in France*, 392

Burnham, James, *Managerial Revolution,* 377

Burrows, Candace, 196

Busch, Adolf, 23, 37, 255

Busoni, Ferruccio, 155, 209, 249

Byrne, David, 30, 128; *the Knee Plays,* 168, 169

Cage, John, 8-9, 23, 30, 48, 56, 69, 72, 115-122, 222, 349; Charles Eliot Norton Lectures, 115-122; *4'33",* 30, 121; *Imaginary Landscape No. 1,* 23, 121

Callas, Maria, 273, 273*n,* 274, 277, 278

Cambridge University, 362

Cardew, Cornelius, 54

Carlos, Wendy, 223

Carlyle, Thomas, 117

Carlson, Carolyn, 165

Carnegie Hall, 38, 95, 101-102, 103, 127, 235*n,* 244, 246, 249, 251, 281, 282, 314

Carroll, Lewis, *Alice in Wonderland,* 31, 80, 116, 400

Carson, Johnny, 125

Carter, Elliott, 29, 32, 47, 48, 56, 60, 69, 69*n,* 71, 79, 93, 117, 349, 403; Piano Concerto, 49-52, 54

Caruso, Enrico, 268, 270, 274-275, 278

Carvalho, Eleazar, 51

Casadesus, Robert, 23, 243

Casals, Pablo, 227

Cassidy, Claudia, 26

Central Opera Service, 131

Chadwick, George, 70, 71*n*

Chagall, Marc, 99

Chamber Music America, 351

Chapin, Schuyler, 135, 152

Charles Eliot Norton Lectures, 115-122

Charlip, Remy, 165

Chausson, Ernest, 80

Chavez, Carlos, 60, 116, 116*n*

Chicago Lyric Opera, 32, 40, 134, 146, 147

Chicago Symphony Orchestra, 23, 238, 305, 375, 400

Childs, Lucinda, 165, 173, 174, 175, 176

Chopin, Frédéric, 37, 45, 50, 51, 83, 231, 233, 239, 240, 243, 249

Chorus America, 403

Christian Science Monitor, 119

Christo, 379

Chung, Myung-Whun, 295

Cilea, Francesco, 99

Cincinnati Symphony Orchestra, 50*n*

Clemenceau, Georges, 260

Clementi, Muzio, 250; *Gradus ad Parnassum,* 242

Cleveland Institute of Music, 318, 321

Cleveland Orchestra, 23, 26, 295, 305, 321, 326, 375

Cleveland Quartet, 68

Cliburn, Van, 37, 227-229, 235, 239-240

Clurman, Harold, 27

Coates, Albert, 249, 288, 289, 290, 292

Coates, George, 146

Cocteau, Jean, 27

Coleman, Ornette, 69

Collingwood, Lawrance, 289

Columbia Artists Management, 8, 49, 307

Columbia University, 9, 135

Coming to Our Senses (Arts, Education, and Americans Panel report), 409-410

Commentary, 13, 54, 56*n,* 67*n,* 68*n,* 94, 248*n,* 268, 294

Conant, James Bryant, 122

Concord Quartet, 68

Conklin, John, 146

Connections Quarterly, 377

Consoli, Marc Antonio, *Afterimages,* 79-80

Copland, Aaron, 20, 21, 22, 27, 29, 46, 48, 52, 54, 56, 60, 69, 70, 71*n,* 77, 79, 116, 116*n,* 156, 204*n,* 250, 299, 300, 349; *Music for the Theater,* 297, 299, 300

Corigliano, John, 32, 110, 153, 261
Cornelius, Peter, 296
Cortot, Alfred, 243
Covent Garden, 270, 291
Cowell, Henry, 22-23, 56, 70
Cox, Nash, 146
Crawford, Bruce, 107, 108, 259, 261
Creighton, James, 256
Creston, Paul, 68
Crompton, Louis, *Byron and Greek Love*, 194
Crosby, John, 146, 147, 148
Crumb, George, 31, 32, 88, 95; *A Haunted Landscape*, 84, 85
Cummings, E. E., 116
Curtis Institute of Music, 21, 26, 158, 363
Czerny, Karl, 250, 252

Dahl, Ingolf, 60
Dalgleish, Julie Gordon (and Bradley G. Morison), *Waiting in the Wings*, 380-384
Dallapiccola, Luigi, 28
Dalrymple, Jean, 139
Dante, 117, 389-390
Darling, Ann Farris, 138
Davies, Sir Peter Maxwell, *Ave Maris Stella*, 79, 80
Davis, Andrew, 295
Davis, Anthony, *X*, 105, 106, 149-150
Davis, Peter, 172, 246, 294, 304
de Groat, Andrew, 173
De Groot, Steven, 229
de Luca, Giussepe, 275n
de Mille, Agnes, 27, 349, 405
de Shauensee, Max, 26
Debussy, Claude, 84, 87, 91, 245, 299; *Nocturnes*, 80, 299, 301-302; *Pelléas et Mélisande*, 277, 311
Del Tredici, David, 31, 113; *All in the Golden Afternoon*, 79, 80-81
Dello Joio, Norman, 153

Dexter, John, 98
Diaghilev, Sergei, 27
Diamond, David, 29, 44, 72
Dissent, 372
Dodge, Charles, 30
Dohnányi, Christoph von, 295, 321
Domingo, Placido, 94, 202, 207
Donatoni, Franco, 73
Donizetti, Gaetano, 273; *Lucia di Lammermoor*, 270, 273n, 274, 274n, 277
Donne, John, 117
Douglas, Barry, 234
Dove, Arthur, 348
Dowis, Jeaneane, 51, 57
Downes, Olin, 26, 281
Druckman, Daniel, 80
Druckman, Jacob, 31, 32, 75, 76, 78-79, 82, 83, 84, 153, 261; *Aureole*, 89
Duchamp, Marcel, 379, 380
Dukas, Paul, 153
Duke University, 393
Duncan, Isadora, 349
Dunn, Susan, 40
Dvorák, Antonin, 21, 256
Dynamic Subscription Promotion (DSP), 381-382, 384

Eakins, Thomas, 348
Eastman School of Music, 26
Easton, Florence, 290
Ehrling, Sixten, 266
Eichendorf, Joseph von, 309
Eisenberg, Alan, 146, 148
Eisler, Hanns, 158, 162
Elgar, Edward, 60; *La Capricieuse*, 256, 257
Eliot, Charles W., 122
Eliot, T. S., 116, 280; "Tradition and the Individual Talent," 66, 74, 287, 292
Elman, Mischa, 255
Emerson, Ralph Waldo, 119, 405, 428
Emerson Quartet, 68, 73

Emmons, Beverly, 173
English Chamber Orchestra, 39
Erickson, Robert, 33
Estes, Simon, 263, 264

Falla, Manuel de, 60, 153, 243
Fassbänder, Brigitte, 264
Federal Theatre Project, 158
Feghali, José, 234, 235
Feinberg, Alan, 82
Feinstein, Martin, 214
Feld, Alan L., 333-344
Feldman, Morton, 30
Feltsman, Vladimir, 127, 237, 244-246
Fenley, Molissa, 165
Fiedler, Arthur, 49
Fine, Irving, 117, 118n
Finney, Ross Lee, 29
Fischer, Edwin, 243
Fitzpatrick, Robert, 146, 168
Flagstad, Kirsten, 291n
Fleischmann, Ernest, 126, 126n, 318; "The Symphony Orchestra Is Dead. Long Live the Community of Musicians," 320-328
Fleisher, Leon, 25, 27, 227
Flesch, Carl, 256
Floyd, Carlisle, 29, 140; Of Mice and Men, 29, 134, 140; Susannah, 29, 140; Willie Stark, 29, 143, 146, 150, 198
Foote, Arthur, 70, 71n
Ford Foundation, 178, 397
Fort Worth Symphony, 235
Foss, Lukas, 32, 72, 72n, 76, 87; Baroque Variations, 87-88
Fountain, Clarence, and the Five Blind Boys of Alabama, 151
Frager, Malcolm, 233, 297-298
Frankenstein, Alfred, 26
Franklin, Benjamin, 71n
Frick Collection, 348
Friedenberg, Daniel M., 372

Friedman, Gary William, 146
Friend, Jonathan, 108
Frost, Robert, 116
Fry, Howard, 289
Frühbeck de Burgos, Rafael, 202, 207
Fuchs, Marta, 267
Fukuyama, Francis, 419
Fuller, Buckminster, 119, 120
Furtwängler, Wilhelm, 111, 266, 291, 306, 313

Gaddes, Richard, 146
Gaisberg, Fred, 287
Galbraith, John Kenneth, 360
Galli-Curci, Amelita, 275n
Gans, Herbert, 422
Gardner Museum, 348
Garment, Leonard, 287, 397
Gershwin, George, Lullaby for String Quartet, 60, 71n; Porgy and Bess, 110, 261
Getty Trust, 14
Gibson, Jon, Voyage of the Beagle, 150-151
Gielen, Michael, 50n
Gieseking, Walter, 243
Gigli, Beniamino, 270, 274, 275, 275n, 278
Gilels, Emil, 227
Gill, Dominic, 256
Gingold, Hermione, 161
Giordano, John, 233
Giulini, Carlo Maria, 249, 273n, 277, 320
Glass, Philip, 31, 33, 55, 64, 69, 83, 95, 104, 107, 110, 122, 127, 164, 165-166, 211; Akhnaten, 105,106n, 153, 171-173, 215; Einstein on the Beach, 11, 33, 131, 164-165, 173-180, 215; The Photographer, 165; Satyagraha, 170-171
Globokar, Vinko, 87
Gluck, Christoph Willibald, 137
Gockley, David, 146, 148
Goethe, 66, 283, 296

Goode, Ruth, 281*n*

Goodman, Alice, 110

Goodman, Paul and Percival, 372

Goodwin, Richard, 364

Gordon, Eric A., 157

Gore, Leigh Gibbs, 195

Gould, Morton, 22

Gounod, Charles, *Faust*, 199

Graham, Martha, 27, 349, 355, 405

Grand Street, 188

Grant, Micki, 146

Greater Miami Opera, 270

Grieg, Edvard, 133

Griffes, Charles, 70

Griffiths, Paul, *The String Quartet*, 69, 69*n*, 70*n*, 71

Grillparzer, Franz, 258

Group for Contemporary Music, 76, 81

Grove's Dictionary of Music and Musicians, 255

Gruen, John, 194; *Menotti*, 203

Gruenberg, Louis, 156, 204*n*,

Guarneri Quartet, 68

Guthrie Theater, 383

Haas, Kenneth, 326

Habich, Eduard, 290

Hadley, Henry, 71*n*

Hammerstein, Oscar, 162; *Oklahoma!*, 142

Hanayagi, Suzushi, 168

Handel, George Frederick, 38, 40, 87, 104, 152, 270, 273, 283, 299, 301

Hanks, Nancy, 365, 391-402

Hanson, Howard, 21, 26, 44, 56, 60, 70, 71*n*, 204*n*

Harbison, John, Concerto for Violin and Orchestra, 81

Harris, Dale, 179

Harris, Joan, 146

Harris, Roy, 20, 21, 56, 60, 68, 69, 70, 79

Hartley, Marsden, 348

Harvard University, 70, 115-118, 122

Hassid, Josef, 254-258

Hastings Law Journal, 342

Haugland, Aage, 264

Hawthorne, Nathaniel, 349

Haydn, Franz Joseph, 45, 63, 67, 126, 133, 251; Sonata in E-flat major, 231, 249

Heath, Edward, 354

Hefner, Hugh, 348

Heger, Robert, 111, 290

Heifetz, Jascha, 95, 255, 278

Heine, Heinrich, 162

Henahan, Donal, 91, 108, 172, 202, 246, 304

Hendrix, Jimi, 69

Henze, Hans Werner, 88, 153, 155

Herbert, Victor, 204*n*

Heritage Foundation, 350

Herrmann, Bernard, 25

Hesse, Hermann, 309, 310

Higgins, Dick, 30

Higginson, Henry Lee, 348

Hill, Edward Burlingame, 117, 117*n*

Hiller, Lejaren, 30

Hindemith, Paul, 20, 47, 49, 71, 79, 87, 99, 116, 116*n*, 137, 153, 155, 208; *Mathis der Maler*, 155, 261

Hodsoll, Francis S. M., 147, 407, 410, 413

Hoffman, William, 110

Hoffnung, Gerard, 87

Hofmann, Josef, 243

Hofmann, Peter, 263, 264

Hogwood, Christopher, 38

Holden, Stephen, 177

Holinshed, Raphael, 211

Holland, Bernard, 125

Hollywood Bowl, 320

Hollywood Quartet, 68

Homer, Louise, 275*n*

Homer, Winslow, 348

Honegger, Arthur, 29

Horne, Marilyn, 38, 94
Horowitz, Joseph, *Understanding Toscanini*, 278
Horowitz, Vladimir, 23, 45-46, 95, 234n, 237, 243, 245, 247-253, 278
Hotter, Hans, 266, 267
Houseman, John, 157, 160, 162
Houston Grand Opera, 143, 145, 146, 171, 197
Howard Gilman Foundation, 178
Howells, William Dean, *The Coast of Bohemia*, 373
Hoyle, Fred, 119-120
Humanité, 168
Huneker, James, *Painted Veils*, 373
Hurok, Sol, 97, 281, 281n, 284
Hutchens, James, 378-380
Hutt, Robert, 289
Hwang, David Henry, 110

I Ching, 119, 121
Ibert, Jacques, 60
Ilgenfritz, McNair, 337
Imbrie, Andrew, 29, 72, 72n
Institute for Advanced Study, 363
International Tchaikowsky Competition, 37, 227, 228, 239
Irving, Washington, 405
Istomin, Eugene, 25
Ives, Charles, 22, 69, 71n, 77

J. D. Steele Singers, 151
James, Henry, 349
Janssen, Herbert, 267
Jarnach, Philipp, 155
Jarrell, Randall, 1, 10
Jenson, Dylana, 61
Johannesburg Festival, 320
Jommelli, Niccolò, 184
Jones, Bill T., 165
Jowett, Benjamin, 65n, 223
Joyce, James, 120; *Finnegans Wake*, 80, 120

Juilliard American Opera Center, 188, 189, 190, 191, 197, 203
Juilliard Quartet, 47, 68, 300, 300n
Juilliard School of Music, 26, 46-47, 95, 99-101, 103, 166, 363, 373, 374, 375
Julius, E. Haldeman, 405

Kabalevsky, Dmitri, 45
Kapell, William, 25, 38
Karajan, Herbert von, 111, 262, 266, 273n, 296, 304, 306, 307, 312, 313-317
Kavafian, Ida, 79, 80
Kazanjian, Dodie, 210
Keene, Christopher, 104, 106
Keens, William, 1-15
Kennedy Center Opera House, 202
Kerner, Leighton, 202
Kernis, Aaron Jay, 84-85, *dream of the morning sky* (Cycle V), 83, 84
Keynote, 123
King, Martin Luther, Jr., 87, 171
Kipling, Rudyard, 117
Kipnis, Alexander, 23
Kirchner, Leon, 29
Kirkpatrick, John, 22
Kissinger, Henry, 395
Klee, Paul, 53, 183
Kleiber, Erich, 111
Klemperer, Otto, 111
Klimt, Gustav, 390
Klose, Margarete, 267
Knappertsbusch, Hans, 111, 266
Knussen, Oliver, *Where the Wild Things Are*, 105, 106
Kodály, Zoltán, 28, 155
Kogan, Judith, *Nothing But the Best*, 125
Kohon Quartet, 71, 71n
Kokkonen, Joonas, 155
Kolb, Barbara, *Chromatic Fantasy*, 82-83
Korngold, Erich, 155, 296
Kostelanetz, André, 78
Koussevitsky, Serge, 24, 111, 303, 305, 306

Krainik, Ardis, 32, 146, 147, 148
Kramer, Hilton, 3
Krauss, Clemens, 111, 260
Kreisler, Fritz, 19, 255, 256
Kronos Quartet, 68-69

Laderman, Ezra, 100
Lakes, Gary, 108
Landowska, Wanda, 23, 37
Landry, Richard, 165
Lapham, Lewis, 66-67
Larrocha, Alicia de, 94
Larsen, Libby, 34-35, *Symphony: Water-music*, 33-34
Larson, Jack, 189, 190, 193, 194
Lateiner, Jacob, 49, 50*n*
Lawrence, D. H., 86
League of Composers, 27
Lehar, Franz, *The Merry Widow*, 133
Lehmann, Lotte, 23, 37, 266, 290
Leibowitz, René, 120*n*
Leider, Frida, 289, 289*n*, 290, 291, 291*n*
Leinsdorf, Erich, 49, 294, 295-297, 299-303
Leisner, Emmi, 290
Lenau, Nikolaus, *Faust*, 254
Leoncavallo, Ruggero, *Pagliacci*, 154
Leppard, Raymond, 76, 79, 80, 295
Lerdahl, Fred, *Chords*, 81
Lerner, Alan Jay, 162
Leventritt Award, 228, 233, 298
Levi-Strauss, Claude, 87
Levine, James, 94, 98, 99, 108 109, 112, 152, 259, 261, 265, 266, 285, 306, 307-308, 311, 375
Levine, Rhoda, 146
Levy, Marvin David, 261
Lhévinne, Ròsina, 46
Liberace, 237-241
Lichtenstein, Harvey, 164
Lichtenstein, Roy, 164
Lieberson, Goddard, 72*n*

Lincoln Center, 95, 96, 101, 278, 367, 375; Alice Tully Hall, 33, 95; Avery Fisher Hall, 95, 101, 286, 295, 297, 299, 302; Chamber Music Society, 38; New York State Theatre, 105. *See also* Juilliard School of Music, Metropolitan Opera
Lind, Jenny, 405
Lipman, Samuel, "American Music: The Years of Hope," 56*n*, 67*n*; "American Music's Place at Home and in the World," 67*n*; "Art Education Without the Mess," 13; "Berlin on Two Coasts," 307; "Copland as American Composer," 54; "From Avant-Garde to Pop," 55; "Horowitz: King of Pianists," 248; *The House of Music*, 55, 68*n*, 248*n*; *Music After Modernism*, 54, 248*n*; "The Real Vladimir Horowitz?" 248*n*; "Schooling for All,"13; "Yesterday's New Music," 54; "Zeroing in on Karajan," 307*n*
List, Emanuel, 289
Liszt, Franz, 31, 45, 50, 223, 231, 238, 243, 249, 296
Ljungberg, Gota, 289, 290
Loeffler, Charles, 71*n*
Loesser, Frank, 162
Loewe, Frederick, 162
London Symphony Orchestra, 320
Lorca, Frederico García, 31
Lorentz, Pare, 21
Loriod, Yvonne, 246
Los Angeles Chamber Orchestra, 322
Los Angeles Philharmonic Orchestra, 23, 25, 320, 322, 326, 400
Louis, Morris, 174
Lowe, Robert, 370
Lucier, Alvin, 30
Ludwig, Christa, 108
Luening, Otto, 30
Lully, Jean-Baptiste, 184
LuPone, Patti, 161

Lupu, Radu, 229

Ma, Yo-Yo, 38, 94
Maazel, Lorin, 321
Macdonald-Wright, Stanton, 348
McEwen, Terence, 32, 149
McLuhan, Marshall, 119, 120
Mahler, Gustav, 80, 86, 87, 89, 91, 112, 118, 284n, 286, 323
Manhattan School of Music, 95, 103
Mann, Robert, 300
Mann, Thomas, 27; *Doktor Faustus*, 74
Mannes School of Music, 95
Marherr, Elfriede, 289
Marin, John, 348
Marsalis, Wynton, 38
Martin, Frank, 28
Martino, Donald, 32; Triple Concerto, 81, 82
Mason, Daniel Gregory, 71n
Massenet, Jules, 256, 270
Masur, Kurt, 295
Mathews, Max, 30
Mayer, Martin, *Grandissimo Pavarotti*, 271
Mehta, Zubin, 4, 8, 76, 77-78, 83, 84-85, 86, 94, 97-98, 104, 111, 113, 278, 285, 286, 291n, 294, 295, 296, 303, 304, 305
Melchior, Lauritz, 266, 267n, 289, 290, 291
Mell, Randle, 161
Mellon Collection, 348
Melville, Herman, 349
Mendelssohn, Felix, 249
Mengelberg, Willem, 111
Mennin, Peter, 29, 71n, 100
Menotti, Gian Carlo, 29, 153, 201-209; *Amahl and the Night Visitors*, 29, 153, 203; *The Consul*, 203, 204; *Goya*, 201-209, 214-215; *Juana la Loca*, 203, 204, 205; *The Medium*, 29, 202, 203, 204, 205; *The Telephone*, 29, 203, 204

Menuhin, Yehudi, 257-258
Merrill, Robert, 277
Merriman, Nan, 277
Messiaen, Olivier, 80, 403; *Oiseaux exotiques*, 47; *Vingt regards sur l'enfant Jesus*, 127, 237, 244-246
Metropolitan Museum of Art, 348, 363, 405
Metropolitan Opera, 10, 12, 24-25, 32, 94, 98-99, 103, 104, 105, 107-110, 134, 137, 146, 147, 152-153, 188, 197, 202, 259-267, 268, 269, 271, 282, 283n, 285, 287, 295, 348, 363, 374, 375, 405
Metropolitan Opera Chorus, 275
Metropolitan Opera Guild, 364
Metropolitan Opera House, 95, 311, 312
Metropolitan Opera Orchestra, 308
Meyer, Ursula, *Conceptual Art*, 379
Michaelson, Edward, 102
Michelangelo, 117
Milhaud, Darius, 20, 46, 57, 71, 74, 155, 209, 297
Miller, Arthur, 10
Mills College, 20
Minnesota Opera, 33, 182
Minnesota Orchestra, 23, 33
Mitropoulos, Dimitri, 23, 77, 111, 301, 303
Mitterand, François, 354
Mocsári, Károly, 234
Modern Music, 27
Molière, 21, 184
Moll, Kurt, 108
Mollicone, Henry, 133
Momaday, N. Scott, 84
Mondale, Joan, 161, 331, 341, 352
Monk, Meredith, *Dolmen Music*, 150
Montale, Eugenio, 86
Monte, Elisa, 165
Monteux, Pierre, 23, 37, 46, 111, 283, 284n, 302, 304, 313
Moore, Douglas, 56; *The Ballad of Baby Doe*, 105n, 153; *The Devil and Daniel*

Webster, 21, 153
Moore, Gerald, 256
Moorman, Charlotte, 30
Morgan Library, 348
Morison, Bradley G. (and Julia Gordon Dalgleish), *Waiting in the Wings*, 380-384
Morris, James, 108, 266
Morris, Mark, 165
Morris, Thomas, 326
Morris, Tim, 165
Moynihan, Daniel Patrick, 149
Mozart, Wolfgang Amadeus, 37, 39, 45, 63, 66, 67, 99, 104, 137, 152, 154, 178, 183, 211, 219, 243, 249, 257, 260, 286, 307, 314n
Muck, Karl, 292
Munch, Charles, III, 295
Munkacsi, Kurt, 173
Murrow, Edward R., 283
Museum of Modern Art, 348, 363
Musgrave, Thea, *Harriet, the Woman Called Moses*, 33, 198
Musica Elettronica Viva, 88
Musical America, 26
Musical Courier, 26
Musicians Union, 96
Mussorgsky, Modest, 106
Myers, Philip, 86

Nabokov, Vladimir, 116
Namath, Joe, 353
Nancarrow, Conlon, 69
Nation, 26
National Art Education Association, 360
National Association of Schools of Art and Design, 345
National Council of Art Administrators, 378
National Council on the Arts, 1, 5, 10, 58, 139, 142, 143, 152n, 210, 403, 407-408, 412-413, 414

National Endowment for the Arts (NEA), 41-42, 58, 76, 135, 136, 137, 140, 141, 142, 143, 145, 146, 148, 152n, 178, 210, 331, 340-341, 345, 350, 351-352, 355, 357-359, 365, 391-402, 397-402, 403-416
National Endowment for the Humanities, 352, 420
National Gallery of Art, 363
National Institute for Music Theater, 351
National Interest, 420
National Opera Institute, 136, 144
National Orchestral Association, 48
Naumburg Prize, 228
NBC Opera Theater, 269
NBC Symphony Orchestra, 23, 25, 26, 235n, 304
New Amsterdam Theater Group, 103
New Criterion, 1, 3, 19, 44, 63, 75, 94, 115, 121, 131, 157, 164, 181, 201, 219, 226, 237, 248n, 254, 259, 280, 306, 307n, 318, 331, 345, 360, 371, 377, 391, 403, 417
New Grove Dictionary of American Music, 71n, 238
New Republic, 393n
New Swingle Singers, 76, 86
New York, 172, 246, 294, 304
New York Choral Artists, 76, 87
New York City Ballet, 349
New York City Opera, 24-25, 32-33, 94, 96-97, 103, 104, 105-107, 134, 143, 152, 153, 171, 181, 182, 197, 198, 203, 204, 205, 208, 215, 295, 375
New York Herald Tribune, 26
New York Journal-American, 26
New York New Music Ensemble, 76, 79
New York Opera Repertory Theatre, 188, 195, 197
New York Philharmonic Orchestra, 8, 12, 23, 25, 26, 31-32, 37, 48, 94, 97-98, 103, 110-114, 235n, 267, 281, 294-305, 322, 348, 374, 375; "Horizons '83," 31, 75-93
New York Review of Books, 194

New York School of painters, 10, 349
New York State Arts Council, 76
New York Times, 26, 42, 51*n*, 63, 64, 76, 91, 95, 96, 97, 98, 101, 102, 104, 106, 108, 112, 119, 123, 125, 162, 170, 172, 177, 178, 191*n*, 194, 202, 229, 238, 246, 281, 296, 297, 304, 371, 375, 389
New York World-Telegraph, 26
New Yorker, 39, 171, 190
Neway, Patricia, 204
Newland, Larry, 76, 82
Newman, Danny, 381
Newton, Ivor, 256
Nikisch, Artur, 112
92nd Street Y, 56, 63, 67, 74, 95, 123
Noland, Kenneth, 174
Nolen, Timothy, 146, 148
Norman, Jessye, 108, 285-287, 291*n*
Norrington, Roger, 126
North Texas State College, 26
Norton, Charles Eliot, 117, 122

Oakland Symphony Orchestra, 320
Offenbach, Jacques, *Tales of Hoffman*, 132
O'Hare, Michael, 333-344
O'Horgan, Tom, 146
O'Keeffe, Georgia, 348
Oistrakh, David, 227, 255
Oja, Carol J., *American Music Recordings*, 72*n*
Oklahoma Arts Council, 353
Oldfather, Christopher, 84
Oliveros, Pauline, 30
Olympic Arts Committee/Festival, 167-168, 170
Olszewska, Maria, 290
Opera America, 132, 136, 139, 145, 149, 351; *Profile: 1983*, 132-135
Opera News, 203
Opera Theatre of St. Louis, 146, 197
Oppenheimer, J. Robert, 379
Oppens, Ursula, 50*n*, 82

Orchestra of St. Luke's, 322, 326
Orford Quartet, 71
Ormandy, Eugene, 24, 249, 305, 306
Ortiz, Cristina, 229
Ostrow, Stuart, 146, 148
Owen, Wilfred, 86
Oxford University, 362, 427
Ozawa, Seiji, 4, 307

Paderewski, Ignacy Jan, 19
Paganini, Niccolo, 254
Paine, John Knowles, 117, 117*n*
Palma, Donald, 87
Papi, Gennaro, 303
Papp, Joseph, 146, 148
Paris School of painters, 348
Pater, Walter, 247
Patrons Despite Themselves (Twentieth Century Fund report), 333-344
Paulus, Stephen, *The Postman Always Rings Twice*, 33, 133, 197, 198
Pavarotti, Luciano, 37, 94, 125, 240, 268, 269-275, 277
Peerce, Jan, 24, 277, 282
Pell, Claiborne, 341
Perahia, Murray, 39
Perle, George, 72
Perlman, Itzhak, 37, 38, 94, 254, 255, 278
Perry, Herbert, 196
Persichetti, Vincent, 29, 100
Pew Memorial Trusts, 178
Pfitzner, Hans, 155; *Palestrina*, 60, 155, 260
Philadelphia Orchestra, 8, 23, 24, 26, 48, 102, 305, 306
Philharmonia Orchestra of London, 38, 314*n*
Piazzolla, Astor, 69
Pinza, Ezio, 275
Pirandello, Luigi, 47, 214
Piston, Walter, 21, 44, 56, 68, 69, 70, 71, 117, 118, 118*n*; Symphony no. 4, 60, 61

Pittsburgh Symphony Orchestra, 26

Plato, 223; *The Republic*, 65

Pleasants, Henry, 67; *Serious Music and All That Jazz*, 66

Poe, Edgar Allan, 349

Porter, Andrew, 171, 172, 190, 191, 191*n*

Porter, Quincy, 70, 71

Portland String Quartet, 71

Posseur, Henri, 87

Potter, Stephen, 226, 231

Poulenc, Francis, 29, 60, 134, 99, 243

Powers, Marie, 204*n*

Previn, André, 320

Price, Leontyne, 12

Price, Monroe, 342

Prince, Harold, 139, 140, 144

Prokofiev, Sergei, 45, 48, 49, 60, 79, 133, 150, 153, 155, 243; Concerto no. 3, 46, 234, 243; Sonata no. 7, 46, 243, 250

Public Broadcasting Service (PBS), 10, 198, 201, 202, 205, 226, 230, 269, 271, 375; "Live from Lincoln Center," 10, 285

Puccini, Giacomo, 96, 106, 137, 154, 183, 203, 208, 214, 261; *La Bohème*, 11, 98, 212, 260; *Madame Butterfly*, 132, 336; *Tosca*, 212, 214; *Il Trittico*, 132-133; *Turandot*, 32, 132, 206

Queen Elisabeth Contest (Brussels), 227

Rachmaninoff, Sergei, 49, 60, 240, 243; Concerto no. 3, 49, 228, 234, 240, 249, 250

Raeburn, Andrew, 230, 231, 232, 235

Ramey, Samuel, 285

Randall, Tony, 82, 83

Rands, Bernard, *Canti del Sole*, 86-87

Raphael, 223

Ratner, Leonard, 46

Ravel, Maurice, 87, 90; *Gaspard de la nuit*, 243, 245

RCA Victor Records, 26

Reich, Steve, 31, 55, 64, 83, 95, 122, 127, 165, 166

Reimann, Aribert, 155

Reiner, Fritz, 23, 111, 249, 283*n*, 284*n*, 305

Reise, Jay, *Rasputin*, 105, 106

Respighi, Ottorino, 60

Rex, Charles, 81

Rich, Maria F., 131

Richter, Sviatoslav, 245

Riegger, Wallingford, 60

Riley, Terry, 55, 83, 127, 166

Rimbaud, Arthur, 86

Robinson, Joseph, 89

Rochberg, George, 31, 32, 69-70, 70*n*, 91, 95, 133; *Imago Mundi*, 87

Rochester Philharmonic Orchestra, 295

Rockefeller, John D. 3rd, 353, 395

Rockefeller, Nelson, 391, 394, 395

Rockefeller Brothers Fund, 395, 396

Rockefeller Foundation, 145, 149, 178, 377

Rockefeller Institute for Medical Research, 363

Rockwell, John, 64, 91, 92, 96, 123, 170, 177, 179, 375

Rodgers, Richard, 84, 162; *Oklahoma!*, 142

Rodzinski, Artur, 24, 111, 267, 295

Rorem, Ned, 29

Rosen, Seymour, 102

Rosenfield, John, 26

Rosenman, Leonard, *Foci I*, 81, 82

Rossant, M. J., 333

Rossini, Gioacchino, 10, 133, 152

Rothstein, Edward, 97

Royal College of Music, 270

Royal Festival Hall, 347

Rubin, David W., 53

Rubinstein, Arthur, 23, 37, 95, 227, 243, 252, 253

Rupp, Franz, 284*n*

Ruskin, John, 117

Russell, Anna, 264

Rzewski, Frederic, 32, 87, 90; *The Silence of Infinite Spaces*, 87, 88

Sackler, Arthur, 336
St. Denis, Ruth, 405
St. Louis Orchestra, 23, 320
St. Paul Chamber Orchestra, 182
Saint-Saëns, Camille, 283
Sallinen, Aulis, 69, 155
Salomon Quartet, 126
Salonen, Esa-Pekka, 39
Samuel, Gerhard, 191
Sandow, Gregory, 179
San Francisco Opera, 25, 32, 134, 146, 152, 348, 363, 375
San Francisco Symphony Orchestra, 23, 25, 26, 283, 284n, 304
Santa Fe Opera, 146, 147, 375
Sarasate, Pablo de, 256
Sargent, John Singer, 348
Sargent, Malcolm, 111
Sarnoff, David, 269
Satie, Erik, 74
Scalero, Rosario, 158
Scarlatti, Alessandro, 37, 249, 403; Sonata no. 23, 87
Schenk, Otto, 108, 261, 262, 263
Schickele, Peter, 87
Schippers, Thomas, 205n
Schlesinger, Arthur, Jr., 364
Schmitt, Jacqueline, 51
Schnabel, Artur, 23, 37, 243
Schneider-Siemssen, Günther, 262
Schoenberg, Arnold, 20, 21, 27, 30, 31, 67, 79, 83, 87, 120n, 137, 158, 209, 285, 299, 300, 300n; Concerto for String Quartet and Orchestra, 299, 300-301; *Gurre-lieder*, 87, 300; *Moses und Aron*, 32, 99, 110, 153, 155, 261
Schonberg, Harold C., 31, 98, 189-190, 191, 191n, 229
Schorr, Friedrich, 23, 289, 290

Schub, Andre-Michel, 229
Schubert, Franz, 37, 63, 67, 127, 233, 243, 244, 246, 258, 283, 284; Symphony no. 8 ("Unfinished"), 314, 315, 316
Schuller, Gunther, 76, 89, 321; Concerto no. 2 for Orchestra, 89, 90
Schuman, William, 21-22, 26, 27, 29, 47, 56, 57, 60, 68, 69, 70, 71, 71n, 72, 77, 79; *Colloquies*, 32, 86
Schumann, Elisabeth, 23, 290
Schumann, Robert, 57, 127, 190, 232, 243, 244, 246
Schuster, J. Mark Davidson, 333-344
Schwantner, Joseph, *Sparrows*, 87, 88
Schwartz, Boris, 255
Schwarz, Gerard, 44, 52, 58, 61, 118n, 220
Scionti, Silvio, 26
Scriabin, Alexander, 49, 245, 250
Sculthorpe, Peter, 69
Seidler-Winkler, Bruno, 267
Sellars, Peter, 213
Sendak, Maurice, 106
Senofsky, Berl, 227
Serafin, Tullio, 111, 273n, 277
Serkin, Peter, 246
Serkin, Rudolf, 23, 37, 48
Sessions, Roger, 21, 56, 68, 69, 70, 71, 71n, 73, 116, 116n, 156, 209, 349; *Montezuma*, 156, 197, 198
Shakespeare, William, 198, 211
Shankar, Ravi, 166
Shapero, Harold, 117, 118n; Quartet no. 1, 72, 72n
Shell Companies Foundation, 384
Shelton, Lucy, 87
Shostakovich, Dmitri, 45, 48, 60, 67, 79, 125, 134, 137, 153
Sibelius, Jean, 26, 60
Sills, Beverly, 32, 96, 103, 104, 105, 153, 182, 203, 205, 375
Siloti, Alexander, 158
Sisson, C. H., 408

Skrowaczewski, Stanislaw, 233, 235

Slatkin, Leonard, 320

Smetana, Bedrich, 21

Sollberger, Harvey, 81

Solti, Sir Georg, 109, 111, 266

Sondheim, Stephen, *Sweeney Todd*, 144

Sophocles, 151

Sorel, Magda, 204

Sousa, John Philip, 375

Speculum Musicae, 76, 87

Sperry, Paul, 86

Spoleto Festival, 197

Spotlight, 184

Stanlis, Peter J., 392n

Starr, Cornelius, 336

Steber, Eleanor, 24

Steichen, Edward, 349

Stein, Gertrude, 21, 27, 188, 195

Steiner, George, 67; "Archives of Eden," 66

Stereo Review, 241

Stern, Isaac, 25, 27, 100, 101, 254

Stevens, Risë, 24

Stevens, Roger, 397

Stieglitz, Arthur, 349

Stillman, Charles Chauncey, 116n

Stock, Frederick, 238

Stockhausen, Karlheinz, 30, 48, 54, 73, 87, 361

Stokowski, Leopold, 24, 60, 111, 204, 305, 306, 313

Straight, Michael, 340, 364, 365; *Nancy Hanks*, 391-402

Strategy to Encourage Lifelong Learning (SELL), 382-383

Strauss, Johann, 316

Strauss, Johann II, 315-316; *Die Fledermaus*, 132

Strauss, Josef, 315, 316

Strauss, Richard, 91, 137, 155, 183, 184, 185, 186, 270, 285, 314n; *Arabella*, 99, 153; *Le Bourgeois Gentilhomme*, 184, 186, 186n;

Death and Transfiguration, 89, 309; *Elektra*, 77, 77n, 185, 260; *Four Last Songs*, 308, 309-310; *Der Rosenkavalier*, 80, 260; *Salome*, 31, 80, 260, 283, 283n

Stravinsky, Igor, 20, 21, 27, 37, 47, 79, 87, 89, 99, 116, 116n, 137, 184, 185, 186, 233, 250, 260; *L'Histoire du soldat*, 83, 254; *Oedipus Rex*, 99, 134; *The Rake's Progress*, 99, 133, 156, 185, 186, 261; *Le Rossignol*, 99, 134

Stravinsky, Soulima, 233

Street, Tison, 91; *Adagio*, 89, 91

Stresemann, Wolgang, 233

Subotnick, Morton, 30, 32, 84, 90; *Ascent into Air*, 82

Sullivan, Louis, 349

Surrey, Stanley, 334

Susa, Conrad, 146

Sutherland, Joan, 268, 270-274, 276-277

Sutherland Williamson International Grand Opera Company, 270

Sutton, Sheryl, 174, 176

Szell, George, 24, 111, 235n, 305, 321

Szigeti, Joseph, 23, 255

Szymanowski, Karol, 80, 245

Tagore, Rabindranath, 171

Takemitsu, Toru, *Far calls. Coming Far!*, 79, 80

Takhmizian, Emma, 234

Talking Heads, 68, 169

Taubman, Howard, 281

Taylor, Deems, 156, 204n

Tchaikowsky, Peter Ilyich, 106, 171, 190, 240, 256, 299, 300; Concerto no. 1 in B-flat minor, 227, 234, 234n-235n, 235, 240, 243, 248, 249, 252

Telson, Bob, 151

Tennstedt, Klaus, 295

Terry, Megan, 146

Tessmer, Heinrich, 290

Theater unter den Linden, 289

Thomas, Dylan, 86

Thomson, Virgil, 20-21, 26, 27, 28, 34, 56, 70, 71*n*, 72*n*, 117, 188-200; *Four Saints in Three Acts*, 21, 156, 188, 189, 190, 195; *Lord Byron*, 188, 189-197, 198, 200; *The Mother of Us All*, 156, 188, 189, 190, 191, 195; *The State of Music*, 28

Thoreau, Henry David, 119

Thorne, Nicholas, 32; *Symphony from Silence*, 84, 85-86

Times (London), 69

Tighe, Mary Ann, 341

Tigranian, Armen, 133

Tippett, Sir Michael, 134, 156

Tokyo String Quartet, 232

Tolstoy, Leo, 171

Tomita, 223

Tomowa-Sintow, Anna, 308, 311

Toscanini, Arturo, 21, 23, 37, 111, 235*n*, 248, 249, 251, 277-278, 277*n*, 278*n*, 281, 295, 304, 306, 313

Toward Civilization (National Endowment for the Arts report), 410

Town Hall (New York), 95, 101, 102-103, 281

Traubel, Helen, 24, 267

Trilling, Lionel, 116

Trollope, Frances, 348

Tsontakis, George, 42, 63, 73-74; String Quartet no. 3, 73-74

Tucker, Richard, 24

Tudor, Anthony, 22

2001 (film), 84

Ussachevsky, Vladimir, 30

Van Cliburn International Piano Com petition, 226-236

van Gogh, Vincent, 390

Vantage Point, 1-15

Varnay, Astrid, 266

Vaughan, Roger, 307*n*

Vaughan Williams, Ralph, 85

Vehanen, Kosti, 284*n*

Velikovsky, Immanuel, 171

Verdi, Guiseppe, 133, 137, 152, 154, 183, 190, 260, 282, 362; *Aida*, 12, 260; *Rigo letto*, 132, 212, 271, 272, 273*n*, 274, 274*n*, 275, 275*n*, 277, 277*n*, 278; *La Traviata*, 270, 271, 272, 273*n*, 274, 274*n*, 277, 277*n*, 278

Vergara, Victoria, 207

Viardo, Vladimir, 229

Vienna Philharmonic, 266, 285, 314-317

Villa-Lobos, Heitor, 45, 243

Village Voice, 122, 179, 202, 371, 374

Virginia Opera, 198

Vitali, Giovanni Battista, 88

Voice of America, 203

Vollenweider, Andreas, 128

Votapek, Ralph, 229

Wagner, Cosima, 308-309

Wagner, Richard, 54, 89, 106, 137, 152, 167, 183, 265, 270, 288, 290*n*, 292, 295, 296, 309, 310, 311-312, 418; *Die Meistersinger*, 288, 289; *Parsifal*, 260, 265, 291, 292, 309; *Der Ring des Nibelungen*, 107-108, 211, 259, 261-262, 266, 290-291, 309 (*Das Rheingold*, 107, 292, 315; *Die Walküre*, 107, 108, 108*n*, 259, 261-267, 285, 290; *Siegfried*, 107, 288, 290-291, 292; *Götterdämmerung*, 107, 288, 289*n*, 291, 291*n*, 292, 309); *Siegfried Idyll*, 308-309, 311-312; *Tannhäuser*, 80, 262, 265, 286; *Tristan und Isolde*, 90, 265, 285, 286, 288, 289, 291*n*

Wagner, Siegfried, 292, 308

Wagner, Wieland, 262, 263

Wagner, Wolfgang, 263

Waleson, Heidi, 51*n*

Walker, Charles, 196

Wallace, Henry, 393*n*

Wall Street Journal, 119, 178-179

Walter, Bruno, 23, 24, 37, 111, 249*n*, 266, 267*n*, 290, 295, 306, 313
Walter, Paul, 146
Walton, William, 88
Ward, Robert, 133
Warren, Leonard, 24, 277
Washington Opera, 202, 215
Washington Times, 13, 14
Waterloo Music Festival and School, 44, 45, 57, 58-61, 219
Webern, Anton, 30, 31, 69*n*, 79
Wechsler, Gil, 263
Wedekind, Frank, 211
Weill, Kurt, 99, 162, 134, 214; *Die Dreigroschenoper*, 158, 161, 214
Weill, Suzanne, 146-147
Weisberg, Arthur, 76, 81, 84, 85
Weisgall, Hugo, 29, 46-47, 57, 71, 73, 156, 209; *Six Characters in Search of an Author*, 47, 153, 156 197, 198, 214
Welitsch, Ljuba, 283, 283*n*
Welles, Orson, 160
Weston, Edward, 349
Wheeler, Kimball, 82
Whistler, James McNeill, 348
Whitman, Walt, 349, 405, 431; *Democratic Vistas*, 424, 425; "I Hear America Singing," 424-425
Whitney Museum of American Art, 367
Widdop, Walter, 289, 290, 290*n*

Wille, Hans-Christian, 234
Wilson, Charles E., 394
Wilson, Robert, 153*n*, 166-167; *the CIVIL warS*, 167-170, 178; *Einstein on the Beach*, 11, 33, 164-165, 173-180, 215
Wilson, Robert W., 106-107
Winston, George, 128
Wittgenstein, Ludwig, 119
Wolf Trap Center for the Performing Arts, 375
Wolfensohn, James, 101
Wood, Pamela, 82
Woods, Jessie, 147
Woodward, Joanne, 271
Wright, Frank Lloyd, 349
Wuorinen, Charles, 32; *Reliquary*, 89

Xenakis, Iannis, 79

Young, La Monte, 127, 150, 165
Ysaye, Eugene, 227

Zandonai, Riccardo, 133
Zane, Arnie, 165
Zeffirelli, Franco, 98, 260
Zimbalist, Efrem, 255, 256
Zorn, John, 69
Zukerman, Pinchas, 38, 94, 254
Zwilich, Ellen Taaffe, 42

About the Author

BORN IN CALIFORNIA in 1934, a pianist and former member of the National Council on the Arts, Samuel Lipman is publisher of the *New Criterion*, artistic director of the Waterloo (N.J.) Music Festival, and music critic for *Commentary*. He is the author of *Music After Modernism* (1979) and *The House of Music* (Godine, 1984). Mr. Lipman and his wife, the pianist and teacher Jeaneane Dowis, live in Manhattan with their son, Edward, a student in Classics at Columbia.